2012
COACH OF THE YEAR CLINICS
FOOTBALL MANUAL

Edited by Earl Browning

www.coacheschoice.com

ISBN: 978-1-60679-218-6
ISSN: 1534-925X

Telecoach, Inc. Transcription: Emmerson Browning, Kent Browning, and Tom Cheaney
Diagrams: Steve Haag and Travis Rose
Book layout and cover design: Bean Creek Studio

Cover photo (front): ©Patrick Green/Cal Sport Media/ZUMA Press
Cover photos (back): ©Manny Flores/SCG/ZUMA Press
                     ©Marvin Gentry-US PRESSWIRE

Special thanks to the Nike clinic managers for having the lectures taped.

Coaches Choice
P.O. Box 1828
Monterey, CA 93942
www.coacheschoice.com

Contents

ZONE GAP SCHEMES: IMPLEMENTATION/UTILIZATION

Temple University

It is a pleasure to be here today. I am not one to get up here and preach because I am an offensive line coach. When we played against Ohio University this year, the night before the game, we had a local minister come in and speak to our team. He said, "As iron sharpens iron, so one person sharpens another" (Proverbs 27:17). That proverb stuck with me.

I thought about our football team. I thought our team had to sharpen our team. We had to bring each other up and bring the best out of each other. We had to be a team when we took the field on Saturday afternoon. That is an important concept that seems to be leaving football now. The team sharpens the team and our coaches have to bring the best out of each other.

It does not matter if it is college or high school coaches, we have to complement each other and bring out the best in each other. It is the same with a marriage. The husband and wife have to complement each other and bring out the best. That is what that proverb means to me. I wanted to share that with you.

I want to share with you something I got from our strength coach. This summarizes just who we are.

THE PROFESSIONAL FIGHTER

I am the last of a dying breed. I will tell you the truth even if you do not like it. Many of you do not like me and are even afraid of me because I tell it like it is and you do not like to hear it. I am always there for my friends. I will tell them the truth even if they do not like it because that is what a friend does. Strength and honor are my bloodline. I will back my friends and stand with them even if there is an army standing in front of us. I will fight to the end. Death before dishonor is our motto. I am a man with honor.

That inspired me when I read it. This is the essence of building a football program and team. That is what it is all about, and it is our job to convey that to our players. That might not be in vogue right now, but that is the way it is and what the sport of football is all about.

Mike Sherman was the head football coach at Texas A&M last year. He wrote a letter to the Texas High School Coaches Association that I want to mention. At Temple, this is what our program is all about. It is about our core values. I have plagiarized this letter from Coach Sherman on how to build a program.

If a player learns anything from me, it is that there are specific core values by which to live your life. The core values are a guiding light followed not only as a football player but also as a man. Our core values for our team are simple. They are truth and love. I believe they are essential elements to running a football team, a business, an organization, a government, or a family.

Let us speak first of truth. Be who you say you are, do what you say you will do, and be truthful to yourself and others. Be accountable, with no excuses. Speak the truth, demand the truth, and tell the truth. Live the truth because if there is no truth, there is no trust. If there is no relationship, there is no value or substance to what you are doing. As coaches, we must never lie or mislead a player.

It is simple. He has to trust you and you have to trust him. There is no trust when truth is not at the forefront. You cannot fix something unless there is absolute truth. Never let a player get away with lying to you and go to the nth degree to confirm that what he is telling you is the truth.

They have to know that you will not accept dishonesty and that there are consequences for not being honest. Without absolute truth, there is no relationship, and without a relationship, there is no chemistry. Without chemistry, you lack a major component for winning a championship.

The second component is love.

Love your God, family, friends, and country. Love your freedom and those who protect your freedom. Love your teammates, coaches, and school. Love the game of football, competition, and winning. Love all the things that equate to winning. Love is the passion that brings great success to your life and your team. Love is the one emotion that plays out positively for your team. It is the glue for your team and promotes great chemistry.

I wanted to share those two core values with you before I get going on football. Those are the most powerful things I have ever heard. I wanted to make sure you had a chance to listen to that letter, and I hope it struck you the same way it did me. Urban Meyer once said, "Great talent would get you seven wins. But to win a championship, you need leadership, chemistry, and unselfishness." Talent will get you seven wins, but how do we win the championship?

Many people think it is the X's and O's. All the offenses and defenses work regardless of the schemes. The secret is to coach the fundamentals of the game. Then, you motivate the players to play with great passion and energy. You coach them to respect the game and make them understand it is a privilege and not a right to play the game. Those are the important thing for winning championships.

I was a high school coach for seven years, and it was the greatest time of my life. In those seven years, I felt like I had an effect on kids. Your job is the greatest job there is because that is what you do every day. The scheme stuff is highly overrated. Be a great fundamental teacher, motivate, demand, be a great role model, hug them, and love them, and you will win a championship.

My talk is about the implementation and utilization of the zone/gap schemes for our spread and two-back offense. I want to tell you our core values for winning football games.

CORE VALUES FOR WINNING FOOTBALL

- Play great defense.
- Run the football.
- Play great special teams.
- Score in the red zone.
- Do not turn the ball over.

That is our plan to win at Temple. It is on the board and the first thing you see when you come into the locker room. In order to play great defense, you must be able to control the ball. When you run a zone/gap scheme, you work with double-team blocking. With this scheme, it does not matter if you are under the center or in the shotgun set; they will both work. You cannot run the ball unless you create movement on the line of scrimmage. Penetration by the defense stops running games. Gap schemes are double-teams to a backside linebacker, and zone scheme are double-teams to a playside linebacker. Those two schemes make up our entire offense.

The backfield action or ballcarrier is completely irrelevant to me. When our offensive linemen puts their hands on the ground, they are going to rock off the ball with a zone or gap scheme. They will hit you in the face for four quarters. I do not want to offend anyone in here, but I am going to tell you what I believe.

If you are a no-huddle team, it gets the defensive coaches fired. If you have great players, anything will work. However, if you go three-and-out and the defense has to come back on the field, you are not playing team football. Too many offensive coordinators worry about their stats. If they score points, it helps their careers. The winning takes second place to the excitement of scoring points. Being tough is not in vogue. In vogue is how many points you can score, and I think that is bull.

PHILOSOPHY

- We are a multiple zone/gap scheme team.
- This keeps you from being predictable within certain personnel groupings/formations.
- This system creates stress on a defense having to defend both styles of offense.
- Use a system that has carryover for the O-line from spread and under center.

- We want to conflict the defensive ends and slow down the linebackers.
- The defensive ends will never know whether they are being kicked, logged, or read.
- The linebackers will be slowed down by multiple misdirections, jets, and motions.
- Each year, we are trying to create these conflicts.

We call our zone scheme on-to-on. The double-team occurs on a playside lineman to a playside linebacker. We call the gap scheme on-to-off. We double-team an onside defensive lineman to an offside linebacker. We want to build a wall on the offside linebacker.

The rules system in our zone scheme is easy. We do not have a lot of time to teach and rep, so the system must be sound and simple. It is so easy that a player can play guard, tackle, or center and know his assignment. That allows you to play with your five best linemen on the team. You do not play with the eighth offensive lineman because he is a tackle and not a guard.

The center has to identify a defender and assign #0 to him (Diagram #1). Once he identifies the 0-defender, the remainder of the linemen count to find their assignments. The center identifies anyone on or over him as the #0 defender. The playside guard blocks #1, the playside tackle blocks #2, and the tight end blocks #3 in this scheme. The backside linemen do the same thing.

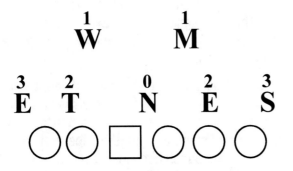

Diagram #1. Number System On

The numbering systems correspond to our blocking rules. If we call a zone play, the tight end knows he has to block the #3 defender (Diagram #2). The playside tackle has the #2 defender. The playside guard sees the #1 defender off the line and knows he has to call for the tackle on a

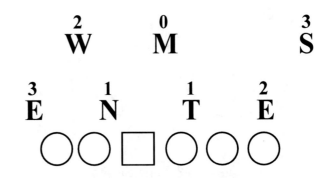

Diagram #2. Number System Off

combination block to block him. The center blocks #0. To the backside, the guard sees #1 off the line of scrimmage. He calls the tackle and tags a combination block on the #1 and #2 defenders to the backside. If there is a #3 defender, we block him with a second tight end, a fullback on a split zone, or a receiver in motion.

In the first diagram, if the nose were aligned in a 1 or 2i technique instead of shading the center, the guard would combination-block with the center instead of the tackle. However, the rules are simple. If the lineman's blocking rule is off the line of scrimmage, he will combination-block with the lineman adjacent to him.

You can choose your own words to designate the combination blocks. We use Ted for the tackle and tight end. Tag is the tackle and guard combination, and Scoop is the center and guard combination block. It is not rocket science, and that is how we coordinate our zone plays.

In the second diagram, the tackle and tight end use a Ted combination for the end and Sam linebacker. The guard and center use a scoop combination for the 3 technique and Mike linebacker. The backside guard and tackle use a Tag call for the nose and Will linebacker.

When we merged the two-back offense with the spread offense, there was no tight end in the original spread formation. In our play calling, the single digits are zone plays. One of our zone plays is 94. Ninety is the series, which means we are blocking the #3 defender to the playside with a tight end. The number four in 94 is a zone play to the right. Odd numbers are left and even numbers are right. The teen series indicates an openside run (Diagram #3). A play run to the openside left is 15.

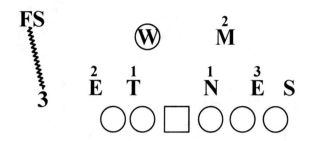

Diagram #3. Teen Series

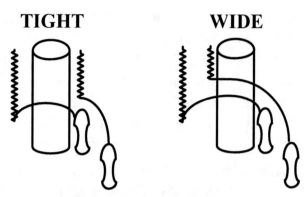

Diagram #4. Zone Step Board Drill

The center identifies the first linebacker in the box to the callside, working outside to inside at the #0. That means there is no #3 defender to the openside.

This series also indicates that the playside tackle is responsible for making an out call against any #3 defender that may show up. If the defense rolls a secondary player down to the outside, the tackle has to make an out call. We never leave any frontline defenders unblocked.

The difference between the 90 series and teen series is that the tackle does not have to worry about the #3 defender in a 90 series play. In the teen series, he may have to be responsible for a #3 defender.

ZONE SCHEME DRILLS

• Boards
• Boards to linebackers
• Sled progression
• Crowther™
• Two in takeoff
• Deliver/takeover
• Generic zone
• Pods
• Inside drill

To teach the zone scheme, we use a number of different drills. I need to talk about fundamentals instead of just the schemes. I do not want to bore you, but it is like building a house. You have to pour the foundation first. Every day in practice, we work on boards. It is simple footwork.

The first drill aligns the lineman with his outside foot against a board (Diagram #4). This is tight zone footwork. He makes a lateral step with the outside foot over the board and runs down the board with short choppy steps. The inside foot does not cross the board because we want to vertically knock the defender back. We are not trying to stretch the play. The running back action is tight and the lineman's step is tight. We call those plays 2 and 3 tight zone plays. They may be 92 or 13 zone plays.

The next part of the drill aligns the lineman in the same position; however, he steps over the board with his first and second steps. This is footwork for the wide zone plays. The target on the tight zone is the playside number, and the target of the wide zone is the playside armpit. We do the same drill with a linebacker bag holder. The difference is the bag is at linebacker depth. The footwork is the same and the target area is the same. One drill is on the line and the other drill is off the line. When we come off the ball on the zone block, we want to knock the defender off the ball. We do not want to push him sideways. It is a tough, aggressive block.

The sled progression is next. When we start, we put the sled against the wall. I do not want to drive the sled. We work on our first step, hand placement, and punch.

The next part is a fire the fist drill. We take the first step and cock the hands and arms to explode on the second step, which is the contact step. On the second step, we put the face and pads on the blocker and punch him in the sternum with the hands. We want to do this with a flat back.

In this drill, we are not in a stance. We simulate being out of the stance and going to the second step. In the next progression, we put it all together from the stance. We call this "one, two: fire the fist." They come from their stance on one and "fire the fist" on two. I have them chop their feet to get used to finishing the block.

We use the Crowther sled for one reason. It teaches balance. We teach the combination block by using the Crowther sled. When the blocker comes off and delivers the forearm on the combination, they have to stay square and not lean into the block. If you lean on a Crowther sled, it will spin out. Blocking the Crowther teaches the blocker to keep his balance and not lean. It forces the linemen to play within their hips, legs, and thighs.

From the Crowther, we go to a flipper drill. We put a partner with a bag on the shoulder of a lineman. He comes off with the one-two footwork, delivers the flipper, stays square, and drives the bag off the ball. We follow that with the flipper drill coming from under the chutes. When he comes off the ball, there is not a hesitation or pause. He drives through the defender with his eyes on the linebacker.

The leverage drill is the greatest drill in football for offensive linemen. The bag hold puts pressure on the offensive blocker. The offensive blocker fits his face into the bag and drives the bag without using his hands on the dummy. The offensive blocker has to stay square on the bag. He steps one foot at a time in almost a slow-motion step to get maximum push on each step. He goes slow and plants the foot each time he steps. The bag holder keeps pressure on the blocker and makes the blocker drive him backward. The blocker drives the knee forward and push with maximum push off his legs. He drives his opposite arm with each step to keep his shoulders square but does not put his hands on the dummy or dummy holder. He plants the next foot, drives the knee forward, and pushes off with his legs. This is the essence of blocking.

The punch starts the block and gets the blocker going, but the legs have to drive the defender and finish the block. Too many players punch and wrestle with the defender by using the upper body. The legs are what moves a defender. This is a slow and meticulous drill. We overemphasize the legs. The chest is down and parallel with the knees as the blocker steps each time. We stomp the foot into the ground and push forward with the knee. We plant the foot again and push forward with the other knee. We go step-by-step and move the arms as we go. We stay square on the dummy and drive. We do this drill all winter long to learn how to play with leverage.

The takeoff drill is a 1-on-1 drive drill. This is a simple come-off-the-ball drill. They apply the blocking steps that you have practiced individually. We want to focus on acceleration coming off the ball. We do not want them to punch reset and push. We want them to come straight out, punch, and accelerate through the block. The second part of the takeoff drill is to put them under the chute and do the same thing.

The deliver takeover drill is a great football drill (Diagram #5). This is an everyday drill as a leverage drill. We put two offensive blockers in a fitted position on one defender. We put the second defender behind the down defender as a linebacker. The blockers are hip to hip with their outside hand free. This is the flipper drill for both blockers. One blocker does an inside flipper and the other does the outside flipper. The drill begins with the blockers taking the down defender off the line of scrimmage with their outside hands free. The linebacker moves to one side or the other.

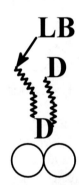

Diagram #5. Deliver/Takeover Drill

We have four eyes on the linebacker. When the linebacker moves to the outside, the inside blocker knows he is the takeover blocker and starts to work for the outside armpit of the down lineman. The outside blocker shoves the down defender to the inside and comes off on the linebacker. If the linebacker went to the inside, the techniques of the linemen reverse. This teaches the linemen how to come off combination blocks. We do this sequence daily.

The drills that we do are generic drills. They apply to the gap and zone plays. We do not have to spend time drilling things that fit only one scheme. The drills we do apply to everyone on the line of scrimmage. The only difference is we have one blocker covered and the other uncovered. The blockers can be the tackle and guard, the guard and center, or the tackle and tight end. The technique is the same for any of them. The uncovered lineman comes off the ball toward the covered lineman, keying the inside foot of the defender; if the foot comes to him, he works the deliver/takeover drill. If the foot goes outside or stays straight ahead, he works up to the linebacker.

How do we attack the field? Our tight zone play is an inside zone scheme run (Diagram #6). The running back in the tight zone has an aiming point as the backside hip of the center. We want to attack from the backside A gap to the backside B gap. The tight zone uses onside down linemen to onside linebacker combo blocks (on-to-on).

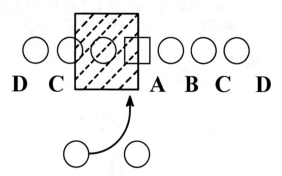

Diagram #6. Tight Zone Attack Area

All the inside zone plays have code words. The play would be 92 or 12, which is the inside zone play, followed by a code word. The code word is a job description in a play. The first code word is Bible. This is a read play on the defensive end.

The play I am going to show you is from the pistol set with a tight end in a wing set off the offensive tackle to the backside (Diagram #7). The defensive end is the read key. We bring the tight end flat to the line of scrimmage at the defensive end. The defensive end does not have time to think about what he should do. With the defensive end coming at him, the handoff vision is cloudy to him.

It puts the defensive end in conflict as to what to do. He must make an immediate reaction. He has to turn his shoulders and close or the ball breaks into the hole. From the pistol set, the play looks like a midline option. The action allows the quarterback to make a read and be sure of what he sees. The tight end leads the play outside if the quarterback pulls the ball.

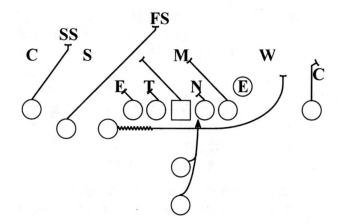

Diagram #7. Bible

We have a middle zone attack. On this attack, the running back aiming point is the inside leg of the playside guard. He attacks the frontside A gap to the backside A and B gaps. In our play call, the middle zone is 94 or 14. If we ran the play to the left, it would be 95 or 15. The code words for the middle zone are read, book, triple, tres, crunch, and zombie. Read means we read the defensive end. Book means we read the defensive end but put a conflictor in the scheme. Triple means there is an option component to the play. Tres means there is an option component with a conflictor added to it. Crunch means we hand the ball off with no read involved. Zombie means we are going to block the backside end and put the fullback on the linebacker.

I will show you our crunch concept (Diagram #8). This is a split zone concept. If the fullback lined up in the backfield, he goes to the left and the running back goes to the right, which makes a split zone play. In the diagram, we align the fullback in that position and run the play. We have a tight wing outside the tackle to the backside of the play. The tight end or fullback in the wing set blocks the #3

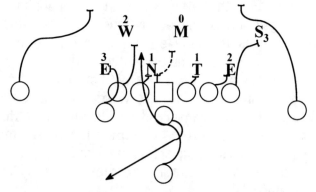

Diagram #8. 94 Crunch

defender on the backside. There is no read by the quarterback. We run the 94 zone to the right and block the #3 defender to the left side.

The zombie is a switch call on the backside for the fullback (Diagram #9). The play is 95 zombie. We block 95 inside zone to the left. On the backside, zombie means we block man on man with the backside guard and tackle. The fullback folds inside on the linebacker. There is no read. It is a straight give play.

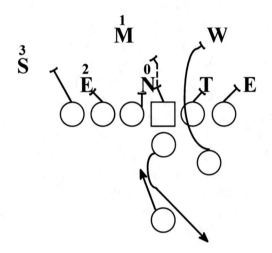

Diagram #9. 95 Zombie

When we use the code word book, we align a tight end to the backside or set him off the line of scrimmage to that side. That makes the defensive end to that side extend his technique and align wider. The blocking does not change. If we run 14 book, we have a backside tight end to the backside. His present widens the defensive end and makes his reaction easier to read. It also gives the defender more space to cover. We generally get the tight end to fake an inside movement toward the defensive end to freeze him. If the defensive end moves inside to stop the book, we block the tight end down on him, pull the tackle, and run the outside zone. The book play puts the defensive end in conflict.

If the defense is a bear front defense or shifts to the bear defense, we read the 3 technique defender (Diagram #10). The backside tackle influences the defender by faking a down block and climbs to the linebacker. Everything else on the play remains the same.

The stretch zone attacks the playside A gap to the playside D gap. The running back's aiming point

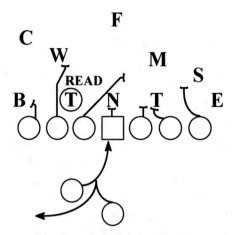

Diagram #10. Bear Defense

is the butt of the playside tight end (or the ghost tight end). When we run this play, we want to use stretch zone aiming points. We want to work for the outside armpit. We still want vertical push, but the stretch of the play comes from the wider aiming point.

The outside zone is our last zone play, and it attacks the perimeter. The ballcarrier's aiming point is to break containment and get the ball on the perimeter. The landmark may be two yards outside the tight end, and the play may be an option. We use lock-the-box principles and outside zone aiming points on outside zone plays. We want to rip, reach, and overtake defenders to lock the box and get the edge for the ballcarrier.

In our gap scheme, we have some general rules. The blocking rules in under center and spread carry over in our gap schemes. The offensive line must understand the track of the ball and backfield action to dictate the combos used. However, the rules and targets are the same.

GAP SCHEME RULES

- *Playside tackle:* B gap to backside linebacker
- *Playside guard:* A gap to backside linebacker
- *Center:* backside A gap to backside B gap
- *Pullers:* kicker/reamer based on code word

In the gap scheme, everyone must account for a gap. In this scheme, there is a ream blocker and a kick-out blocker. This offense falls into our 80 series. The 80 means the play is a counter. The 6 or 7 as the second digit means right or left and is a gap scheme play. The number punch 86 is a counter run to the right with gap scheme blocking.

The center in the blocking scheme identifies the second linebacker in the box, which is the defender we run the gap scheme to. In the diagram, the second linebacker in the box is the Will linebacker. The play is 86 punch (Diagram #11). "Punch" is a tag word for the gap scheme. With the fullback aligned behind the tackle, the word *punch* indicates that the fullback is the reamer on the play. His assignment is the Will linebacker. On the play, the playside guard and tackle gap block the A and B gaps to the Mike linebacker (backside linebacker). The center blocks backside for the pulling guard.

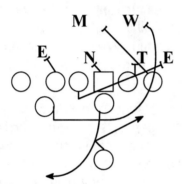

Diagram #11. 86 Punch

The guard pulls and kicks out the first defender past the tackle. When the guard pulls, he uses a convention pull with his shoulder pointed to the sideline. The fullback follows the pulling guard, turns inside his kick-out block, and blocks the Will linebacker. The fullback tries to enter the hole with his shoulder square to the line of scrimmage. That way, he turns up in the hole and does not drift to the outside. He wants to do that in case has to turn back on the Will linebacker.

If we run an 86 topper, everything on the play remains the same except the guard and tackles pull and the fullback cuts off the backside C gap. The guard is still the kicker and the tackle becomes the reamer and blocks the Will linebacker.

When we run this gap scheme, it is a vertical gap scheme. We tell the back to run the play in the A gap until he cannot. If he cannot get into the A gap, he follows the puller, but he does not want to bounce the play outside.

The code words we assign to the gap scheme are Mickey, hammer, Mickey-bash, punch, topper-bash, and shovel. The straight power play is Mickey. It gets its name from our strength coach. Hammer is the power bounce play. Mickey-bash is a power play with a speed sweep to the field. Punch is the counter play. Topper-bash is a guard and tackle speed sweep into the field. Shovel is another name for the dig play or Utah pass play.

The vertical power is Mickey. This play is 96 Mickey (Diagram #12). Because we are in a tight end set to the right, it is a 90 series play. Six tells us it is to the right and Mickey means A gap power. The offensive line blocks its rules. The fullback is the kicker and kicks out the first thing outside. The guard pulls and turns up on the Mike linebacker. When the guard pulls on the power, we use a skip pull. He does not turn his shoulder parallel to the sideline. He keeps his shoulder square to the line of scrimmage so he can plant and get upfield square. The playside guard and tackle combo-block for the 3 technique defender to the backside linebacker.

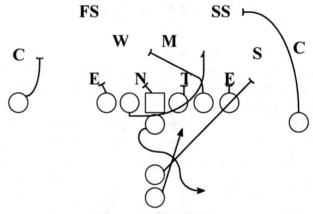

Diagram #12. Mickey

The running back hits the A gap if he can. If he cannot, he slides to the hip of the puller and finds the hole. The tight end on this play blocks the defensive end. On occasion, we flip the backside tackle and tight end if we are having troubling handing the defensive end with the tight end.

The hammer play is the bounce play that Stanford University runs. We run this from a three tight end set. The third tight end is the wing into the playside. It is a gap scheme, and we try to sell the linebackers that it is a Mickey play. The tight end and wing combo-block on the edge of the defense and cave it to the inside. The running back holds the A gap and bounces the play to the outside. If the A gap is open, the back takes it into the A gap. However, we are coaching to sell the A gap, bounce, and get on the hip of the puller.

We are trying to create a formation so the fullback ends up on the corner instead of the Sam linebacker. If the spill player is the corner, it is a mismatch. Everything else on the play is the same. We start in the A gap and bounce to the outside. We get a softer edge, and the play is a wider fit than the linebackers normally play. It becomes a difficult play for them to fit.

The Mickey-bash is a read play with gap scheme blocking (Diagram #13). On this play, we read the playside defensive end instead of kicking him out. We align the quarterback in the shotgun with the running back to the backside of the play. On the snap of the ball, the running back comes in front of the quarterback and over the ball. If the read defender stays inside and closes the hole, the quarterback gives the ball to the back on a speed sweep play. If the defensive end jumps outside on the running back, the quarterback keeps the ball and runs the quarterback power off gap scheme blocking.

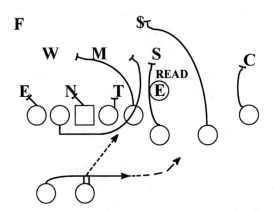
Diagram #13. Mickey-Bash

This play presents a problem on the inside linebackers. If we hand the ball to the running back, the ball gets to the perimeter in a hurry. If the quarterback pulls the ball, he has a downhill power play against linebackers running laterally.

We have a Q-Mickey, which almost looks like this play. The difference is we do not read the defender. The quarterback pulls the ball and runs the power following the puller. We kick him

out with the fullback and run the power with gap blocking. We like this play in a goal line situation.

The punch play is the counter. The guard is the kicker, and the fullback is the reamer. If you are going to run the power game, this is a good play to put into the scheme. It is not only a counter, but the kicker is a guard and not the fullback. That gives the fullback a break from the kick-out block. If you are a power team, it is brutal on the fullback if that is your scheme. This is a good change-up with the same blocking.

We can run a Q-punch, which is the counter action with the quarterback carrying the ball. It looks like the Mickey-bash play. Teams play the Mickey-bash by rotating their secondary to the field. We show them the Mickey-bash set, let the quarterback fake the running back, pull the ball, and run the punch into the boundary. It has the guard as the kicker and the fullback/tight end as the reamer.

The punch-plus means we are going to run the punch play to a tight end. We make the defensive end align wider in an extended position on a tight end. That puts more space between him and the inside 3 technique defender. It gives us more space to run the kick-out and gives the defender more space to try to close.

The topper-bash uses the guard and tackle pull with the bash scheme (Diagram #14). The quarterback reads the defensive end to the wideside of the field. If the defender comes up the field, he keeps the ball and runs the quarterback counter into the boundary. If the defensive end closes, he gives the ball to the running back on the speed sweep into the wideside of the field.

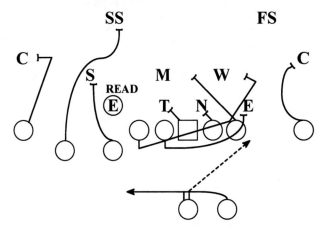
Diagram #14. Topper-Bash

I think this is good systematic football. You have gap schemes and zone schemes. You have a downhill running game. That puts a tremendous conflict on the defense because of the reaction components of them.

The last play in the gap scheme is the shovel pass. This is a triple option play with gap scheme blocking. We block the gap scheme and pull the tight end behind the line of scrimmage. He looks for the shovel pass to the inside by the quarterback. The quarterback reads the defensive end. If the end attacks him, the quarterback shovels the ball inside to the tight end. If the defensive closes on the tight end, the quarterback keeps the ball and runs an option on the support defender coming up the field. The pitchback is the running back.

We have talked about zone and gap schemes. We can run them both with multiple groupings, meaning we can use three tight ends or three wideouts and run the plays. We read, kick out, and log defensive ends. We can get the linebackers flat-footed with the counter and hammer schemes.

I started out talking about core values, and I want to end up talking about leadership. Last year, we played Penn State and lost in a tight, closely played football game. We had to play Maryland the next week and did not know how our players would react. I told them the story about the coal miners recently trapped in South America. The story was an international story, and they tabbed their story as "nine out alive." I told them the story about the adversity the coal miners went through in their life and death situation.

The leader of the coal miners held his men together and gave them hope and a belief that they would be rescued. While in the mine, they strapped themselves together in an attempt to keep from being swept away by the water that filled the cavern. In a dramatic scene on TV, they were rescued and brought up to the surface one man at a time. Their leader was the last man rescued out of the mine.

I told my team the only way we would beat Maryland was if we all linked up to the line so we could bring the best out of each other. We must have leadership, and the seniors have to be players that can be held accountable and can lead if it does not go well at the beginning of the game. If we link together, fight for each other, and block selfishness out, we can overcome anything.

If you want to know what we are about at Temple, this is what we are all about. The scheme is great and I like it, but that is not the secret to winning. You have to link your team together. You must get the staff linked together and find your leaders on the team.

I was an assistant coach for a long time, and I loved it. I coached high school football coach and the offensive line, and I am proud of it. I have been to the top of the heap and all the way to the bottom. I have had some great experiences, and I loved every minute of it. I was 62 years old before I got my first head coaching job at Temple.

In the business, you must have the will to keep going and the passion for what you are doing. You must believe in yourself, and you must surround yourself with good people. I invite you to come to see us, and I hope you will feel like you are a part of Temple. I appreciate the opportunity to be here, and I wish you nothing but the best. Thank you very much.

WIN WITH THE KICKING GAME

Virginia Tech

I want to start this off by thanking Nike® for all they do for football. It is a pleasure to be here. It is always encouraging to see all the high school and college football coaches. You are great people. It is five hours to Blacksburg from this area, and we encourage coaches to come down to visit.

We have won a lot of games at Virginia Tech, but we have not won the national championship yet. We have won 10 games in eight of the last 10 years. Four of the last five years, we have been to a BCS bowl. We have won big games to get to the big ball game. What we need to do is win that one big ball game. We have knocked on the door and are in the top 20 every year, but we need to open that door.

We know it takes players to continue to be successful as a program. I appreciate the fact that many of our players come from the coaches in this room. You do an outstanding job, and I appreciate that.

My topic is the kicking game. I do not know if this would be a good year for me to speak on this topic after this past year. We had a bad year in relationship to the kicking game. I used to say, if you have a good kicker, you should have a good kicking game. We put a lot of emphasis on it, devote practice time to it, and spend a lot of time on it in other areas. It is an important part of the entire program.

If you go back to the bowl game against Michigan, our kicking game broke down. We dominated them in the first half, but a mistake in the kicking game was our undoing. On a fourth-down play, we roughed the punter, and gave them a first down, which led to their first touchdown. On the ensuing kickoff, we fumbled the ball, which led to another bizarre play in the kicking game. They lined up for a field goal, had a bad snap, but ended up getting a tipped ball for the first down. The tipped ball happened when two of

our players ran together and an offensive lineman caught the ball for a first down. They did not score a touchdown, but they did get a chip shot field goal out of the play.

On a fourth-and-one, we ran an option rugby punt. It was an option to kick or run the ball, and we screwed it up. The game went to overtime, and we missed a field goal in the overtime. The topic of the talk is a true statement. The "Quickest Way to Win" a game is also the quickest way to lose one if you do not take advantage of the kicking game. During spring practice, we will get back to work on the kicking game and get it back to what it was.

To understand the importance of punting the football, you must understand field position. The reason I am into the kicking game—and particularly the punting game—is field position. The offense's chance to score is directly related to where they start each drive. The punt is a 40-yard offensive play. It amounts to 40 yards of field position when you kick the football.

CHANCES OF SCORING

Yard Line	Chance of Scoring
-20	1 out of 30
-40	1 out of 8
50	1 out of 5
+40	1 out of 3
+20	1 out of 2
+10	1 out of 2

It is a fact in winning a football game. If you play the field-position game, you have a better chance of winning. Part of the lecture is "making the kicking game important." That is a challenge to all of us. Most of the players today want to play offense or defense, but you have to make them play special teams. We do the opposite of that. We try to make the kicking game important so the players want to play special teams. We have an offensive, defensive, and special teams goals chart. This is our special teams goals for 2011.

SPECIAL TEAMS GOALS 2011

Pride

- Allow no more than 6 yards per return.
- Down punt inside the 10-yard line.

Kickoff Coverage Team

- Average starting the opponent at the 20-yard line or less.

Pride and Joy

- Average 10 yards per punt return.

Punt Rush/Field Goal/Extra Point Team

- Block a punt, field goal, or extra point, or force a bad kick every game.

Kickoff return team

- Start drives at the 28-yard line or beyond 60 percent of the time.

Field Goal/Extra point

- 100 percent of extra-point attempts.
- 66 percent (two out of three) on field-goal attempts.

No Penalties or Mental Mistakes

Hidden Yardage

- Gain 20 yards of field position in the exchange of punts.

We try to keep the goals simple. I do not want a detailed chart of statistics. I want to talk about the hidden yardage on the goals sheet. During the course of the game, we want to gain 20 yards of field position in our punts and the opponent's punts. Twenty yards of field position is two first downs. It is the hidden yardage in a football game.

MAKING IT IMPORTANT

- Head coach involved
- Most efficient way of operation
  - ✓ Offense, defense, more time for game plan
  - ✓ More time than normal for special teams game plan (four hours on Pride and Joy)
  - ✓ One new rush every week
- Head coach with special teams players
  - ✓ First four periods
- Help your pro career
- Never come before practice; never stay after practice
  - ✓ Middle of practice (everyone stops)
- Privileges by playing special teams
  - ✓ Pride and Joy during conditioning (get off early)
  - ✓ Pride and Joy verses Pride (less sprints)
- Same awards
  - ✓ Player of the game (offense, defense, special teams)
  - ✓ Big hit (Kahuna—do in front of team)
  - ✓ Goal chart
- Meeting time for kicking teams (Monday–Friday)
  - ✓ Pride: five minutes (Monday–Wednesday) before individual meeting

If you are going to make the kicking game important, the head coach must be involved with that part of the game. He does not hand the responsibility over to someone else. He is directly involved with the game. If he is involved, the player will feel it is more important. I oversee the entire game. I have coaches that coach each special team we have. They all are involved with the kicking game.

I found the most efficient way of operating the special teams program is to put one coach in charge of each aspect of the special teams. An example,is Bud Foster is in charge of the punt and kick block teams. From an operation standpoint, we want to spend the time in practice working on special teams. We want to game plan for the special teams as we do for the offensive and defensive game plans. As we watch film of the punt or kick protection teams each week, we generally find different ways to rush kicks each week. We add one new rush scheme each week.

We work our special teams the first four periods of each practice. The special teams players who do not play much during the other parts of a game begin to feel more a part of the team when you put the emphasis on special teams and practice it before other things. One thing we point out to our players is it could help those who want to play at the next level. Being a good special teams player can help a player make a pro football roster. It is very seldom that first-year college players can make an impact on a professional team as a starting player. They can affect the team by being a good special teams player.

With the limited roster positions available on a professional team, the player can increase his chance of catching on if he can play special teams. They increase their chances of making a professional team if they can excel in this area.

At Virginia Tech, the special teams never come before practice, and we never stay after practice. We put it in the middle of practice. What this statement says is we do not penalize the players who play special teams by making them come out early or stay late to work on special teams. I want the players to want to play on the special teams, not to discourage them.

The other image I do not want to project is the way we think about practice time. I do not want them to think that offensive and defensive teams are important and we can do special teams at another time. When we do our special teams work, we do it in the middle of practice; everyone stops and takes part.

We want to make playing special teams a privilege. During conditioning, members of the Pride and Joy teams get to go in early. When we work our punt block versus our punt return, we let them run less sprints during the conditioning period. They did their sprinting during the special period and run less than other players. We want the players to feel it is a privilege to play special teams.

If you reward players for offensive and defensive achievements, do the same thing for the special teams. We have a player of the game on offense, defense, and special teams. We have a "big hit" called Kahuna, which we give to a player on special teams.

A couple of years ago, I started having meeting time for kicking teams. I think it is tremendously important. That way, we can get out of the teams exactly what we want. If we have a punting drill on one day, the next day we show them the film of that drill. I think it is important to learn from what the players did the day before and use it as a teaching tool. Do not try to wait until the end of the week to show them their mistakes and correct them.

Our practice schedule for special teams stays the same throughout the year. I want to talk about our *Monday* practice schedule. The first thing we do on our Monday practice is kick a field goal. We give the field goal kicker a chance to kick a field goal. We get him in front of the team, and he gets one shot at the field goal. I try to do that as many times during the week as we possibly can. That makes him focus as if it were a game situation.

The second period is kickoff and kickoff return. I feel we overlook that area of the kicking game. We align our kickoff team against the kickoff return team. We put vest and helmet cover-ups on one team. Sometimes, it is hard to do that because of duplicate players on both teams. If you can, that is the simple way to work both teams at the same time.

After we finish the kickoff drill, we go to an individual period, pass skeleton period, and an option period. We follow those periods with the Pride (protection) scheme. We follow that period with an inside Pride and Joy rush. We finish the practice with three more drills that are offensive types of drills.

On *Tuesday*, we have the special teams drill right in the middle of practice. We work our Pride and Joy teams. The Pride team is our punt protection and coverage team. The Pride and Joy team is the punt block and punt return team. When we get into this drill, we can isolate the coverage team and look at what we want to see.

We can send the headhunters, wide coverage players, and watch their angles of coverage. You can send the interior players and watch to see if they fan and get into their lanes of coverage. I used to run this drill from five to eight reps of coverage. I now do two reps and get the type of effort I want. That is better than running eight reps and getting half-speed effort on half of them.

When we isolate on our coverage elements, we punt the ball to the Pride and Joy team. The returner catches the ball and does something with it. The headhunters coming down have to maintain leverage on the returner.

We have a special period during our practice (Diagram #1). The special period is more for backups instead of the front line players. In one area, we have the kickoff man working on pooch kicks, directional kicks, onside kicks, and pop-up kicks. We have the place kickers, holders, and kick blockers working in another area. The place kickers kick to the kickoff return men down the field. On the other side of the field, we have the snappers, punters, and punt returners receiving punts. We have coverage people covering and trying to touch the returners.

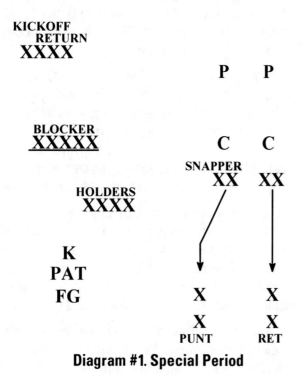

Diagram #1. Special Period

In this drill, we work a kick blocking drill (Diagram #2). The kick blockers start out on a line with the ball in the middle of the line. The blockers want to get as close to the ball as they can without aligning offside. If the protection scheme is zone blocking, the defender attacks uphill. He does not attack to the inside. He wants the zone to spread to the outside and not contract to the inside.

In the zone blocking scheme, as the defender attacks outside, the blocker puts up his outside arm and tries to force the defender outside with his hand. The defender does one of two things. The first thing is to dip and get his shoulder under the hand of the blocker, fire up through the hand, and penetrate around the blocker inside. The second thing he does is react like a pass rusher. He uses his outside hand to club the outside hand of the blocker. At the same time, he swims over the blocker with his inside hand.

Once the defender disengages from the blocker, he bends inside, and attacks the landmark. The landmark is one yard in front of the punter. In the drill, we mark the landmark with a practice vest or flat spot marker. If the defender knows he cannot block the kick, he pulls off and goes past the punter to his side. If the defender hits the landmark and does not block the ball, he will not fall into the kicker. We want the defender's hands to come out from in front of him as he runs to the spot. If he reaches across his body to the side, his body will hit the kicker if he does not get the ball.

He has to keep his eyes open and not turn his head to the side (Diagram #3). When we block the ball in this drill, we use a deflated ball. We want to practice blocking the ball off the shoe. We practice blocking the ball off both sides and up the middle. If the outside rusher aligns on the headhunter and cheats back inside to rush the kick, he must take the proper angle. If he does not start upfield on the outside of the blocker, he will not get to the landmark. He has to get to his original position to make his rush. If he rushes from wide, his angle will take him into the kicker.

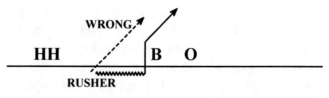

Diagram #3. Proper Angle

The punt formation we see so much today is the shield type of punt (Diagram #4). If the defender comes up the middle on the shield, I feel he has to

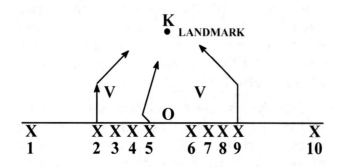

Diagram #2. Kick Block Drill

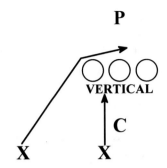

Diagram #4. Shield Punt Block

get to the shield blocker and use a vertical jump. He cannot jump horizontally into the shields. He wants to get height in front of the shields. If he comes from the side of the shield, he has to be under control on his run up. When he reaches a point on the shoulder of the outside shield, he bends inside in front of the kicker.

If the defender tries to come off the edge and not bend, he goes into the punter. I want know where the punter kicks the ball. If he comes directly up the middle, I want to jump and block it. If he steps to the side, I want to come off the edge.

I want to get back to Tuesday practice. We work the special period in the middle of practice.

Kicking

- Pride (priority) versus Pride and Joy (rush)
- Field goal versus field rush
- Pride and Joy (return) versus Pride (scout pride)
- Onside prevent
- Punt safe versus Pride (priority) pooch kick
- Kickoff return (squib, pooch)
- Pride and Joy versus Pride (scout pride)

We use the onside kick about three times a year. However, when you have to use it, you must be good at it. When you use an onside kick, the game is generally on the line. When we work on the squib and pooch kickoff, we practice the ball kicked close to the sideline. If we can let the ball go out-of-bounds instead of fielding it, we want to do that. You have to practice judgment and situational football. I used to rep these teams numerous times. I have gone to getting a fewer quality reps at full speed. During this time, we bring the field goal kicker out and let him attempt one field goal.

In our *Thursday* practice, we work a number of things. We work kickoff return followed by kickoff coverage. We use the Pride and Joy team in a rush drill versus a half-line scheme. In the half-line drill, we work the normal punt set first (Diagram #5). In this formation, we work five defenders on four blockers. In the normal set, the kickers count the defenders from the inside going out. We stack over the guard, and the defenders get the offensive count of #1 and #2.

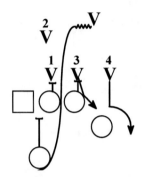

Diagram #5. Half-Line Punt Block

The defender outside the tackle is #3, and the defender outside the wingback is #4. The free defender blitzes between the guard and tackle. He is the defender who will block the kick. The free rusher must attack the line of scrimmage. Too many rushers get to the line, wait to see if the hole opens up, and then rush. You have to attack right away and go for the ball. If the blockers block the outside defenders, the defenders should stop their forward rush and start working for width. We only want one player to block the ball. If we have two players, they probably knock each other off the block path.

The reason we work outside is to hold up the eligible receiver if the punter tries to throw the ball. In some cases, the punter sees the block about to happen and runs the ball. In that case, the outside defenders work outside and make the tackle instead of letting him run for the first down. We work the same drill coming from the outside on the block. The half-line drill is good to work on the block.

We have two regular team periods and come back with more special teams practice. In that part of the practice, we use the Pride team. We work on a fake punt, pooch kick, and punt safe. In our situational punting, we work on Frosty, which tries to draw the defense offside. We have a fan on set, which means we kick the ball right away. We can also call the headhunters in from their wide alignments. We have another regular drill and conclude the special teams work with the field goal and field goal block team.

When we go to *Friday's* practice, we cover all the situational plays in a game.

Pride

- Grimm (callout)
- Frosty
- Fan on set
- Pooch versus punt safe
- Kicking out
- Kick at three seconds
- 11-man rush
- Take a safety
- Bad operation (-5, -6-yard line)
- Kick blocked behind line of scrimmage; run for first down

Kickoff Return

- Pop-up
- Squib
- Kickoff after safety

The Grimm callout is to combat the confusion on the sidelines during some games. To eliminate any confusion about which team or situation we want on the field, we have one coach call out what we want. When we practice kicking out, we place the ball at the -1-yard line and punt the ball. We use the kick at three seconds when we try to take time off the clock in the fourth quarter. On the 11-man rush, the punter takes a rocker step and kicks the ball. The only concern in that situation is to kick the ball somewhere. If we have a bad operation inside the five-yard line, we want to take a safety. If the ball is on the six-yard line or farther out, we pick up the ball and attempt to make something happen.

On Friday, we go over all the calls for Pride and Joy. We have one player on the team who makes all the calls.

Pride and Joy

- Pickle (callout), Boykin, and Reidy (punt return)
- Pride and Joy or field goal block on punt safety +40-yard line
- Jump
- Ball blocked (behind or past line of scrimmage)
- Peter or short versus return
- Kicker loses protection
- Block kick close to line of scrimmage
- Fake punt
- Spread

Pickle callout is like the Grimm callout in the punt-protection game. Boykin and Reidy are punt-return schemes. The term "jump" is about when to jump on a punted ball. If we block the ball behind the line of scrimmage, we want to pick it up and score. If the ball is close or over the line of scrimmage, we want to get away from it. The kicker losing his protection is like the quarterback throwing the ball. You cannot rough him after he has taken one step after kicking the ball. With the number of teams using the shield punt formation, we have to cover their responsibilities on the spread coverage personnel. We cover the same point with the field goal block team. The difference is when the field goal is blocked on third down. We want to secure a blocked kick on third down. On fourth down, you can try to pick it up and score. If we muff the ball and the offense recovers, we still get the ball.

Kickoff Coverage

- Huddle
- Squib
- After 15-yard penalty
- After safety
- Onside (feet team)

The thing we talk about is what happens when we kick off from the 45-yard line instead of the 30-yard line. We do not want to kick the ball through the end zone. We want to kick the ball high and drop it on the goal line. We want the high kick so we can cover deep and back up the offense. The feet team consists of the fast players. We want speed covering onside kicks.

What we tell our players on a punt safe play is to cover to the sidelines. We play our defense and make sure they kick the ball. We do not want to retreat down the middle of the field and let the ball come down on our heads. When we cover back, we cover to the sidelines.

I like the way we kick off and cover on kickoffs (Diagram #6). On our kickoff team, we have headhunters, coverage players, and safeties. The headhunters in the diagram are players #1, #4, #7, and #10. They can align at different places in the formation, but their responsibility is always the same. The headhunters are our more reckless players with good football instincts. They will go down and make a tackle. The coverage players take on blockers, read where he is trying to block them, and play across his face. After they get across the face, they return to their coverage lane and go to the ball.

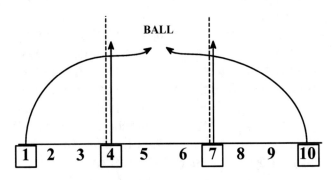

Diagram #6. Kickoff Headhunters Coverage (Middle)

On our coverage scheme, players #1 and #10 go straight to the ball. If the ball is in the middle of the field, they should arrive at the same time. Their assignment is to make the ball change directions. The worst thing for a kickoff cover team is to have the ball coming straight up the field. If the ball changes directions and starts sideways, we can get to it.

Players #4 and #7 cover five yards outside of the outside headhunters. The outside headhunters go to the ball, and the inside headhunters are five yards to their outsides. The ball is the only thing that makes any difference in our coverage. The ball determines the landmarks for our coverage team. If the ball moves right, the outside headhunters go to the ball and the inside headhunters cover five yards outside them.

If we kick the ball outside the hash marks, the #1 or #10 headhunter has a different angle to the ball (Diagram #7). If the ball goes to the left, the #1 headhunter does not bend in so far and has a more direct path to the ball. The #10 headhunter has to take an acute angle to get to the ball. The inside headhunters take their angles according to the ball and the headhunter to their side.

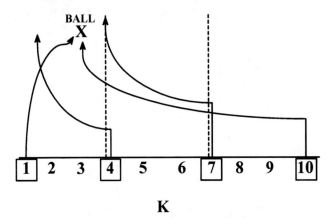

Diagram #7. Headhunters Kickoff Coverage (Side)

The coverage players get their landmark on the ball (Diagram #8). They cover down the field, keeping leverage on the ball. When they get 15 yards from the ball, they encounter the blockers. They lock out on the blockers and walk them back into the ball. As soon as the ball gets to them, they shed the blockers and attack the ball. They engage the block, keep leverage, and squeeze the ball. They play through the blockers to the ball.

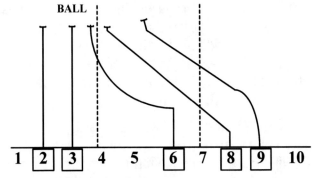

Diagram #8. Kickoff Coverage Players Coverage

Coverage players #3 and #8 are always outside the ball. Players #2 and #9 are the contain players on the kickoff. The #6 player covers down the middle of the field and never goes across the hash mark if we kick the ball outside the hash marks. We do not want to get the coverage team stacked in their coverage.

The last elements of the coverage team are the safeties (Diagram #9). The #5 players and kicker are the safeties. If the ball is outside the hash mark, the #5 player covers in that area of the field. The kicker covers down the hash mark to that side. I want the safeties to be between five and eight yards and no more than 10 yards behind the coverage players.

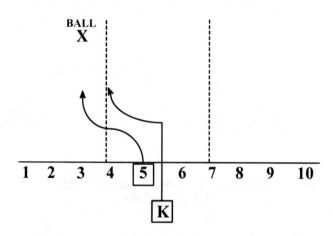

Diagram #9. Kickoff Coverage Safeties

I want to cover a couple of things on the punt return (Diagram #10). The outside rushers are #2 and #9. They make sure the offense punts the ball. They peel back to the inside and get inside out leverage at the ball. Blockers #3, #4, #7, and #8 jam the coverage team at the line of scrimmage and retreat with their assignments, getting inside leverage on them. The #6 rusher goes over the top of the center and forces the ball up the middle. He slows down the center with his charge. The #5 blocker retreats through the middle of the field and becomes the personal protector for the return man.

The #1 and #10 blockers are deep with the return man. They are responsible for the headhunters coming from the outside. They want to get inside leverage on them and block them to the outside. If the offense has a good punter, we probably will end up fair-catching the ball.

We call the return I like against the shield protection scheme "full rush, return right" (Diagram #11). I like this return because you threaten the punter with a rush scheme. The

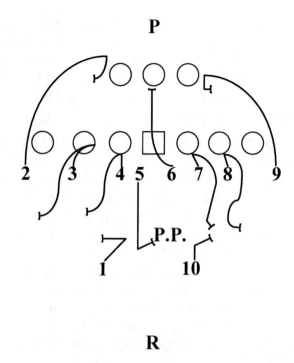

Diagram #10. Middle Return vs. Shield Punt

blockers do not release the line of the scrimmage and cover with no regard for the block. It slows down the coverage. This is a full rush on the shield. The #5 and #6 rushers in the middle cross their path as they attack the middle shield blocker. We feel that may confuse the blocker about who to attack. The #1 rusher comes through the punter and sets up at the rear of the return.

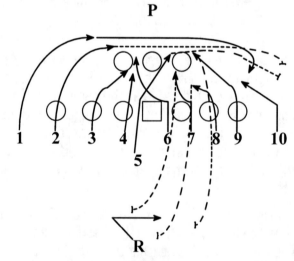

Diagram #11. Full Rush, Return Right

I like this scheme because we get pressure coming off the edges of the formation. The left side rushers fan through the formation and wall to the right of the punt returner. The right side rushers do not try to get into any type of wall to the right. They peel off and get into the middle of the return, blocking coverage players coming from the punt returner's left side.

The next return is a combination of the first two I showed you (Diagram #12). We have six rushers forcing the punt. Rushers #3 through #8 force the punt from the edge and inside. The #2 rusher is away from the wall and has the outside headhunter man-to-man as his blocking assignment. We want to wall the coverage to the outside. The #9 rusher has to keep the right headhunter on the line of scrimmage as long as he can. When the coverage escapes the line of scrimmage, the #9 rusher runs with him, keeping outside leverage.

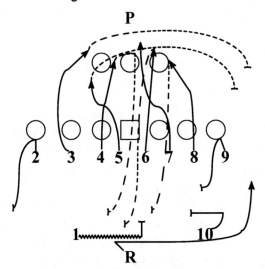

Diagram #12. Right Return

The #1 back becomes the personal protector and blocks the most dangerous man coming down the middle of the field. The #10 back has to get the returner into the wall. He takes the most dangerous man, coming down the right side of the return. As in the last return, the left side rushers continue their path through the kick formation and form the wall to the right side of the returner. The left side rushers fan back through the middle, looking to pick off coverage people. This gives us the best of both returns. We get security on the ball and rush on the punter.

We have a return called "double" (Diagram #13). We like to return the ball up the side. On this return, we double-team the coverage team

to the side of the return. Rushers #2, #3, and #4 are responsible for forcing the kick and setting the wall. The right side rushers double up on the coverage personnel at the line of scrimmage. The #5 and #6 rushers double on the guard. We single block the tackle with #7. The #8 and #9 rushers double the right side headhunter.

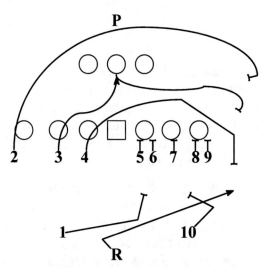

Diagram #13. Right Return Double

When we double the coverage personnel, we let one blocker attack the coverage, and the other blocker sits. That allows us to see what the coverage is going to do. We normally attack from the inside of the coverage man. The outside blocker sits and waits to see the reaction of the coverage man. The #1 back takes the headhunter coming down the left side and secures the catch. The #10 back takes the most dangerous threat coming down the middle of the field. That is usually the center covering down the middle. The #10 blocker wants to get the returner into the wall. We form the wall with the left side rushers, forcing the kick and setting the wall.

I like this return because we keep the coverage on the line of scrimmage to the side of the return. That gives the return man a chance to get started back upfield. If he can gain 10 yards on the return, that is one first down. If he gets 20 yards, that is two first downs. We can run the return either way. If we run the returns to the left, we reverse the assignments for the blockers.

You are always welcome at Virginia Tech. I appreciate your attention, and come down to see us if you can. Thank you very much.

BASIC PRINCIPLES OF MAN-TO-MAN COVERAGE

Robert Morris University

Everything I have learned in football, basically, I learned from Coach Dan Radakovich. I have been fortunate in that I had a great teacher. Coach Rad has done everything, and he has coached everything. The one thing he taught me is very simple: "If it doesn't make sense, then you are not supposed to do it." He always tried to make it simple for the athletes.

My lecture is about man-to-man principles. We run a lot of pressure packages, and it requires good perimeter play. I have talked with high school coaches who say they do not have the athletes to play man-to-man defense. My feeling is this: we do not have the linebackers to cover man-to-man. We try to make sure when we use man-to-man principles that we are getting our linebackers to apply pressure and to get after the offense.

We like to keep one safety free. We do not play a lot of zero coverage. The pressure applied by the linebackers really helps us on the quick throws and the deep throws. Our philosophy consists of:

• No fourth quarter touchdowns
• No completions +25
• Create three turnovers
• No 100-yard receiver
• No 225-yard passer
• Quarterback rating under 68 percent
• No missed tackles
• No missed checks
• Win

I know some of the other defensive coaches have talked about no big plays. That is a part of our philosophy as well. We feel the quarterback must earn his completions. If he is to drive the ball downfield, he will have to complete some passes, and we know we must tackle the receivers once they catch the ball. The essentials of a good secondary are as follows:

• Line up properly.
• Key properly.
• Communicate.
• Use proper technique.
• Develop great footwork.
• Take proper leverage angles.
• Have great play entry.
• Develop great ball skills.
• Study your opponent.
• Never ignore the fundamentals.
• Practice for perfection.

We think teaching stance is important, particularly for the corners. They have to see one-half of the field. Safeties have to see both sides of the field. We do not use a backpedal much in our coverage. We are a shuffle-step coverage type of team. The reason is this: the transition in the hips from the takeoff takes some time. If the defender uses a backpedal, he does not know when to get out of the backpedal. So we prefer to use a shuffle step.

A good stance allows you freedom for quick movement and permits correct steps:

• Flex ankles, knees and hips
• Hips are cocked in slightly
• Weight on forward foot and balls of feet
• Shoulders forward
• Head up and chin out over toes
• Arms hanging loosely
• Eyes focused on keys
• Alert but relaxed

I will say by not using the backpedal—and using the shuffle—on intermediate routes, there is a little more difficulty in the shuffle technique. To eliminate some of the difficulty, we like to use pressure. We tell our corners on the perimeter to be quick and to be deep. On the intermediate plays, it is up to the linebackers and line to get pressure on the quarterback and force the pass.

When we talk about man-to-man coverage from a front standpoint and a gap-cancellation front, we want to make sure we contain the quarterback, assign pass contain, and assign the pressure lanes. We want contain lanes and pressure lanes when we are talking about bringing heat. From a perimeter standpoint, we want to be able to key the depth of the quarterback.

BACKPEDAL

The objective of a good pedal is to enable you to change the angle of your drop without crossing your legs. The longer you stay square, the more effective your coverage will be.

- Weight is centered over your front foot.
- Shoulders should be in front of hips.
- Bend at the waist.
- Push off front foot, and step with your back foot.
- Shoulders remain level at all times.

The only reason we backpedal is for our safeties. We want them to be two-way players. Coach Rad was not a huge backpedal guy, and I had to adjust to that. However, getting out of the transition is important.

MOVEMENT

- Pedal—takes time and you better do it a lot.
- All movements should be natural and relaxed.
- Back foot must move first.
- Do not turn hips until the wide receiver forces you.
- Stay square through 14 yards.
- Study angle of wide receiver's hips to determine deep or intermediate routes.
- Shuffle and open.
- Fish tail.
- Key three-step drop.
- Eyes on quarterback after second quarterback step, settle, and eyes back to wide receiver.
- Read, shuffle, run.

I read a great deal. In coaching in college, often you force the players off the field into meeting rooms. I took a quote from Coach Tomlin of the Steelers. He was asked what makes a good cornerback.

"It is a physically taxing position. You have to have a great deal of God-given ability and belief in that. Now, how do you measure their belief in their ability? Not by what they say, but by what you see on tape: how they play, how they respond to positive things, how they respond to negative things. All of that helps you build a profile, if you will."

I believe that action speaks much louder than words. It is not what they say, but what they do. Players will say, "Yeah, Coach. I got you. I will take care of it in the game." I do not want to hear what they say. I want to see it on the tape. It is important for us to see it on the tape. What we see on the tape is evaluated. We want to see how they respond to positive plays and, more important, how they respond to negative plays.

It is obvious defensive backs are going to experience a "burn period." It does not matter if it is at the Pop Warner level to the NFL; you are going to get beat. It is part of the game. As much as we work on stopping the offense, they spend as much time as we do working to beat the defense. It is critical how the players will respond when they get the ball thrown over top of them. We are looking for a player who has thick skin, does not tuck his tail, and can rally and make another play. We want to teach them in terms of the mental preparation as much as possible.

MAN-TO-MAN DEFENSE

You must understand that, when playing man-to-man, we are bringing pressure up front. Thus, we are trying to cause havoc behind the line of scrimmage. If we do not succeed, and the quarterback gets the ball off, our goal is to:

- Stop the big play
- Deny the reception of 10+ yards

We will not have a high interception ratio in man-to-man, and that is to be expected.

Basic Principles

• Know the type of blitz, balanced or overload. Know where your help is.

• Focus on the hip of the receiver nearest your leverage.

• Maintain your leverage. Never be driven to head-up position.

• Keep the feet moving, do not brace down (weight on the heels).

• Versus all out routes, drive through the outside number to ensure the tackle and to avoid leaving yourself vulnerable to the out-and-up.

• If beat, do not panic. Run to the catch hand.

We are teaching "knock downs and not interceptions." That may be counterproductive to what defensive coaches think. We do not have a high interception rate because we want our defenders to play through the receivers.

Our philosophy is to *dominate the short game and the deep ball*. Make them earn intermediate routes. In our superman blitz package, you will always have post help with the free safety. You will align outside the crotch of the receiver in normal split alignment. In wider plays on an inside technique, *you will never be wider than the numbers in man-to-man.*

Your eyes should be on the quarterback for the quick or three-step pass. If it is going to be either one of these, the quarterback's shoulders will turn as soon as he starts away from the center. When you clear the three-step, then you want your eyes to go directly to the inside hip of the receiver. You must maintain leverage (inside/out) as long as possible. If the ball is not thrown quickly, you will be forced to turn into the receiver and run with him.

We encourage our players to coach each other. In our film sessions, it is not just me up there teaching them. I will have one of our players come up front and have him coach the rest of the secondary. We have questions come up all the time. For example, they will ask, "Why are we lining up outside the numbers when it is an oversplit when we know that number is coming back inside?" It is a simple thing, but we have to constantly remind our players of the little things. The little things are important. Coaching players at the college level is similar to coaching the high school players in this regard. You have to constantly remind them of the fundamentals.

When we talk about the three-step, we are talking about the quarterback's release. If the quarterback is in the shotgun, it is the catch and when his shoulder turns. If he is under center, in the quick game we are talking about that second step as a drive step. He settles, and then we get the directional step.

From a depth standpoint, we have our corners playing 7 to 10 yards deep. They key the quarterback through the three steps. Once the quarterback settles, we settle and get our eyes back on the receiver. We have to train our eyes. This is one of the most important tools they have, and we teach them to train their eyes. We do not want them looking at the quarterback, and then when he throws the ball they try to find the wide receiver. On the quick game and the out or slant routes, we tend to overplay one or the other.

As I said, we want to train the eyes. Once we key the three steps, our eyes are back on the wide receiver. Where they catch the ball is where we are going to force them. If the ball is below the number, we use the 12th man, which is the sideline. We force him outside and out-of-bounds. If the receiver catches the ball inside the numbers, then we are going to force him to the free safety.

In the passing game today we see 55 percent of the quick passing game. A lot of teams are reverting to the "now" passing game. As soon as the ball is snapped, the quarterback is throwing the ball *now!* It comes down to their athlete versus your athlete. You must decide how to defend in that situation. You must ask your players where the receiver is catching the football. You cannot take anything for granted because a five-yard hitch route could turn into a 65-yard touchdown. So we want to teach them if the receiver catches the ball below the numbers, we want to use the 12th man on the sideline and force them out-of-bounds. If they catch the ball inside, we want to force the receiver inside to the safety.

KEY THE TRANSITION

Throughout the process, you must concentrate on the receiver's inside hip, searching for transition signals.

Transition Signals

- Hips sink
- Feet pitter-patter
- Hand breaks

We teach our corners the 5-10-15 yards phase, and the intermediate phase. A lot of the kids want to key the earhole. We see it on our films. We see them lined up on the wide receivers, and they are looking at the receiver's helmet. The first thing that is going to drop in the transition for the receiver is his hips. We want to make sure our backs have their eyes on the receiver's hips and they are seeing that transition.

A drill we use to help our backs is the trace drill. We teach our backs to mirror the transition. If that wide receiver steps to us, we give ground. If he uses a slide-shuffle step, we give ground. We mirror what he does. If he steps back, we step up. We want to get comfortable where that three-and-a-half yard cushion breakdown area is.

Once he separates and gets broken down at three yards, we key his route. We will give up the long throw to the outside to the sideline, but we are not going to give up the deep ball.

WIDE RECEIVER CLEARS UPFIELD

If the receiver continues upfield, your vision should come off his hip and go to his head gear. It is important, as you turn and run, to continue to search the receiver's hip until you are convinced he is going vertical. You want to keep your pads just on the upfield side of his pads. When his head gear turns to find the ball, you should now see his eyes and hands. If you have top side position, you want to lean into the receiver, club him with your near hand, and cut him off as you turn your head back inside to find the football.

Continue to run throughout the process. If you are not on top of the receiver when he looks to catch the ball, forget about making the interception. Now, you must play his catch hand and deny the reception. You must avoid making contact with the receiver. Do not be afraid to be an actor at the last second, pretending to look for the ball.

BUMP-AND-RUN

They call this technique bump-and-run for a reason. It is not called run-and-run. We see film where corners allow the receiver to come off the ball and just run around the corner. When we teach bump-and-run, we want to take something away from the receiver. We want to split the receiver's inside foot in our alignment. We want to see the corner with his hand up and active. Bump-and-run is something we like to use to take away the short throws. The guesswork is out in terms of the routes.

The things we want to focus on are his *feet, face,* and his *hands!* We want to match up with his feet, and we want to look where we are jamming him. There are a lot of different ways to teach bump-and-run. Some coaches teach the defenders to look at the hips on the release. We do not think this is the best way to teach it. We want to teach the defender where he is the strongest, and that is up top. Our eyes are going to be up on his eyes. We want to look where we are jamming the receiver.

If you teach the defender to keep his eyes on the receiver's hips, what happens is this: the defender gets overextended and low, and he has to reach for the receiver as he comes off the ball. When he gets low and he reaches, the wide receiver blows past him. We want to match and mirror the wide receiver.

We do a mirror drill most every day. We take a wide receiver, and line him up between two cones that are six or seven yards apart. We have the wide receiver work back and forth between the cones. We want to mirror on the line where he lines up. The feet are the most important thing. If you are not athletic with your feet and cannot move your feet, you can't jam. If you are going against a poor athlete, you can jam him on the line and shock the receiver. We would rather teach it where our feet have to be in position. We want to be athletic before we jam the receiver. This is the most important thing.

The hands are the last part of the technique. That jam does not have to happen on the line of scrimmage. It can happen two or three yards down the field. If the defender is real good and can jam the wide receiver on the line, that is great. Most of the wide receivers that we are facing are not the same as the receivers as in the SEC.

Bump-and-Run Basic Principles

- Square balanced stance as defined in stance section.
- Eyes on the receiver's mid-section.
- Wrists cocked, ready to collision the receiver.
- Approach the line of scrimmage with a plan of attack. You dictate to the receiver what type of release you will give him.
- When playing inside man position, *do not* honor an outside fake, be patient, stay square.
- Make a receiver release through your body position. Maintain a square alignment to the line of scrimmage to decrease running lanes. *Use your hands!*
- On outside release, use your off-hand jam and take the proper cut-off angle to squeeze the receiver into the sideline and take away fade. Do not retrace the receiver's footsteps, cut off, and squeeze the upfield route.
- On an inside release, clamp and squeeze the receiver down to the ball, and do not let him get his shoulders turned upfield.
- When running upfield with a receiver, focus the eyes on the far hip for an indication of breaks in route. Move the eyes to the outside shoulder area as the receiver moves out of the break area.
- On breaks into your position, force the receiver to go over the top of your position, run him out of his route with your body position.
- On sit-down routes, drop your weight and turn into the receiver.
- If playing press on a slot receiver versus a double width formation, be prepared to defend a quick fade up the seam.

There are three things we talk about. After five yards, we want to get a jam. We emphasize to our players that the jam does not have to happen at the line of scrimmage. This is particularly true on an outside release. We want to stay square as long as we can match the receiver. Once he commits outside, then we are going to jam him. We do not want to open up the gate too soon as the receiver comes off the line of scrimmage. We want to stay as square as we can as long as we can.

Three Phases of Bump-and-Run

- *Fight:* This occurs first five yards
- *Chase:* 10 yards, eyes on hips
- *Finish:* 15 yards plus—The most important!

If he comes inside on your leverage on the bump-and-run from the inside position, we want a two-hand jam, and we want to be physical in the jam. We want to drive him all the way. If he comes inside on his release, we are going to jam the crap out of him and drive all the way down inside.

We try the two-hand jam as much as we can. Again, the three phases of the bump-and-run techniques are the fight, chase, and the finish. We use the jam on the fight for the first five yards.

The chase is the 10-yard phase. Now, the eyes must be on the hips of the receivers. We tell the defenders to get an arm's length away, to get their eyes on the wide receiver, to get into a natural position, and to get his eyes on the hips of the receiver. When that receiver gears down, that is the first thing that gears down.

The finish is 15 plus yards. Once he clears the 10-yard window, the defender now looks at the earhole. We use the eye indicator to look for the ball. There are two ways to teach it: in phase and out of phase. In the out phase, you have to run to the receiver's hands. Do not look back to the football. If we can put our hands on the receiver, we are going for the "basket" he makes with his hands as he reaches for the ball. If we are in phase, we are going to look the ball in. If the wide receiver is in phase, we are going to "look," and then we are going to "locate."

The finish to me is the most important. You must find players who will finish. You must emphasize the finish in the film sessions. You can do everything right, but if you are not a finisher, you will have a hard time playing a defensive corner.

Some of the things we talk about in bump-and-run include staying square. It is similar to a pass rusher in that you must have a plan of attack. You must know the down-and-distance. What blitz is our defense using? Where are you in terms of the field position?

We want them to be aware of the distance between the field and the boundary. We tell our boundary player to be very aggressive. We tell our field player in man-to-man to play a little more cautiously. Also, we tell him to play deeper, and to play cautiously.

COMMON MISTAKES IN PRESS COVERAGE

- *Spread feet:* Do not get too wide with your feet.
- *Hands lead:* Think feet, face, and then hands.
- *Open gate:* Must pay the toll first before leaving.
- *Step up:* Be patient with all receiver fakes.
- *Cross over:* Stay square for as long as you can.
- *Punch extension:* Do not get overextended, which will get you off balance.
- *Peeking:* Do not look back at quarterback.
- *Looking back too soon:* Three levels = 5-10-15. Fight/chase/finish!
- *No separation:* Keep the receiver on your hip. Don't push off. You want to feel the receiver.
- *When do I look back:* Receiver's hip in the chase, then indicator, which is eyes to receiver's hands.
- *Finish:* Get in a good habit of finishing the play!

I will take questions as we go through the film. Thank you.

SHORT PASSING GAME AND SCREEN PASS

Baylor University

I know the last speaker on Saturday night is a good spot for me to be speaking. That is what I love about being where I am right now. If they told you to name the 10 top football teams in America, I am not sure anyone would mention Baylor. That to me is very inspiring and invigorating. I am like the dog they left outside in the backyard and everyone else gets to go in the house. I have been left out a bunch of times in my coaching career, and I like working my way to get in the house.

That is like the players we recruit at Baylor. I do not want players who grew up on silk sheets. I want players who grew up with no sheets. I want players who think outside the box and do not want to follow the path of others. They want to create the path. It has been a fun four years at Baylor. We do not think we have arrived as a prominent power. We know we have a long way to go.

We have a ways to go both on the field and off it. We have a long way to go as far as recruiting and earning national recognition. However, we are getting closer, and that helps us. Now we are a school that is getting some respect. When I first went to Baylor, having people respect us was one of my main goals. I wanted people to respect us when they played us. I feel we have done that.

When we line up, it will be a 60-minute game, and we will play our butts off for those 60 minutes, regardless of the outcome. We were behind in 7 of the 10 games we won this year. We were behind in 6 of the 7 conference games we won.

Our players are fighters, and most of them were not premier players coming out of high school. However, it is not how you start but how you finish that is the important thing in this game. They believe in finishing strong and fast. It has been a fun deal this year at Baylor.

We have just finished recruiting, and this is one of my days off before we go back to work. I wanted to be here. I love talking football. My father was a high school coach. I have been around football all my life, and I have never done anything else and do not care to do anything else. I have coached every day of my life in the state of Texas.

In 1984, I got my first head coaching job at a little 2A school in west Texas. From 1984 until now, I have been a head coach every year except for the three years when I was an assistant at Texas Tech. It has been a lot of fun, and I have had a good run. I have been blessed to be in very good situations with good people. I think it is harder to sustain a program than it is to build one. I have gone into situations that many coaches did not want.

In 1988, I took the head coaching job at Stephenville High School. They had not been to the state playoffs since 1952. I stayed there 12 years, won 4 state championships, and had a bunch of players go on to play in college. I had some good people that played for me. I had some players that were hungry. They had a mission and a plan, along with discipline and determination to go with it. That is how we won some football games.

You do not show up at a school and tell them we are going to do things a certain way. At the high school level, you must play with the players you have. You must adapt your philosophy to the personnel you have on your team. That is what I have always done. In 1985, I started throwing the ball around at Hamlin High School, a little 2A school. That year, we went 13-0-1.

In the mid-1970s, I played football at the University of Houston for Bill Yeoman in the split back veer. I am a good example of never getting a second chance to make a first impression. If I had gone to Houston and treated people with no respect and been a bad actor, I would never have gotten the chance to be the head coach there 30 years later. When I became the head coach at Hamlin in 1984, we ran the split back veer and the wishbone. When we played against better people, we got beat. I knew we had to do something different to have a chance to win.

That next year, we went to a shotgun, one-back set and started throwing the ball around. We progressed from there to now in our passing offense. I figured out if you wanted to beat teams that had better personnel, you had to do something different. That is where our philosophy came from back in the mid-1980s.

I got my first college job in 1999 at Texas Tech under Mike Leach. I was the running backs coach and coached some great players. I had a player by the name of Wes Welker. He had one scholarship offer coming out of high school. We signed him a week after the signing date. No one wanted him. When you put on the tape, he did everything and never came off the field. He punted, kicked off, did the place kicking, returned punts and kickoffs, and played safety on defense and quarterback on offense. He was the best player on the field.

When they brought the tape to me and asked me what I thought, I told them it was a no-brainer. I told them if he makes those kinds of plays in high school, he would do the same thing in college. He made the plays in college and now he makes the same plays at the pro level. It only made sense. A football player is a football player at every level. It did not matter that he was 5-9, 178 pounds, and ran the 40-yard dash in 4.48. He was a football player.

In 2003, I got the head coaching job at the University of Houston. It was the lowest-paying job in Division I football. The program was down, and no one wanted the job. They had not been to a bowl game in 13 years and had not won a conference championship outright since 1979. The attendance was dropping, and no one cared. I cared because I played there and had three children graduate from there. I loved the school. It is a great city, and I thought it was a great opportunity to make a run at a good program. We were fortunate enough to have some great players. We had Kevin Kolb, who now plays for the Arizona Cardinals. He started for us for four years and at one time held most quarterback records in the nation. We had a wide receiver by the name of Donnie Avery, who became the first receiver taken in the pro draft in 2008.

Donnie had one scholarship offer coming out of high school. He caught nine passes as a senior in high school. It was between Arkansas State and us.

I stayed at Houston five years, and we had some good football players and won one conference championship, played in the Liberty Bowl, and lost to South Carolina. I got the job at Baylor in 2007, with the first season being 2008. I had a player that came with me by the name of Robert Griffin III. He came from high school as a midterm graduate. He had the best times in the nation in the high school immediate and high hurdles. He could have gone back for his senior year in track and broken all those high school records.

However, he wanted to play football. That is what I loved about him. He was the premier track athlete in America, and he wanted to be a football player. That meant a lot to me. I was fortunate to have him for the last four years. I watched him develop, lead, and grow as an outstanding person. He is a great ambassador for football in general. I am talking about football at all levels. Robert Griffin III has it all together. It is not a front because what you see is what he is. He is a winner and why he stands a chance to be the first pick in the draft this year.

At Baylor, we have good players. Three years ago, we had the second pick in the draft in Jason Smith, who went to St. Louis. We had two first-round picks last year, and we will have two this year. Kendall Wright will be a first-round pick along with Robert Griffin III. We have had good players that have produced for us on the field. That is what the game of football is all about. It is about production and performance on the field. You practice to perform and produce. You do not practice to be the best receiver at Baylor. We want them to be the best in America. When they are the best players in America at their positions, that means something.

I want players that want to be the best in America. That is the only way you win at the national level. They pay the coaches to produce those kinds of players. That is what we are trained and paid to do because that is our job. I hope Baylor does not falter because we lose Robert Griffin III. I am not completely stupid, and I understand that he is a dynamic football player that can do amazing things. However, that is why we coach.

He was hurt the year before in the third game, and we had to fight our butts off the rest of the season. We won some big games coming down the stretch. We have to hang on, keep fighting, and keep producing to keep the program going at the level we are now. If football is all you think about, care about, and all you do, then you have a chance to stay in the game for a while. I want to coach another 10 years because it is fun to compete. There is nothing like a happy locker room after a big win. There is nothing more satisfying than to get a player to play his heart out for his college. It is inspiring, and it takes inspired people to make it happen.

In the players, I want big-butted linemen and players that can run. I want players that are going to fight on the field and fight their butts off to win. At the end of the day, that is the name of the game. Everybody has good people. You have to find an edge so you can win. It could be the mentality, physicality, or athleticism, but you must find something to separate us from the other teams so you can win.

We are looking for things that will give us a chance to win. Twenty years ago, I might have phrased that as the "keys to victory." There are no keys to victory. If there were, we would all do it. These things go on in our coaching room that will give us a chance to win.

Keys to Give You a Chance

- "No" is never an answer.
- Surround yourself with passionate coaches.
- Understand the difference between playing a game and playing to win.

In our staff meetings, if someone asked a question about trying something new or doing something different, the answer is always yes. No is never an answer, and we will find a way to get the job done if it helps our football team, our student athletes, or our university. That one thing eliminates many negatives. We will find a way to get it done.

You have to surround yourself with passionate people. I know you hear that all the time, but I hope you believe it because it is true. You must have coaches that are passionate, inspired, and care enough about others to perform at a high level for

them. It is critically important to your program. Everything you say or do must be done that way. Your players are watching how you conduct yourself and are trying to read you. They want to know if you are in the job for yourself or for them. The coaches have to make sure the players know that you care about them as a person, not just a football player. They need to know you care about their lives.

You have to understand the difference between playing the game and playing the game to win. You cannot worry about consequences. We finally decided this year to play every game to win, especially offensively. We played every snap to win. We were not trying to set up touchdowns, get down to third-and-one, or situations like that. We tried to score on every snap within the game structure. We did not try to go to the body to set up the knockout shot. We wanted to come out and play fast, fearless, and physical.

I want to show you some stats we compiled on offense this year.

Baylor Offense

- *#1 total offense:* 587 yards/game
- *#4 passing offense:* 352 yard/game
- *#10 rushing offense:* 236 yard/game
- *#1 in first downs:* averaged 29/game
- *#1 in explosive plays.*
- We averaged 568 yards and 40.2 points versus ranked opponents, which was #1 in the country.
- We punted less than any team in the country.

We were #1 in total offensive in the country of all the major conferences. We were #4 in passing offense and #10 in rushing offense. We were the only offense in the country with 200 yards rushing and 200 yards passing in every game. The thing that is misleading about us is our rushing offense. We will run the football and run it effectively.

I do not know if you saw us in the Alamo Bowl. The defensive staffs were sweating that day. It got crazy in that game. Sometimes, that happens. In our bowl game, we set the all-time bowl record with 777 yards of total offense and a bowl record 67 offensive points.

QUARTERBACK DRILLS

I am going to talk about some quarterback drills. The drills I am going to talk about are:

• Quick release

• Stand parallel (lock it in)

• Stance: easy and hard way

• Walkaway: easy and hard way

• Backpedal

• Walk forward

• Shuffle in pocket

• Lateral: easy and hard way (screen throws)

• Ball security

You want to have a purpose for every throw. Every throw is a big throw. It does not matter if you are warming up or throwing in a game. We take a lot of pride in that. Robert Griffin III had 13 interceptions in the past two years and threw the ball 800 times. He is a smart quarterback and knows how to take care of the football.

The first drill is a feet parallel drill (Diagram #1). We align the quarterbacks 10 yards apart from the receivers and make them stand on a line. They throw the ball with both feet on the line. They do not step or stride into the throw. We work on ball placement and snapping the hips. The throw starts from the ground up. The first movement we work on is the arm movement.

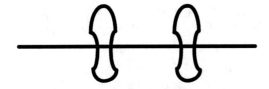

Diagram #1. Parallel Drill

The next drill works on the throwing stance (Diagram #2). They align 10 yards apart with their normal stance for their throwing arm. If they are right handed, their left foot is on the line, with the right foot dropped back off the line. I want the toes pointed slightly outside. They do not get foot movement involved in this drill. They stand with the nondominant foot forward and the dominant foot back and then throw the ball. They do not move their feet during the throw of the ball. They should end up on their toes when they deliver the ball. We

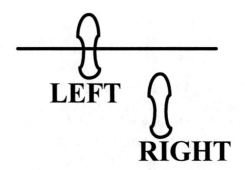

Diagram #2. Throwing Stance

do the drill on command, with the coach giving the command to throw.

The ball is in the throwing position, waiting for the command. On the command, the quarterback wants to get the ball out fast. The longer the quarterback holds the ball, the more time he gives the defense to move. When the coach calls "Hup," he throws as quickly as they can. I tell the quarterback, if you do not have the ball, the defense will not hit you. If you hold the ball, it will.

We call the next drill the easy way (Diagram #3). It is a combination of the parallel throw and the throwing stance drills. The quarterback begins the drill with his feet in a parallel stance, facing away from the target. On the command, the quarterback does a quarter turn to his left (right handed) to face the target and executes the throw from the throwing stance drill. In every drill, we want the quarterback to throw a catchable ball.

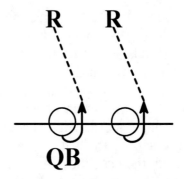

Diagram #3. Easy Way

The hard way drill is just the opposite of the easy way. It is the same drill, except they turn to their dominant arm. If the quarterback is a right-handed quarterback, he turns to his right side to face his target. This is a more difficult movement to get the feet set properly. He cannot simply make a quarter turn to be in position. He has to make a half turn to get his feet into position. The emphasis is to turn and not hop.

Each one of the drills we do is a progression to his drops and throws. This is the walkaway drill. We do this drill to the easy side and the hard side. The quarterback starts on the line. On the command, he turns his back to the target and walks away from it. It is a slow walk. On the second command, he executes the throw, doing the easy way drill. We run the same drill, making him turn to the hard side of the throw. The emphasis on turning to the hard side is to turn and not hop. Hopping is the mistake that most of the quarterbacks make.

The backpedal drill is like the walkaway drill. The quarterbacks align on the line. On the first command, they begin to backpedal. On the second command, they set their feet and deliver the ball. As they throw the ball, they end up on their toes. That makes the quarterback use his butt and twist his hips.

Instead of backpedaling, the next drill has the quarterbacks walking forward. It is the walkaway drill in reverse. The difference is they walk forward. On the command of the coach, they still have to step their feet and throw the ball. We want every throw made in the least amount of time. All these drills are quick-release throws. We want to get the ball out of the quarterback's hand as quickly as possible. The key is to make a catchable throw.

Everyone in America does this next drill. This is the shuffle in the pocket drill (Diagram #4). The coach stands in front of the quarterback line. On command, the quarterbacks shuffle back off the line. The coach gives the quarterbacks a directional movement with his hand. They shuffle in that direction. It is a shuffle wave drill with the quarterbacks reacting to the movement key. On the next command, they set their feet and deliver the ball. We want the quarterbacks to observe all the same principles from the other drills. The ball is high in their carriage, the eyes are up on the target, and the feet are ready.

We drill our quick screen releases from the shotgun formation (Diagram #5). We are about 80 percent shotgun. In this drill, the quarterbacks align straddling the line with their left shoulder to the side

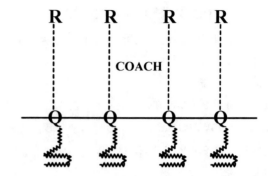

Diagram #4. Shuffle in the Pocket

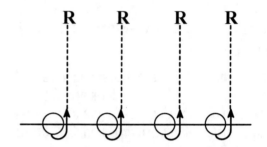

Diagram #5. Quick Screen Release

of the target. We want to simulate the snap from a shotgun snap. On the command, the quarterback tosses the ball into the air. He catches the ball and immediately turns to his target and delivers. If the quarterback is right handed, this is the easy throw. The throw to the left is easier for the right-handed quarterback. He throws the ball the way he catches it. He does not spin the ball to find the laces.

After they execute that throw, they face the other way and do the same thing. With the right shoulder to the side of the target, they have to spin to the other side to make the throw. This is the hard side. Throwing the ball in the air makes the quarterback concentrate on catching the ball before he delivers it. It is like watching the snap come back in the center snap.

I watched a film about Joe Namath the other night. In 1973, they had him taking five- and seven-step drops. At that time, he could barely walk. If they had put him in the shotgun at six yards, he could have played five more years. When you find a quarterback, his success is all about getting in the right system and letting him play.

We work the same drill without tossing the ball in the air. Now we can assimilate the quick screen from under the center. We face them right and left and turn them to deliver the ball to the target. The emphasis in all the drills is to get rid of the ball.

The ball security drill is like a handoff gauntlet (Diagram #6). The quarterback takes the snap, sets the ball, and drops through two lines of ball strippers. He gets the ball in his high ball-carriage position and shuffles back through the gauntlet. After he reaches the end of the players, he changes direction and moves forward through the gauntlet. The players on each side of the line try to punch, pull, and strip the ball from the quarterback's hands.

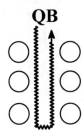

Diagram #6. Ball Security Drill

I want to give you an example of our quick passing game (Diagram #7). In our quick screen game, we want to get five yards from the play. We do something a little different from other teams. If we think we have man coverage on our outside receiver, we do not try to block the defender. We release the receiver and take the defender out of the play with a pattern. The throws we practice in the drill work are the ones we use in the quick screen game. In our screen game, we have one goal: We want to advance the ball in a positive fashion.

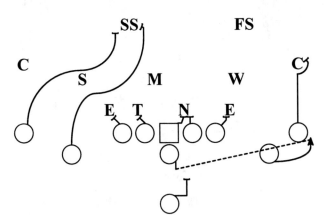

Diagram #7. Quick Screen

The receiver we use many times on this screen only weighs 161 pounds. We do not want him to try to run over someone. We want him to catch the ball and make five yards. When the pressure comes, we want him to get what he can get and get down.

I do not watch much pro ball, but I did watch San Francisco play the New York Giants. I watched Aaron Ross of the Giants return punts. He is a Texas high school player that played at the University of Texas. I watched him return punts. He was smart. He caught the ball, got all he could, and got on the ground. On a punt, the offense will get the ball as long as the punt returner catches it. He does not have to make any yardage. Aaron secured the football and secured his body. That is a situational play.

In football, you must understand situations. That is what we coach our players to do. We are not so much into X's and O's as we are into situations. We let them know in a particular situation what should happen from offensive, defensive, and special team standpoints.

The quick screen thrown to the left is easier for a right-handed quarterback than the throw to the right. We are a tempo team, and the quicker the quarterback can release the ball, the more yardages we make. When the quarterback is under center, as he receives the ball, it is important for him to get it to his chest as quickly as he can. We do not try to seat the ball. We want the ball to come up to his chest as quickly as possible and into the throw. He works on those mechanics in those drills in practice.

The quick throw is all about rhythm. It is almost like dancing. If the quarterback feels comfortable, he can execute. The quarterback has to feel good about how his footwork feels. You build that confidence and rhythm in drill work in practice. The more relaxed the quarterback can feel, the better he performs.

The biggest thing in the success of our offense was the tempo at which we played. We pushed the tempo and ran a ton of plays each game. I want to be the fastest team in America as far as the number of times we snap the ball. The more times we snap the ball, the more yards we can make. People do not pay money to come to a game and watch a slowdown offense. If they go to the restroom, I want them to come back and say "What happened while I was gone?" They will miss something if they leave the game. When we have the ball, we will do something with it. You only get 12 possessions a game, and we want to get our money's worth.

The difference in the shotgun and under the center in the quick screen game is the quarterback's grip on the ball. In the shotgun, however the ball comes back is how the quarterback throws it. Under the center, he gets the laces of the ball because of the way the ball comes up from the center. Another thing we think speeds us up is using a verbal cadence instead of a foot or hand signal to the center. We are verbal every chance we get.

When you get in the shotgun, the one point people overlook is the snap. We had a great center this year. The snap has to be perfect to execute the quick screen play. That was an advantage for us this year. You cannot have a quick passing game if the quarterback tries to field the ball at his feet or on the shoulder. He does not need the laces, but he does need the ball delivered at the chest. We want to play fast and get as many plays as we can. When we played the University of Washington in the Alamo Bowl, we were down 18 points on two different occasions. Us being able to snap the ball fast and get the number of plays we had won the game for us.

When you watch game tape of the quarterback, the only thing you want to see is the ball being up and his feet in the proper position. In our quick game, we have some one-step and two-step drops. The mechanics are the same as the quick screen. When we use this game, the quarterback has a chance to use his eyes to move the defense before he throws. He looks off safeties and throws the other way.

We want the quarterback to stand tall and step small. A six-foot three-inch quarterback should play at that height. He stands tall in the pocket so he can see. His stride into the throw is a small step. A short quarterback in the pocket should stand as tall as he can and not reduce his height by taking a long stride into the throw. A quarterback who stands 5-9 becomes 5-6 if he takes a long stride to deliver the ball. He should always stand tall and step small to improve his accuracy. The other part of the equation is to throw with the hips and butt.

The quick deliver helps the receiver. Throw the ball when the receiver breaks open. Do not hold the ball as he breaks open and then try to hit him. Defensive reaction is too great these days. The quick release does not require a step in some situations. If the receiver is going to clear, get the ball out. The drills I talked about earlier are the ones we do in practice daily. The only day we do not do the drills is during Friday's walk-through.

This past year, Robert Griffin III was good at not hanging the receivers out in a bad situation. He is intelligent, has great vision, and understands what is happening on the defensive side of the ball. The slant pattern is a dangerous throw. Receivers will catch a low ball on the slant. However, a high thrown ball on a slant play puts the receiver in a bad situation and leads to many tipped balls. Tipped balls in the middle of the field become interceptions. When we throw the slant, we try to throw it below the waist in the gut.

I will show you one of our bootlegs. It is the same type of throw (Diagram #8). We run most of our sets from multiple wide receiver looks. We run doubles, trips, and no backs. We use motion to get from one set to the other. On this play, we align in a trips set to the boundary and motion to a double slot set. The motion man goes to the flat and the split end runs a curl combination. The inside receiver from the backside runs through the middle on a crossing pattern. We play-action the inside zone and pull the guard. If the corner clears with the split end, we throw the motion in the flat.

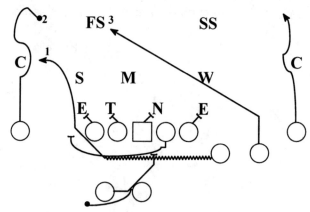

Diagram #8. Bootleg

This is not a play to get the quarterback on the edge. If the motion comes open immediately, throw the ball to him. It is like the quick screen. The quarterback does not have to be on the perimeter to throw the ball. He can throw the ball from behind the tackle. If we want to get him on the edge, we do it with some type of naked bootleg. When we throw on the naked, we want him to run through his throw. We do not want him to set up and throw.

When the quarterback throws on the run, it is important that he square his shoulders—whether he runs to the right or left. Running to the left is harder for the right-handed quarterback. He has to square his shoulders so he does not throw across his body. He has to open his hips and run through the throw, going to his left. The mechanics of the ball carriage is the same going right or left. He has to have the ball up and ready to throw at all times.

March 22 at Baylor University is our pro day. Most NFL head coaches will be there. Robert is not going to the combines to throw. He is not going to throw in Indianapolis. He is going to wait until he gets back to Waco to throw there. It is going to be a big event, and those coaches will see a big-time player. Robert has a tremendous arm and is very accurate.

Before I stop, I want to talk about the zone read play. I want to show you some of the drills we use to practice the play. We use the read drill every day in practice. We use it as a two-ball drill (Diagram #9). We align with a quarterback, tailback, and pitchback. On the defense, we have a read key for the quarterback. The second ball is in the hands of a manager standing to the outside of the read key. You can run it from the shotgun set or under the center. The quarterback takes the ball and rides the zone back. He keys the zone key for his read.

If the key comes down, he pulls the ball and runs the zone option to the pitchman. If the read key forces the handoff, the quarterback continues down the field with the pitchback. The manager standing behind the read key pitches a second ball to the quarterback. The quarterback continues with the pitchback and pitches him the ball.

We run the drills both ways and try to get as many reps in as we can. They are rapid-fire plays. We do the same type of drill with the speed option (Diagram #10). We can run it from the shotgun, under the center, or from the pistol. It is the same type of drill. From the pistol set, the quarterback runs at the pitch key and gets his read off that defender. He keeps the ball or pitches it to the pistol back. The pitchback needs a relationship to the quarterback of one yard in front and four yards outside of the quarterback.

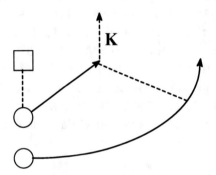

Diagram #10. Speed Option

The third drill we do is the lead isolation drill (Diagram #11). We have a blocking back, quarterback, and tailback. On the defense is a linebacker. The block can come from the backside or from outside with motion. The quarterback hands the ball to the tailback, he follows the blocking back into inside zone hole, and he breaks off his block on

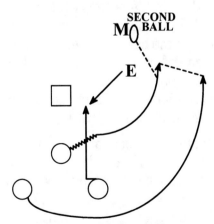

Diagram #9. Read Key

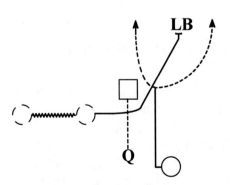

Diagram #11. Inside Lead Play

the linebacker. If the linebacker comes inside, the fullback blocks him in and the back breaks out. If the linebacker goes outside, the blocking back turns him out and the tailback cuts inside.

We spend eight minutes daily on the run option game. We want to get maximum reps during that time. When we teach the relationship between the quarterback and pitchback, we try not to overcoach it. We feel that if you try to coach too much technique into a simple skill that it is not good. We want them to react rather than think too much. We feel that if you are thinking, then you are not reacting and going at full speed. We want players to be active. If they make a mistake, we talk about it later.

On the inside zone play, we read the defensive end as the key (Diagram #12). If the end closes, we pull the ball and the quarterback runs the option. There may or may not be a pitchback on the play. If the quarterback ends up carrying the ball, he gets all he can and gets out of bounds or to the ground. The line blocking is the same scheme used by everyone else on this play. The two guards, center, playside tackle, and tight end use a combination scheme to block the inside 3 and 1 technique linemen and the two linebackers. The backside tackle seals the backside B gap.

Will linebacker to his side. The quarterback reads the movement of the wide 5 technique defensive end. The backside tackle zone steps into the B gap and stops any penetration from that side.

We have a zone scheme from our trips tight end set (Diagram #13). The tight end loops outside the 7 technique defender or read key. If the linebacker fills, he goes to the safety. On this play, we fan the backside tackle out on the 5 technique defender. The backside guard and center double on the 1 technique defender. The playside guard and tackle double on the 3 technique defender, with the tackle working for inside leverage on him. The playside guard comes off on the backside linebacker, and we let the frontside linebacker fill the C gap unblocked. If the read key shuffles inside, the quarterback reads that as a handoff key.

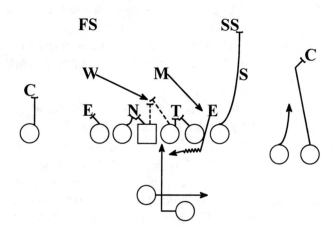

Diagram #13. Tight End Loop

The shuffle read is hard for the quarterback. However, in our scouting report, we assess the athletic ability of the defensive end, quarterback, and tailback. If the defensive end is not extremely quick, we give the ball. We feel that if he shuffles down instead of crashing, then he will not tackle our tailback. From the pistol, the quarterback opens to the playside and the tailback runs downhill at the inside leg of the offensive guard.

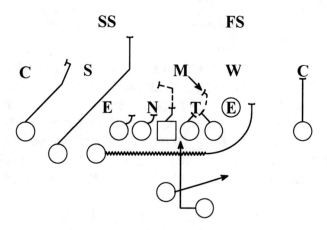

Diagram #12. Read Zone

In the diagram, the tight end comes in motion from the trips set left and blocks to the callside. We use a combination block on the 3 technique defender with the playside guard and tackle. The center and backside guard combination block for the 1 technique defender and the backside linebacker. The tight end comes in motion and locks with the

The mechanics of our backs will not be anything like the University of Nevada. Those coaches do a great job with the pistol offense. We run the pistol on occasion and not as a steady diet. We do not get into the fine points of the pistol offense. As I said before, we do not overcoach any technique that we may not use every week.

If we feel the quarterback can outrun a shuffling read key, the quarterback pulls the ball and gets off to the races. However, if there is any doubt, we hand the ball to the tailback. If the quarterback gets outside the defensive end, the free safety has to make the play. We can get our five to six yards and get out of bounds. The quarterback has to be smart and know the defensive personnel he faces at the defensive end positions.

I want to show you a wrinkle we use from time to time (Diagram #14). We set the trips set into the field. The tailback sets in the boundary side, with the quarterback in the shotgun. We bring the inside slot (tight end) in motion and snap the ball as he reaches the gap between the fieldside offensive guard and tackle. We use a combination block on the boundary side 3 technique with the guard and tackle. The center and backside guard combination-block the 1 technique defender. The fieldside tackle fans on the 5 technique defender.

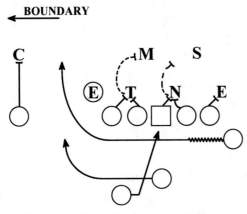

Diagram #14. Quarterback Power

We run the read zone play to the tailback and read the boundary side defensive end. The split end blocks the corner to his side and the motion tight end comes around as a pulling lineman for the quarterback on the keeper into the boundary. The only thing left on the boundary side should be the free safety, and we have a blocker for him.

People forget that we run the football, and we run it effectively. That is the way you win football games, and we understand that. We like to do what we do, and we do it fast. However, we do like to win. You are not going to win a lot of football game consistently unless you can run the ball. It will be windy, raining, no artificial turf, muddy field, and you will not be able to throw the ball. You must have some running schemes, and you had better be ready to go. You have to run with intelligence, and we try to sell that to our players. We just do not run the football; we run with a purpose and a plan.

If you ever want to come to Waco, we would love to have you. We share a great deal with high school coaches. We want to make the game better, and there is no better way than sharing and learning from high school coaches. I feel that high school coaches do the real coaching. You cannot recruit for your needs. You have to play with what is in the school. We understand and know what you coaches go through on a daily basis because we have been there. I appreciate you, and our door is always open. Thank you very much.

ORCHESTRATING A TURNAROUND

Portland State University

I want to give you a little information on my background so you will know where I am coming from. I am originally from Sacramento, California. I attended Jesuit High School. I played football at the University of Washington and graduated in 1999. My first job was as an office accountant/auditor at Deloitte & Touche. I was 23 years old, and I was making about $40,000 a year. It sounds as if I was in a great position. However, I hated every minute of the job. That lasted about six months.

I had a friend who was the offensive coordinator at the University of South Florida. I ended up taking a job there as a graduate assistant defensive backs coach. In 2001, a friend told me about a job opening at Portland State University. I applied for the job and became the defensive backs coach. In 2003, I moved to Oregon State University as a defensive backs assistant. In 2008, I was the defensive coordinator at the University of Nevada. In 2010, I was named the head coach at Portland State. That is a quick rundown on my coaching days.

I have always said that my number one priority is to help prepare my players for life after football and be a positive influence throughout the rest of their lives. It is much more important than winning football games. When I die, the thing I want people to remember me by is not the number of friends I had but the number of lives I touched. That is one of my mottos for life.

I considered talking about recruiting and about our thought process. However, it did not take me long to realize how boring that could be. The thing that sticks with me now is the number of people that ask me how we turned the program around at Portland State. In my first year, we went through a year of pain in 2010. It was a rough year. We had to step back and examine ourselves to figure out what we needed to do to turn the program in the right direction. In the first year, we ended up with a 2-9

record. We had a lot of close games, but the fact of the matter is, we lost.

2010 SEASON

- 2-9 overall record
- 1-7 (eighth in the Big Sky Conference)
- 2.69 team GPA
- Several players left program after the season.

Our GPA was respectable but not great. Players left our program, and I took that personally. If we are to be a big influence in our players' lives, we must teach them that the game is more than just wins and losses.

2011 SEASON

- 7-4 overall record
- 5-3 (third in the Big Sky)
- 3.05 team GPA
- No players left the program after the season

As you can see, we made some improvement during the 2011 season. Our record improved to 7-4, and our team GPA improved to 3.05. We have not had one player leave our program this year. At the Division I level, there is always attrition. We have 80 players on scholarship, and we have 25 walk-ons. Those players stayed because they want to be a part of our program. I think that is cool for us.

The questions are, "What changed? What happened?" We had the same players. In fact, we had 18 returning starters coming back. Most of the staff remained the same. We did get a new defensive line coach in Malik Roberson, and we hired a new special teams coordinator in Ikaika Malloe. I got a chance to move John Ely over to work with our running backs. Our offensive and defensive systems remained the same. We did not get a new training facility or new techniques.

Again, what was the difference? The first thing we did to turn the program around was a big step. We go on an annual staff retreat right after recruiting and the national signing day is completed. It is probably our most productive time. It allows us to step away and take a look at where we are.

The first thing that came out at the retreat was the fact we needed to make it clear that the pressure was on *us, not* on the players, to get better. We decided when we started spring practice that the players needed to see a different staff. We wanted them to see a different program, even though it would be with most of the same coaching staff. The principles and core values remained the same.

I read a book by Coach Pete Carroll called *Win Forever*. In the spring, Coach Carroll would have his staff give what he called the "first speech of spring." It was to galvanize his crew. Each assistant coach would have his individual group give the speech to the staff and the players when they started spring practice. The assistant coaches would practice the speeches in front of each other. Each coach would get in front of the assistant coaches and talk about his group and what they were expecting to accomplish. The coaches did not have any of those fancy PowerPoint presentations or a lot of film to view. All they had was notes to go by. They covered the things they would teach their group that would make them better football players. So, we did the first speech of spring with our staff.

Next, our staff started talking about research projects. We wanted to find things that we could do that would improve us as a staff. We studied third-down plays and turnovers. We selected several different things that would make us a better staff, and we did the research on those areas of the game. It was an amazing process.

The first speech of spring that I remembered the most was by our quarterback coach, Bruce Barnum. Bruce has a brother that is working in Japan. As you recall, a huge earthquake hit there last year. Bruce got up in front of the group and put up a simulator that you could go on the Internet to see all of the earthquakes and aftershocks going on in Japan. Remember, his speech was for quarterbacks. But you could go online and view a map of Japan and then all of sudden this huge, large red surge similar to a lightning bolt flashed in the center of the screen. It showed the epicenter of the earthquake and how far it extended. It showed a time lapse of the aftershocks.

The whole idea was to give a visual of what those people were going through over a course of a month. The people in Japan were worried that they may have a nuclear accident as a result of the damage by the earthquake. What Bruce was trying to convey to the quarterbacks was this: in times of stress, pandemonium can break out, especially when you are struggling.

Bruce went on to talk about his brother and how he had to keep his family together, and he had to keep his company together. People were bailing out, and a state of confusion existed all around him. He had to stay calm and make sure to move everyone in the right direction.

Bruce went on to tell the quarterbacks this was similar to what they faced with the football team. "It is your responsibility to keep the team together when things are not going good. The quarterback has to be calm during the aftershocks, and he has to be a leader." Bruce gave us an unbelievable visual for our players, and I will never forget that presentation.

John Ely came up with an unusual presentation as well. He wanted to give a special identity to our special teams, and he called them the "S.W.A.T. Unit." He went on to tell the team that we would no longer refer to our punt team. Our punt team will now be called the "Bomb Squad." We are calling them the Bomb Squad because if they make a mistake, people die. He went on to tie in all of the things related to the special teams. He called our kickoff return team the "Seals" because he expected them to react to something that had just happened and we need something positive to take place. When he finished, all I could say was that that was an awesome speech. He delivered an inspiring presentation, and our team bought into it hook, line, and sinker. We had an outstanding special teams this past year, and it all started with John as he got the players to buy into what we needed to do to make our special teams a special group. That all happened the first week of spring practice.

The first step for us as a staff was the fact that we understood that it all had to start with us. Now, it all did not come together just because of us. It started with the players that were coming back for another year. That was the start.

The next point we stressed was this: we have to be ridiculously positive energetic every day. It could not be just a game day thing. We could not have high and low days when it came to being positive and being energetic. When people come to our practices, I want them to think we are football junkies. I told the assistant coaches I did not care what they had to do; go get coffee or get something to eat or whatever turns them on. But when we hit the field, I wanted them to go crazy.

In practice, we made a big deal out of positive plays. We encouraged our players to make a big deal out of a touchdown or a big play on defense. Not only did the players go down to the end zone to congratulate the players that scored, but some of the coaches did the same thing. We did not stop them from having a blast to celebrate excellence in practice. We juiced up practice with a lot of noise and a lot of enthusiasm. We told the players they could not do this in a game, but in practice, we would encourage the team to make a big deal out of the big plays.

The press would come to our practice, and they would say we were nuts. "They have players and coaches running out to congratulate individuals on plays. They high-five every positive play." All of this made practice fun, and it increased the competition level.

When I took the job at Portland State, I had been a coach at colleges that had winning records. At the University of South Florida, we took a program that was 1-AA and moved it up the ladder, and at one time, we were the #2 team in the country. When I was first at Portland State, we won seven games that year. I went to Oregon State, and we had the most wins in the program in a span of time. We had 19 wins in two years. I got to Nevada, and we won seven games. Coach Chris Ault was ready to fire all of us because that was not a good season for them. They were accustomed to winning.

So, when I took the head job at Portland State, I was used to winning. When I played at the University of Washington, I was used to winning. It was a lot of fun when I went there. Do you know what you do when you want a winner to respond

when he fails? You kick him in the butt! You show him the films and tell him that the opponent kicked his butt. You ask those players if they are going to allow the opponents to kick their butts. In 2010, the players did not have that burning desire to win.

It is obvious that we must recruit better. Randy Shannon, the former head coach at the University of Miami, is a friend of mine. When Miami built that great run of teams, they built the program one way. They recruited players that loved the game. Ray Lewis had no scholarship offers in his senior year of high school. He has ended up as one of the best linebackers in pro football.

Our staff talked about going through a process to recruit football players that want to play football. It is slow, and it may have cost us some players. In the end, it has also helped us eliminate some mistakes.

We want to recruit players who are better students and *love* the game of football. I want to discuss our system.

EVALUATION SYSTEM

- Highlight game film and transcript evaluation
- Live evaluation (camps, workouts, or games)
- Social media research (Facebook, Twitter, etc.)
- High school coach and recruit interview ("Does he love it?")
- Uninvested party interview (lunch lady, security guard, etc.)

We never ever offer a player a scholarship off of a highlight film. I put his highlight films together, and we study the game films. We also want to get a live evaluation of the player. We go to a great deal of football camps. We have our own camp as well.

One thing that we do that separates us is that we dig a little deeper about our prospects. We check their Facebook and if they have information on Twitter, etc. We check this out. We check with the players' high school coach. Most coaches want their players to get a scholarship because they care about them. What we are trying to figure out about the player is this: "Does he love the game?

The last aspect that we look into are the uninvested party interviews. We go to the high schools, and we talk with the lunchroom lady and even the security guards. They will be able to tell you everything you want to know about them. This has helped us in not making mistakes on players.

Everyone talks about competition within his program. We wanted to re-emphasize the competition aspects in our program. We call this showcasing or showdowns. We do our tackling drills, our Oklahoma drill, and our route drills, and we keep charts on third-down plays and fourth-down plays in practice. We keep score in practice. We do it in the game, so why wouldn't we do in it in practice? We do it for competition for the players. If they lose in practice, they have to run.

We want to create an atmosphere of positive peer pressure. You were only allowed to be a certain way within our program. The players made it this way. If you were not with us, you were told to leave. If the players do not want you in our program, then you can't be there.

We posted our study hall hours in the locker room. We listed what the players had in certain aspects of the study hall. On the report that was posted, there was a column that accidentally had the players' GPAs listed. Most of the time, I think players do not care about their grades that much. But in this case, the players got after a player who was not doing as well as they thought he should have been doing. They got after him. He was embarrassed, and he should have been.

Every now and then, when we are lifting weights and a player is late, we run the whole group. Now the players are on the player who is late. To have to go out and run at 6:30 a.m. in 25-degree weather is not a lot of fun.

We did a coaches challenge where we took the team and divided it up into groups. We gave them exercises for the workouts: bench, squats, power cling, this, that, and the other. The group that had the largest percentage increase would win a prize. The prize was to go to dinner anywhere in the city on Coach Burton. Anywhere! They had to go to a restaurant that was respectful. That was the only rule.

They could get bonus points if their position coach lost any weight. If you could see our staff, you would see that we have not missed a lot of meals, myself included. This got the coaches working out more than before. In the end, the linebacker group won the challenge. They went out and had a nice meal. It created a positive atmosphere and created peer pressure in our indoor program. We posted the scores each week, so the players knew where they stood as a group.

Then, the players created a buddy system where they worked out together in the summer. If a player missed a workout, not only did the player who missed the workout have to run, but his buddy had to run as well. This is a good way to create positive peer pressure.

One of the problems we face with the group of players that was coming back to our program was the fact they did not know how to be leaders. So, we started a program of leadership training. We started with a group of 16 players. This was not a leadership council. We had five leaders to start with, and those five players selected the others to be leaders in the group.

The key to the program was this. It was not a group of coaches' boys. It was not a group that the coaches thought were good guys. We picked a quarterback and a couple of other players and then the team picked the others in the group.

We told them there can be no dark corners. You know what I mean. You have the groups working together, and all of a sudden, you have one player who is sitting over in a dark corner and not involved in the group.

With that group, they talked about the five characteristics or traits of a dysfunctional team. We gave them a lot of materials on how to be a leader. What is important? What are our options? The seniors gave the presentation, not the coaches.

We have a set of core values. We had a core values presentation by the leaders. We talked about integrity, responsibility, accountability, hard work, and perseverance. Those are our five core values. They are on T-shirts, they are on signs in our office, and they are everywhere.

The group had a chance to meet with the athletic department heads. They did not like what was going on in the training room, and they did not like what was going on in the equipment room. They were able to sit down with those people and make some changes. They saw that their leadership did have an effect on a change in the program. They actually helped with the equipment order and with the uniform selection.

This is the best thing we did on defense. We had problems with players who did not understand what they were doing. During the winter, we would meet for one hour each week to teach our defense. When we got to spring football, our players knew what to do. Our coaches do not say a word on defense. Each player knows on the first day we are going to go over cover 4. We had players who could teach the younger players the system. We created trust in the defensive players, and it gave them accountability for the defense. It was a great deal for us.

I talked about contingency planning and the ideas I got from Coach Pete Carroll's book *Win Forever.* We visit with the players in practice and ask them a lot of what-if questions. We have plans to communicate to the players what they will need to be prepared a little better for the upcoming game. Now there is no panic in the players when they see something different. We cover the contingency that may happen if something comes up that we have not planned for.

We placed more emphasis on academics. The reason I say this is because we had a few players that were struggling academically. We had a daily cap and gown meeting for select players. We added another round of progress reports. We asked the players to hand-return their progress reports to our coaches to force the player/ professor communication level. We emphasis the importance of attending office hours when they have meetings scheduled. We focus on 100 percent return of progress reports. We make more class checks during our quarter system. We know early if a player is having a problem.

The last thing I want to discuss is our schedule. In 2010, we had seven road games. When I came in, I wanted at least six home games. As you can see by our schedule for the five-year period, we are trying to have a balanced schedule, with six home games and six away games each year.

- 2010: four home games
- 2011: six home games
- 2012: five home games
- 2013: six home games
- 2014: six home games

In closing, I want to invite you to come to visit with us. We have our camp schedule on our website (http://www.goviks.com/sports/2012/2/9/ FB_0209123359.aspx?path=football). Give us a call if we can do anything for you. I appreciate your time.

THE DOUBLE WING OPTION OFFENSE

U.S. Air Force Academy

Thank you. It is good to see all you coaches up early on a Saturday morning. If you are ever in Colorado Springs, you should come by and see us. We would love to have you.

I know many coaches today are in the shotgun set. About 25 percent of what we do comes from the shotgun set. The rest of the time, we are under the center; however, we try to keep a balance in what we do. We are one of those teams in the top 25 in passing efficiency. We also run the ball well.

At the Air Force Academy, our academics are extremely high. We are looking for 3.5 GPA students. He must have at least a 25 ACT and 1150 SAT score. After graduation from the Academy, the student has a five-year commitment to military duty. Everyone must pass a fitness test to get into the Academy. They must run a mile-and-a-half in 11 minutes. We are 7,100 feet above sea level and that becomes a difficult feat. Because of that, we have small football players. Both the offensive tackles were in the 245-pound range. The center was 242 pounds, and the left guard was big for us. He weighed in at 248 pounds.

There are no red-shirt players. You go to school and graduate in four years. While you are there, you must take two levels of calculus, two levels of physics, two levels of chemistry, aeronautical engineering, along with other academic courses. They push you to the hilt in the classroom. Our graduates have 140 semester hours when they graduate. That is not 12 hours a semester. They take a full class load each semester they are there.

During the summers, they are training at some base throughout the world. They do not stay on campus. They are training to be leaders within our country. They will be officers in the United States Air Force. They do an internship during the summers. They are learning the job they will do after they graduate.

As a coach, sometimes, I would like it to be more about football. However, at the Academy, there is a different mission. We get them before practice for about 35 to 40 minutes, and we do have some time in the weight room before practice. However, on a school day, the longest practice we can have is 90 minutes. That is the way we have to work, but they expect us to play good football teams.

The way you do it is to tap into what makes up these players. All the intangibles make them special people. We have to funnel that in a way so that we are ready to go on game day. We will play anybody. We are in the Mountain West Conference, which is one of the six best leagues in the country. We play non-leagues, and we try to find the toughest teams we can find. In the last few years we played the University of Notre Dame twice, we played in Norman, Oklahoma, against the University of Oklahoma. Next year, we are going to the University of Michigan to play them in The Big House. In addition to those games, we still play Army (United States Military Academy) and Navy (United States Naval Academy).

I know when you come to clinics you want to talk some ball. I am going to show you a bunch of stuff, so stop me if you have any questions. We ran a little gun zone read this year. We want to create some three-back concepts with two blockers on the perimeter. We want a receiver on the outside to block the defensive back and an extra blocker coming around to check the linebacker coming from the inside.

In the eight-man box, you need the extra blocker to handle the additional defender in the box. There is also a strong safety who aligns outside the box; we want to account for him.

The first play is an inside zone play (Diagram #1). We read the first defender over the offensive tackle. In most cases, it is the 5-technique defender.

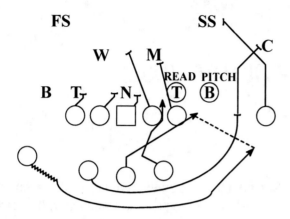

Diagram #1. Inside Zone

He is the read key, and we pitch off the next defender, usually a 9-technique defender. From the right guard to the backside, we run an inside zone play. We have small offensive linemen. We need them to take wide line splits. Our line splits should never be anything less than two-and-a-half feet. We will expand the splits to five feet. In the offensive linemen stance, we want weight on the balls of their feet and their knees inside their toes. That way, they can push off and move in a lateral direction.

We are in a three-point stance with our hands on the ground. Each week, we want to create a three-back look. We have two backs in the backfield with the quarterback in the shotgun set. We have three receivers on the field. In one week, we may have a fullback as one of the perimeter blockers, and in other weeks, we may bring the slot in motion and he becomes the second perimeter blocker.

The read key is the 5-technique defender on the offensive tackle. The pitch key is the Sam linebacker outside the tackle on the line of scrimmage. We must locate the safety for the extra blocker's assignment. If the defense has an eight-man front with the safety in the box, the extra blocker has the scraping linebacker to the safety as his blocking assignment. If the safety is a secondary player, the blocker arcs on his release.

With the safety inside, we like to get a switch call between the wide receiver and the fullback. The wide receiver comes down on the safety, and the fullback blocks the corner.

If the offensive tackle has a 5-technique defender aligned on him, he releases to the Mike linebacker. If he is blocking for the zone back, he works to the inside number of the linebacker. If he blocks for the quarterback, his target is the outside shoulder of the linebacker. In this case, we want the tackle to take the linebacker right down the middle with his head on the sternum. He gets two hands on him and drives him in the direction he wants to go.

We have plays in our offense where there is no read, and we either run the zone play or the quarterback keep. If the tackle blocks for the zone back, he blocks the inside shoulder. If it is a quarterback-keep play, he blocks the outside shoulder. On the read zone, he is down the middle.

If the defender aligns in a 4i technique or a 4 technique, the tackle steps with his inside foot. If the defender slams inside, the offensive tackle does a quick swim technique back to the outside and comes outside the slamming defender. He wants to get on the scraping linebacker and close the space immediately.

The playside guard and center combo block on the nose to the backside linebacker. The backside guard and tackle seal the backside A and B gaps. They block normal zone blocking.

The pitch relationship for the pitchback is four yards in front of and no deeper than two yards. We want the pitch delivered so the pitchback can catch the ball on the move and accelerate to the perimeter. The pitch has to lead him into the perimeter, not make him stop to catch it.

On the perimeter, the lead back and the wide receiver run a switch scheme for the inside safety and the corner. The coaching point for the wide receiver on any crackback block is to make the block at least three yards up the field. We never want to make the block on the line of scrimmage and never behind the line. The wide receiver takes three steps off the line and goes for the crack inside. The amount of distance he can press the corner off the line depends on the safety. We want to be able to crack on the safety within three yards of the line.

The lead blocker blocks the corner. He wants to track the outside shoulder of the corner. If the corner widens, he continues to work the outside shoulder and drives him out-of-bounds. If the corner drives inside, the lead back attacks him and drives him out.

The fullback on this play is the lead back, and the slot coming in motion is the pitchback. The quarterback runs the inside zone play to the right halfback and reads the 5-technique defender. If the defender charges upfield or plays straight, we give the ball to the running back. If the read key slams inside and takes the running back, the quarterback pulls the ball and attacks the pitch key.

The quarterback wants to force the pitch key and make him react and do something. He attacks the inside of the pitch key as if he were going to turn up inside with the ball. That forces the pitch key to attack him. We do not attack his shoulder. We want to attack inside of him. The reason we do that is so the quarterback does not start to chase the inside shoulder of the pitch key. That allows the pitch key to string out the play. We want to attack inside and make the pitch key do something. If he does not, the quarterback stays inside and runs the ball.

The wide receiver's normal split to the field is the inside edge of the numbers. The split into the boundary is to the outside edge of the numbers. We have other alignments called "wide." When we call "wide," the outside receivers align three yards from the sidelines. At other times, we put them in close splits. That puts them six yards from the tackles.

If we want to change the perimeter blocker, we can bring the slot in motion and snap the ball as he crosses behind the quarterback. That means he is the lead block and the fullback becomes the pitchback.

We have a number of different formations from which we can run this play. You can run the play with a tight end as the lead blocker on the perimeter. You can run it from a 3x1, using the tight end or inside slot as the lead blocker. You can create ways to change the pitchback and lead blocker without changing the mesh or the mechanics of the quarterback. However, the blocking scheme for the offensive linemen does not change.

Everyone runs some kind of zone option. When we run our zone option, we run it to the tight end side (Diagram #2). In the blocking scheme, the playside tackle and tight end combination block on the C-gap defender. If the defender aligns in a 7 technique on the inside shoulder of the tight end, the tackle and tight end combo block for that defender to the inside linebacker. The center and playside

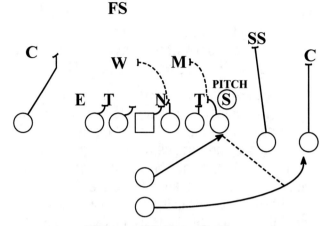

Diagram #2. Zone Option

guard combo block the A- or B-gap defender to the backside linebacker. The pitch comes off the D-gap defender. If the defense aligns in a shade, 5 technique, and 9 technique, we combo the shade and 5 technique, and pitch off the 9 technique. If they align in a 3 technique and 7 technique, we combo both those defenders and pitch off the D-gap defender, whoever he is. It could be a linebacker or the support safety.

This play gets to the edge immediately. The center leads the quarterback with the snap. We want the quarterback moving to the playside as he catches the ball. We want him three feet to the playside when he catches the ball. We have to make up for some of the quickness we may lack. The pitch relationship is the same for the pitchback. He has to hustle because the quarterback attacks downhill in a hurry. If the quarterback attacks the pitch key to the inside, the defender cannot force a pitch from the quarterback and get to the edge to tackle the pitchback.

On this play, the tackle and tight end work with their splits to put space between the pitch key and the quarterback. The guards are two-and-a-half feet, and the tackles and tight end have three-feet splits. The linemen have good angles, and the ball gets to the edge.

The wide receivers stalk block on the defensive backs. When we use the stalk block, we want to work at a 45-degree angle toward the outside number of the defender. He wants his hips slightly turned to the inside. We want to influence the defensive back to widen. If he wants to come inside, the wide receiver latches on and drives him to the inside. If he does that, it gives us the sideline. All this blocking takes place on their side of the line of scrimmage. I do not want the wide receiver blocking on our side of the line of scrimmage.

On the 7-technique or 6-technique defender, we have a fundamental scheme we teach. The tight end comes off the ball as fast as he can and puts his inside hand in the outside armpit of the defender. The tight end hangs on the defender as long as he can or until the linebacker shows over the top. The thing he can never do is use his outside hand on the block. If he uses the outside hand, his shoulders turn, and he cannot block the linebacker. The tight end is the deliver blocker, and the tackle is the overtake blocker.

The linebacker in their scheme aligns in a 10 technique (playside shade of the center). They have time before he can get to the C gap. They want to work and establish position on the 7-technique defender before the linebacker gets there. As the linebacker scrapes outside, the tight end shoves the 7 technique on the tackle's block and climbs up for the linebacker. We want the tight end to punch with the inside hand and get the defender turned.

If the C-gap defender is in a 5 technique, the tight end's aiming point changes. Instead of going to the outside armpit, he attacks the near side hip of the defender. We go to the hip because the angle is better and we can turn him easier going to the hip. That allows him to help the tackle move in the overtake block.

Fundamentally, the teaching for the tackle and tight end are the same techniques we teach to the center and guard. If the guard has an inside shade on him, he is the deliver blocker, and the center is the overtake blocker. The technique is the same with the hand placement and technique. The only difference is they work to the backside linebacker instead of the playside. We have an option if we chose to use it. The guard can make a man call to the center. In that case, the playside guard man-blocks down on the shade defender, and the center goes immediately to the backside linebacker.

If you want to run the play from under the center in a conventional offense, nothing changes for the offensive line. The perimeter blocking changes from

a stalk block for the twin receivers to a switch block with the fullback and wide receiver.

The farther the wide receiver drives the corner off the line, the easier it is for the fullback. The wide receiver cracks the strong safety, and the fullback blocks the corner. The fullback takes a lateral step with his outside foot and turns his shoulders to the sidelines. He takes three steps to the outside on that line to get his width to the outside. He wants to attack the outside shoulder of the corner.

The quarterback under the center has to get off the line slightly because of the combo blocks on the line of scrimmage. The stepping by the takeover blockers is a lateral step down the line rather than out. The quarterback's first step is at 6 o'clock. That takes him off the line of scrimmage. He runs three steps laterally and attacks the inside of the pitch key.

This play is not different from the other zone play in how we get into the play. We have a number of different formations that can adapt easily to this play. By using motions and different backfield alignment, we can run the play from all our formations.

If, for some reason, the linebacker stays inside, the tight end stays on the block with the tackle. He does not come off the double-team until the linebacker shows up.

This is a great goal line play (Diagram #3). Against a 6-2 goal line look, nothing changes for the offensive line. The playside tackle and tight end combination block on the 5-technique tackle and Mike linebacker. The center and playside guard combo for the playside 2-technique defender and backside linebacker. The backside guard, tackle,

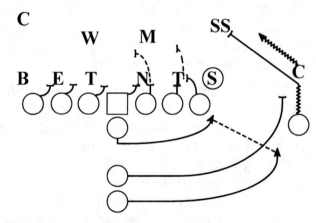

Diagram #3. Goal Line

and tight end cut off their inside gaps. The wide receiver has the important block. He has to crack the strong safety. However, in this situation, the defense may be in man-to-man coverage. He cannot push the corner off because of the depth of the strong safety. He has to get inside to block the strong safety on his side of the line.

With man coverage in the secondary, the wide receiver has to fight inside, and that brings the corner with him. That gives us a good chance to get on the edge. We usually do not tighten our splits in short-yardage or goal line situations. If there is an adjustment, it is minimal.

The option scheme I like is the shovel option (Diagram #4). We read the defender over the playside tackle. He gives us the key to run the outside option with the back or uses the inside shovel pass to the underneath back. If the 5 technique comes up the field for the quarterback, we shovel to the underneath back. If he slams inside, the quarterback keeps the ball and pitches off the 9-technique defender. On this play, there is a mesh in the form of the lateral to the underneath back. However, if the ball hits the ground on the shovel, it is a forward incomplete pass. You can run the shovel from many different sets. In the diagram, we are in a 2x2 set with the quarterback in the shotgun.

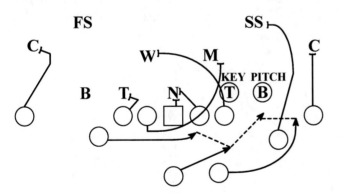

Diagram #4. Shovel Option

The shovel back can be a tight end, wide receiver, fullback, running back, or any type of thing you can dream up. You can use motion or alignments to get into position. The line blocking is simple. We block our open-end power scheme to the playside. The playside guard and tackle combination block the playside A and B gaps. If there is a 3-technique

defender on the guard, the guard and tackle use a double-team on him to the backside linebacker. The center blocks back, and the backside guard pulls for the frontside linebacker.

The backside guard on his first step has to find the playside 5-technique defender. If the defender is outside, he turns up past the double-team block and blocks the Mike linebacker. If the 5-technique defender slams inside, he goes around the outside of the defender and up on the linebacker. We call that a wrap-around technique. The backside tackle has to seal the backside. He steps inside before he turns back. However, if the shovel back comes from outside of him, he cannot come off the line of scrimmage. He has to step flat to the inside and back. In the diagram, the slotback is the shovel back and follows the pulling guard. He is already on the level with the guard and does not need to adjust his depth.

The shovel back is four yards behind and two yards inside the quarterback as he starts his path to the outside. If the shovel back was a fullback aligned to the side the quarterback, he has to take three steps to the line to get on the level of the pulling guard. On his third step, he runs parallel to the line of scrimmage behind the pulling guard. This is a great third-and-six play.

The quarterback catches the ball and takes a lateral step to the playside. He knows after his third step what he is going to do. On the third step, if the 5 technique is up the field, he pitches the ball underneath to the shovel back. He cannot work downhill on the first three steps. If he does, he is too close to the shovel back. If the tackle slams inside, the quarterback focuses on the pitch key and runs the option downfield.

This is a simple play, and it gives you the option the defense has to prepare to play against. This makes the defense play assignment football and negates some of the things they like to do with the blitzing and stunting game.

I want to show you our orbit series. Our number-one run is the outside zone, and our number-two run is the inside zone. We are a zone team, and we run it with a little option. We change from week to week the scheme we want to use. However, we condense the techniques for the offensive linemen so much that they do not have a problem with this.

Our week-to-week adjustments are not hard on our players. In addition to them being tough, they are extremely smart.

I am going to show you this series from under the center and out of the shotgun. We use both of those formations. The first one is an I formation pro set (Diagram #5). We align the sweeper as the pro back one yard outside the field hash mark. He comes in motion toward the ball. We time the play so that we snap the ball when he is four yards from the C gap. The tailback's toes are six yards from the line of scrimmage. When the sweeper hits the C gap, he adjusts his path through the heels of the tailback on the back in the I formation. The tailback takes one lateral step and heads directly into the A gap. The only cut we allow him to make is from the frontside A gap to the backside A gap.

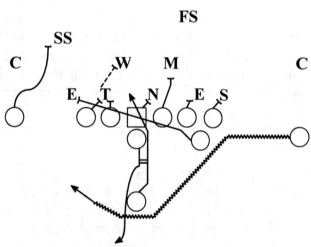

Diagram #5. Orbit Zone

The quarterback has to reverse out to past 6 o'clock with his feet. He has to let the tailback clear into the playside A gap. He cannot force the tailback wide. The linemen come off the line hard and aggressive, but we do not ask them to hold their blocks too long. We want them to drive on the defender; if they can give us one foot of movement, they have done a good job. We use our shoulders more when we block. We still use our hands, but we get the shoulders into the defenders.

On this series, we have a dive play, a sweep, and a play-action pass. We block a gap scheme to the playside, except we do not pull a guard. In the diagram, the kick-out blocker aligns in a tight slot, comes behind the formation, and kicks out on the

5 technique to the playside. That can be a fullback or a tight end. The line blocks back to the backside all the way. We combo block the 3-technique defender to the Will linebacker.

The center and backside guard can combo block or man block the nose and Mike linebacker. The backside tackle and tight end seal the backside defenders. The sweeper using the orbit motion hits the tailback's position as the quarterback comes back and fakes the sweep.

This is the zone play. The back knows he cannot cut until he gets into the feet of the offensive linemen. When we talk about the cutback, it is what we call "cut north." It is a slight cut. We want to stay inside and get yards. The snap of the ball depends on the speed of the sweeper. If he is a fast runner, we may have to snap it when he is five yards from the C gap. You must time that part of the play out in practice.

The kick-out block may be aligned in the fullback's slot in front of the tailback. In that case, he goes straight for the kick-out. Bringing the fullback from his position helps sell the zone play. We want the 5-technique defender to close inside and run the sweep outside of him (Diagram #6). When we run the sweep, the offensive line blocks the play the same as the zone play. We use this play when the 5-technique defender tries to close hard on the fullback's block. If he does not close, we can still get outside of him.

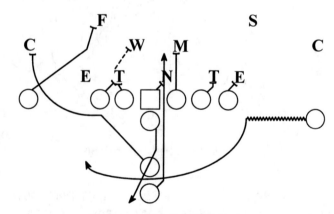

Diagram #6. Orbit Sweep

The wide receiver cracks the force on the play. If there is no one in that position, he climbs to the safety. The playside tackle on the zone play gets to the inside number of the B-gap defender. When we run the sweep, he wants to get to the outside shoulder of the defender. The fullback influences on the 5-technique defender as if he were going to kick him out. He bypasses the defender and goes to block the corner. We can run the play without the motion. We align the sweeper behind the tight end, and he moves on the snap count. Everything else is the same.

The play-action pass from this series is orbit bootleg (Diagram #7). The tight end runs a chip flat pattern. He comes off and assimilates a block on his blocking assignment. He runs a chip flat pattern. The depth of the pattern at the sideline is three yards. The cross pattern comes across the field and has to reach the opposite hash mark before the quarterback on his action reaches that hash mark. We want to do that so the quarterback does not have to throw across his body to throw the cross. The wide receiver to the side of the boot runs an 18-yard comeback.

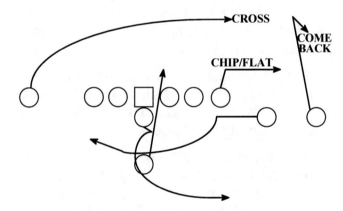

Diagram #7. Orbit Bootleg

When the receiver runs the comeback, we want him to come almost directly down his stem. We want him to catch the ball two yards outside his stem. The quarterback fakes the zone, sweeps, and rolls to the playside. He looks for the chip, cross, and comeback in that order. The offensive line blocks the inside zone play but does not go downfield. This is also a good red-zone play. When we run the play, the quarterback ends up nine yards deep at the apex of his drop. When he begins his roll, he is right between the uprights.

The coaching point for the chip block is to be aggressive on the defender's outside shoulder. When he comes out, he wants to be flat to the line

of scrimmage and gain depth as he runs the pattern. However, he does not get over three yards up the field.

The comeback receiver in the red zone pushes to within two yards from the end line of the end zone. At that point, he comes inside and pushes to the pylon at the back of the end zone, which is on the hash mark.

This is a simple package. It is easy on the linemen and it gives you a good misdirection play for the red zone. After watching our cut-ups, we should lead the country in horse collar tackles. We broke so many long run and passes last year but they always ran us down with a horse collar tackle.

We have another pass off this series (Diagram #8). We align in an I pro formation. We run the orbit motion. The single receiver runs an alley read pattern. He reads the alley for any deep defender inside of him. If there is a defender, he cuts his pattern off at 12 yards just outside the hash mark. If there is no deep safety in the alley, he goes for the end zone.

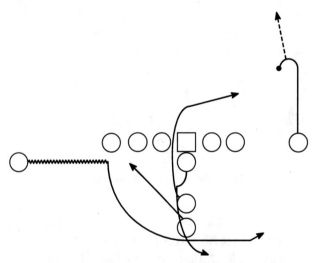

Diagram #8. Orbit Pass

If the quarterback goes for the deep pattern in the alley, he wants to throw the ball to the middle of the field and not drive the receiver back outside with a throw. He wants to take the easy throw because this is probably a touchdown. He wants to make it an easy catch for the wide receiver.

We run the outside zone play. We ran this play when I was with the Denver Broncos. We run the outside zone because it is simple, aggressive, and allows us to play fast. It gives us a downhill run for the tailback. This play takes the pressure off the quarterback and helps him out. We run it from the shotgun, pistol, and under the center. It also gives us a chance to create some throws. Our defense needs to see these schemes because we have to play gap-control football.

On the outside zone, the tailback aligns at seven yards (Diagram #9). His aiming point is the tight end or ghost tight end. The tailback takes a lateral step, and his first key is the defender playing on the tight end. If he sees any kind of stretch to the outside, he makes a downhill cut to the inside. He cannot make two cuts or dance. He makes one cut, and the ball has to go north. His goal is to get the ball back to the line of scrimmage. The fullback does the same thing. He blocks the edge; however, if he sees any outside movement, he plants his foot, goes north, and blocks the first color that shows.

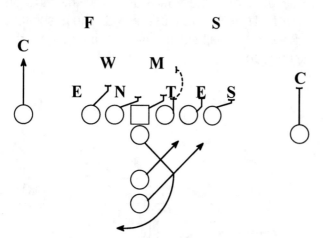

Diagram #9. Outside Zone

The two-man block on the outside zone is slightly different from the inside zone. If the playside tackle and guard are involved in a two-man block, the techniques are not hard to teach. The covered lineman wants to takes his lateral step and gets his face in the outside armpit of the defender. His inside hand and foot must work together. The

inside hand goes to the sternum of the defender and the inside foot is in the middle of the crotch. The 5-technique defender playing gap-control defense should widen to keep his gap-control position.

The uncovered linemen, takes his lateral step to the outside and attacks the defender. He wants to put his chin in the throat of the defender. That is the way he is moving. If the defender disappears, he climbs to the linebacker.

If the defense has a 3 technique over the guard and a 5 technique over the tackle, the tackle is alone on the block. He has no protection coming from the inside. His outside step and target are the same. He still lateral steps and puts his face in the outside armpit. The difference is the inside hand. He does not take the inside hand to the sternum. He uses the inside hand as a catcher if the defender tries to get inside. He places the inside hand on the inside number. That allows him some control on the inside move so he can redirect on his charge. The width of his first step depends on the width of the defender. If he is wide, the tackle has to take a wider step. If he is tight, the tackle takes a tighter step.

If you have linemen that will come off the ball and be aggressive, you can play smaller linemen. They have to use their quickness to get hand and head position on the defenders.

We would love to have you visit. Colorado Springs and the Air Force Academy is a special place. It is a small school with only 4,000 students. These students could go to any school in the country academically. These players are training to serve their country.

You should never think that what you do is insignificant. What you do for the young people you coach and teach is beyond measure. They need the thing you provide. They need the structure, discipline, and the leadership you can give them. You are the rock that holds the people together. I respect you for it. Thank you.

THE HYBRID 3-4 GAP CONTROL DEFENSE

University of West Georgia

Thank you. I want to spend a few minutes talking about our general philosophy. We call our defense a hybrid 3-4 gap control scheme. I am going to talk about our practice sessions, the things we do on third down, and what we do on the goal line. We will go over some game film so you can see what we are doing in the games.

The teams that use the 3-4 defense use the standard terms for the linebackers as Sam, Mike, Will, and Jack. Jack is the linebacker to the weakside of the formation. We keep our Jack to the field, behind our defensive end. You will see this in our film.

We establish basic position rules for our defensive linemen, linebackers, and defensive backs. Our defense is simple, and it is sound. We use a lot of cover 3 and cover 4. We disguise our coverage and our blitzes. As a secondary coach, we never want to give away our leverage. We use an open stance, and we align six to seven yards off the receiver. We come to a square stance when we are in cover 2, and a crossover running technique in cover 4. We want to make everything look the same as we align in a cover 2 look.

Our defensive linemen are in a consistent alignment. Our defensive ends are always going to be lined up straight on the defensive tackles, and the noseguard is head-up with the center. We ask them to penetrate through their man, and to play strong in their gap. We want them to stay where they are once they are in the gap.

Our linebackers must know the hot gaps in their pre-snap reads. They read the backs through the offensive line. We do not want any false steps. When they see the ball, they go after it.

Again, for our defensive backs, we want to hold our disguise. We stress to the defensive backs to use their eyes. Eyes! Eyes! Eyes! We want to make sure their eyes are on the proper reads. We tell the defensive backs they must know their leverage and their assignment!

In cover 2, our outside men key the tackles, and our safeties are looking at the guards to key their run/pass read. They must know their leverage, and they must know their assignment. Sometimes our leverage is inside, and sometimes it may be outside. It is based on our coverage. We never, ever get head-up on a receiver. We may start outside and move inside on the receiver, or start inside and move outside. We want to make sure when the ball is snapped that we are doing what we supposed to be doing.

Our safeties are the quarterbacks of our defense. Regardless of what is going on with our defense, the safeties make all of the calls. They are the guys who tell the linebackers and cornerbacks what we are doing. We always make sure our safeties are communicating with our other players.

I want to move on to tell you how we practice. In the first part of our practice with our defense, we are going against each other. We call it pre-practice in regards to what we cover in the first 10 periods every day.

PRACTICE

- Tackling circuit
- Turnover circuit
- Trey drill (run fits)
- 1-on-1 pass rush
- Skeleton versus offense
- Scout team focus—You're only as good as your scout team.

The first thing we have is a tackling circuit (Diagram #1). We have four coaches running four different tackling drills.

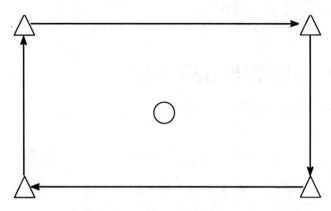

Diagram #1. Tackling Circuit

A timekeeper stands in the middle of all four drills. Each period should last two minutes and 30 seconds, giving a few seconds for transition. At the end of each period, the timekeeper should blow a whistle or horn to alert all groups to rotate.

I will show you the four drills we do at each station. First is the one-man sled drill (Diagram #2). We use two coaches working together on this drill.

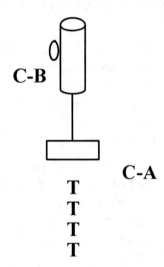

Diagram #2. One-Man Sled Drill

One-Man Sled Drill

- Two coaches—Coach A and Coach B
- One-man sled and ball attached to a long string
- One line five yards in front of the sled
- Coach A says, "hit" and watches form
- Coach B positions the ball on the dummy
- Tackler: Facemask on the ball
- Tackler: Dip, lift, shoot arms, run feet
- Coach B resets the drill

Next is the shield block angle tackle drill (Diagram #3). We can use one or two coaches in this drill.

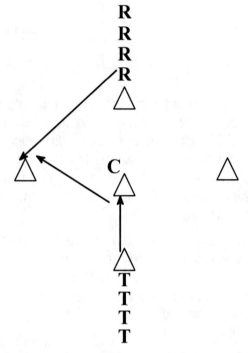

Diagram #3. Shield Block Angle Tackle Drill

Shield Block Angle Tackle Drill

- One or two coaches
- Forearm pad and two footballs
- Coach stands in the middle with the pad facing the tackler.
- Coach points direction behind his back for the runner.
- On "hit," the tackler approaches the coach with the pad
- With eyes on the blocker, the tackler shocks, extends, and sheds the blocker away from the runner
- Tackler sees the runner out of his peripheral, never stops his feet, and finishes the angle tackle
- Runner and tackler switch lines

The next part of the circuit is the angle tackle drill (Diagram #4). We can run this drill with one or two coaches.

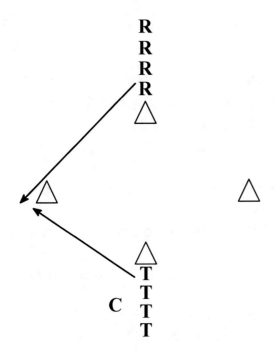

Diagram #4. Angle Tackle Drill

Angle Tackle Drill

- One or two coaches
- Four cones and two footballs
- Set up cones in a diamond formation
- Two equal lines
- One runner and one tackler at a time
- Coach stands behind the tackler
- Coach silently directs the runner to a cone
- Proper angle form tackle
- Players switch lines

The last circuit is our cut block angle tackle drill (Diagram #5). We need two coaches for the drill.

Cut Block Angle Tackle Drill

- Two coaches
- Four cones and two footballs
- One line of cutters
- One cutter, two runners, one tackler
- On "hit," runner takes cut one.
- Runner continues to cut two.
- Runner times up on second cut.
- Coach B blows whistle on contact.
- Tackler becomes the runner.

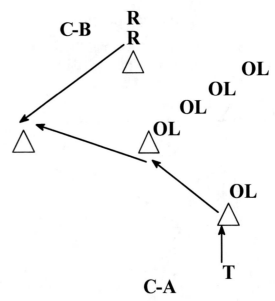

Diagram #5. Cut Block Angle Tackle Drill

- Runner goes to cut line.
- Cutter one becomes the tackler.

The next period is our turnover circuit. We work different drills to teach our players how to create turnovers. We may work on how to pick up fumbles, tip drills, and other drills to help us with the turnovers. I will cover four of the drills we use in our turnover circuit (Diagram #6). We start out the same as we do with the tackling circuit.

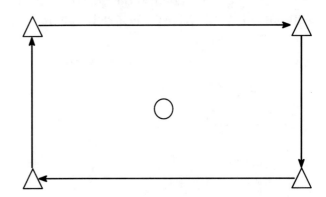

Diagram #6. Turnover Circuit

A timekeeper stands in the middle of all four drills. Each period should last two minutes and 30 seconds, giving a few seconds for transition. At the end of each period, the timekeeper should blow a whistle or horn to alert all groups to rotate.

TURNOVER CIRCUIT

The first turnover drill is our 2-on-1 strip drill (Diagram #7). You can run this drill with one coach.

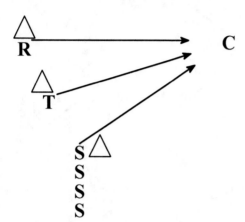

Diagram #7. 2-on-1 Strip Drill

2-on-1 Strip Drill

• Two footballs
• One line with three positions
• One runner, one tackler, one stripper
• Runner goes on "hit"
• Tackler fits the runner up
• Stripper pursues and punches the ball out

Next, we go run the strip the quarterback drill (Diagram #8). We need two coaches to run this drill.

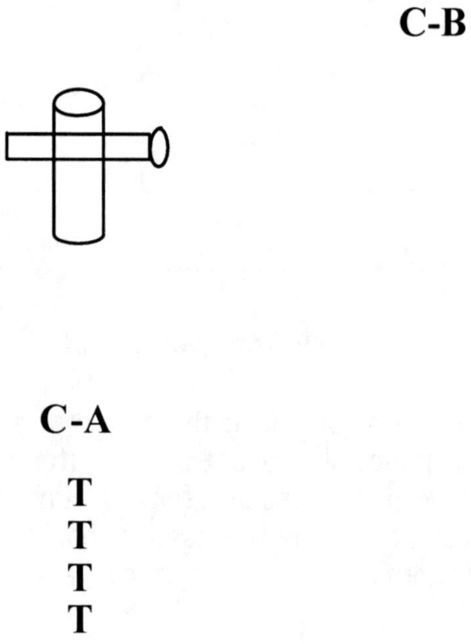

C-B

C-A

T
T
T
T

Diagram #8. Strip the Quarterback Drill

Strip the Quarterback Drill

• Two coaches
• Forearm shield pad, pop-up dummy with arms
• Velcro on back arm, away from defender
• Velcro on two Nerf® balls
• Coach B sets up quarterback dummy with attached Nerf ball
• Coach A stands in the middle with the pad facing the tackler
• On "hit," the tackler approaches the coach with the pad
• With eyes on the blocker, the tackler rips/swims past
• Tackler rakes the throwing arm of the quarterback on the tackle and pops up to find the football

Our third turnover circuit drill is our Oskie drill (Diagram #9). We use two coaches in the drill.

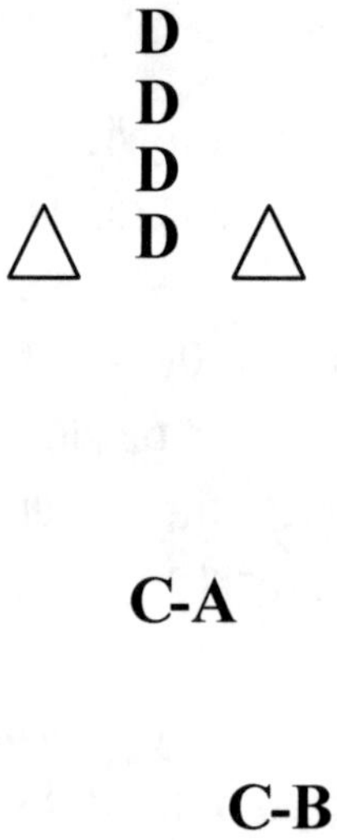

D
D
D
△ D △

C-A

C-B

Diagram #9. Oskie Drill

Oskie Drill

• Two coaches
• Two cones and two balls
• Coach A signals the defender to go
• Coach A then throws the ball
• The defender tries to catch, and says "Oskie"
• The defender runs the ball to Coach B
• Coach B gives the next ball to Coach A

Our last turnover circuit drill is the scoop-and-score drill (Diagram #10). We use two coaches in the drill.

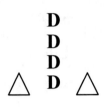

C-A

_____

C-B

Diagram #10. Scoop-and-Score Drill

Scoop-and-Score Drill

- Two coaches
- Two cones and two footballs
- One finish line
- Coach A signals for the defender to go
- Coach A then drops the ball
- The defender attempts to scoop by grabbing the ball with both hands on the fat part of the ball
- Coach B ensures the score, gives the next ball to Coach A, and takes the ball from the last player to score

The next thing in our practice schedule is our trey drills (run fits). Then, we move to the 1-on-1 pass rush drills. After that, we go to our skeleton drill versus our first offense. The following is the way we work on this drill:

- First-and-10 on Monday
- Second down on Tuesday
- Third-and-long on Wednesday
- Red zone on Thursday

In our scout team focus period, we yell at our scout team more than we yell at our first team players. For us to be good, our scout team has to be great. We believe "you are only as good as your scout team." I know some teams are limited as far as the number of players available for the scout team, but we carry 105 players on our roster. We make the scout team players watch the films of our opponents.

DEFENSE VS. SCOUT TEAMS

Focus on efficiency for maximum reps. "You are only as good as your scout team prepares you to be." The trey drill is an offensive drill, but we use it to teach our defense to understand where their gap responsibility is. We stress the defensive players must stay in their gaps.

Our offensive line coach added to our 1-on-1 drills by involving the offensive linemen. They work on pass protection against our defense, and we get more players involved in the drill this way.

We work on the skeleton drill every day. It may be coming in from the 50-yard line, or going from the fringe, which is from the 25-yard line going in for us. We work the drill from the one-yard line coming out. We try to cover all situations. We move the ball up and down the field. We run five or six plays, going as fast as we can. We get our calls in on defense, and the offense gets to call the plays they want to work on. We call the plays from the sideline. We do not care about the results; we are working on plays. We have the play on script, and we want to make sure our defensive players get the calls.

Cover 2

I want to cover a few points in our base defense. We want to make everything look like it is cover 2 for our corners and safeties when we line up. Our orange call is our cover 2 man coverage.

In cover 2, the defensive line slants away from the strength (field) to the boundary. In cover 4, our defensive line slants toward the strength to the field.

In our show package we run the following two types of defenses:

- Bail—max cover
- Blast—max pressure

In our bail call, we are using max cover. We line up the same as in cover 2. We make it look as if we are going to blitz on the play.

- Two defensive ends contain rush
- Nine defenders in coverage

We have four defensive backs lined up seven to eight yards deep. We want to make it look like it is man-to-man coverage. We want it to look like we are all coming on the snap of the ball.

Once the ball is snapped, we are going to open up, look for the run, and then get to a spot. Our corners are two yards on top of the numbers, our safeties are two yards inside the hash marks, and our linebackers drop to a spot. They have curl, curl, and flat. On bail, we want to make the quarterback pump the ball. We want to make him pat the ball. As soon as the defensive backs get to their spot, their eyes are going on the quarterback.

We script eight plays, and the grad assistant has eight big cards. If we script 10 plays, he will have 10 cards. His job is to make sure the players understand what they are doing on the play. We try to rotate the players because we want to have quality reps.

If we call a blast, we are applying maximum pressure. It is the opposite of bail. Now we are going to go after the quarterback.

Bail—Max Cover

- Two defensive ends contain rush
- Nine defenders in coverage

Our calls in our base defense are arrow-2 and slant-4. The arrow means the defensive line is going to slant away from the strength. The strength is always going to be to the field—always. The strength is to the field, and our linemen slant away from the strength.

In cover 4, if we call arrow-2, that is the way we are going to play. The defensive line is slanting away and into the boundary. In cover 4 slant-4, the line slants toward the field.

Our linemen may get beat up at times, but their job is to stay in the gaps and control the offensive line, and let our linebackers run. To us, cover 4 is nine men in the box. This is true if our safeties make a proper read. That is the reason we have the safeties lined up so it looks as if we are playing cover 2.

I want to talk about our third down and long defense. This is situational defense. We are in our shell look. We are not going to show bail or blast. We go back to our arrow-2 look. It is our slant toward look. We are giving a two-shell look. The key is what is behind the arrow-2 call. We are running orange behind the call. One is where we just match up with the receivers. The corner has the first man outside, Will has the #2 man, and our Jack has the #3 man. Mike is covering the spot. We do not run any two-man under coverage unless it is third-and-long. We run it late in the game when the offense is driving but they have a long way to go.

We use three colors to designate what type of coverage we use. We have an orange, black, and we have white. Our colors are used in third-and-long situations.

Our red zone defense is our cover red 7. We call this inside the 12-yard line. It is our four-down package. We use our stunts and pass rush games in this package. It is still our situational defense.

Red Zone Defense

- Coverage: Red 7
- Call inside the 12-yard line
- Four-down package
  - ✓ Stunts
  - ✓ Pass rush games
- Pressure

Very quickly, this is our goal line defense. The call is smoke.

Call: Smoke

- Smoker—thigh/cut/climb
- Man coverage (go with motion)
- Defensive line wants low penetration
- Stress importance weekly!

If you want to visit us, you are welcome. Our head coach, Daryl Dickey, is not opposed to having coaches come to practice or to come by to see us. We love to have coaches come to see us. We love to talk football as much as we can. If you want to contact me, I would love to hear from you.

COMPONENTS OF THE 3-4 DEFENSE

Fresno State

I appreciate your attendance. I do not appreciate the scheduling of having to follow Jerry Glanville. Coach Glanville does a great job, and I do not know if I will be worthy to follow him. I do appreciate the opportunity to come back to Western Pennsylvania and talk to coaches. I used to recruit in Western Pennsylvania and know the great job you guys do coaching. I have been blessed in my coaching career. I have had a chance to recruit in the states of Ohio, Pennsylvania, Texas, and California. There are not many places much better than that to recruit.

Today, I would like to go over some of the options we have in our defensive package. We believe these are the components of a championship defense. We will take these and implement them at Fresno State. We developed these while we were at Texas A&M University. Coach Sherman challenged us, when we first got to Texas A&M, offensively and defensively to come up with four or five major points that would be our central core values for our offense and defense. These are things we want to hang our hat on. These were not so much scheme-wise, but would be our core values. I will go over them and how it, in turn, made us a better defense. I also want to go over our base 3-4 package and why we do it the way we do. I will cover what the advantages are and how we set our personnel in our defense.

We sat down as a defense and wanted to find out what are the things that make a difference between winning and losing. Of course, everyone talks about stopping the run, you play great red zone defense, and we had a discussion about a lot of things that make up a great defense. When you put everything on a young man who is going to class and worried about girlfriends and many other things that are on their mind, they tend to lose their focus. We just want to have four or five things we can hang our hats on. These are the things that we came up with.

COMPONENTS OF CHAMPIONSHIP DEFENSE

- Takeaways—get the ball back
- Stops—run game; 3.25 yards per carry; win on third and/or fourth down
- Fanatical effort—maximum level of speed or strain to the completion of the play
- Play physical—finish the play in a dominant position
- Fundamentals

When we look at takeaways over the past five or six years with defenses I have been a part of, really, the biggest difference as to whether we had an outstanding season or we did not has been our turnover margin. This will be the stat that we emphasize most on defense while at Fresno State because it is a team stat. All of the other stats are nice to look at, but really the stats that make a difference are takeaways and turnover margin. Defensively, our job is not to just stop offenses; it is to take the ball away and give it to our offense in an advantageous position. If you look throughout all of pro, college, and high school football, the team that wins the turnover margin usually wins the game.

Sean Payton for the New Orleans Saints talks about how to make it simple for his guys to always think about takeaways on defense. He came up with four Ps. This is all taken from Coach Payton and the Saints.

COMPONENTS OF TAKEAWAYS

Preparedness

- Know our defense inside out. I do not want our kids to go on the field and worry about whether they are stepping with this foot or the other foot. I just want it all to be second nature to them.

- Know the opponent. Study them in film and know their personnel tendencies. Know their down-and-distance tendencies. The ultimate bottom line is if you are playing faster than your opponent and attacking before he expects you to because you know your opponent, that is where this philosophy will turn into takeaways.
- Play our fastest.

Population

- Fanatical effort to the ball. This is getting guys to the football.

Physicality

- Club, chop, strip, pull, and snatch the ball away from the offense. We teach this just like everybody. This is drilled every single day. Again, this is something that is part of our core values, and we do not just talk about it; we enforce it every day with what we do.
- Knock the opponent to ground violently.

Purpose

- Know that no matter where the ball is, our primary objective is to get the ball back for our offense or score ourselves. This is like next evolution in thinking for a lot of players. Defensively, when our kids first start learning our package and schemes, they have to understand that their job is not just to line up properly; their job is not just to make the tackle; their job is to take the ball away. When we get in that mentality, we are going to force the takeaways that make a difference in the ballgame.

In 2006, I was at the University of Nevada. We led the country in takeaways with 37. I went to the U.S. Air Force Academy for three years and we had 30 plus takeaways. At Texas A&M, we dropped a little bit. We only had 25 takeaways. Our goal every single year is going to be 30. If you will get your guys to believe in the four Ps I truly believe your takeaways will go up. It is that mentality of a player that their job is not just to tackle somebody, but to rip it away. With emphasis from you, they will find a way to do it.

The next definition we have to talk about is stops. We have two components to stops. First of all, we talk about stopping the run. The way we defined stopping the run is the hold the opponent to 3.2 yard average or less per carry. We looked at the top 20 defenses over the past five years and found if you stop people to an average of 3.2 yards per carry, you are going to be in the top 25 in the country. If you face a triple option team like the Air Force Academy that is going to run the ball 60 times, it probably is not a realistic goal to say you are going to hold them to less than 100 yards. I feel if we can give our team a goal of less than 3.2 yards per carry, and go through the entire year, we are going to win 90 percent of those games.

Getting stops on third and fourth down is the second component. Stops for us on third down means to hold the opponent to 33 percent or less conversion on third down. When we held teams to that rate, we won a lot more games than not.

We now need to talk about the definition of effort. Coach Sherman wanted a definition that was good for our entire team, whether it be for offense, defense, or special teams. A definition everyone could look to and say, "This is what we are talking about on fanatical effort." Not just good effort or great effort, we want fanatical effort. Our definition is: we want the maximum level of strain or speed to the successful completion of the play. We grade our guys, like I am sure you do, on every single play. Sometimes, our kids will tell me that they are trying hard and they are hustling, but I ask them, "Is that your maximum level of speed or strain?" If we cannot, or they cannot answer yes to that question, we mark them down. It is very definable for them.

Everyone talks about physical play. Physical play for us is defined as finishing in a dominant position. Did you finish in a dominant position? Again, this is offensively, defensively, and special teams. This is very simple for guys to understand and figure out.

Again, to make it clear to our players, we define the components of fundamentals. This covers all phases of the game. No matter what your responsibility is, this is a common theme we talk to everyone about.

COMPONENTS OF FUNDAMENTALS

Eyes

- Your eye level represents the "leverage position" you have on your opponent.
- Your eyes must be below his eyes.

Hands

- The placement of your hands inside the framework of the body represents the control position you have on your opponent.
- Your hands must be inside his hands. We teach our players that our thumbs should be in the 12 o'clock position. This helps our hands go inside naturally.

Feet

- Your foot position represents the balance and power you have on your opponent.
- Keep your feet slightly outside the hips and shoulder upon contact. It does not matter whether it is a blocker or a defender.

We keep it simple so our players can remember it. Eyes, hands, and feet are the fundamentals that we are going to stress and teach.

At Texas A&M, there is a lot of talk about the wrecking crew legacy. The year before we got to Texas A&M, they only had six wins. We were also 105th in the country in scoring defense. Just by incorporating these things with a brand-new scheme, we went from six wins to nine and from 105th to 24th in the country in points per game scoring defense. We were 36th in the country in takeaways, but my biggest disappointment was we were not over 30. On third down, we got to 36 percent, which was an improvement but not to our 33 percent goal. We still ended up in the top 24.

Let us talk about why we run a 3-4 type defense. In most of the places I have been, we have not been able to find those dominant types of players in the 3 technique, you need to get four guys to beat five guys blocking and get pressure on the quarterback. More and more today in college and even high school football teams are spreading out the ball. The backer comes down so you can get pressure on the quarterback. Even in the pros today, teams cannot get pressure with just four guys rushing the quarterback. They have to bring that extra linebacker as the fifth guy.

ADVANTAGES OF 3-4

Personnel

- Get better athletes on the field.
- Easier to recruit linebackers than defensive linemen. We think, personnel-wise, we can recruit better by getting more linebackers because there are more of those guys available. There are not many 6'5" 290-pound guys that can run for you. We can find some smaller guys who can play with fanatical effort, though.

Multiplicity of Fronts, Coverages, and Pressures

- Any of four linebackers can easily be in the rush. These guys need to be disruptive.
- Offenses must prepare to block all or none of them.
- Easy to disguise. We can get guys in the over front or under front at the drop of a hat as long as you have guys who can do it.

Different

- Offenses have one week to prepare. Most teams are not a 3-4 defense and, therefore, the offense is not used to competing against it.
- Where is the shade-3 technique? Most offenses want to know where the shade of the 3 technique is. If you are lined up in a 50, you are not giving it to them.
- Simplified game plans. On Saturdays, we see about half the plays of what we have seen teams run against other teams. A lot of teams do not even attempt to run some the plays they would normally run because of the structure of our defense. We have a guy on the line of scrimmage who is uncovered that they need to account for. Now, they have to change their mentality of: are they going to go four wide, or are they going to put two tight ends on the field?

The following is how we set up our 3-4 personnel.

Defensive Line

- *Two ends (left/right):* Really, these are just two defensive tackles, but we want to make them feel better about themselves so we call them defensive ends. You can set them up anyway you want to, but we go left to right. We would like our defensive ends to be 6'3" or taller. They are going to be playing in a 5 technique or a 4i technique, or occasionally in a 3 technique.

- *One noseguard:* This guy can be a sawed-off guy, but we would like a guy with some girth. We are looking for a 300-pound plus guy. At the Air Force Academy, where we were running this, we did not have those types of guys. We got by with a 255-pound guy who was extremely quick. You can run this with smaller guys, but they have to be quick and you change up the charges.

Linebackers

- *Outside (Sam/Joker):* Our Sam linebacker lines up to the field. Our Joker lines up into the boundary. When we get to our four-man rush, our Joker is usually the better pass rusher. Our Sam is usually our better coverage guy.

- *Inside (Mike/Will):* Our Mike is our more athletic linebacker. Because of the open offenses that a lot of teams are running now, our Mike linebacker has become more like our old traditional Will linebacker. Our old Mike linebacker, who was limited more coverage-wise, has become our Will linebacker now. Again, this is kind of flipped from the traditional view because of the spread offenses. This gets back to the mentality of always having nickel-type personnel on the field on all downs.

Secondary

- *Two corners (left/right):* If I have a corner I am a little bit leery of, I will probably want him to the field more often than not. Our theory is we play a lot of 6 coverage where we have quarter, quarter, half. If you go 3x1, we are going to put that corner to the boundary. We want him to cover the receiver who is not quite as good. We have been fortunate at Texas A&M, where we

have the personnel, that we can just make them left and right.

- *Two safeties (strong/free):* Our strong safety lines up to the field. Our free safety lines up to the boundary. If we have the ball in the middle the field, we are going to have the strong safety go toward the passing strength. Passing strength is a phrase we will use a lot. To us, passing strength is always the speed receiver or the lightest #2 receiver. In our terminology, open or closed determines where the tight end is. Strong and weak do not define where the tight end is. Strong and weak determine where passing strength is.

This is what our base alignment looks like against a 2x2 (Diagram #1). Our Sam is going to line up over #2. We are going to start out in a 2 shell with just about everything we do. Our ends are going to line up head up to the offensive tackles. We are going to try to get as much ball as we can until we find out what kind of athlete they are. Same thing with our nose on the center. In a 2x2 set, our Mike and Will linebackers are going to be in 20 alignments. They are going to be four and a half yards deep for a generic down and head up over the guard. Our Joker, if #2 is attached, is going to line up in a loose 9 technique. Our secondary is going to be in a 2 shell with our safeties lined up anywhere from 10 to 14 yards deep pre-snap. Our corners are going to be lined up in a press and are five or six yards off the line of scrimmage, outside the #1 receivers. We will start rotating from there.

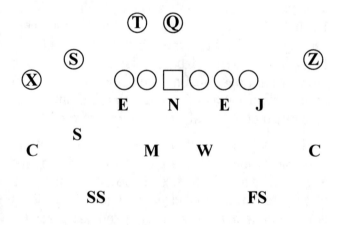

Diagram #1. Base Alignment vs. 2x2

If we get a 3x1 set, the Sam, again is going to line up relative to #2 (Diagram #2). The only guys who

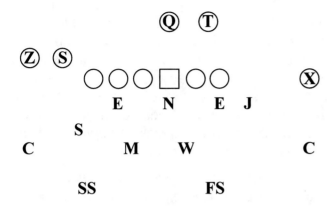

Diagram #2. Base Alignment vs. 3x1

change will be the Mike and the Will. They will bump over one half of a man. Instead of being lined up in 20s, they will be lined up in 30 and 10. Our Joker lines up relative to his #2. Since #2 is in the backfield, he is going to play a 6 technique on the open air side. If we get a removed #2, the Joker is going to expand. Nothing changes to the frontside. On the backside, the Joker will line up relative to his #2.

As we install our base 3-4 defense, we have the ability to rush a variety of different ways. Even though we line up with three linemen, we are only going to just rush three linemen about 5 to 10 percent of the time. About 40 percent of the time, we are rushing four players. Really, we consider our base defense as bringing a fourth guy as part of the rush. The first questions you have to ask yourself are: who and where do I want to bring that fourth rusher from? How does the coverage tie into that?

When we set our front, we go either open or closed. What we mean by open is the outside linebacker who is aligned to the open inside, away from the tight end; he is going to be the fourth guy in the rush. If we call closed, everything is opposite. If I am lined up with the tight end to me, I am going to be in the rush. We are not a one-gap principle team.

We can also align it by field or bench. When we play up-tempo offenses, we have used more of this type of package in just getting lined up. This helps us get lined up fast and gives our guys a better chance.

We also run a Mac and Mo. Mac is going to be an inside linebacker rush from the closed side. Mo is going to be our inside linebacker rush from the open side. Just like open or closed is for the outside

linebackers, when we call Mac, the Mike lines up to the field. If he has a tight end to him, he is going to be the extra guy in the rush. If the tight end is into the boundary, the Will linebacker is going to be the extra guy in the rush. Strong and weak refer to passing strength in our terminology. It has to do with formation passing strength and not where the open and closed are.

We can set our formation based on tite or what we call opposite. The tite is where the offset back is. If we see a one-back offset formation, that defines our tite. If we are playing against a two-back set, and there is an offset fullback, that will define our tite. It is just a way we can set our front and a way we can attack protections.

I mentioned earlier that coverages have to tie in with this. We cannot just say we are going to set a particular front and make our linebacker adjust to every coverage. We have to have everything tied together. We are going to be zone in our base coverage most of the time. We run a lot of 6 coverage and 3 coverage. We play both one- and two-high safety coverages. The big thing that makes us go is our zone pressures. That is another clinic entirely.

As we set our coverage up, if we call open, we are going to run double-digit coverage with it. We might run open 63. Opposite of that would be closed 36. Bench is going to be single-digit, and field is going to be single-digit—like bench 6 or field 3. Mac and Mo are going to be 4 coverage. The 30 tite is where we rush three and play a loaded Tampa 2 coverage behind it.

Let me start out with open 63 (Diagram #3). We are going to bring the fourth rusher from the openside. Coverage is going to be double-digit. We could play man, which we do sometimes particularly out of nickel, but let me just talk about our base. We will call 6 coverage, or cover 6, which is a modified quarter, quarter, half coverage. It will depend on where that #2 receiver is.

We line up in our same shell. Our corner to the field, since he is to the strongside, we are going to play cover 6 to the left. That corner side or modified side turns him into what we call a lock corner. He is responsible for all uphill routes from the #1 receiver. We give him the ability to line up in

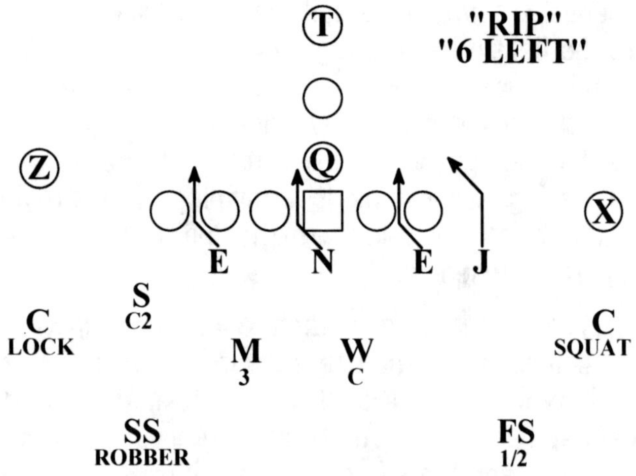

"RIP"
"6 LEFT"

Diagram #3. Open 63 vs. Pro

press alignment, veil alignment, or off alignment. We want him mixing it up during the game. We want that corner to have some ownership and use the different tools he has in his toolbox to be able to play a lock technique.

The strong safety will line up in the 2 shell and make a robber call to the corner, which puts him in lock. He will also tell the Mike linebacker that he is here. That lets him know that in that particular front, with two backs in the backfield, we are going to go to an eight-man front. The Sam linebacker is a curl/pick-up player in pass. He is a force player in run. He has a 9 technique and is responsible for the D gap. Any gap scheme to him, he is going to squeeze on back in. He is responsible to curl/pick up anything that crosses his face, which he will pick up in man-to-man coverage.

In the robber, the strong safety keys on the #2 receiver. He will stem from this to go down to a point where he is 8x1 outside of the tight end. His read is on the tight end. If the tight end has a vertical release, he has him anything past 10 yards, man-to-man. If the tight end stays in to protect, he will play robber technique. His eyes go from the tight end to the #1 receiver. He is a curl/dig post player on #1.

Our Mike is playing a 30 technique. He is our middle-read 3 player in pass protection. Our Will linebacker is our curl player, and he is playing a 10 technique or a scrape 10.

Our front linemen are going to get as much of the ball as they want. We are going to take a six-inch power step away from the direction of the call.

Here, the openside is to the right, so we are going to make a Rip call. Everyone is going to be taking a six-inch power step to their left. We drill this a lot. Our linemen have to have a balanced stance and go wherever we want them to go. The six-inch power step is at a 45-degree angle. We want them punching with their inside or away hand and engaging on the lineman right away.

Our Joker is in the rush here and is playing in a ghost 6. Depending on down-and-distance, he is our edge rusher. We are playing half coverage into the boundary. We have our corner disguise his initial alignment, but he is keying inside first for run. He is our force player to the boundary. His number-one responsibility is force for the outside run. If the outside run is away from him, he does not care. If the outside run is to him, he has to put himself in a force position. We want him to beat the receiver underneath to the inside right away. With normal spacing, he can do it. As receivers cheat their spacing out, he may not be able to do it. What we drill them to do is to find the point where he does not have to go outside of the receiver and create a seam. We want him attacking inside right now and pushing the ball up the field.

Our safety plays in half field coverage. We are going to open crossover and run for three steps and key the #1 receiver. It is important that the corner force from the inside. If you do not win, you have to make the running back run deep and wide. We have to be a factor in the run game with our corners to affect the path of the running back. We want him to force inside and make the running back go vertical. That is how we set against a pro set with a robber side and a half field side.

Against pro sets, we are going to run cover 6. Against slots, we are going to run cover 3 (Diagram #4). Again, we have to define for our players what a pro set is and what a slot set is. A pro set is where passing strength and the tight end are lined up on the same side. In a slot set, the tight end is lined up away from the passing strength. When we are playing double-digit coverage, if we get a change in strength motion, the coverage will change. It will go from 6 to 3 or from 3 to 6. The front does not change. The outside linebackers will always stay in that coverage. That is the advantage to playing open 63. We play it mostly against teams that will

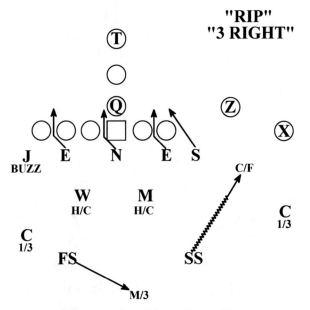

"RIP"
"3 RIGHT"

Diagram #4. Open 63 vs. Slot

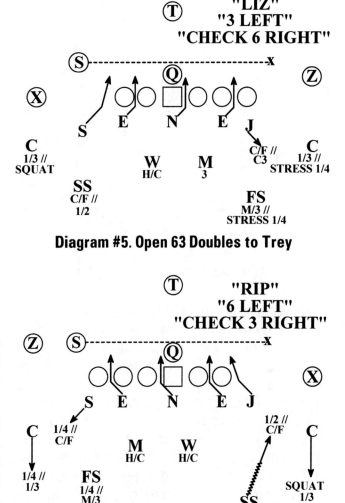

"LIZ"
"3 LEFT"
"CHECK 6 RIGHT"

Diagram #5. Open 63 Doubles to Trey

"RIP"
"6 LEFT"
"CHECK 3 RIGHT"

Diagram #6. Open 63 Trey to Doubles

be in 12 or 21 type personnel. We like to bring some stunts off of the openside. Sometimes, we will see that out of 11 personnel based on down-and-distance tendencies.

The Sam linebacker is now to the openside and will start over #2 and creep late. He is in the charge. It is still a Rip call because the openside is to the right. Will and our strong safety are starting out in a 2 shell. We tell the strong safety, the free safety, and the Sam linebacker they are tethered together. As that Sam starts to creep down, whether it is a disguise or if he is in the charge, the tether has to bring the strong safety with him. Everything has to be tied. As the strong safety pulls down the free safety, he gets pulled to the middle third. Sometimes, we will show this type of coverage as a disguise and then spin back to a cover 6.

When we are playing this, we want the openside outside linebacker in the rush. Change of strength will look like this (Diagram #5). Here it is an open left, and we will call Liz. We are going to play cover 3 because the tight end is away from passing strength. As soon as the receiver goes in motion, it changes things, and we go check 6 right. The Liz does not change.

If they go from trey to doubles, it will look like this (Diagram #6). When we have a Rip call, we are playing quarters at the bottom. If motion changes to the strength, we are going to jump with the strong safety and play curl/flat, and play cover 3.

Let me show you closed 36. Once they have learned open 63, closed 36 gets a little easier for our guys to understand. Once our guys understand their reads and keys of what a scrape linebacker is and 30 linebacker is, a six-inch step to either the left or the right, the Rip and Liz are all just the same. The coverage, however, is just the opposite (Diagram #7). We are now going to be running true cover 3 against pro sets and 6 coverage against slot sets.

With change of strength motion, it is double-digit coverage, so we change from 6 to 3 or 3 to 6. The front does not change. Everything should look exactly the same at pre-snap, but instead of a Rip call to the open, we are going to go with the Liz call. Everyone is stepping opposite the call. We play cover 3 with a curl/flat strong safety and Joker. Our Mike and Will linebackers have hook/curl responsibilities.

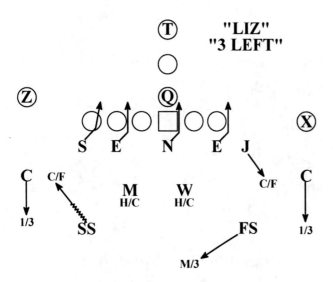

Diagram #7. Closed 36 vs. Pro

Against a slot set, we are going to play quarters to the strongside (Diagram #8). The corner is going to read inside of three steps. Then his vision goes to the #2 receiver. The strong safety lines up inside the #2 receiver anywhere 10 to 14 yards deep, depending on down-and-distance. He is keying #2. If we are getting a vertical release on #1 and #2 to the flat, the corner is going to buy time. He is lined up 6x1 outside. He will rally late to the flat. As long as #2 goes vertical, he is going to continue. We do a lot of practice work in combination to where the corner and the strong safety switch.

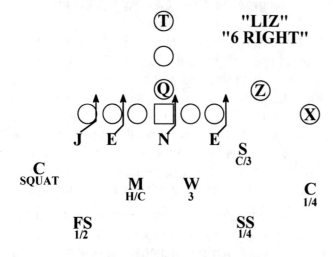

Diagram #8. Closed 36 vs. Slot

This is what the change of strength looks like. As soon as we get a change of strength motion, the outside linebacker does not change, but we are going to spend our safety down and play cover 3 to the boundary (Diagram #9).

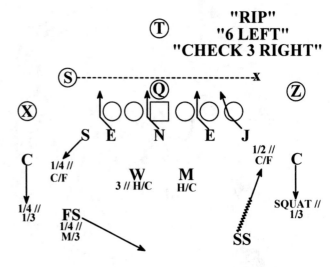

Diagram #9. Closed 36 Doubles to Trey

We can also do the look from trey to doubles (Diagram #10).

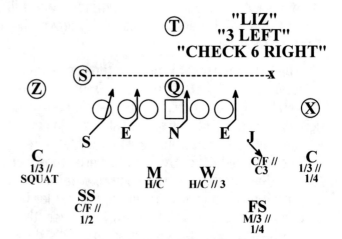

Diagram #10. Closed 36 Trey to Doubles

I have a few minutes to go over bench. We have run this more in the last couple of years because of the fast tempo of offenses we are facing. Same concept as before except the fourth rusher is always coming from the boundary. If the ball is in the middle of the field, he calls to the weakside of the passing strength (Diagram #11). Our coverage is going to be quarter, quarter, half to the field. In quarters, you will always be to the field regardless of the passing strength. It is single-digit coverage. It is cover 6.

We do not have a built-in change of strength for motion (Diagram #12). In motion, we are just going to play six to the field. We may not be in

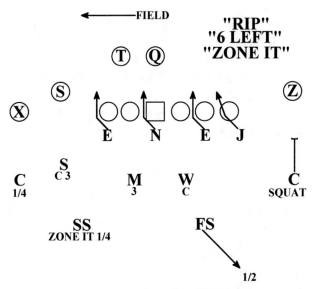

Diagram #11. Bench 6 GF Denver

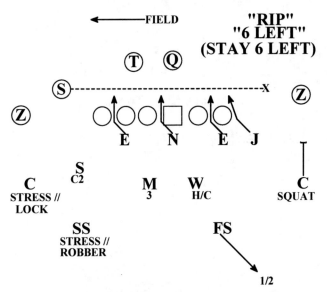

Diagram #12. Bench 6 Change of Strength

the perfect front, but it makes it a lot easier for coverage. Everything should look the same as if we are playing close 36, and we teach it that way.

Once they have learned from the beginning, all of this falls in line, and they can learn it a lot easier. All the calls and techniques are the same.

I am about out of time, but let me put up the diagrams for what some of our other calls are.

With field 3, our fourth rusher is coming from the field. Coverage is four under and three deep, rotating the safety to the field (Diagram #13). We

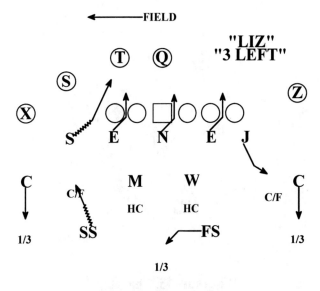

Diagram #13. Field 3

have the constant threat of the Joker or the Sam coming. We want to be disruptive on the edge and to be able to bring guys.

Our coverage is single-digit, and there is no change of coverage with motion (Diagram #14). We are only rushing four, but it appears to be a blitz.

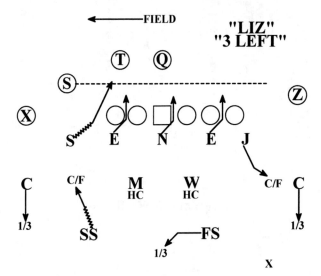

Diagram #14. Field 3 Change of Strength

In our Mac or Mo rush, the fourth rusher is the closed side inside linebacker for Mac or the open side inside linebacker for Mo. Our Mike aligns to the field and our Will aligns to the boundary. We have to identify where the tight end is. It is not a blitz, but the inside linebacker is on a delayed rush. We like this when we are expecting a screen play (Diagram #15).

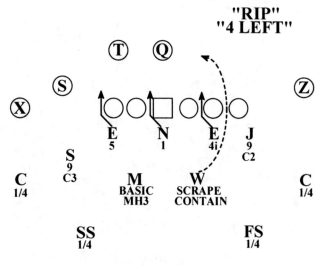

Diagram #15. Mac Gap 4

The last item I have is 30 tite black. This is a three-man rush. Our coverage is five under, two deep with a middle runner (Diagram #17). This changes the tempo for the quarterback from some of the other things we have been running. He is used to getting the ball out quickly, and now it is a three-man rush and he is not sure where to go with it.

We have balanced coverage, and there is no change of coverage with changes in strength motion (Diagram #16).

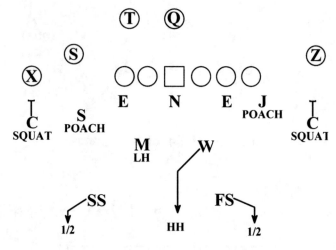

Diagram #17. 30 Tite Black

Guys, I really appreciate your time and attention. Thank you.

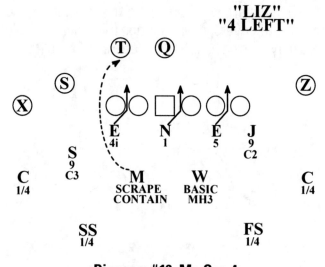

Diagram #16. Mo Gap 4

ZONE BLITZ VARIATIONS WITH STUNTS AND A TWIST

Lafayette College

Thank you very much for having me. It is a pleasure to be here. One of the things that we really like about our defense is the terminology has made it so simple for us to use. It allows us to do a lot. The key is: everything has to be short. Our base zone blitz is fire. That is it. Fire is fire forever and is America's own blitz. It is coming from the field, and everybody knows what they need to do when we call fire.

The thing that we talk about in our office all the time is it is not the number of blitzes that we have; that part is relatively simple. It is the individual techniques our guys have to master. If they have to master seven different things, then we have to practice those seven different things. If they can master just two techniques and run multiple blitzes with those two techniques, it makes it much easier for us and for them. We want to talk about mastering the technique. If you have a solid foundation where they truly understand the ins and outs of the base defense, then it is easy to make a little variation to add onto it.

Techniques

Following are the techniques that we use in our fire zone blitz package:

• *Longcut:* The defensive end has a two-gap movement. This is when he goes from a 5 technique to the A gap.

• *Slam contain:* This is when we are in a 4-3 defense. The 3 technique is to the boundary, and the blitz is coming from the field. The slam is containing to the boundary on the backside. The 3 technique is cutting out.

• *Contain blitzer:* The contain blitzer is the C-gap blitzer. The key for the contain blitzer that everyone in our defense knows is if you are getting zone play, which we have to defend all of the time, the contain blitzer must take the quarterback. If he gets speed option or any kind of that stuff, he has to contain and play the pitch. If he is the contain blitzer, nothing gets outside of him.

• *Spill blitzer:* The spill blitzer is the B-gap blitzer. If he is the spill blitzer and he gets the zone read play, he must take the dive or the tailback. If he gets the speed option, he must take the quarterback.

• *Seam flat:* These are our droppers. Whether it is a safety coming down or a defensive end dropping out, they always have the #2 receiver.

• *Middle hot:* Middle hot is the middle linebacker in the middle of the three underneath defenders. He is going to play the initial #3 receiver to the final #3 receiver.

• *Middle third:* The middle third is the deep post safety.

• *Hot third:* The corners always have #1 and is what we refer to as the hot third.

We can line up our front any way we would like. When we call fire, they just have to know what technique they are to use, and they can run it (Diagram #1). We run this from different fronts, but the concept is the same. The 3-4 defense allows you to be very multiple in schemes because it is balanced.

Let us assume we are on the left hash mark. In this example, our B end will have the longcut across two gaps. The nose has the backside A gap, and the tackle has backside contain. The Sam linebacker will be our C-gap contain blitzer. For any zone read play, he knows he has to sit at the line of scrimmage and make the quarterback hand it off. He has to head it off because he knows the rest of the blitz is coming up the middle. The Mike linebacker is the spill or B-gap blitzer. This is the basis of the zone blitz.

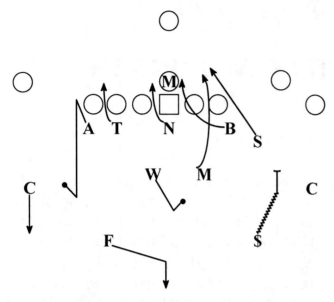

Diagram #1. Fire Stunt vs. 3-4 Look

The corners have the hot thirds and the #1 receiver. We are going to roll down the strong safety to back up the Sam contain blitzer. The free safety is going to be the middle third post safety. We have three deep defenders and three middle defenders. The Will linebacker will be the middle hot defender. He is going to match the initial 3 receiver, and he is going to carry him until there becomes a new #3 receiver. We have two underneath droppers, and they are the seam flatters in our terminology. They are matching the #2 receiver.

Tags

- Direction: Right/left formation
- Paths: Rule of threes
  - ✓ All three underneath defenders
  - ✓ Three-deep droppers
  - ✓ A gap, B gap, C gap filled and contain away

We have ways that we can change up the zone blitz. We do that with tags. The first sets of tags are directional tags. By tags, I mean we can call a blitz based on the tendencies of the offense. It might be toward the tight end or away from the tight end, and it might be toward the field or away from the field. It may be just a left or right call. It gives us a way to call a blitz based on the personnel and tendencies of the offense.

The second set of tags are what we call path tags. This enables us to change up the blitz and

gives us a different look, where we have players going through different gaps. We can do it through different fronts and different alignments of our linebackers. At the end of the day, our guys only have to remember one more word and they are running through a different gap.

We have three rules with the #3 that apply. The first rule is you have to have three underneath defenders. They can come from anywhere. They can even be lineman dropping out of the line into the pass coverage. You have to be smart about what your guys can handle.

The second rule is you have to have three deep droppers. There are two corners and two safeties. Three of those four will be our deep droppers. We tell our guys we are not going to be right all of the time. Nothing in our defense is designed to give up a touchdown, so we want to put those three guys in the best possible position we can to keep form giving up six points.

The third rule is we must have A-gap, B-gap, and C-gap responsibilities, and we must have contain away.

One thing we want to do is to be able to change the package every week. Because of our solid foundation, we are able to build and expand from a small package at the beginning of the season to a larger package by the end of the season.

We like to look at our opponent's tendencies. Do they run it to the tight end? We look at it, as there are not a lot of split end running game plays. We usually have to play a tight end side running game. If there is a blitz, we can bring it to the side of the tight end to put them in a bind.

We want to confuse them with blocking assignments, whether we are in a zone scheme or a gap scheme. We want to know if there is an offensive lineman they like to run behind. On third-and-short, we want to know if they run behind a particular tackle. We designed a scheme to address those situations. We call that a big blitz, and wherever that favorite tackle lines up, we blitzed toward him.

A zone read is just like an option play. It is easy for the quarterback to see our 5 technique and read him all day. We are going to take that 5 technique and move him on the fly so it changes who the quarterback has to read. We are going to try to make the quarterback's job harder. We believe that confusion makes the other team play slower and less confident. Our guys are running through paths so they are more confident and can fly. We believe this is beneficial.

As far as the passing game goes, we are big on trying to figure out protections. The first thing we can do if we know you have a pass protection tendency is to bring our blitz from the other side. If you are a big-on-big man protection team, or if you are a slide protection team, we will adjust to that. If we know which way you are sliding your protection, we are going to hit your quarterback in the back of the head.

If we know you are going to check based on where you see our blitz coming from, we will have a disguise from one side and bring it from the other side. This is done through good scouting and knowledge of the other team.

If it is man-to-man protection, that is better in terms of a passing team picking up our blitzes. However, it is not as good for picking up our twist game. We can build and play twist games with our blitzes to handle that. Let me give you a couple examples of our blitz tag variations. Again, we are on the left hash mark.

This is basically the same blitz package I showed before but with a little twist. We can call torch and bring a blitz to the side of the back (Diagram #2). We can call arson and bring it away from the back (Diagram #3). We can call right and bring it from the right side, left side, and we can bring it from the left, field, boundary, or the split end side. It is all the same blitz, but we do it based on what we see, and then we direct it to the area we want to apply pressure. It is a different name, but it is all the same technique. We are multiple with where we want to bring the twist from and still everyone is doing the same thing. For each individual player, it is not that complex.

Following are some other variations. I will only go over the individual changes. All the other techniques are the same. We are changing the path of the blitz. We are having Sam as the spill blitzer (Diagram #4). The Mike linebacker takes a wider

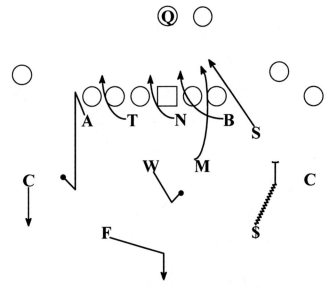

Diagram #2. Torch—Right/Field/Split

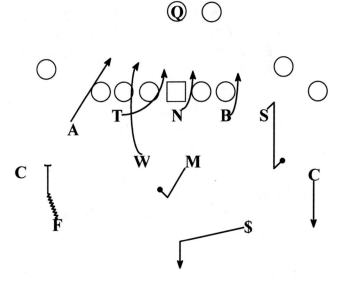

Diagram #3. Arson—Left/Boundary/Tight

path and works for containment. We use this when we think teams are running away from the blitz. We have Sam make a play and chase it down from the backside if he has to. This is a good stunt if you have an athletic Sam linebacker.

A lot of times, the offensive line likes to cheat. I believe that as a defensive coach. They will hold, and they will do everything they can get by with. A lot of times, the tackle will get lazy and see the longcut, and he knows our tackle is going down to the A gap. He knows he is not his man, so he just lets him go. The guard knows our guy is coming and is just waiting on him. To change it up for protection,

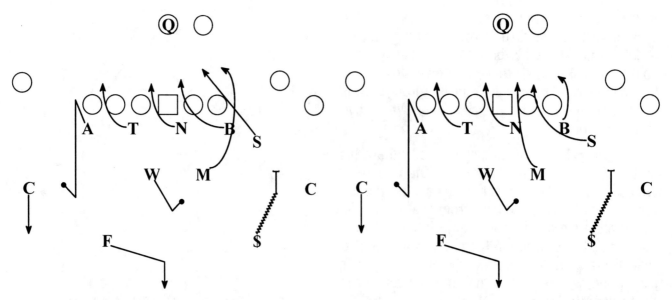

Diagram #4. Sam/Spill Blitzer

Diagram #6. Zone Blitz From Outside the Box

we can send our tackle through the B gap and not run the longcut (Diagram #5). This has given us some free runners at the front just by switching the gap responsibilities.

looking for it, and we have wrecked a lot of zone run plays with that.

If we do not know which way you like to slide your protection, we like to run this particular blitz scheme. If you slide it away from our blitz, we are going to get a 2-on-1 on the backside. If you slide into our blitz to pick the blitz up, the guy who is on an island is the tackle. We can run an up-and-under, especially if he is our best pass rusher, and the nose can get outside and contain (Diagram #7). I believe this blitz puts us in a good situation. The offense usually likes to slide toward our best pass rusher to give them help. This allows us to keep the heat away from him and allows us to get pressure from both sides.

Diagram #5. No Longcut

This next look is when teams are running the zone read. As they are making the read, they figure on a blocking scheme for the four down linemen and the middle linebackers. With the end stepping up and being the contain guy, he is showing a clear give read to the quarterback. The offensive guard and tackle are not used to combo blocking for defenders coming from outside of the box (Diagram #6). We bring him to the inside where they are not

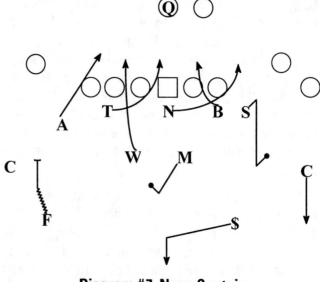

Diagram #7. Nose Contain

This look is similar to the one from before. If this Sam is a playmaker, we can have the Mike run through and the Sam run across two guys (Diagram #8). It is very difficult for the offense to pick it up and get the pass off without getting sacked. Timing is important here because he cannot come all the way from left field. As far as zone schemes go, it is hard to pick this blitz up.

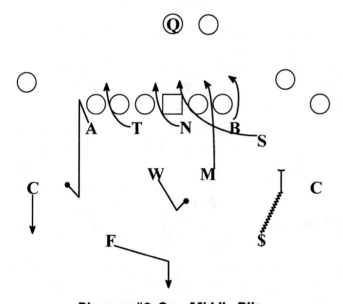

Diagram #8. Sam Middle Blitz

If you know the offense is a big-on-big type pass protection team with man schemes, this is a good look for us (Diagram #9). They may not like the idea of having to slide one way or the other, so they just take care of the four down linemen and the Mike linebacker. We walk the Will linebacker up and put him in the gap and run him through first. This is nothing different than America's number-one zone blitz. This is what we did first, except we are lining him up in the gap and it changes the timing on when he goes. It forms a twist between the Will linebacker and the tackle. This gives us an opportunity to get a back on a defensive end, which is good for us.

I want to touch on a couple of things on the footwork for our defensive lineman. Slamming for contain is one technique we have to work on. This is essentially making a lateral step from a 3 technique. The second step is a vertical step so we

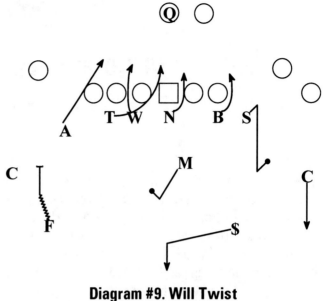

Diagram #9. Will Twist

can get penetration. If the offensive tackle goes away, he needs to keep his shoulders square and penetrate downhill to be the contain man. If the tackle comes down, he is going to go across his face to get outside and contain.

For the nose and any one-gap movement, it is a lateral step and the shoulders are square coming down inside. We do not want him to gain any ground on the first step. Their pad level and helmet level should never change. We practice this in the chute a lot of the time. Your head and your hips get you into the gap, not your feet. As he takes that first step, his head and his hips must cross the offensive player's face. As he takes his first lateral step, his eyes should be on the hip of the offensive lineman he is going toward. If the lineman is coming toward him, he can shorten up that first step as he watches his hips and fits into the gap. If the offensive lineman's hips are going away, we can take a longer lateral first step and gain a little more ground with our second step.

The longcut, which is a two-gap movement, is from a 5 technique. He is going to take a 45-degree angle step, then make a crossover step. On his third step, he is going to try to get back to vertical through the A gap, and he is moving downhill.

Thank you very much for your attention.

THE NO-HUDDLE RUN/PASS OPTION

The University of North Carolina

Thank you very much. It is a pleasure to be here. It is going to be exciting starting out at North Carolina. We are excited and ready to get started. I grew up in Texas and played all the sports. At that time, all that was available in high school were football, basketball, baseball, and track. I went to Austin College and played wide receiver and did a graduate assistant job there in 1986.

I coached high school football at Garland High School in Texas. I stayed there for four years. That is where I learned how to coach football. The things a high school coach has to do, most college coaches do not. From there, I had the opportunity to go to Baylor University and become a graduate assistant at the age of 29. I was 29 years old and had a pregnant wife. I spent one year as a GA, and they hired me as a full-time assistant the next year.

I spent six years at Baylor under Grant Teaff. From there I went to the U.S. Air Force Academy under Fisher DeBerry. I spent two years there, and it was an unbelievable time. If any of you have that academy type of player in your program, that is a place he should look at. It is a special place.

When I got the call to be the offensive coordinator at Middle Tennessee State University, it was time for me to step outside my comfort zone. I wanted to find out if what I believed in and my philosophies in an offense could be successful. Coach DeBerry advised me not to take the job because it was a 1-AA school, and he did not think it would be good for my career. He thought it could be the end of my career. It could have been if I had not believed in what I was doing.

In 1999, I installed the spread/no-huddle offense at Middle Tennessee. Tulane University was the only other team in the country that ran that type of offense. We put in the offense and had success with it. From there, I went to the University of Florida

with Ron Zook for three years. I spent three years at Oklahoma State University with Mike Gundy. I took the head coaching position at the University of Southern Mississippi and was there for four years before I took the job at North Carolina.

In the no-huddle offense, in addition to all its values, it kept the offensive linemen from running in and out of the huddle. The huddle is seven yards off the line. That meant for every game, the offensive linemen ran probably 1,000 yards running to and from the huddle. We can accomplish everything at the line of scrimmage that we do in the huddle.

My goal today is to give you one thing that will help you be a better football coach or one thing that will help your team. That gives you an idea of where I come from. I want you to know is where we came from and who we are. When we start practice at North Carolina, we have to instill our philosophy on offense, defense, and special teams. We have to change a culture, and that is what our job is. In the previous years, that culture has been more of an NFL-type mentality.

We are going to run this program the same way we have run it since 1986. We are going to roll up our sleeves, get them to work hard, make them compete, find out who the players are, and go win some football games. That is it, and there is nothing special about it.

I want to tell you who North Carolina is going to be in the future. We are going to be a team that plays *smart*, *fast*, and *physical*. We started our offense back in 1999. This offense is a one-back, one-tight-end, and three-wide-receivers scheme. We call that personnel grouping "11 personnel," and we are going to be in it the majority of the time. We will be in multiple formations and multiple tempos.

In 1999, no one had heard of multiple tempo offenses. Today, everyone is talking about tempo and playing fast. We have done this since 1999, and it is no big deal for us. We have done this every year, and there are great advantages to it.

It is the offense that we started with at Middle Tennessee, and the system has not changed. We have the same philosophy. We may have tweaked the plays or taken things out, but the offense has not changed. We project the same philosophy and tweak it to the players we have in the system. Coaches must do that same thing high school coaches do every year.

Smart

- Take what they give you
- Minimal audibles
- Strive for balance

The first thing you must do in this offense is to take what they give you. There are coaches who make up their minds to run the football no matter what the defense does. The defense puts 11 defenders in the box, and they still try to run the ball. That does not make sense to me.

Our deal is to get the job done any way we can. One week, we may rush for 300 yards, throw for 100 yards, and win the game. That is all we want to do. If the next week we run for 100 yards and throw for 300 yards, that is what we want to do as long as we win. All I care about is getting the job done, and I do not care how it happens.

If you come in to watch your films, you will always find places where if the quarterback had changed the play, it would be a big gain. If we did not build that automatic into the game plan, he cannot change the play. Those kinds of adjustments are in-game plans. To keep the quarterback from having to see all those things, we put that in the hands of the coaches. I take it out of the quarterback's hands and put in the hands of the coaches because we watch more film than he does. We call the audible from the sidelines.

When I see the situation on the field, I know what I want to attack. We package runs with passes to take advantage of the defense. That gives us a run/pass option. I want to talk about one of those today. We want to strike a balance. Balance to us is not necessarily 50/50 run to pass.

When we talk about balance, it is your ability to do both run and pass the football. The defense can stop the run or the pass, but they cannot do both of them.

We were one of two teams in the country last year that rushed for 200 yards and threw for 250 yards a game. In my opinion, that is balance.

Fast

- Tempo—multiple speeds
- Average 80 plays a game
- Fatigue creates cowards

We have always been about multiple tempos. We can go fast, give the perception of going fast, go slow, or run at a regular pace. I know the defense does not like a team that changes the tempos in a game. The defensive coordinator likes to go to a huddle and call the blitzes he wants to run. We do not allow the defense to do that. We have five and sometimes six tempos in every game.

We were one of five teams in the country last year to run 1,000 plays in the season. The more plays you run, the more opportunities to score. Every play you run is an opportunity to score. We want to put as much stress on the defense as possible. We want to stretch the field to create vertical seams in the defense. When we can create seams in the defense, it gives an opportunity for a big play.

We like to dictate the speed of the game. When I was at the Air Force Academy, we did not have a lot of game plan; however, the defense did not have much time to prepare for us. They had two days, which meant you saw two fronts, two coverages, and one blitz, and it was dangerous to blitz us. We want to approach the game in the same way. We want to keep the defensive coordinator from calling the blitz.

If we go fast, the defensive coordinator has to do something that week to make sure his players play fast. We want to run the defense from sidelines to sidelines so they have trouble lining up. If they work off a wristband, the tempo almost eliminates that. I love to see wristbands on defensive players. They are looking at the wristband, and we are running the play.

This scheme creates cowards. Fatigue creates cowards of us all. We want to get our players in the best shape possible and get them accustomed to running with speed. This scheme deflates the defensive linemen. They live for the sack. They like to dance around, perform their act, throw out their chests, and get the crowd jacked up. They are like sharks circling. One of them makes a play, and the rest of them get in the feeding frenzy. I want the defensive linemen running 53 yards every play. We want to create a situation that tires the defensive linemen. We want them breathing so hard they cannot keep their hands on the ground.

Physical

- Believe it—mentality.
- Run the football.
- Be the most physical team on field.

I believe physical is a mentality you build into your team. You have to believe you are physical. I think it is getting harder to create that culture. People are not tough anymore. I am not as tough as my dad is, and he was not as tough as his father was. It is because of the way we live. It is about instant gratification. If things are not going right, do not do it. Football is a hard game, and the people who play it have to be hard and tough.

It is something we talk about all the time. I talk about it in our team meetings, and the position coaches talk about it in their individual groups. The strength coach talks about it in his program. The manager and secretaries talk about it. Everyone involved with our program talks about being physical.

If the team hears it and thinks it, they will be physical. If you do not think you are physical, I promise you, you will not be. We coach it, teach it, and talk about being tough. It does not matter whether it is a punter, kicker, quarterback, the offensive line, or the defense line; they are going to be tough. We are going to be physical, and we will win football games. We are going to be tougher and more physical than our opponents are.

To be able to run the football effectively, you must be physical. The last five years, we have averaged running the ball for 205 yards a game. I look at teams that run the ball all the time, and they do not run for that many yards. We average

205 rushing yards out of the spread offense. Since I have run the spread offense, we averaged over 190 yards rushing the football. I am proud of that fact because we believe in running the football.

We want to be the most physical team on the field. We want each of our units to be the most physical. We spend a lot of time coaching effort and knockdowns. We spend time praising and talking about knockdowns, whether they are cutting defenders or finishing blocks. We treat those players better. We talk about it and reward them for that kind of achievement.

If a player does not give us the effort we want, we call him into the "Tar Heels Circles." In our scrimmages, practices, or games, we record all the lack-of-effort plays. We have criteria for loafs or lack of effort. If a player, running to a play, changes his rate of speed, that is an example of lack of effort. At some time, we circle up as a team. The coach gets in the middle and calls out a name. The player runs to the middle of the circle, repeats his name, and tells everyone the number of times he let the team down by loafing. If he had four loafs, the team does four up-downs. We repeat this until everyone on the team has announced his number of loafs. I have been in scrimmages where the team did 235 up-downs. Eventually, the team starts to understand about loafing.

This makes the players responsible to one another. What they do affects the players on their team. A player who causes the team to do 12 up-downs does not want to go back in the locker room.

BOUNCE PACKAGE

I want to show you what we are doing. This is a run/pass option. Most of you will be disappointed because you are doing better things than I am. All the formations in the diagrams will go from a 20-personnel grouping to a 10-personnel grouping (Diagram #1). We start out in a shotgun set with two backs in the backfield and three wide receivers with no tight end. That is the 20-personnel grouping. We motion the left halfback into the wide slot receiver side. The formation goes from a 2x1 set into a 3x1 formation, or 10 personnel.

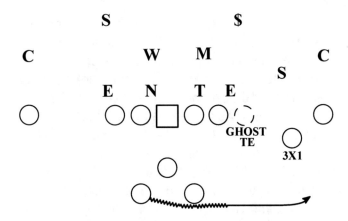

Diagram #1. 20 to 10 Personnel

From this package, we have runs, screens, and play-action passes. We call them based on the way the defense plays against us. The motion scheme creates a problem for the defense. We add the third receiver to the formation, which generally means a secondary communication to account for the third receiver. You have to remember, we are pressing the tempo, which makes it harder on the defense to adjust.

I want the defense to adjust on the run quickly. They have to think. The defense does not want to think; they want to chase the ball. I want to get the defense out of their gaps and their alignments. I want the front to misalign and the corner in the wrong coverage because he did not hear the communication.

When I talk about the run/pass option, we are talking triple option. This goes all the way back to when I coached at Air Force, except we are doing it out of the shotgun. When we were at Air Force, we tried to talk Coach DeBerry into throwing the ball more because we were getting only one type of coverage. He told us we were going to throw it more; it was just going to be backward as a lateral in the wishbone.

The quarterback is creating an audible on this play, but no one knows it. He is making decisions. I am not going to talk about the line blocking and schemes. If you want that, you have to talk to the offensive line coach. I am going to talk about the mechanics reads, and responsibility of the quarterback on these plays. I will show you how he decides to run or pass.

I am going to talk about how we make a decision to run or throw and how we are going to attack the defense. The first thing I want to talk about is the zone run attached to a perimeter screen (Diagram #2). We put the backside back in motion and run a zone play to the single receiver side. If a team has two high safeties, we do not count them. The first thing the quarterback looks for is someone covering and moving with the motion. We start the count from the ghost tight end to the outside.

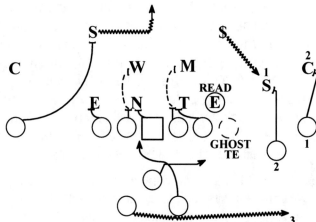

Diagram #2. Decide—Run or Throw

Since we have no tight end in the formation, we call the alignment of the missing end the "ghost alignment." If no one moves, the defense has two defenders on three receivers. That means we have three receivers against two defenders into the three receivers' side.

If the safety rolls down into coverage, there are 3-on-3 to the outside, and that is no advantage. If they move a linebacker to the outside, we still have no advantage to the outside. That is how the quarterback starts this process in his mind. He has to decide if he has the numbers to throw the football to the motion back. If we are two receivers on two defenders, the quarterback throws the ball, and we want to get four yards from that play.

All I want is four yards out of a run or quick screen to the motion back. Our team understands that. If the play gains four yards, that makes me happy. If it gains more than four yards, that success belongs to the team. However, if the back does not get four yards, he comes to the sidelines and stands by me because we have the wrong player on the field.

The perimeter screen is a four-yard run in my way of thinking. I am not trying to hit the home run on the screen. I am trying to stretch the field so the defensive linemen have to run. The only run I will show you today is the zone; however, all the base runs will work from this formation.

We want to attack the defense where it is weak. If the defense moves someone with the motion, the quarterback knows he has six defenders in the box. We outnumber them in the box, and they cannot cover all the gaps. With the running quarterback, they are one gap short. If one safety rolls down, the other safety goes to the middle of the field. They have no run support player from the secondary to the single-receiver side. You will always have one more player than the defense unless they play zero coverage all the time. Teams will not do that.

When there is movement in the secondary, everyone knows we will run the ball. We run the zone play to the single-receiver side. The quarterback reads the backside end for an option read. If the end closes on the running back, the quarterback pulls the ball and runs downfield. We tell the quarterback, if he is not sure on the end's movement, to give the ball to the running back.

This is a simple play and a simple read for the quarterback. There is nothing tricky about the play. The quarterback reads the numbers to the receivers, or if someone moves, he knows he has numbers in the box.

When we run the screen because the defense did not roll someone into motion, it is like a toss sweep. We throw the ball to the back with two blockers in front of him. We use the screen for two reasons. We want to control the blitz from the outside and attack defenders in space. We want to attack the defense with a numbers advantage.

When we run the play and throw the screen, the linemen block the zone play. The zone back runs the zone play. On the zone play, the two receivers blocked as if we threw the screen. The quarterback called an audible and told no one. The motion back knows when he sees no movement that there is a possibility of a pass to him.

With no movement with the motion, there are seven defenders in the box and there is run support from the secondary to the single-receiver side. The quarterback knows his numbers are good for the screen and throws it. The wide receiver wants to work for outside leverage on their blocking assignments. We tell them if his head is on the outside, it is a 3 technique. If his head is on the inside, it is a 1 technique. They do not have to be knockdown blocks, but they must make a block. We tell them to get on the defender and take him wherever he wants to go.

When the quarterback throws the ball on the screen, it is the job of the motion back to make that the right decision. He has to get four yards.

The next phase of the bounce package is the play-action pass. We run the run action fake with the quarterback faking the zone play. He performs what we call "three fast footwork." We run two schemes on this play-action pass to take advantage of the rotation of the secondary.

The defense comes into a game with maybe two adjustments to the motion. They rotate down with a safety and go to a three-deep scheme or stay two-high and try to get a linebacker out in the screen. When they stay in the two-deep look, they try to rally to the screen and keep it to a minimum gain. They may think you will not run the screen enough to hurt them.

If they rotate, we throw a play-action pass to take advantage of that (Diagram #3). The X-receiver (single) runs a seven-step glance. That pattern is a skinny post. The running back has a check pattern to the flat. The quarterback keys the backside safety. The field safety rotates down with the motion. If the boundary safety rotates to the middle of the field, the quarterback works from the glance to the flat. He does not look to the field side.

If the backside safety does not go to the middle, the quarterback peeks at the pattern up the seam. If quarterback does not like what he sees, he works the curl route by the outside receiver or the swing pattern of the motion back. The quarterback does not work the entire field. He knows where to go off the reaction of the backside safety. If the safety goes to the middle, he works glance to flat. If the safety backs up and stays to the backside, he peeks

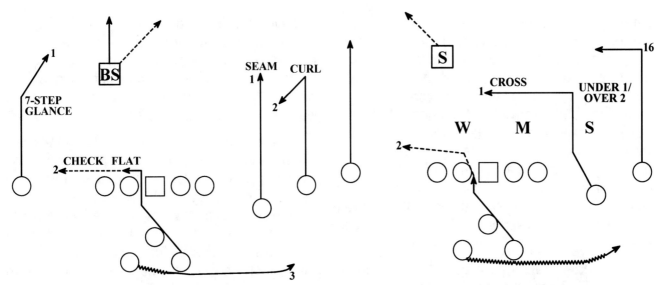

Diagram #3. Play-Action Pass

Diagram #4. Play-Action #2

at the seam, curl, and swing. Secondaries that try to disguise their coverage against normal tempo are simply trying to align because of the tempo of the offense. It cuts down on the secondary disguise. If there is no rotation, we work to the motion side.

The quarterback takes a fast three-step drop. They are not really steps. He runs the fake, takes one step back, and delivers the ball on the glance. If backside safety goes to the middle of the field, the quarterback throws the glance like an out pattern. As soon as he hits the third step, he releases the ball. The receiver has not taken his break step when the quarterback releases the ball. The quarterback throws the ball to an area and not the receiver. The receiver breaks into that area. We tell the quarterback, if the linemen turn their defender loose, he should still get the glance off. He will get hit, but he should get the pass away.

When the safety rolls down, the quarterback knows he is going to the backside. His primary key is the drop of the boundary safety; however, he must look at the backside linebacker. If he does not respect the fake and drops straight back from his position, the quarterback has to throw to the flat and come off the glance.

The second play-action pass keys the boundary safety, also (Diagram #4). This route takes advantage of the safety rotation. This pattern is a basic route we run with all our passing games. This concept is our best third-and-long pattern. The

X-receiver runs vertical. We say this is a yes-or-no pattern. If the corner has tight coverage with no safety support, the quarterback can throw that pattern right away. This happens before the snap as the quarterback looks at the alignment of the defense. The vertical is not in the progression once we snap the ball. The back runs the check flat route.

In practice, we work competitive fade drills. We send the receiver on a vertical with a defensive back in press coverage. We make the ball a catchable ball every time and see who comes down with the ball. We find out about the receivers and the defensive backs. We find out who will go up and get the ball.

The slot receiver in this diagram, or the #3 receiver in a trips set, runs the cross. He goes under the first linebacker and over the second linebacker. If the second linebacker does not drop, the slot is 8 to 10 yards deep. If the linebacker drops, the slot could be 12 to 14 yards deep. If the coverage is zone, he finds the window and sits down. If it is man coverage, he keeps running across the field.

The quarterback has to decide on the "yes/no" to the X-receiver before he snaps the ball. If the safety bails on the vertical, the quarterback works high to low in his progression. He looks high for the cross pattern to low for the flat. He works only two receivers. We do not count the "yes/no" as an option once we snap the ball.

The thing that takes the quarterback off the cross pattern is the Mike linebacker and strong safety squeezing the cross pattern. If the strong safety jumps the cross, the quarterback comes off the cross to the dig behind the strong safety. The quarterback works two receivers, whichever side he decides to work. He does not work the entire field. The safeties take him from one side to the other. On occasion, we designate the area we want the quarterback to throw. We do not have a lot of passing game, but we are good at what we do. We run these patterns repeatedly. You do not need 10 choices in a third-and-long situation. We may run two plays six to seven times. You get the reps in practice.

The next play in the package is the slow screen (Diagram #5). This is the same motion as the other plays. Nothing changes in the looks of the motion or the play-action. The quarterback fakes the zone to the back, flashes the bubble screen to the motion back, and then buys time before throwing the screen back to the zone back.

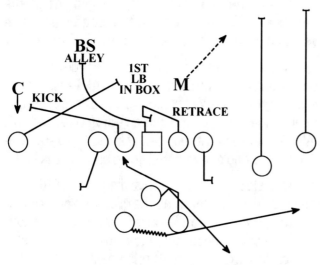

Diagram #5. Slow Screen

Both offensive tackles block their normal protection, which is EMOL (end man on line of scrimmage). If the defender zone drops into coverage, the tackle goes and gets him. What we want him to do is sit soft and let the defender beat him up the field. That way, the tackle can run him deep and out of the play. The guards and center set soft on the half-man of their defenders and let him beat them. If the defender does not charge, the guard torques him and throws him.

This is a two-count screen. The guards and center release their men on a two count. The playside guard releases his man, goes flat down the line of scrimmage, and kicks out the corner to the outside. We call that "pigs on ice." If the tackle does not come flat down the line or tries to block the defensive back high, the corner makes him look like a pig on ice. We tell the offensive lineman to throw on the corner and not stay up on him.

The center is the alley blocker after the count of two. The backside guard loops to the playside B gap and turns back for any defender who is retracing his steps to get back into the play. The running back sets up behind the playside guard in his pass protection check. When the guard leaves for the kick-out, the back flares into his pattern, turns back, and presents himself to the quarterback. If for some reason the guard cannot get out, the center replaces him and the center comes late into the alley.

The X-receiver cracks on the first linebacker in the box, generally the Will linebacker. The quarterback has to buy time if he gets a blitz and get the ball to the back. He gets back, pumps to the motion, pumps the ball downfield, and buys time until the throw. The wide receivers and motion back are decoys and run off defenders.

I appreciate your time. If there is anything we can do for you at North Carolina, let us know. You have access to what we do in football. We will install our offense, defense, and special teams in our first five days of spring practice. If you want to see it put in for the very first time, you are welcome to visit with us. Thank you very much.

OUTSIDE ZONE RUNNING GAME

Rutgers

Thank you. I want to get right into the topic. I am going to talk about the outside zone play. The track on this play for the running back is the midline of the tight end. We want to press that track. That means we want to make the cut as close to the heels of the tight end as we can. The thing that can get the back off his track is the feet of the offensive linemen coming off the line of scrimmage. If the defense is a basic 4-3 defense, the feet of the right guard could get into the track of the running back.

He has the block on the 3 technique defender. If he cannot get movement on the defender, he may have his feet in the way. For this play to have success, the offensive line has to win the line of scrimmage on the playside. You do not have to knock them 10 yards off the line of scrimmage, but you must win there. We also must cut off the backside defenders if we expect this play to work. Both of those things must happen.

We want the running back's toes at seven yards (Diagram #1). That is deep for a running back on this play. However, this year, we had a freshman running back that aligned at seven-and-a-half yards. We backed him up because he was too fast to the line of scrimmage. The saying for this play is "Slow to the line of scrimmage and fast through the line of scrimmage."

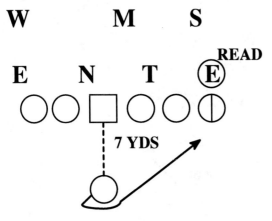

Diagram #1. Outside Zone Scheme

If you have a big running back, when he enters the line of scrimmage, there should be a very discernible change in his speed. The speed to the line of scrimmage and through the line of scrimmage should not look the same. You should be able to see when the running accelerates through the line of scrimmage. When a running back makes his decision to cut into the line, I should be able to see it.

In my opinion, if the running back turns his shoulders to the sideline, he has made the wrong decision. On the outside zone play, the back reads the first down lineman from the outside defense alignment to the inside alignment. The secondary read is off the second down lineman. If the back can read the first down lineman, you did a good job of teaching. I have yet to see a back read the second down lineman in his run. However, people swear he can do it.

I coach the running back to read the first down lineman to the outside. As the back runs the play, if the read tells him to go outside but he has to turn his shoulder to the sideline, do not go outside. The defensive lineman has stymied the offensive lineman and is waiting for the back to make a cut. If the back cuts outside, the defender sheds the offensive lineman and makes the play on the running back for a loss. If the back never turns his shoulder to the sideline, it will save you many negative plays.

We coach the running back to drop-step with his backside foot. The second step is with the playside foot. We pick it up and put it back down to align his course to the midline of the tight end. When the running back thinks he wants to make his cut, he takes two more steps and cuts. Backs always want to make their cuts early.

If we want to run the outside zone to the right, we call that force (Diagram #2). In the 4-3 scheme, the center is responsible for the Mike linebacker.

The playside guard blocks the 3 technique defender. This block can end up in a combination block, with the center and playside guard on the 3 technique defender and the Mike linebacker. The tight end and playside tackle block the C gap defender up to the Sam linebacker. The tackle has the C gap defender and the tight end has the Sam linebacker. The backside guard is responsible for the 1 technique defender, and the backside tackle blocks the Will linebacker. Their rule is to block the backside number #1 and #2 defenders.

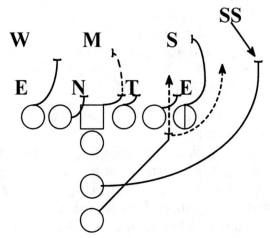

Diagram #2. Force Blocking

This play is 60 force. The "60" tells us the play goes to the right and "force" tells the fullback he blocks the force defender on the play. The fullback knows he only blocks the force defender if the ball goes to the outside. If the ball does not go outside, the fullback becomes an extra blocker on the play. That means the fullback has to read the first defender. He can clean up on a lineman's block that is slipping off.

The technique for the fullback on the force play is to open step at the inside leg of the playside tackle. He runs three steps at the inside leg of the tackle, reading the defensive end/Sam linebacker stack. If the tackle reaches the C gap defender, the fullback is to the outside and blocks the force defender. It may be the strong safety or a rolled-up corner. If the tackle does not reach the C gap defender, the fullback turns inside and cleans up any trash he sees. We refer to that as cleaning the hole or sponging the blocks.

The coaching point for the fullback is to run as fast as he can so he gets separation from the

running back on the play. When he sponges the block, he puts defenders that are coming off blocks back into the blocks of the linemen.

We have a variation of this play called 60 arc (Diagram #3). On this play, the tight end arc-blocks on the force defender. The fullback switches responsibility with the tight end and blocks the Sam linebacker. The remainder of the blocking scheme is the same as the force scheme. He helps the offensive tackle on the C gap defender on his way to the Sam linebacker. We run the same blocking scheme with one minor change on the outside blocking.

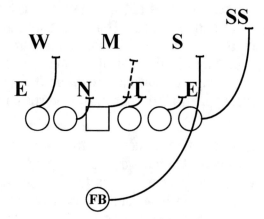

Diagram #3. 60 Arc

The next play is 60 stretch (Diagram #4). When the fullback hears "stretch," he goes to the backside of the play. The blocking scheme for the offensive line is the same as the 60 force play. The play is the same play except we have a split flow play read for the linebackers. On the 60 force and 60 arc, both backs go the same way. That is a full flow play. When we add the split flow play, we begin to start the basis for our play-action passing.

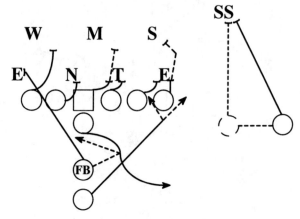

Diagram #4. 60 Stretch

We can use variations of the fullback's path on the stretch play. We can start him on his 60 force track for three steps. On the third step, he sticks his foot in the ground and goes to the backside to block the defender coming off the edge. Any time we send the fullback to the backside of the play, the Z-receiver has to handle the force player on the playside. He gets into position by alignment or motion. He has to do the job of the fullback on the force play. In the huddle, we make a huddle call that says "Z can motion." That tells everyone that the Z-receiver might come in motion depending on the alignment of the force defender. The huddle call is to keep anyone else in the scheme from going in motion.

The quarterback is not responsible for sending the Z-receiver in motion. The decision to go in motion or not is the Z-receiver's decision. He decides if he can block the force from his alignment or if he has to get into a better position.

Some coaches want to give the quarterback the option of throwing the ball based on the alignment of the strong safety's movement. If you are an offensive line coach, if you want to run the ball, do not give the quarterback the option of running or throwing the ball. We have plays with run/pass options for the quarterback. However, if you want to run the ball, do not let the quarterback have the option to throw it as an automatic. The secret to the motion is not to motion only when you want to crack on the force. You must disguise what you are doing to keep the defense off balance.

We call the last look for this play 60 stretch/insert. The term insert aligns the fullback in an offset position into the backside of the play (Diagram #5). This alignment is very popular in the NFL. "Insert" means the backside of the play locks up in a man-blocking scheme. The backside guard blocks the 1 technique defender. The backside tackle blocks the 5 technique defender. The fullback blocks the Will linebacker. The playside of the play is the same blocking as the force play.

The reason we use the insert play is to help the backside tackle. The backside tackle has trouble cutting off a Will linebacker on a full flow play. By putting the fullback in the insert position and blocking out on the 5 technique defender, this gives the fullback a chance to make that block on the Will

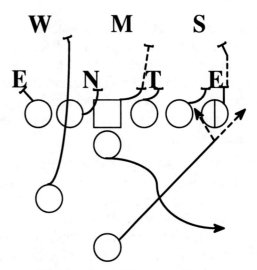

Diagram #5. 60 Stretch Insert

linebacker. It gives the linebacker a different look and slows him down. This gives the defense four different looks on the same play.

If the defense runs the under front, the best play to run is the 60 stretch insert (Diagram #6). In the under front, the defensive line shifts to the weakside and the Sam linebacker aligns on the line of scrimmage on the tight end. The center blocks the playside shade defender aligned on him. The playside guard and tackle run a combination block on the 5 technique defender and the Mike linebacker. The tight end blocks the Sam linebacker. The Sam linebacker is the first down lineman to the playside and becomes the read defender.

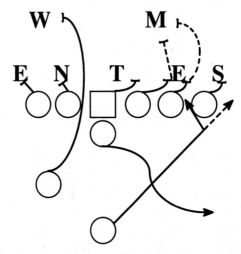

Diagram #6. 60 Stretch Insert vs. an Under Front

On the backside, the backside guard and tackle block the 3 technique and 5 technique defenders. The fullback from the insert position goes through the A gap and blocks the Will linebacker. The tight end wants to cover up the Sam linebacker and knocks him off the ball on the angle he attacks. Insert plays started in the NFL because the tackles could not cut off the Will linebackers. They put the fullback on him because he was a better player with more speed and agility.

The 60 force plays gave us a strongside running game. On our weakside running game, we use names to call them. The 70s series goes to the left. We call this play 70 Woody (Diagram #7). The word Woody puts the fullback on the Will linebacker. The center and playside guard combination-block on the 1 technique defender, up to the Mike linebacker. The playside tackle blocks the 5 technique defender. The fullback comes through the B gap and blocks the linebacker. The backside guard and tackle combination block on the 3 technique defender, up to the Sam linebacker.

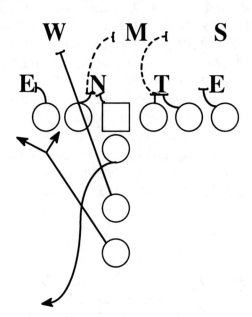

Diagram #7. 70 Woody

This is nothing more than a weakside isolation play on the Will linebacker. The difference is the running back's track. He threatens the outside leg of the offensive tackle. He can break in or out depending on the block of the tackle. That makes it a moving isolation. Instead of running the isolation downhill, we move it sideways.

The twists and counters of any play depend on how the defense plays against a particular play. When the guard blocks heavy on the 1 technique

defender, the Will linebacker will play hard inside on the fullback's block and spill the play to the outside. His play picks off the guard and keeps him from getting to the Mike linebacker. The Mike linebacker plays over the top of the spill block and stops the play. That is how some defenses will try to stop this play.

The counter to that scheme is 70 Molly (Diagram #8). The word Molly tells the fullback he isolates the Mike linebacker instead of the Will linebacker. The center blocks the 1 technique defender. The playside guard and tackle run a combination block for the 5 technique defender and the Will linebacker. The backside linemen block the same backside combination on the 3 technique and Sam linebacker. The fullback comes through the hole and isolates the Mike linebacker.

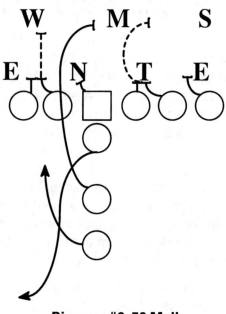

Diagram #8. 70 Molly

You can see how simple it is for the players. I am constantly teaching the same thing to the players. We go over the techniques repeatedly. The repetition of the blocks teaches the players how to execute.

I want to show you one more play to the weakside. We call this play 70 Woody Y-insert (Diagram #9). In the NFL, we called this formation the Christmas tree formation. In this formation, we offset the fullback to the weakside of the formation. We insert a tight end in the offset position to the backside of the play. The play we

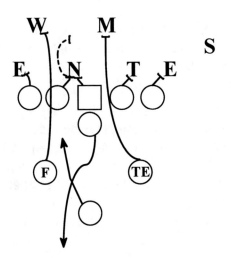

Diagram #9. 70 Woody Y-Insert

run is 70 Woody, which I talked about earlier. The difference is the backside guard and backside tackle use a man-blocking scheme on the defenders aligned on them. That is their insert rule. The offset tight end goes through the A gap and blocks the Sam linebacker.

That puts the defense in a dilemma. If it tries to scrap the Mike linebacker over the top of the Will linebacker, we run the ball backside and isolate the Sam linebacker. If the Mike linebacker stays in the middle, we run the ball at the Will linebacker. If you wanted to run 70 Molly Y-insert, you could do that. The playside blocks the Molly scheme and the backside blocks the insert scheme. We block both outside linebackers and key off the play of the Mike linebacker.

All the combination blocking is the same regardless of which players the block involves. The combination block between the center and guard is the same technique as between the tackle and tight end. You teach the idea of covered and uncovered. You teach double-team blocking and slipping to the second level. It is the same in every combination.

In this situation, the ball is going to the right (Diagram #10). In each situation, we have a covered and uncovered lineman. The covered lineman tries to strike the defender with his nose on the playside armpit of the defender. He wants to leave the line of scrimmage and cover him. The uncovered lineman opens his hips and attacks the face mask of the down defender. We do not overlap the defender. We do not step under the covered lineman's position so

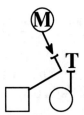

Diagram #10. Center/Guard Combo

as to overtake a block. The covered lineman may reach him or he may not reach him.

If the defender slants inside, the center takes him and the guard climbs to the second level for the Mike linebacker. If the defender plays straight ahead, the center and guard stay on the defender and drive him off the line of scrimmage at the angle he charges. They both stay on the down defender until the Mike linebacker forces one of them off the block. If the linebacker attacks in the A gap, the center shoves the defender into the guard's block and comes off to block the Mike linebacker.

If the down defender works outside on the guard, the uncovered lineman has a three-step rule. If the center does not encounter the 3 technique defender by his third step, he has to climb upfield to the linebacker. He snaps his shoulder off and gets ready for the linebacker coming inside or running to the outside. If the 3 technique defender works outside, the linebacker has a gap responsibility in the A gap and fills there. The combinations are the same technique for any two offensive linemen.

The uncovered lineman is the most difficult to teach. You have to coach the uncovered lineman to get to the double-team first and then find the linebacker. The center comes off the ball and looks at the 3 technique defender. As soon as he hits him in the face mask, he snaps his head and looks for the linebacker. Uncovered linemen that come off the ball looking for the linebacker never get any movement on the down defender.

The center and guard must assault the down defender. The center is not being cautious going to the double-team. I want speed to the double-team and literally assault him. The mentality of the uncovered lineman has to be "Get to the double-team and then find the linebacker!"

I am going to show you some under looks and show you how we help the center. Against the Okie front, the playside guard sets the combo block to the tackle and they work on the 5 technique defender to the Mike linebacker. The tight end blocks the Sam linebacker. The backside guard and tackle block the backside #1 and #2 defenders. The fullback blocks the force unless the read key says to go inside.

That scheme looks good on paper. Our second noseguard we work against in practice every day is probably not as good as the ones we play on Saturday. If the center can win the match-up with the noseguard every week, this scheme is great. Sometimes, we can win those match-ups. We coach our noseguard that his first priority is to beat the hell out of the center. He does a good job of it. Most defensive coaches teach their noseguards to do the same thing.

To help the center, we run a scheme called 60 force rub (Diagram #11). To us, "rub" means to turn the combination blocks backward. Instead of the guard combination blocking with the tackle, he works with the center. The center and playside guard combination-block the noseguard to the Will linebacker. The backside guard and tackle work their combination block to the 3 technique defender to anything coming from the backside. The playside tackle single-blocks on the 5 technique to his side and the tight end blocks the linebacker aligned on him. On the rub call, the fullback isolates the Mike linebacker to the playside.

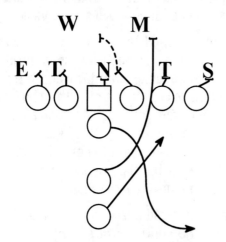

Diagram #11. 60 Force Rub

The movement of the back makes the isolation block a moving isolation play. The center is the player who calls all the blocking schemes, and he is the one who knows when he needs help. When we

game plan, we must know if our center can block their noseguard 1-on-1. If the center can handle the nose, we run 60 force. If the center cannot handle the nose, we run 60 force rub.

If we called 60 arc and the defense shifted to a under or Okie front, the playside tackle is covered and must block the defender aligned on him. The tight end cannot arc on the force because the tackle is covered. In this case, 60 arc becomes 60 force, and we run that play. That is the rule we have. If the defense covers the tackle, arc becomes force.

The weakside runs have the same rules against the Okie front. On Woody, the fullback isolates the Will linebacker. The center and backside guard run a combination block for the noseguard and Mike linebacker (Diagram #12). The playside guard and playside tackle use a man-blocking scheme on the 3 technique and 5 technique defenders. The backside tackle and tight end run a combination scheme for the 5 technique defender and the Sam linebacker.

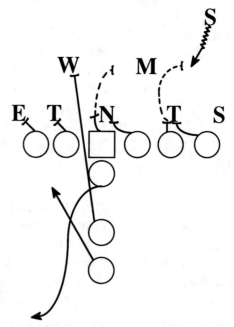

Diagram #12. 70 Woody Safety Call

If the strong safety walks down into the box, we make a safety call. On the safety call, the tight end comes down on the combination block with the tackle on the 5 technique defender, working up to the strong safety in the box. If there is no threat of a safety down in the box, we work to cut off the Sam linebacker.

This last play makes it easier on the players. If we play an odd front defense, we adapt our Molly play. We call 70 Molly F-insert (Diagram #13). We block the Molly play to the left side of the formation. We insert the fullback to the backside of the play. That means he offsets to the backside, and the backside linemen block insert rules, which is man-to-man. We can align the fullback in the offset position or motion him into that position. That gives you some variation with the play. We want the fullback to the backside because the Mike linebacker aligns to that side.

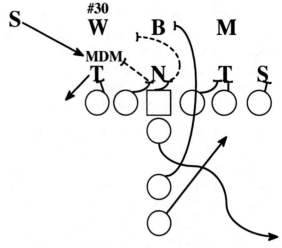

Diagram #14. 60 Buck

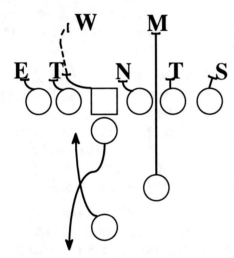

Diagram #13. 70 Molly F-Insert

To the playside, we run the center guard combination for the 3 technique to the Will linebacker. The tackle reaches the 5 technique defender. The backside guard blocks the shade noseguard and the fullback comes through on the Mike linebacker.

We are a Mike linebacker–driven blocking system. For us to block a play, the center has to decide who the Mike linebacker is in a defensive alignment. If we play a 3-3 stack alignment, we designate the defender aligned on the tight end as the Sam linebacker. The Mike linebacker is in the stack over the tackle to that side. The middle stack linebacker is Buck and the tackle stack linebacker away from the tight end is the Will linebacker.

When we play those types of teams, we run a play called 60 Buck (Diagram #14). The word in the play tells the fullback he blocks the Buck linebacker. By using this scheme, we take away all the spill/scrape combinations of the defense. The

tight end blocks the Sam linebacker as he always did. The playside guard and tackle combo-block on the tackle stack for the Mike linebacker. The center and backside guard combo-block the noseguard to the backside Will linebacker. The backside tackle blocks the MDM (most dangerous man).

We call the jersey number of the linebackers after we make the line calls. For example, the center makes an A-30 call. That means he is working with the backside guard in the backside A gap to the linebacker wearing jersey #30. The backside tackle knows he is not blocking linebacker #30 because the center called his number. He works through the inside shoulder of the 5 technique defender to the most dangerous man. If there is, a safety dropped down in the box that could be his block. The two combination blocks have good leverage on the defenders and the fullback has good leverage on the Buck linebacker.

When you set the system, you have to decide what player you want the fullback to block. If you want him to block the Mike linebacker, you call 60 Mark or some other "M" name. That changes your combination blocks to the middle and weakside stacks, and the fullback takes the Mike linebacker in the tackle stack to the playside. That seems like a lot of stuff to throw at you, but from a player perspective, it is very simple.

I want to show you some of the ways we drill our linemen. We simply use a 1-on-1 blocking drill to teach the covered lineman technique. The first step the lineman takes is with his outside foot, and it sets the angle for the lineman to the defender.

The second step drives the backside knee to the defender. We want to gain ground and not cross over the feet. The hands and arms strike the target with the thumbs up and the elbows tight to the body. When we strike with the hands, we want to lift the defenders so we can stay on them.

A coaching point to the reach block is to pin the defender on the playside of the play. Running the outside zone does not mean you run the play outside. It means the track of the back takes him to the area where no one is in his way. The ball going outside is not the objective of this play. Stretching and cutting the defense are what we try to do. The blocker hits his target and tries to win and pin the defender to the inside.

The defender re-establishes his position to the outside of the block because he does not want the blocker to pin him to the inside. If the blocker cannot win and pin the defender, he wants to run his feet as fast as he can so he takes the defender to the sideline. We want the defender so wide that the gap to his inside is too big for the linebacker to handle. I coach the linemen to hit the target and win the block. If they cannot win, I want them to run the defender wide.

When we teach the combinations, we block two blockers on two defenders to start the drill. The covered blocker works the 1-on-1 drill. The uncovered lineman has to be committed to the double-team and watch nothing else. He cannot look at the linebacker until he hits the down defender. The coaching point is to watch the head of the uncovered lineman. If he turns to look at the linebacker before contact on the down defender, you must correct that error. Additionally, when the uncovered lineman comes off the double-team to block the linebacker, he gives a double-handed shove on the down defender into the block of the covered lineman.

In the drill, you want the down defender moving outside. As the uncovered lineman comes for the double-team block, he applies his three-step rule. If the defender runs away from him, he climbs to the linebacker. He has to vacate the line of scrimmage on his third step.

The rule for the center as to the combinations depends on the alignment of the Mike linebacker. If the Mike linebacker aligns in a zero or plus technique to the playside, the center works to the playside combination. If the Mike linebacker aligns in a minus alignment, the center works the backside combination with the backside guard.

When we drill this technique, we work a three-on-three scheme. I have three offensive linemen and three defenders. We work one combination block and one reach block. We work on the Mike linebacker position and calls from the center.

That is all the time I have. I hope you got something from this talk. Thank you for your time and attention.

DEFINING YOUR PROGRAM

The University of Mississippi

Thank you for that introduction. I do feel that I am a high school coach at heart. I still run the same plays I ran on offense and call them the same thing I did in high school. However, more things go into the job of a college coach. Obviously, you have to recruit, but the same philosophies we used at Briarcrest Christian High School, Lambuth University, and the other places I coached and played are still the same. We are under a bigger microscope, but few things have changed.

I want to share some things with you today. Before I get to that, I want to talk about things I think are overlooked in teaching and coaching. One of these things is being clear with your players of what your expectations of them are. I want talk to you about the things we want to do at Ole Miss. We know we have our work cut out for us and have numerous challenges that lie ahead.

I wake up in the morning feeling and understanding that, but it excites me and it always has. I have a great group of men who have joined me in this endeavor. We need the high school coaches to help us and come see us. Sometimes, you come to clinics and do not get all you want from a particular coach. If you want to come to our place, I will give you whatever I have and give you access to anything you want.

We want to make it happen at Ole Miss. We are going through some characteristics at Ole Miss that may be helpful to you. The first thing is to know what "it" is. We want to make it clear to them. The "it" for the offense is to be a *fundamentally efficient scoring machine*. When I go into those meetings and ask our players what their "it" is, they should respond with the correct answer. I believe there is power in the way you think and talk to your players. We want to hear and see that daily. We post it on the walls and envision that thought. That is our "it" offensively.

When we refer to the "it" on defense, we have a different meaning. On defense, we want to *relentlessly pursue the football and knock the ever-living stink out of the opponent*. That is what our players hear in every meeting with our defensive staff. When I ask our players what the defensive "it" is, I want to hear them say that. I want it to be a clearly defined statement of our expectations of them.

It does not matter what your ambitions or goals are in life. If you do not have a clear understanding of your "it," all the things that life can throw at you can distract you. That is why we clearly define our "it."

We have an "it" on our special teams. Our special teams "it" is *to provide the winning edge*. I am not a great kicking coach and never have been. I do not relate well with some kickers. I like an athletic player to be our kicker. If he is an athlete, he understands competing and how I feel. I tell our kickers, if they think it will be all right with me if they miss a 25- or 36-yard field goal, they have the wrong coach. If a quarterback throws an interception, I will be all over him. If they miss a 30-yard field goal, I want to know why. We want them to know how important the kicking game is and how important they are to us. We want them to provide the winning edge.

This next point will not apply to all the coaches in here, but we have an "it" for our coaches. We have a recruiting "it." The recruiting "it" is to *develop dynamic relationships with the student athletes and those involved in the decision making process.*

The coaching staff "it" is to capture the hearts and minds of our players. I do believe the coaches I hired are coaches who care and want to make an impact on the players' lives. That includes their playing days at Ole Miss and the times after they have finished playing for us. I believe we can get more from our players if we capture their hearts and minds. Our coaches understand this.

The players have an "it." We call them the "three wills."

The Players' "It"

- I *will* give great effort in the classroom.
- I *will* conduct myself in a manner that leads to a positive image of our program.
- I *will* prepare myself to win.

We post these in the locker room and ask our players to live by them. I have to give credit for these three wills to a coach by the name of Steve Roberts. Steve coached football at a number of colleges in Arkansas and was head football coach at Arkansas State University. This was the battle cry for his teams for many years. He did a magnificent job of making sure these three things took place with his players.

The first "will" is to give great effort in the classroom. At Ole Miss, we have some challenges in that area right now. Our position coaches have to capture the hearts and minds of their players. They have to make sure our players understand the effort it takes in the classroom to get the job done.

The second "will" is to conduct myself in the manner that leads to a positive image of our program. We want to be positive in the community. We want the community to say the team is representing the university, coaches, and families in a manner that brings a positive image. Unfortunately, that does not always happen in our profession.

We have a gift box at our place, which we bring out almost every week. The gift box is a wrapped present that comes from an opponent's player who made a bad decision. I hope that our players will learn from the poor decision of others and not go through the experience themselves.

The third "will" is to prepare to win. There is a big difference between people's desire to win. Everyone says he wants to win. However, the winning comes from those players who prepare themselves to win. It can be in the weight room, off-season, or spring practice. That will determine the wins and losses in the next season.

This sounds good, and we can talk about all the "its." We can post them on the wall and ask the players to recite them. That is good, and I think it is important. However, the players have to envision where they see themselves going and what the offense or defense looks like on the field and in film. You have to see those things when you turn on the film and watch your team perform. After saying all of that, if you do not have a game plan, you are spinning in the wind. You must have a game plan to accomplish what you want to achieve.

HOW WE BUILD THE FOUNDATION

- Family atmosphere
- Communication
- Trust and respect
- Common purpose

We start to build with a family atmosphere. We talk about the family and the core values that the family represents. Within those core values, we have separate themes. The themes form an acronym made up of the first letter in each of the themes, which spells out "FAMILY."

Themes

- **F**aith
- **A**ttitude
- **M**ental toughness
- **I**ntegrity
- **L**ove
- **Y**ou

Faith in the good Lord above and faith in each other is important to us. Attitude and accountability is important for us. In the few short weeks I have been at Ole Miss, we have done something that has helped me everywhere I have been. We formed accountability groups. We assign every coach on our staff a particular team. We have 10 teams with 10 coaches above them.

In our staff meetings, I have the position coaches name their most accountable player. I want them to tell me the player who does everything right. They give me his name, and we list him on team one. We go to the next position coach and ask the same question. We list his name on the second team. After we go through the 10 position coaches, we should have 10 teams with the most accountable players on them. After we get the most accountable players, we begin over with the next most accountable players.

The further you go through the roster, the harder it is to come up with a name. However, we fill all the teams with a mixture of players. We have players who do things the right way, players who do things the right way most of the time, and players who struggle to make proper decisions. After we finish assigning players to the teams, we draw out of a hat the names of the coaches who will be responsible for those teams.

The team is accountable for the behavior of everyone in the group. If anyone on the team misses a class, is late for a class, misses a tutoring session, or is late for a tutoring session, it bears consequences for the entire team. If anyone on the team embarrasses our team by the decision he makes, the entire team and the coach report to the stadium at 5:30 in the morning. The players must learn the decisions they make effect their teammates.

The "M" in family stands for mental toughness. I hope they pick up some of that from the other themes. Integrity comes from the players telling each other the truth all the time. The "L" is for love, and the "Y" stands for you. We define "love" the same way with did our "it." Love is the *ability to handle the inconveniences that come with the relationships*.

When you combine your team and bring them together, you will have 120 players from different cultures and backgrounds. They will not agree on everything. The one thing they must all agree on is that they will love one another even if they disagree. When they care for one another, it will lead to success in the football program at the university. The core values of a family start with communication and respect. We want to say what we mean and mean what we say.

COMMUNICATION

It is the province of knowledge to speak, and it is the privilege of wisdom to listen.

—Oliver Wendell Holmes

- Listen—truly get to know kids and staff.
- Make decisions you feel are right per the feedback and input from assistants.
- Make sure all parties understand the defined description and task at hand (i.e. ask kids to repeat instructions). Remember that there is:
  ✓ What I said
  ✓ What I think I said
  ✓ What he heard me say
- *"Believe nothing you hear and half of what you see."*

We must have trust and respect. I have this quote in our locker room already. *"The mark of a man is how he treats people that can never do anything for him."* That quote comes from Darrell Royal, the great Texas coach.

TRUST AND RESPECT

- Janitors, trainers, managers, and walk-ons are as important to our family and team goals as our stars. Our bench's attitude has won a bunch of games.
- You completely control your integrity, your honesty, and your attitude. Always do what you know to be right.
- Always treat people the way we want our family to be treated.
- If you cannot say something positive about someone, do not say anything.
- Embrace cultural diversity (socioeconomic, race, and education)
  ✓ Thanksgiving day
  ✓ Tell life stories
  ✓ Dedication game
  ✓ No depth chart or starting lineup

I believe that major college athletics and the money it generates has created a monster. The Internet and the diverse ways our sport is covered have made administration of college programs difficult. Sometimes, our players have a sense of entitlement. That is the attitude I want to fight against every day. That goes to the treatment of the equipment managers, trainer, and janitors by the players. I want our players to see the respect they give other will affect the way they see themselves.

Spirituality is important to us. I am a man of faith, but I am far from perfect. Spirituality is the inner makings of a man. That leads to how he competes on a daily basis.

SPIRITUALITY—NEVER GIVE UP

- Strive for excellence
- Positive attitude
- Commitment
- Solid character
- Belief in self and teammates

I want to say something about our weight-training program and strength coach. When I hired Paul Jackson, I knew I had the right man. If you are searching for new techniques and ways to do things in the weight room, you need to come visit us. He is phenomenal and is doing some great things that will change the way we work. I think it will pay off on the football field and you will see a more physical football team.

PHYSICALITY—PREPARE YOUR BODY FOR BATTLE

- Willingness to hit and be physical
- Explosive power
- Endurance
- Speed
- Agility

I am an emotional coach, and we never want to lose the mental battle. I want our players to play with emotion. I want them to play on the edge because football is an emotional game.

MENTAL—NEVER LOSE THE MENTAL BATTLE

- Execution
- Knowledge
- Preparation
- Confidence
- Communication

We are 100 percent in control of the mental aspect of the game. The difference in many games is the team that is ready to play and perform to the maximum. We must commit 100-percent hustle on each play, and take one play at a time. We must play with intensity, desire, effort, pride, and enthusiasm.

This next topic is what I need to talk about the most. We said our offensive "it" is to be a fundamentally efficient scoring machine. I want to spend some time on the game planning for the offensive team. We must have a way to become a fundamentally efficient team. If all you have are words on a board, it means absolutely nothing. You must have a plan.

GAME PLAN FOR OFFENSIVE "IT"

- All about the ball
- Tempo (two-minute drill the entire game)
- Stay on schedule (no negative plays)
- Create a swagger/confidence and belief
- Enjoy the process and have fun

The game of offensive football will always be about the ball. If you do not take care of the football, your chances of winning go down. Everyone knows that, but you must put an emphasis on it. We practice on Sunday and take Monday as our off day. On Sunday, we have "ball security Sunday." We have 15 minutes on Sunday dedicated to ball security. The drill has everyone on the offensive team participating in the drill, including offensive linemen.

Our tempo is important to us. We prepare to go with the two-minute drill the entire game. That is how we practice. If you use this type of tempo, you must practice that way. The biggest challenge for us this year will be the offensive linemen. They will not be used to that type of play. The same thing was true when we went to Arkansas State. They were a two-back power team and had not played with that tempo. The first year, it was a struggle to get the offensive linemen to play at the tempo we desired.

When you use the tempo we use, you must stay on schedule with the down-and-distance. The worst thing that can happen to a tempo offense is a three-and-out situation. That affects your defense. If the offense uses a hurry-up tempo and goes three-and-out, the defense does not have a chance to rest. If you do not stay on schedule, you will have a nightmare of a game. The most important people in staying on schedule are the coach and the quarterback.

I spend the entire week with the quarterback about how to set the protection schemes. We cannot have negative plays. A negative play is not a punt or an interception. A negative is a sack. We cannot take sacks. We spend an enormous amount of time with the quarterback as related to timing. He counts one-thousand-one, one-thousand-two, and uses his feet. We obviously would like to have an athletic quarterback, who can scramble and make positive yardage and avoid the sack.

You must create a swagger and confidence within your players. You have to talk about it with your receivers, backs, and quarterback. The offensive linemen are who they are. They will get the job done if the offensive line coach does his job right. They will work hard for you because that is the makeup of the offensive line. The other cats in the offense need a little swagger. They need something to believe in. They need some kind of saying or motivation technique. In our accountability groups, we come up with a saying or question every day. We hope it will spur their minds to start to think of themselves differently.

If we can do all those things, we still have to find ways to have fun and enjoy the process. The football journey is difficult. The length of time we spend with our players can wear them down and grind on them.

We do a pace period every day. Most of our practice is centered around pace. We do not spend a great deal of time on the practice field. We go an hour and 45 minutes on the practice field. However, everything we do is fast.

TEMPO HINTS FOR PACE PERIOD

- Create a simple communication system—signal/ flip chart
- Scout coach—two footballs
- Do not chase incomplete balls—injured player/ manager
- Hand the ball to the nearest officials.
- Do not change personnel or formations in order to be your fastest.
- Whistle to stop every play.
- Script the first seven plays (excluding third down) in order to get a good start.
- Indy plays (five plays)

The number-one thing in this type of tempo is to create a simple communication system. There are different methods of doing that. I am sure you know more about that than I do. We use a variety of methods. We use signals and flip charts. We vary that from game to game. You must practice the entire week on the changes you plan to make. On our flip charts, we color code the schemes. The colors indicate the type of protection scheme, and the numbers indicate automatics. We have live numbers and dead ones. We have five concepts in the passing game, and the numbers indicate the concept we want to use.

The scout coach has two footballs and keeps the ball spotted so it does not slow down the drill. In a game situation, we want to hand the ball to the nearest official. Do not drop the ball on the ground. The faster the official marks the ball, the faster we can snap the ball. At Arkansas State, I worked with the chain crew. I wanted a young man on the downs marker. I wanted him to run to the next spot and set up as quickly as he could. The faster that occurs, the faster we can go.

We have three tempos. We have NASCAR, Talladega, and Indy. They all mean something different with relations to speed. If you want to be at your fastest tempo, do not change personnel or formation. We want a whistle to spot the ball in the pace drill.

I have gone back and forth on scripting plays. In some games, I see something the defense is doing and get off the script. However, I do have in mind what we will do the first seven plays. I like to script the plays because I feel like it will get us off to a good start in the game.

You want to script plays that your players understand and have answers to every situation.

However, when you play tempo football, you will get into some bad plays. There will be times you run something into a bad look for the offense. You can only hope it does not become a disaster. You have to live with that, knowing that the pace will pay off down the road.

When we talk about staying on schedule, we must convert on third down. When you convert on third down, you get another set of downs. On *third and less than one yard* for the first down, we carry one play in our game plan. We rep that play twice during the week. On third and less than one yard, our players know what we will run. The same thing is true on *third-and-one to two yards* for the first down. We have one play from the left hash mark and one from the right hash mark.

On *third-and-three*, we have one play from the middle of the field and one play from each hash mark. We run the same play, and we stay with them. We work extremely hard on third-down situations. On *third-and-four to six yards and seven to 10 yards*, we have two plays from the left, right, and middle of the field. We have a section of practice on Thursday that we call "third down Thursday." We work on hash marks and landmarks on the field. If the situation is 11-plus yards, we need some help.

We have *"red zone" landmarks*. When we cross the 50-yard line, we already have landmark plays from the 45-yard line to the 10-yard line. At each interval of yardage, we have plays listed on the call sheet. If we cross the 35-yard line, I have a number of plays that I want to call. We know the plays we want to run, from which hash mark, and what area of the field.

We always have the freedom on these landmark sheets to run any running play we choose. We do not list running plays unless it is a special play for a particular team or particular situation. If you have special passes or plays where you want to take a shot at the end zone, we list them on the red zone landmark sheets. If we have a special throw we like against a particular defense, we list them in those situations.

Obviously, if you are running the ball well, when you reach the red zone landmarks, you continue what is successful for you. We do not shift to a passing routine if we continue to move the ball with the run. However, if you want to get out of the box, you have no problem because you have worked on those plays during the week. We cover the landmark plays twice during the week. We actually walk through them on Friday with our team and quarterbacks. When the rest of the team is working on special teams work, the quarterback is walking through our landmark plays with the offensive coordinator or me.

We work with him on what we think and what he will see from the defense. We talk to the quarterback about trick plays, shots, or special plays in these areas. We carry special plays from week to week and keep them as part of the play selection, even though we may not use them. This is the time to reinforce the special plays and discuss when you want to take the shots at the end zone. Opponents will break down what you do, so you want to vary the places you take your shots.

Special plays are all about stealing points. Anytime you can steal points or make the opponent work on things that you do that are unconventional, you are stealing their practice time. If an opponent plays us in the fourth or fifth game, they have some things to work on in their practices. We do not use the special plays only once during the season. We repeat them, as they are part of the offense. They are not always successful or even great plays. Nevertheless, the defense has to spend time working on them.

Sunday practice is about corrections, ball security, introducing the next opponent, and putting up the special plays we want to use. We put the special plays in on Sunday. We have a book of them and change them from week to week. This allows us to work them in pre-practice all week long. Following is an example of some of the things that appear on the Sunday practice schedule.

When we practice, we do not stretch together. I went to that last year and loved it. Our position coaches are responsibility for stretching their groups. The strength coach helps each group with their stretching routine. On Tuesday, after we stretch in our positions groups, we go straight into period one, which is our special team period.

SUNDAY PRACTICE SCHEDULE

Period	Time	Type	Offensive Line
1	15 min.	Individual fundamentals and corrections	Capture your position
2	20 min.	Special teams	Everyone
3	10 min.	Intro team defense visual	Intro front seven and secondary
4	10 min.	Team corrections	What we screwed up
5	10 min.	Communication on Daytona	From the sideline vs. top look
6	5 min.	Trick plays	Things that stress the defense and coaches
7	15 min.	Conditioning	
8	0	Off	

In period two, we go straight into a run drill. We want to get the practice going with a physical drill. We go best against the best. It does not matter what the defense runs or what the offense runs. We go four plays with the number-one teams and four with the number-two teams.

The third period is an individual period. The backs work on ball security, the blaster, and handoffs. The offensive line works their schemes and a good deal of teaching by the coaches. The receivers work on individual catching and pattern drills.

The fourth period gets into group drills. The backs and receivers work in a skeleton passing drill. The receivers work on the concepts of our passing game, and the backs work on protection schemes and route running. During this period, the quarterback works on the concepts against one- and two-high safeties and man coverage. The O-line works on their protection scheme.

During the next period, we work on the inside run. We work against an odd, even, and blitz front. We work four plays from the right hash and four from the left hash. After the inside run period, we set the tone for the rest of practice with the pace period. In addition to working on plays, we work on tempo. We follow that with practice involving our personnel groupings. We work seven five-minute periods with our personnel groups, wildcat, and special plays. We work 20, 10, 11, 12, and 21 personnel groups in these periods.

Tuesday practice is a full-pad practice. During this practice, we work on our gap scheme blocking. We work the gap schemes during the personnel grouping period. We could mix in some zone schemes with the gap scheme on Tuesday.

The Wednesday practice is a repeat of Tuesday's practice with the exception of the concentration of plays. The format is the same for the first seven periods. We work the best-on-best during the second period followed by the individual period. We work the skeleton shell work, inside run drill, and the pace period. In the next periods, we work on the third-down situations I talked about earlier. We follow that with our red zone landmark drill and finish up with the Indy and Talladega plays. The emphasis on this day in the running game is the zone scheme. When we work on our red zone offense, we want to score touchdowns.

Thursday starts out with a special teams period. During this time, the quarterback is with the offensive coordinator, working through his landmark reads and shots. The second period is a skeleton shell period with the offensive line working on protection schemes.

THURSDAY PRACTICE SCHEDULE

Period	Time	Type	Offensive Line
1	20 min.	Special teams	Indy
2	10 min.	Skelly vs. scouts	Protection
3	10 min.	First seven plays Talladega	Everybody on sideline
4	15 min.	Third-down calls	
5	15 min.	Landmark review	
6	10 min.	Personnel grouping "play specific"	
7	5 min.	Fourth-down call (2) two-point conversion (2) special plays	
8		Off	

When I refer to "play specific," they are the auxiliary runs or things out of the norm for our offense.

FRIDAY PRACTICE SCHEDULE

Period	Time	Type
1	20 min.	Special teams
2	10 min.	First seven plays
3	15 min.	Red zone landmarks
4	5 min.	+ 10 red zone
5	5 min.	Coming out
6	5 min.	Specials, third-down situations, two-point conversion, tricks
7	5 min.	Hail Mary Victory formation
8	Off	

When we work on the red zone plays, we work from both hash marks. We want to make sure they have a great understanding and feeling for our landmark plays. We want to get off the field on Fridays in about an hour.

We have a sign posted as our players walk out of the locker room.

Practice Winning Every Day

As Coaches and as parents, we can only teach our kids that life is a series of options, just like football. If you make good decisions, you are likely to succeed.

Once a decision has been made, do not look back. It is our job to make the decision work. Do not second guess!

In the pace period in practice, I am in charge and actually run it. That is my exercise for the day. I am not a big runner, but I have the whistle, and I make the players work. On occasion, I make some of the players run 50 yards to get into the play. The pass may only travel five yards; however, I control the whistle and stop the ball when I want to stop it. I have the managers and ball boys sprinting from hash mark to hash mark and up and down the field to get the ball set.

You have to game plan to achieve what you want to accomplish. However, the last point I want to make is to stay the course. You have to stay the course to complete the journey. It is a blessing for coaches to deal with kids. I have three daughters of my own. The statistics tell us there is a tough road ahead.

Tough Road Ahead

- 40 percent of all girls will become pregnant by the age of 19.
- 750,000 teens become pregnant each year.
- 1 million teenagers run away from home every year.
- 6,000 teenagers become alcoholics every day.
- 3 million teens are "problem drinkers."
- 13 teenagers commit suicide every day.
- 1 million teens attempt suicide every year.

I read all that material, and it scares me. The community entrusts us with the opportunity to affect the lives of so many young people. It is great for us to win game, and I know we all are driven to do that. At the end of the day, I hope we can stay the course and have an impact on our players and young people by the way we conduct ourselves. I hope they see the great passion we have and the energy and love we have for them. It is a blessing to be a coach, and I hope you accept that as seriously as I do. The calling is a challenge.

I do not read many books, but every summer I read one book. I try to write a character trait from the book. As a coaching staff, we get together after the film work and discuss the character traits. The last book I read had a character trait, which said, "The buck stops here." That is what we have to learn at Ole Miss. No matter what has happened in the past or what the issues have been, the buck stops with you. We are driven to do it the right way, and we need your help.

Thank you very much for your attention.

GOAL LINE AND SHORT-YARDAGE DEFENSE

Former College/NFL Coach

Thank you. It is good to be here. I want to you to stand up and stretch a little. If there are any defensive line coaches in here, you need to move down front. You are going to get a little workout and some knowledge. If there are any offensive coaches in here, you can go to the bar.

Back when I was coaching high school football, I got a call from the coach at Eastern Kentucky, Roy Kidd, who wanted me to come to Louisville to interview for a job. I was supposed to meet Coach Kidd in the lobby of the Brown Hotel. I got there early and ran into the coach at Western Kentucky, Nick Dennis. He offered me a job and I took it. Eastern and Western Kentucky were rivals in the Ohio Valley Conference at that time.

If you like defense, this is what I do. I am a full-fledged bump-and-run corners coach. That is what I am. But remember this, you will not be successful everywhere you go. You have to take the players you have and try to make them better. I went to Hawaii as the defensive coordinator because I liked June Jones. We had a corner that could cover me. You could watch our games around midnight back here on the mainland. We had a quarterback by the name of Colt Brennan, who was a good player. On defense, we were awesome. We had a bunch of Samoans playing for us. and they stole everything. They would steal the football or your car.

Do you remember a person by the name of Bobby Beathard? He was a big-time general manager for the Washington Redskins. At that time, I was coaching in Houston with the Oilers. We beat him to death. He went to San Diego, and we beat him there. I went to Atlanta while he was still at San Diego, and we beat him again. He told me something one day that I would never forget. He told me I had new players, different skills, different teams—and they all played like the same team.

That is what high school coaches do every year. From year to year, the players change. The high school coach takes what he has and coaches them. He gets the best out of the players he has in his school.

Our front is an under front (Diagram #1). In our four-man front, we will play with a nose in a 3 technique to the openside of the formation. The end to that side is on the outside shoulder of the offensive tackle. The strongside tackle plays a shade on the center to the tight end side, with the defensive end on the outside shoulder of the offensive tackle. We have a linebacker on the line of scrimmage on the tight end.

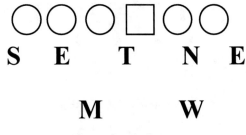

Diagram #1. Under Front

We built our short yardage defense off what we do. Not many coaches that coach on the defensive line know the things we do. When I coached at Portland State, we did not have any players play professional football. In fact, we did not have any players that should have played college football. Oregon State crushed Southern Cal when they were #1 in the nation. They used the zone-blocking scheme and ran up and down the field like a lawnmower. They crushed Southern Cal. We played them next week in Corvallis. The little running back that gained all the yards against Southern Cal was a nonfactor in our game. Their offensive line plays changed against us, and they could not block us.

If you watch San Francisco run their plays, the backside guard pulls on every play. What are you going to do about that? How are you going to help your players handle those plays? When you play short yardage defense, you must play with a certain mentality. When you practice your short yardage, you should feel you got the offense right where you want them. They are in third-and-one. They are toast.

The first thing I want to show you is Montana. We play this against what we call green. That is a two tight ends, two backs, and one wide receiver formation (Diagram #2). We take the defensive tackle and align him head-up with the guard. His job is to run through the guard and push him into the backfield. It does not matter if the guard reaches him. If the guard reaches the defender, he becomes the cutback player. The defender pushes the guard into the backfield and continues his pursue angle.

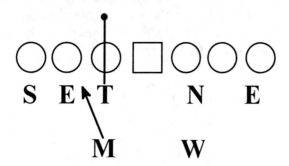

Diagram #2. Montana

If the guard reaches the defensive tackle, he continues to push the guard back and pursues off the butt of the offensive blocker. The linebacker stacked behind him jumps to the outside. He is going to blitz and jump over the line of scrimmage.

Blitzing got me in trouble when I was with Atlanta in 1977. The Los Angeles Rams had just signed Joe Namath from the New York Jets. That was supposed to be the piece that brought them the Super Bowl championship. Chuck Knox was the coach of the Rams at that time. We played the Rams in the third game of the season. That was the last game that Joe played. They packed him in ice; he did not play again and retired at the end of the season. Leeman Bennett was the head coach. He was in the press conference, and I was in the shower.

He came in after the press conference and asked me if I blitzed every play. I told him I did not because I remembered two plays where I did not blitz. If you have something that works, keep doing it. In 1977, we blitzed almost every play and gave up 129 points and 2 rushing touchdowns in the NFL for a season. When I coached in Hawaii, we gave up 5 rushing touchdowns.

Let me get back to the even technique on the guard. If we get in the even technique on the guard, we do not worry about the double-team from the guard or tackle. In an even technique, the guard will try to handle the block and the tackle will combine with the tight end on the defensive end and the linebacker. If we get the double, we play straight ahead and try to push the guard back off the line of scrimmage. I do not tell the defender to knock the guard back, but do not let him reach you. That is an impossible play for the guard.

The defender knocks the guard back. If the guard reaches him, he keeps on going. The nose does not have frontside flow. The nose plays the same technique as the even technique over the guard. He plays over the guard and drives him back off the ball. If the guard tries to cut him off, he becomes a cutback player. The linebacker jumps over a gap because the nose is playing the cutback lane. The linebackers play the fastest reads you will ever see. The nose does not hang back and wait for the cutback. He attacks off the butt of the guard from the backside.

Last year, Nike had Jim Harbaugh speak at one of their clinics, and I followed him. He is the best quarterback position coach I have ever heard. If quarterback coaches listen to him and take his advice, it will change their lives. His offense will change the defensive coach's life unless you clean up what you do against him.

Every play they run has a backside puller involved in the play. There is not a double-team block and kick-out block without a backside guard pulling. They do not have a zone block without a backside guard pull. The pulling guard does not make crushing blocks. He does not knock anybody out, but he gets in the way of the linebacker. He takes the great hit away from the linebacker by getting in the way.

When we play against this type of scheme, we use what we call a wraparound (Diagram #3). We have a 3 technique defender aligned on the backside guard. If the guard pulls to the tight end side, we pull the defender on our side of the line of scrimmage and fit into the play as the guard turns up on the runside of the play.

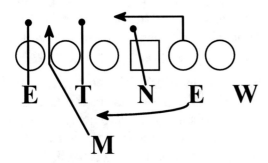

Diagram #3. Wraparound

There was a coach in Dallas that thought of this before I did. I coached against him. Tom Landry was the coach in Dallas who came up with this idea. I was in Detroit at that time. Tom Landry played what he called the flex front. Teams that run the power-O add the pulling guard at the point of attack. If the offense adds a blocker to the point of attack, the defense has to add one. If you do not have enough defenders to take up the blocks of the offense and have a free runner coming into the hole, you will not have success against those teams.

The first clinic I ever went to, I was coaching at Lima Central Catholic High School. We won most all our games. The monsignor was the principal of the school. On the way to the playoffs, he got on our bus and told me he could not believe how well we had done, and he wanted me to lead the team in the rosary. I told him I would love to, but I could not because I was not Catholic. There was dead silence from the monsignor. He told me I did not tell him that before I took the job. I told him he did not ask me if I was Catholic. Therefore, he delivered the rosary and got off the bus. That means do not tell everything you know or you will not get the job.

I am going to teach the shin. I teach the defensive linemen this technique. In this technique, the defender's nose is down to the ground and his butt is in the air. He looks like a frog. We use the technique in situations of one yard or less for the first down or touchdown. We want to hit the offensive linemen two inches above the patella. The offensive line can use any type of scheme they want, but nothing on the line of scrimmage moves. In the shin, the linebackers jump over.

When you run the shin technique, you have big piles of people but no movement. I was at Georgia Tech when, one day, I got a call from Bear Bryant at Alabama. He saw us run the shin and wanted me to come to Alabama and coach it. We went up to play Michigan State. Their offensive line blocked out the sun when they broke the huddle. We shinned them and had piles of humanity all over the place.

We teach the shin, even, wraparound, and the jump over. We put all the down linemen in even techniques and tell them not to worry about the reach block. We teach penetration at all costs. We play the defender over the tight end in an even technique. We teach to penetrate the reach. You cannot stay on the line of scrimmage. To my way of thinking, in America, nothing good ever happened at going 55 miles per hour or staying at the line of scrimmage. The government tries to pull off those two fallacies on the public. It is all bull.

With the field tackle in a strongside shade and the under defensive nose in a 3 technique alignment, the quarterback will think he can sneak the ball into the under A gap. The first thing I call is left, which shifts the line into the even alignments to the left (Diagram #4). We give an able call and bring the 3 technique defender into the A gap.

Diagram #4. Able

Another thing we do is run the linebacker through the gap (Diagram #5). With the tackle in the even technique on the guard and the linebacker stacked behind him, we run the linebacker through the B gap. The linebacker runs through and goes for penetration. The even technique tackle gets into the A gap. The backside linebacker is still in his jump mode. He is jumping over the line.

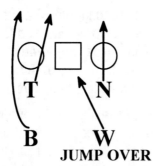

JUMP OVER

Diagram #5. Linebacker Run-Through

In the secondary, we play bump-and-run coverage. Offensive coaches say we cannot play like that because they can throw the ball deep. That does not scare me. When we coach bump-and-run in practice, we take the outside arm and put it behind our back. That is how we teach bump-and-run. We only jam the receiver with the inside arm.

We lead the nation in deep fade routes run against a defense. Sometimes, they complete those throws. The only time the outside hand and arm are used is when the receiver tries to release inside. If he tries to release inside, the defensive back opens and uses the outside arm to drive the receiver flat to the line of scrimmage and run him down the line to the inside.

If the defensive back cannot play bump-and-run, he gets off the receiver and plays inside leverage on the receiver. He makes him run out breaking patterns. With the college hash marks where they are, the quarterbacks have trouble throwing the ball outside the field hash marks. If he is on the boundary side hash mark, he has a hard time throwing the ball outside going into the field. It requires accuracy and arm strength.

When I was coaching at Detroit, we played Sonny Jurgensen and the Washington Redskins. I told the defensive backs to take away the inside on Jurgensen's receivers. We did that, and at halftime, they had completed 11 out patterns on us.

Coming off the field at halftime, the head coach asked me what I was going to do to stop the out pattern. I told him not to worry about that pattern. We were ahead 6-0. We won the game, and we did not worry about the out. It is hard to win the game throwing outs and three-step passes. If they catch it, make the tackle. If you make the tackle, three-step passing will not beat you.

The linebackers in a short yardage situation react to the angle of the backs. They mirror the angle of the backs in short yardage and goal line situations. If the backs move right or left, the linebacker attacks at 45-degree angles and jumps over the line. The only time the linebacker is not in a jump over technique is when the fullback comes directly at the linebacker. The first thing the linebacker does is wham the whammer. How are you at coaching this technique? How do you attack a blocker that tries to read your linebacker?

We coach this situation is three ways. The first time the fullback comes inside, the linebacker is going to check him out. We are going to wham the whammer and take on the fullback. We are going to knock him back or he will knock us back, but we are going at it man on man.

The second time we take on the fullback, we hit him two inches above the patella. We hit him in the thigh. That is awesome. It turns him upside down.

The third time he comes, we jump, turn, and matador him. The fullback will whiff on the linebacker. You blow him up on one play, destroy his knees on another play, and jump out of the way on another play. You need a plan to take on the fullback. You have to change up the way you attack the fullback. You had better have a plan, especially if the fullback knocks the linebacker on his back when you wham the whammer. That slows the fullback down and keeps him from teeing off on the linebacker. It puts doubt in his mind.

The corner coach has to be involved in short yardage and goal line run defenses. Corner backs play a role in the running game in a short yardage defense. Because of the way we play the linebackers, the wide receivers will try to crack on the linebackers in their scheme. We have to teach the corners to replace the linebacker when the wide receiver cracks to the inside.

Is anyone in here an offensive or defensive coordinator? Does anybody in here know who Joe Bugel is? Joe Bugel was the offensive coach at Western Kentucky and went on to become the offensive coordinator of the Washington Redskins. I was the defensive coach at Western Kentucky. We coached together one year at Western Kentucky. We went to a clinic together. When we got back to Bowling Green, Coach Nick Denes asked us if we learned any football. We wanted him to make us offensive and defensive coordinators, but he never would.

Joe is a great line coach. He is probably the best offensive line coach I have been around. He was running the combination blocking and slide blocking schemes at Western Kentucky in 1966. I was also running a four-man front at that time.

You must understand that the players and the plan are the most important things in football. I played high school football in Ohio. My senior year, I went to Ohio State on an official visit. I watched Ohio State play the Stanford Indians. That was a long time ago. Stanford had a quarterback named John Brodie, and Ohio State had a running back named Howard "Hopalong" Cassady. Woody Hayes was the head coach at that time. When it came time for the signing date, he pulled my scholarship offer.

Years later, I was coaching at Georgia Tech. Woody Hayes called and asked me to coach the defense for him. He told me I could only run monster to the field. He gave me a list of things I could do on defense. I told him that was not what we do on defense. He told me that was all we do on defense because that is what the players can do. It is not what the coaches know. It is what the players know and can do. He did not care about the scheme. He played what the players could play.

Bud Carson coached at Georgia Tech when I was there. He took that offensive scheme to the Pittsburgh Steelers and won a bunch of games up there. Tom Moore was at Georgia Tech at the same time and went on to do great things. Our teams were a bunch of pencil-necked, snow-white football players. However, we beat the snot out of everyone we played. The reason we did that was they did what they could do.

You will get on goal line and short yardage what you demand from your players. I learned this from George Allen. He brought me in for an interview when he was with the Washington Redskins, and I learned that from him. I watched what went on within one of their coaching meetings. It was intense, to say the least.

Once the head coach gets on his side of the desk, his attitude is entirely different from the other side. When I became head coach, how many players did I have over to my house to eat? I had none. I was not their daddy. I was the man that demanded things that their moms and dads would not demand. It was not easy to do what I asked, but that was all I would accept. No player ever loved playing for Jerry Glanville until 20 years after he played for me.

I did learn this about coaching: While you are coaching this player in college or high school, he is someone's baby. You are coaching someone's child. I am a demanding coach. Every coach says we are going to run, chase, and hit. There are degrees to everything you do. As a player, if you swear on the practice field, you are done for the day. If you are a coach working for me and you cuss a player on the field, I will fire you.

Bum Phillips was the greatest coach the Houston Oilers ever had. Everyone thinks I followed Bum Phillips as the Oilers coach. There were three coaches in between us. Ed Biles only lasted part of a season. Chuck Studley became the interim coach until Hugh Campbell took over. When I took the Oiler job, coaches wanted to know why I took that job. It was the worst job in football. They were winning two and three games a season. I went to Atlanta. The last game Atlanta played before I got there was against the Detroit Lions. Only 5,000 people were at the game. People wanted to know why I went there.

It was simple. No good team would offer me a job. I got an interview with Jerry Jones of the Cowboys. He flew me to San Diego when the Super Bowl was out there. I got there early and went to the suite. It was a huge suite loaded with food and drinks. There was everything that you could possibly want. He came in, and the first thing he said to me was "Are you going to coach my team or not?" I said, "Who gets to cut the players?" He replied, "See you down the road." That was a five-second interview. Thank God I did not get that job.

The other thing we do on short yardage and goal line is not to cover the slot with one man. We treat a slot as two slots. We treat it like a trips formation; we double-coverage the slot receiver (Diagram #6). We are not going to allow the slot receiver to run a slant or diagonal route to the inside. It may look like single cover, but the second defender will cheat

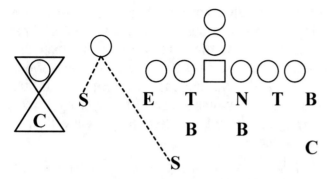

Diagram #6. Double the Slot

at the last minute to stop the inside move. The quarterback can make that throw on the goal line. The fade and outside throws are harder to make with the restricted area in the end zone.

I went to Alabama for one spring practice session while I was at Georgia Tech. I learned something from that. We were winning at Georgia Tech, but we had intensely physical practices. I went up in the tower with Coach Bryant to watch the practice. I would like to tell you we had a two-hour conversation, but he mumbled everything he said and I could not understand what he was saying.

The Alabama team dressed out in helmets and sweats. After practice, Coach Bryant asked me if I had any questions. I told him I was surprised he was not in full gear and doing a bunch of hitting drills. He told me they had 11 games to play next year and if he hit them all spring practice, it would cost him next year. While I was at Georgia Tech, I was bad in my approach to hitting. We probably would have been better if I had learned sooner when to hit and not hit.

Today, I am still demanding, and we hit bags, but we do not hit people with the regularity I used to use. We teach hard pursuit to the football. When the ballcarrier is going down, the defense has to be in the picture. When we stop that tape, I want every player on the defense in the shot. You have to come to the party. There is always room for one more. That is what causes turnovers. How did we lead the nation in college and in the pros in turnovers? You do it with gang tackling. You have to do that in the short yardage situations. You cannot allow the ball to move forward at all. The defense has to win scrums that occur in football these days. You cannot allow the offense to push the pile. You must stop them with great force from more people.

When the tacklers arrive at the ballcarrier, they do come under control, gather, and come to balance, and we do not break down. We attack the ballcarrier with a mass of people coming at 110 miles per hours. Someone may miss a tackle, but if we do, we are coming full speed. If the ballcarrier tries to fake someone out, he is not going to make the first down. In these situations, we do not get finesse running from the backs. If you do not bring it, they make the first down or the touchdown.

In the secondary, we play lockup bump-and-run coverage. With the ball on the boundary hash mark and the receiver into the wideside, the out is not an option. Joe Gibbs coached the Washington Redskins. He ran two routes if the defensive backs pressed him. I called it pogo. That means he ran a post route or a go route. If the defensive back got off the receivers, the receiver had a passing tree with more limbs on it than a Christmas tree. He could run 14 routes if you played off his receivers. There was no way the defensive back could cover that. I make them run a post or a go route.

Leadership

- Truth and honesty
- Fighting discouragement
- Courage

I want to leave you with one thing. I saw the coach at the New York Jets [Rex Ryan] talking about leadership. If you do not have leaders on your team, you can create some. You have to tell them a few things. If you want to be a leader, you have to do three things. You cannot be a leader without truth and honesty. You cannot tell the coach a lie for the betterment of the players and lead the entire team. Truth and honesty are the only way a player can lead his team, and we must tell them that.

My wife is a good person. When we were in Houston, she decided to feed all the runaway children. She worked and organized a big dinner for all those kids. She had a big spaghetti dinner prepared for them. When some of the kids came through the line, they wondered and asked why there were no mushrooms in the sauce or garlic on the bread. The second thing in creating leaders is you have to fight discouragement. Despite my wife's hard work, it was not enough for some of them. She had to fight discouragement. I call it bringing the group with you for the sake of the team.

When I was the head coach of the Atlanta Falcons, we played Pittsburgh in Pittsburgh. They were ahead 3-0, and we had the ball on the three-yard line just before halftime. I had Mike Rozier in the backfield. I could kick the ball and go in 3-3 at halftime or pitch the ball and try to score. I pitched the ball to Rozier, he headed for the corner, and six Steelers tackled him. Time ran out, and we went in behind at halftime. In the old stadium, both teams went through the same exit to get off the field. On the way out, my starting safety said, "We have the dumbest coach in the league." When we got into the locker room, he repeated it again and the other corner echoed his remarks.

My starting strong safety, Tracey Eaton, walked down the bench and bam!—he knocked out the cornerback doing all the talking. He walked over to the second corner and asked him what he thought of the call. The corner replied, "Damn good call!" Because of that, we never lost a game in Pittsburgh. We beat them every time we went up there. The leader has to fight the discouragement of the players that do not like what you are doing.

I am a great believer in this last thing. When I coached against Don Shula, I would tell my team several things. I told them that Miami's coach was a brilliant coach, and they had me as a coach. I told them I had been watching their players, and they were better than we were. They have better players and a hell of a lot better coaches. What can we do? We are all born with the same amount of courage. That means everyone is born with zero amounts of courage. We are not born with courage. The team brings courage to the pot. You have to be the courageous one. If you play with courage, you can overcome a stupid coach or players that lack athleticism. Take that to the short yardage and goal line defense, and you will change your team. Thank you very much for putting up with me. I appreciate your attention.

Al Golden

UTILIZING SAFETIES TO STOP THE RUN

University of Miami

Today, I am going to talk about our pressure package, which involves our safeties. I will take you through a process of how we involve our safeties in the running game. I also want to take you through how we train our safeties to force the ball and how to tackle in those situations. A lot of times, this part is left out. We want to take one big subject and refine it down as best as we can and, through repetition, get good at it rather than cover 100 things at one time.

When I call field, I am talking about where I am going to be putting the 3 and 9 technique linemen. When we call field, we are putting the 3 and the 9 technique to the field. We take the shade and the 5 technique and put them into the boundary. Snake is where we bring the strong safety. 2 sloop is the coverage (Diagram #1). The corner is playing cover 2. The field corner is playing a catch cover 2. He is lined up six to seven yards deep and face-up to the outside pad and jamming #1. He is carrying any vertical until he gets a flat threat. A catch technique is a little softer than a normal cover 2. The strong safety is going to time it up and come off the end man on the line of scrimmage. We want

him about two yards from the line of scrimmage and about four yards wide at the snap of the ball. He is not the force player. Most of the time, when the offense sees the safety coming down, it is trying to block force. The reason why snake 2 sloop is so good is because he is not the force player. He can blow up the play right now. He can spill it to the corner, who is the force player. It allows us to add a ninth guy to the front and show on the strongside.

The rush end for us is a long stick rush. We want our rush end to line up in a 9 technique. Sometimes, he likes to cheat over to a 6 or a 7 technique, but you cannot let him do that. He can disrupt the offensive zone schemes a little better if he stays in a 9 technique. The 9 technique end has a long stick to the B gap. The tackle is spiking to the A gap. The nose moves to the B gap. The end is in a touch technique. The Sam is the sloop or flat defender. Anything that comes to the flat, he has to collect. He has to run under the flat. As a rule, we tell him bottom of the numbers, 10 yards deep.

The Mike and the Will linebackers will be our hook curl defenders. This means they are relating to #2. They are jamming on #2. The weak safety will show post coverage. He will show middle of the field coverage and then close, and he will run to a hat. The boundary side corner plays a cheat half. His rule is 2x10 inside #1, and he is a half-field defender. We try to keep everything simple, and these concepts will repeat over and over again.

Against two tight end personnel, we might look like this (Diagram #2). The Sam is the sloop player. Anytime you are a flat player in football, you are responsible for force. In this case, he is in a wide 9 technique so he can play force from right where he is. The corner will be about 2x10 or 2x8 and will run over the top to play half-field coverage from there. For us, a half is 17 yards deep on the hash when the ball is on the hash. Since it is cloud force to the field,

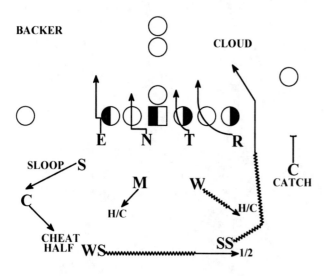

Diagram #1. Field Snake 2 Sloop

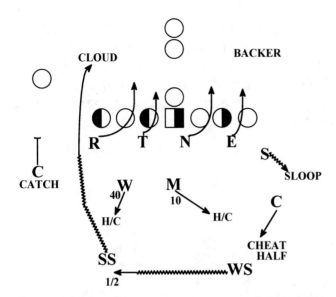

Diagram #2. Field Snake 2 Sloop vs. Two Tight Ends

it is going to throw off the offense that wants to block the force, as long as your strong safety kicks the ball sideways. He will take on any blocker that is leading the ballcarrier in order to kick it down to the Will linebacker, who should be fast off his butt. We instantly become a nine-man front in this type of situation.

Now I want to talk about over snake 9 (Diagram #3). Everything is basically the same except we are playing a five zone. The corners are playing exactly like you play cover 3. The corners are in hot coverage or one-third coverage. The weak safety is our middle-of-the-field defender. The strong safety is coming. Everything else up front is the same. The Sam and the Will are playing seam coverage. The

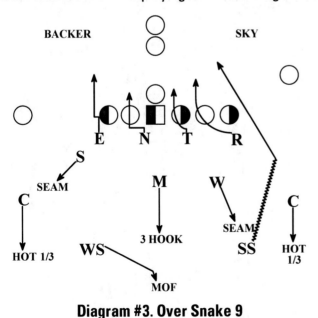

Diagram #3. Over Snake 9

seam coverage is very simple. He is defending #2 from the inside out. He will hold the seam on any vertical. If the #2 goes to the flat, he has him. If he runs a wheel route, he has him. The Mike linebacker is playing the 3 hook.

It is really important to know when you play post coverage or cover 9 how they are going to attack you. When you are playing cover two, all the throws are high to low. When you are playing cover 3 or cover 9, it is a horizontal passing game. Once they understand that, they can really defend it better. When we are talking about cover 9 now, we are talking about the Will and the Sam as the seam defenders and the Mike is the middle defender.

One reason why we like this is because to defend the read option, you want to stay in a two shell for as long as you can. You want to make sure you end up with at least a seven-man box. When you do this, because it is cover 9, the Will is always walking out on #2. He gives the illusion of cover 2. You are also changing the tempo of the read of the option series guys. After they are used to you running your base defense, you are now switching it up on them. The defensive end now is chasing the dive. The strong safety is the quarterback guy and the ball is out quick. The Will linebacker is the pitch player.

One of the reasons why you want to run this as a 9 coverage is you can run it as a field snake, as we just talked about, or you can run it as a formation call. It would be a field snake 9 in that case. The 3 and the 9 techniques go to the side of the tight end. In cover 9, the strong safety is the force player now. The corner is out of it.

If we run against 11 personnel or doubles, it will look like this (Diagram #4). Coming out of the huddle, the Mike will make a call: over snake 9. It is not a field call. "Field" means it is going to the field no matter what. "Over" means to the tight end. The Mike says "Tight left, sky left, and backer right." We now know the force, and we can play. The corners have thirds. The weak safety on the right is in the middle of the field.

Why is it good versus 2x2? It is strong against 11 personnel or if they are a tight end–oriented running team. Also, we can play the #2 man or run to this coverage, and our seam players are always lined up on #2. The seam player is jamming inside out.

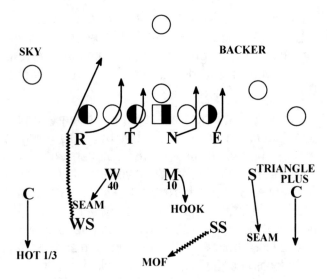

Diagram #4. Over Snake 9 vs. Doubles

We teach it like basketball. We teach it with our hands behind our backs. We want them to stay as square as possible for as long as possible. We tell them to take one more step like they are taking a charge in basketball. As soon as I jam him, I get my eyes inside and see how I am being attacked. I have to understand there is going to be some kind of flat threat. This way, I can hang in the curl for a long time. If I am a seam defender, I am defending inside out.

Now you say you want to be a snake team. The offense is going to start to motion the Z or line up so he can come up inside and crack you. You have to have a crack replacement. Now we have to run cobra. You have to bring your corner. If I am getting cracked on if I am the safety, my job is to turn and face the crackback. Get your hands on him and walk him out. The corner now has to be the force player.

We want to have eight guys in the box to defend all of the read option games we are getting. The way to do it is to drop him down on the snap.

If we call field snake 9, we do not need any other call. If the field is to the right, then we have sky to the right and backer to the left. The corners are playing outside thirds; the safety is in the post. The Sam and Will relate to #2 and are seam defenders.

We do not want to just teach snake. The offense is going to take the Z man and motion him and then have him block. It is going to put a wing over or it cuts the split of the Z man. In any of those cases, the strong safety and the corner are going

to change assignments (Diagram #5). If we were in a snake call, the safety is going to make a cobra call. Nothing else has really changed other than they have changed responsibilities. The weak safety has the hot third and the strong safety has the middle of the field. The corner is coming.

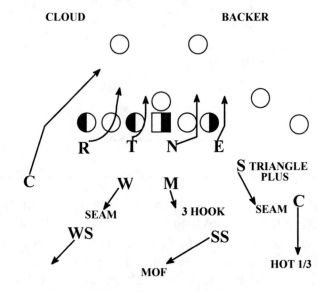

Diagram # 5. Cobra Call

This one is a little tougher. This is over flash combo (Diagram #6). If you are going to play just one of these, this is the one to invest in. We will run this versus everything. "Over" means we are setting the front to the tight end. The 3 and 9 technique guys are going to the tight end side. "Flash" to us means the weak safety. The weak safety is always going to come to the openside. It is a formation

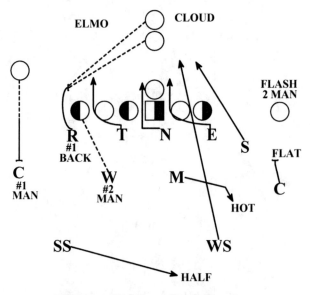

Diagram #6. Over Flash Combo

defense. It is always going to be the weak safety. He is always going to come to the openside. If there is no openside, then he is coming to the weakside.

The long stick by the right defensive end means two gaps. He is lined up in a 5 technique and he has to get to the A gap. The nose is in a RAC technique. This means he is going to go right across the center. The tackle is going to be in a LAT technique. This means loop around the tackle. The rush end is as he was before—a punch player.

If the offense is in a 2x1 pro set or a 2x2 set, we want to play two-man coverage. The right side is going to play #2. The corner on the right is playing as he did with snake. The safety is now coming to cover one half. The Mike is playing hot off of #2. The rush end has the #1 back.

The free safety in flash is the B gap blitz man. The most important coaching point for the weak safety is to chase the long stick. When we do a walk-through practice, we want the weak safety to hit the end's backside. It is mandated. The Sam is the leverage rusher. On over flash (two-man) combo, it is two men to the pressure side and man-to-man on the tight end side.

This is what it looks like versus a pro set (Diagram # 7). The Will is out on #2 and the rusher has the back. The corner has the #1 receiver.

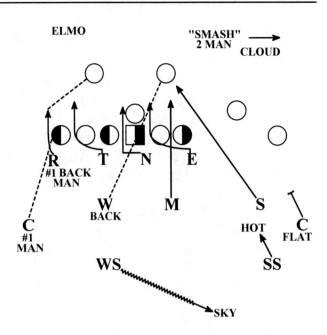

Diagram #8. Over Flash Combo Smash

plan no matter what. We are in the over call, and the tight end is to the left. The corner has #1 and the Will has #2. "Smash" means the flash went to a smash versus two removed. The strong safety stays and the Sam and Mike are coming. This is really simple, and we are still playing two man.

This is what it would look like versus any trips formation. We are playing cover 9 (Diagram #9). Again, let us think about the progression. We started out with snake 2 sloop and then we went to snake 9. This is one call: over flash combo. Any 3x1 is check to cover 9. The rush end and the Mike linebacker are seam players, and the Will linebacker is a three-hook defender. The two corners are one-

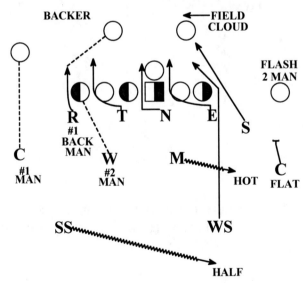

Diagram #7. Over Flash Combo vs. Pro Set

When flash is against a slot, we make a smash call (Diagram #8). The Sam comes and now the safety takes over the hot. This call is in every game

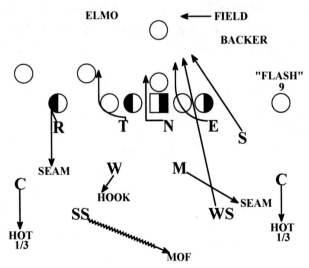

Diagram #9. Over Flash Combo vs. Bunch

third players and the strong safety is in the middle of the field for the post.

Remember, if it is a 2x2 or 2x1, we are playing two man. Any time the safety has two removed inside, we are calling smash. The Sam is going. This is good on first, second, and third down. It is good in the red zone. You name it. If you put a lot of time into this, then it will pay dividends for you. If they are going to give us an openside, we want to rush the openside with the weak safety and the Sam (Diagram #10). The only call that needs to be made is in a trips formation, and the call is between the Will and the rush end. The rush end is the hook hole player, and the Will linebacker is the seam player.

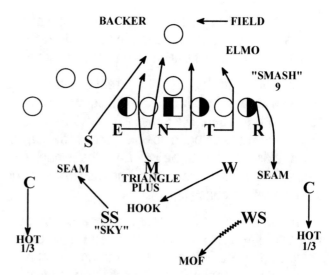

Diagram #11. Over Flash Combo vs. Treys

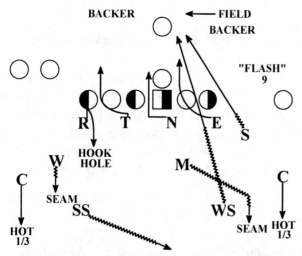

Diagram #10. Over Flash Combo vs. Trips

They get this through repetition. In cover 9, they know there are always two-seam players and a hole player. The corners have their hot third to cover, and there is always somebody in the middle. The safeties are always on a string. The safeties have to work together: one has the middle and the other one is going.

This is what it would look like against treys (Diagram #11). We are going to run smash and the Sam is going.

This is versus pro. We have a slot set. What does the free safety have to say? Smash. That is it. Everyone else is playing a two-man game (Diagram #12).

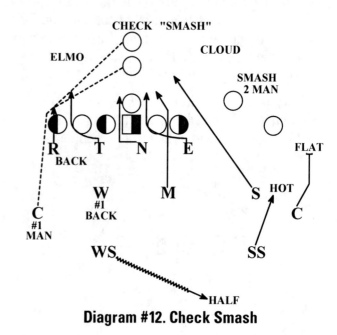

Diagram #12. Check Smash

Let me get to the film so you can see the defense in action. I appreciate your time, gentlemen.

PRACTICE LIKE YOU PLAY

Stephen F. Austin State University

It is great to be here. My dad coached college football. Like a lot of college coaches, he coached at a lot of different schools. I think he coached everywhere in the United States. He coached at Iowa State University, Oklahoma State University, Virginia Tech, the University of North Carolina, and Clemson University, and a few other schools.

My dad played football at the University of Kentucky for Coach Paul Bryant. He coached high school football in Louisville, Kentucky. While he was in Louisville, Coaches Duffy Daugherty and Bud Wilkinson asked him to be the director of the Coach of the Year Clinic in Louisville. He stayed with the clinics several years, but moving around so much, he turned the Louisville Clinic over to Earl Browning, who stills runs the clinic in Louisville.

We bounced around in three different towns when I was growing up. In our home, we always had a room that we called "Dad's room." I can still remember a big poster board from the Coach of the Year Clinic. Back then, it was the Kodak Clinic. That is how far my memory takes me when Bud and Duffy were running the clinics. It is always great to attend clinics, even if you only get one or two ideas that will help you.

Earlier today, I attended the lecture by Coach Les Koenning, the defensive coach from North Carolina, before I came in here. I filled up a notepad of things that he covered in his lecture. I think it is neat when we can all get together and share ideas about football.

It is great for me to come to Charlotte and talk about Stephen F. Austin University football. We are located in Nacogdoches, Texas. Nacogdoches is an interesting place. However, it is somewhat hard to get to the town. This is one of the reasons we have a hard time getting a schedule each year. No one wants to come to Nacogdoches to play us because of that reason.

I remember two years ago, when we played Villanova in the Championship Division (Division II) Playoffs at our place. We tried to make the playoff similar to a bowl game and tried to create the atmosphere that goes with a bowl game. On Friday night, our teams had dinner together and tried to be a good host for the playoff.

On Saturday after the game, their head coach, Andy Talley, came up to me and said, "Coach Harper, I thought this was a great weekend, but we will never come back." Later I sent him a note and asked him what he meant by the comment they would never come back. He replied, "Well, it took us a whole day to travel to Nacogdoches, and it took a full day getting back to Philadelphia."

We are 90 minutes south of Shreveport, Louisiana. We are two-and-a-half hours west of Dallas, and about two-and-a-half hours north of Houston. We are in the middle of the Piney Woods, where it gets hot. There is very little air in the area when it gets hot. Once we get the players in town, we lock them up and have fun playing football. I am going on my seventh year there. I was the defensive coordinator for two years, and I have completed my fifth year as the head coach there.

A lot of the things I am telling you today are to illustrate the fact I have learned a lot as I have progressed in this business of coaching. When my dad was living, we went to a lot of clinics. He had a saying that went something like this: "You are only as good as the last clinic you went to." I think there is some truth to that statement. But there is the other side of going to clinics. Often times you may say, "I like my way better."

In my first season as head football coach at Stephen F. Austin University, we went 0-11. That is certainly a miserable feeling. I was excited to be a head coach, and we were picked number one in the pre-season of the Southland Conference, and we went 0-11. Believe me, it was tough.

My mother is here today because she lives here in Charlotte now, and she and I talked a great deal during that 0-11 season. She has been to a ton of clinics and could understand what I was feeling. My dad passed away two weeks after I graduated from Clemson. He was not around for me to seek advice. So I called my mom a great deal that season. I would ask her, "What would Dad have done?" I had to figure out a lot of what was taking place on my own that year.

The topic for my lecture I was assigned is: "Practice Like You Play." As I kept thinking about the topic, it seemed weird to me. I could not figure it out, and I could not wrap myself around it. You may say the topic should be: "Practice How You Play." No! That is not correct. It is: "Practice Like You Play."

After that first year, I did some things that turned our program around. I took the time to listen to some players at the end of the season. The word "consistent" came to mind throughout those meetings. It became clear to me it is important to be consistent in what we do.

Everything I am going to cover today is about our offense. After that first year, I had to figure out how I was going to keep my job, and I knew the only way that was going to happen was to win. It was more than just winning. I had to win at Stephen F. Austin University. That did not mean we couldn't win anywhere else. I had to figure out how to win. The best way for us to be successful was to be consistent. I had to find a plan where we could be consistent every day and still be a good football team.

The first thing we knew we had to do was to score points. We had to find a way we could score and score a lot. In that first year when we were 0-11, we did not score for 10 quarters. This was a tough pill to swallow. We did not get a point for 10 quarters, not even a field goal. So I was determined we were going to score.

Being a head coach for the first time, I went out and recruited six quarterbacks. We signed six quarterbacks. When I played at Clemson, Coach Danny Ford would always say, "We are going to recruit 10 offensive linemen." I could not figure out why he wanted 10 offensive linemen every year. He said, "Three of them are not going to be very good, three of them are going to get hurt, and we are going to end up with three or four offensive linemen."

I took that same approach when I went looking for a quarterback that year. If we signed six quarterbacks, we could probably get one that could do what we wanted. I found a quarterback by the name of Jeremy Moses who could throw the football. He could make our offense be consistent. He did not look like a quarterback. He looked more like a manager. He was 5'11", and weighed 165 pounds. However, he could sit back in the pocket and deliver the football. I knew we had to build our program around him. As we started building the offense around him, the word "consistency" within our practices became the definition of how we play.

In the last four years, we have not changed anything at all in the way we practice. We start at 7:45 a.m., and we are done at 10:15 a.m. It is amazing how everyone in our program—from the trainers, equipment manager, to the film crew—everyone knows what we do when we do it. If you come to our practice, you are not going to hear a horn, you are not going to hear anything about periods, because we do not need them. Everyone knows this is how we do things. This is how we play as well.

With this consistency, the players have gained confidence, and they know there are no tricks to the game. Everything just flows smoothly, and it is easy for everyone because they know what we do. Everyone knows what to expect.

This past year, we won the first game and then lost the next five games. I made a mistake. I went away from my consistency plan. We did a few things a little differently, and the players made me aware of this fact. During our open date, we went back to what we had been doing, and we won the next five games.

One time I interviewed a person who said, "You must have the capacity for boredom, and yet you must stay consistent in what you do." That is the way we do it at Stephen F. Austin now.

I will be happy to share anything we do with you. Basically, we copied what Mike Leach did with his offense when he was at Texas Tech University. Ruffin McNeil was a graduate assistant for my dad. A few years ago, he was an assistant coach at Texas Tech with Mike Leach. I called Ruffin and asked him what they did. We visited Texas Tech and studied their offense.

Next, I hired a Shannon Dawson. Today, he is the offensive coordinator at West Virginia University. The first year Shannon came to coach with us, we went from 115th in the nation in scoring to 15th in the country in scoring. For the last three years, we have been number one in the nation in passing offense. We are going to throw the football. We are consistent with it. We set the record for the number of passes in a game. We threw the ball 85 times and completed 55 passes. This is in one game! And we lost that game.

We are going to throw the football, and we are going to playside fake. Our tempo is a huge part of what we do with our offense. I want to show you how our practice works so you can see what we do offensively.

People want to know how this type of offense affects our defense. My defensive coordinator has been with me for four years, and he and I get along. For 12 years, I was a defensive coordinator. So I know where he is coming from. We are able to communicate and talk. He likes the fact that we can score points. We have averaged 36 points per game for the last four years. My comment to him is this: "If we score 36 points in a game, we should win, right?" His comment is, "Oh, yes!"

As time has gone by, we have improved our defense, and we have improved our special teams. And, we have kept our offense consistent with what we do best. This is how we have been successful. In the last three years, we have a 17-4 record in our league.

When I got the topic "Practice Like You Play," this is what it is all about. The first thing we do in practice is to have a 15-minute session, and it is going to be our walk-through. This is at 7:35 a.m. If the defense does not want a 15-minute walk-through, it does not matter. I think it is a good thing, but offensively it is a great thing.

Offense is about execution and about rhythm. We probably should extend the time on this drill,

but we haven't gotten there at this point. At West Virginia University, they do 30 minutes on their walk-through. In that walk-through period, we are going to rep the plays we are going to run in our team period that day. We are going to walk through those plays.

The next period we go to what we call our "noose" drill. Some days, we do it for five minutes, and some days we do it for three to six minutes. We are going to see how things go during the drill.

This is a weird deal for me because it is a fun drill. It is strange for me to talk about this point. When I played football at Clemson, there was nothing fun about the way we played. Everything was physical. This has been a learning period for me. I know it works at SFA, and it works for what we do.

If you have a lot of money, you can take those pass rush dummies and use them in the drill. I talked with Coach Dawson, and he said they had pop-up dummies for sale now that can be used in the noose drill. I asked Coach Dawson what he wanted to do with the pop-up dummies and what did they do. He said, "They stand there."

He went on to tell me we would use them every day. I asked him what he was trying to do with the dummies, and his response was, "We are going to do the noose drill." Again, I asked if we were going to use the dummies every day. He assured me we would use them every day for life. I asked him if he knew how much the dummies cost, and he assured me he knew.

I like to spend the money on the players. I do not mean spending money to get players, but to improve the facilities for the players. I want them to have a nice dinner or to have a nice sweat top. When I played at Clemson, we were treated well. I would rather spend money on the players than on those dummies. So this is what we did.

We took big trash cans, and we doubled them up, one on top of the other. We have one can with the bottom on the ground, and the second can is on top of the other can, upside down over the lower can so we have a taller "dummy" (Diagram #1), We screwed the cans together and that is how we got our four dummies. The cans are just standing there anyway, so they work fine.

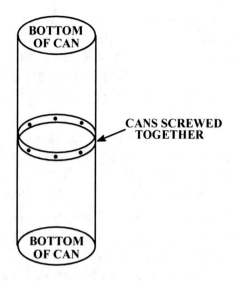

Diagram #1. Tall Dummy—Two Trash Cans

In the noose drill, we have three quarterbacks working in the drill at the same time (Diagram #2). If you have more quarterbacks, you can include more players in the drill. These trash cans are spaced about five to seven yards apart. The receivers are in three groups. They are relaxed and take it easy, waiting their turn in the drill. This is just a warm-up drill for them. The quarterback takes the long snap from the center and looks for the receiver to plant his foot in the ground on his route. We talk about planting the foot in the ground all of the time.

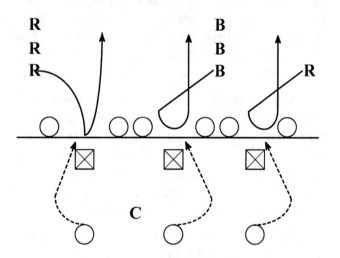

Diagram #2. Noose Drill

If you saw the Orange Bowl, you saw West Virginia University play. Their receivers knew how to put their foot in the ground. They could put their foot in the ground and make a move on the cut in

their pass route. We love those players who can put their foot in the ground. We want to get them the football. Some of our players are learning how to put their foot in the ground in the noose drill. We want players who can "just do it!"

Putting your foot in the ground and making your cut is similar to dancing. It is being athletic. Once the receiver puts his foot in the ground, he comes back to the football. The receiver can run in between the cans as much as he wants. The quarterback is waiting for the receiver to put his hands up to form the target under his chin. With the hands open up under his chin, it simulates the noose. That is why we call it the noose drill.

Every coach in the drill stresses getting the hands up to form the "noose." The players go back and forth, running their routes. They put their foot in the ground, and then put their hands up forming the noose. We carry this technique over to how we play. Again, it is "Practice Like You Play." We are working on releases, footwork, and we are working on staying tight to the body. "Put your foot in the ground, come back to the ball, get the hands up and make a noose, and then take it to the next level and score." We also work on ball security in the drill.

I have a player who wants us to let him run the Wildcat. The Wildcat is not our deal. We do not run the Wildcat. I convinced him last week by telling him this: "Every time you catch the ball, it is your Wildcat." He asked me what I meant by that. I told him we were going to get him the ball every kind of way possible. "When you get the ball on a pass, you can be the Wildcat." I convinced him all he had to do was to stick his foot in the ground, make his move, catch the ball, and then do his Wildcat thing.

In the drills, we have a coach standing behind the receivers, and he stresses ball security after the player catches the ball. The receiver tucks the ball away after the catch and goes to the next level.

This drill may look simple, and it is. A lot of the things we do are based on the fact that we have a 10-hour work week, so we want to do as much as we can in that time span.

Let's talk about the other players in the noose drill. The center is working on his snaps. The quarterback is working on catching the snap from the center. The quarterback sets in the pocket, working on his footwork, and then he delivers the ball to the noose, and we score. All of the quarterbacks are doing the same thing.

If the center is having trouble blocking a defender on his nose, we can work on that aspect. We put a defender on the center and let him work on making the snap and then getting his body on the defender.

We can run the drill in shorts and shoulder pads. We are running this drill now. We have been doing this drill since January. The players reported back to school on January 7, and we do this drill every day. This is what we do.

Now the question is: how does this relate to a game? I will show you how in this film clip. (Film: Here the receiver comes out, sticks his foot in the ground, turns and makes his noose, and the ball is delivered, and he takes it in for a score.)

When we do this drill every day, it is a lot like driving a car. You get used to doing it. It is no different.

Our next drill is our pat-and-go drill. We do not have to blow a whistle to let everyone know what to do. As soon as the last man goes on his noose drill, we move to the pat-and-go drill. If you come to Nacogdoches on Monday morning at 8:10 a.m., we will be doing this drill.

The next question you want to know is: how can we do this legally? Outside of fall practice and spring practice, there are no coaches on the field with them during the drill. If we are not allowed to be on the field with them, they run the drills on their own. The drill runs itself. No one is checking on the players. We do not have a strength coach or anyone else at the practice. They want to run the drills, so we tell them it is up to them if they want to run the drills.

Why do I like this practice setup? Everyone likes to pitch and catch the football. Kids love to catch the ball. The noose drill is fun for the players.

In the pat-and-go drill, we have two quarterbacks lined up in the drill (Diagram #3). First, we are working on the slant route. The receivers release and run their slant routes. It is an easy throw for the quarterbacks. We want the quarterback to throw the ball at the face of the receiver. This type of pass is a face thrown for the quarterback.

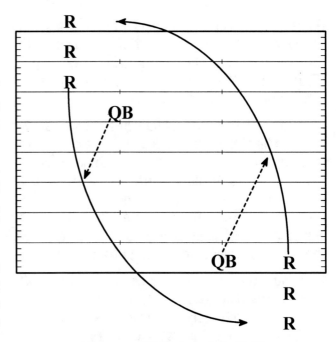

Diagram #3. Pat-and-Go Drill

We can have a coach line up in front of the receivers and work with them on their routes. We can work on the release for the receivers. We can work on the footwork and their hands. We are doing simple things at the same time. There is no real timetable on this drill. They are working on their routes.

This past year, we did take the drill one step further. If the receiver drops a pass during this drill, they do up-downs. We can tell them if they drop the ball today, we want them to do five up-downs. We may say 10 up-downs. We do not drop too many passes. If the quarterback makes a bad read or makes a bad throw, he does the up-downs. This made the drill better.

Now, we are working on throwing the ball down the field. I have attended a lot of clinics, and I have talked to a lot of coaches about the go route. I have talked with coaches about keeping the ball on the bottom of the numbers on the field, and to throw the ball over the outside shoulder. We do not spend a lot of time talking about that. We spend more time talking about getting open on the routes and adjusting to the pass. We want to throw the ball out there, and we want the receiver to get open and then adjust to the ball.

Obviously, we must have room for the quarterback to throw the ball. We find a lot of times, when things are not perfect on the pass, the receiver has to do a great job of adjusting to the football. That is what we work on in this drill. Again, "Practice Like You Play." We want to be consistent in this drill.

We do this drill every day. In the summer, we may not be able to do the drill because a lot of the time the players are not around. In the off-season, this drill is like lifting weights for us. It is what we do. We work on releases and adjusting to the football. We want the quarterback to throw the ball to the outside shoulder with a lot of air under the ball. The receiver must adjust to the football.

Also, we run the same drill where the quarterback does not throw the ball high on the route. The quarterback makes a quicker release on the ball. Primarily, it is just another type of warm-up drill. This is a drill where the coaches can work on the releases and having the receivers adjust to the football.

I want to show you how the drill works in a game situation. You can see the receiver make the plant on his route. More than likely, this is just an adjustment by the receiver and the quarterback. The defender is playing off the receiver, so he runs the slant route. The quarterback can see this on his pre-read snap, and he knows the receiver is going to run the slant route. He throws the ball as the receiver puts his foot in the ground on the cut. This is what we work on every day. It is the pat-and-go drill.

As we look at this film clip, I would like to see Hudl® or some another company come up with a way to isolate the receiver and quarterback, and remove all of the other people in the picture. They would see that this play is nothing more than our pat-and-go drill. We sell this idea to our players. We work on this every day. It is the same principle of working on blocking every day. The consistency of the drills is the most important aspect of our offense.

We run the pat-and-go drill for 5 to 10 minutes. There is not particular timetable on the drill. We do not have a horn that blows to tell us to move to the next drill. We do not worry about that. We work on the drills until we feel we have had enough of it, and then we move on to work on something different.

In this shot, you can see the drill again. The ball is not quite at the bottom of the numbers, and it

is not perfect, but it is a great job by the receiver, adjusting to the football over his outside shoulder. This is what we want. We actually want the pass at the bottom of the numbers, where the receiver can use the distance from the numbers to the out-of-bounds line to adjust to the pass and make the reception.

The play is not always perfect. We do not work in a perfect world. We talk about this fact often. It is important for the receivers to know that when the pass is made, it is not always perfect. That was a hard concept for me to learn.

After Shannon Dawson went to West Virginia University last year, we hired a new offensive coordinator. We hired Mike Nesbitt to take his place. A few weeks ago, Mike joined the staff at the University of Houston as offensive coordinator.

I learned an important point about receivers running routes from Mike. We use a technique for our receivers that we call "stacking." When the receiver gets a certain distance to the defender, he wants to control his body from the top down and actually slow down a bit. He wants the corner to come over the top of the receiver. If the receiver does not make the catch, the defender will be called for a penalty. The defender is stacking on top of the receiver as the receiver slows down to control his body, and to look for the football. That is all a part of the pat-and-go.

Next is our quick game. We have worked on our walk-through, noose, pat-and-go, and now we are working on our quick game. The quick game and routes on air for us are basically the same drill. Quick game is obviously our quick throws. Routes on air are any routes we run on air without a defense (Diagram #4). The difference in the two depends on the drop by the quarterback. It is either a quick throw, or a five-step drop action. The drill is the same.

When we went from 0-11 in my first year as head coach, and not scoring for 10 quarters, I wondered why this offense is so successful. How do you teach a quarterback to make great decisions, and how could the offense execute as well as they did at Texas Tech? How did this happen? The way it happened is this: you must have a capacity for boredom. You must run the same plays over and over again.

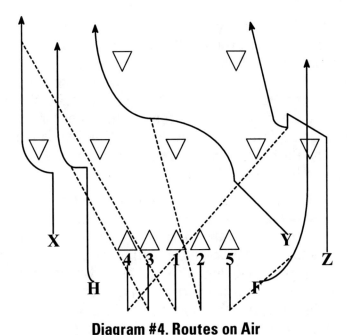

Diagram #4. Routes on Air

Basically, we have eight routes. In practice, we rep them over and over again. I am fortunate in that I am the son of a former college football coach, and to me it is similar to the option teams used to run. When I played at Clemson, they worked on the option every day. Coach Chuck Reedy would work on the give to the first back, and read the defensive end. Then the quarterback would work the ball outside and make the pitch on the option. It is the same concept. So routes on air is really the meat and potatoes of what we do.

We only have three formations. We have a 2x2, 3x1, and a 2x1 formation. If you want to really break it down, we only have one formation, which is the 2x1. We are always in the shotgun set. That is one hundred percent of the time. We never take a snap from under the center. We never work on this. We can get our practice completed in one hour and 15 minutes. Our defense needs more time, so we work with them in this respect.

In the routes on air drill, you need five quarterbacks. You can use a manager or an extra coach if you do not have five quarterbacks. It is important that the quarterbacks stay tight together in the drill. The middle quarterback calls the snap count. Our snap count is simple, and everyone in our league knows our snap count. It is simple: "two-two, set-hut."

When I am at home, my son Michael will ask me if I want to play football. I tell him I do. He gets

the ball, and he calls out, "Two-two, set-hut." To me, I am amazed. He is a seven-year-old kid, and he knows our snap count. Everyone knows our snap count. Why is this snap count so important? It is because of our rhythm. Our offensive line coach is my brother-in-law, and he drives me crazy about other teams knowing our snap count. I tell him we want the opponents to know our snap count. That is good. We have no problem with this fact. We teach rhythm. Again, have a capacity for boredom.

The five quarterbacks must stay tight together in the drill. That is the way it is in the pocket in a game. We want them to get the feeling of tightness in the pocket.

From there, we line up three deep at each position for the five quarterbacks to throw to in the drill. As soon as the first man in line runs his route, the second man steps up and he is ready to run his route. The quarterbacks will be ready to go. They throw the ball on the cut by the receivers. Everyone is catching a ball as all five quarterbacks make their throws. The receiver runs the route we call. We either run our quick game or our 90 game, which is our five-step passing game.

To take the concept one step further, in the consistency and "Practice Like You Play" concept, we have a three-day installation schedule. It is day one, day two, and day three. No matter what we do, we stick to that schedule. After day three, every offensive player knows we are going back to day one. It is one, two, three, and one, two, and three.

Everyone knows what we are doing, and they come to work. They know we are doing a one, a two, or a three day. They know we are going to run the noose, pat-and-go, quick game, and routes on air. It just flows. The quarterbacks know what we are going to do each day. Everyone knows what we are going to do each day.

One thing we were not doing well this past season was catching the football as we had in the past four seasons. As much as we throw the ball, we were not catching the ball very well. The problem was, the receivers wanted to blame it on the quarterback. The quarterback wanted to blame it on the receivers. It was simple. We solved the problem. If they missed a pass in practice, they had to do an up-down. If the quarterback had a bad read, he had to do an up-down. In the routes on air, there are no defensive players on the drill. I told the quarterbacks since they did not have to run, if they had a misread, they would have to do double up-downs. At least the receivers were running their route.

We do a lot of reps on the routes. We run one route, which is our 618, so much that we can run it in our sleep. If you watch our quarterbacks on the play, you see they know who they have to throw to on the play. Again, this is the key to our offense. That is why we are effective in the passing game.

When we run our quick game, they know the ball is coming out of the hands of the quarterback immediately. We combine the noose drills and the pat-and-go, and combined them with our routes on air, and we work on them. Basically, the walk-through is the same thing as our drills, except we use one quarterback. We only have one at the time.

After the pat-and-go drill, the offensive line knows that we are 45 minutes into practice. The offensive line has 45 minutes of individual work. They do what they need to work on during that time span.

Next, we go to our team period. The quarterback is seeing how we carry over the "Practice Like You Play" concept. The receivers run their routes, and it is the same routes we ran in our routes on air drill.

It really goes back to old school, option football. It is getting reps after reps, over and over. The key for the receivers is the fact that they are running the same routes over and over again. We have eight routes. They run those eight routes over and over. The player who is different is the quarterback. The offensive line does the same blocking over and over again.

The quarterback is different when he makes different decisions based on what the defense gives us. He is the person who must make the correct decision as the ball is snapped. As Coach Les Koenning said in his lecture, the defense may not give you what you expect to get on the play. It gets to the point where the quarterback does not care what the defense does, because it is a matter of repetitions, and he makes his decision and moves to the next play.

When Jeremy Moses was our quarterback, he threw for over 13,000 yards. He threw for 121 touchdowns. That was a big difference in what we were doing before we signed him. I timed him on his release. He got rid of the ball in 2.5 seconds. You may ask how he was getting rid of the ball in 2.5 seconds. It is by the way you practice. That is the key. The key is how you practice. I think this is true on offense and defense.

Before I came here yesterday, I had a meeting with our defensive coordinator. I told him we have been doing the same thing for the last four years. We do these drills over and over: noose, pat-and-go, quick game, and routes on air. I asked him how we could get that same rhythm and the same mindset defensively so that when the players come to practice, they know what they are doing and they know how they are going to do it. There is no script for our offense. Can we do that on defense and just rep the defensive plays we are going to see?

I do not want to get into any plays today in this lecture. I will talk about the backside of our 618 pass. Basically, on that play, we are reading the linebacker on the flat player to the frontside. On the backside, we can run the quick slant and other routes.

In our first year with this offense, we only ran one running play. When we first put the offense in, we were very much like Texas Tech in that we wanted big splits in the line. When you take those big splits in the offensive line, you cannot zone block. My offensive line coach wanted to do some zone blocking. So slowly we have cut our splits down, and we run the inside zone and the outside zone plays, and one more play. That is it!

The routes on air drill takes a little longer than the other drills. It depends on the day we are in. Day one, two, or three determines the plays we are going to run. The time for the drill is 12 minutes. The reason it is only 12 minutes is because we are going fast. There is not a lot of coaching going on during this drill. This is the reason we film the drill.

When we get into the skeleton drill, our coaching is to tell the receiver to get open. "Run the route, and get open." We want everyone on the same page on the drill, and they all know that. We tell them to find a window and to get open.

Now, we have the offensive line join us in our drills. This is after those 45 minutes of drills. They become a part of our drills. This is when we do our screen passing game. Our screen passes are a big part of what we do. This is what I think made this offense go. It is the quick screen passing game. Basically, it is a toss sweep outside play, and our tailback screens. We have added a few other screens to our offense.

We love our screen passes because they are the idea why we can keep our snap count as "two-two, set-hut." The reason we run the screens is to get their linemen to run all the way outside to the left, and all the way to the right. We want the defensive coordinators yelling at his linemen, "Get to the ball!" This is what we want. We want to wear those defensive linemen out. We want to run a screen pass early in the game. We are going to run a screen outside and a screen inside. We want to run 80 to 90 plays in the game. We want to make those defensive linemen get outside on those screens so we can wear them down.

After we run the screens, we are going to come back with a draw play. We run the screen, then a draw, and then we are going to throw deep. When we know those defensive linemen are tired, we can go to our five-step game and go deep. We do not go deep early, but we are going deep late in the game.

Our screens are very basic. We have rocket to the right, and laser to the left. Then we have a Randy screen. It is similar to a bubble screen, but it is not a bubble. We do not run the bubble screen anymore. It takes too long to teach. We want the quarterback to look at the outside receiver, and if he is uncovered, he is going to throw him the ball. The big thing we want to do is to go north with the ball.

I can remember when I was at Clemson, and Danny Ford was the head coach. In the game, he would get on one knee on the sideline and yell out to the offense, "Just get us four yards! Just four yards, please!" It is the same thing for us on the screens. We just want those four yards. "Get us four yards."

If we can get the first two plays for four yards each, it is third-and-two. That is the way it works. It is a slow process. We keep working on it, and we work on the tempo. We may throw the ball outside and only get one yard. The offensive line coach may say, "That was a bad play." I tell him it was not a bad play, and that it was a good play. "Look at all of those defensive linemen running over to the ball." Then, we run the screen to the other side. If we can get the receiver to catch the ball, just as he does in the noose drills, we may break it for a long gain. Now the receiver is the "Wildcat" for us. So we gain more yards on the screens. We run our tailback screens in this drill, and we do our quick screens to the outside during this period.

We run three things all of the time. Again, it is consistency and "Practice Like You Play." Everyone knows what we are calling. The offensive tackles run three plays, where all they do is to go backwards. We ran our 618 play 90 plus times last year. On the frontside, we are running our 618 play, and on the backside we are running our nickel play. That is all we tell the receivers. Run 618 to the frontside and nickel to the backside. Then, we incorporate our linemen into the play.

When we run the screens, our two tackles are backing up. We want to take them on over the top. If the defense goes inside, they take the defenders inside. We want the defense to go inside.

We run a running play where the tackles block the same way. We call that our 10 play. We run our 11 play, which is a draw for us. Then, we run our screen pass, and then we pass set. The tackles are doing the same thing on those plays, and they can do a good job. We let them know they are doing a good job. We do not want to coach negative thoughts with them. We tell them they ran three plays: 10, 11, and a pass set.

We want the center to work outside to the numbers on our screens. We want the guard to work far outside toward the center. We want the center and both guards outside on the screens. In a sense, it is like a toss sweep play. We tell the first man who gets outside to the top of the numbers to block the first man that he sees. The next man works up to the numbers, and the third man works inside.

We bring the outside receiver shallow across to restrict the defender down inside. A lot of those receivers do not like to come back inside. Plus, the defense is doing a better job of reading the plays and restricting the effectiveness of the man coming back inside. We are thinking about changing the play some in that respect.

I was a GA at the University of Notre Dame when Rocket Ismail was there. He sort of invented the flanker screen play. He could catch the ball underneath the coverage and rocket up the field. He made it look like a rocket. I think the defense has caught up with this play to a certain degree. He could catch the ball at a position behind the guard and take it up the field.

We tell the tackles if they block on the screen, we will score. All of sudden, they will start blocking. A lot of the success we have with the blocking aspect is because it is fun. Our right tackle in the film is 6'9" and 340 pounds. Going backwards is all he can do on this play. He cannot do anything else on the play. He was invented to go backwards. He would have never played at Clemson when I played. That is what is so great about this offense. It gives everyone a chance to play.

We do run the inside zone play. Our inside zone is a slow tempo play. Our inside zone is our number-one running play. We work on the inside zone and 1-on-1 at the same time. We go from routes on air, screens, 1-on-1, to inside zone. On the 1-on-1, we tell the defense this is an offensive drill. We tell them to play man defense and compete. We run the play off man coverage. It works the same way in a game.

The receiver runs his route, and the quarterback gets him the ball.

The last thing we do in our team segment is our team-tempo drill. We run a play and down the ball after five yards. As soon as the play is over, the manager runs up and spots the ball at the next five-yard marker. We go from where he spots the ball. We do not script the plays from different positions on the field. We do not do that now. We want to go from where the ball is down. The offensive coordinator has to adjust to where the ball is spotted. The players are going to go just like they do in a game.

In this drill, the players know we are only going to move the ball five yards at a time. If we are in a half-field situation, we run six plays down to the 20-yard line. If we go the length of the entire field, we still go every five yards. If I feel we have had a good practice and the tempo is good, I may tell them we will go every 10 yards. That is how we work our team-tempo drill.

We do not stop the plays in this session. No coach can call out, "Run it again." No repeats. You can do repeats on the films. We run the plays, and then go to a second group, and then a third group. It is go, go, go. That is how we do it. We get that in a game because that is how we practice.

I appreciate your attention, and thanks for having me. I will be around if you have any questions.

NCAA ELIGIBILITY CENTER: APPLICATION PROCESS

Long Island University (C.W. Post)

Thank you for the introduction, Brian. I am the Senior Associate Director of Athletics at C.W. Post. Also, I am the Compliance and Eligibility Coordinator. I am a former student-athlete. I graduated from Freeport High School, and as you may know, they have some good student-athletes.

I was a college basketball player and received a scholarship. After my first bachelor's degree, I went on to get my first master's degree from California University of Pennsylvania on a graduate assistantship. I received a second master's degree from Teachers College Columbia University. I did receive a graduate assistant position with them, and I worked for them later.

The titles after my name, ATC stands for certified athletic trainer. I have been around athletics in some capacity for some time. I worked at Columbia and C.W. Post as the head athletic trainer. I have always been in football, and I know some of the ins and outs of the game. I have been associated with the academic side of the game as opposed to the X's and O's you are involved with.

I am here to talk about the requirements your student-athletes need to go on to the college level as student-athletes. Today, we are going to talk about those issues. The program is now called the NCAA Eligibility Center and is no longer called the Clearing House. The NCAA governs all eligibility now.

Overview

- Cast of characters
- NCAA Eligibility Center
- Initial eligibility requirements
  - ✓ Core courses
  - ✓ Nontraditional courses
  - ✓ SAT/ACT scores
  - ✓ Early certifications
- Tips and reminders

WHOSE ROLE IS IT IN THIS PROCESS?

- High school student-athlete (i.e., "PSA" = perfected student-athlete)
- Parents
- High school coaches
- AAU coaches
- High school guidance counselors
- College/University coaches
- College/University compliance department
- NCAA Eligibility Center

We are starting to see a lot of AAU coaches getting involved in the process. We are seeing more and more student-athletes participate on an AAU team and not on their respective high school teams. The AAU coaches are getting involved in the process as a result.

The process can get a little crazy, and it can be stressful for the groups involved. That is why I am here. I want to define some of the issues involved and what is needed to meet the requirements involved.

NCAA ELIGIBILITY CENTER

This is where it all begins. The NCAA Eligibility Center is responsible for determining the eligibility of every (PSA) college-bound student-athlete in NCAA Division I and Division II, using the following two areas:

- *Amateurism Certification:* They determine if the PSA has the college-bound student-athlete jeopardized his or her amateur status? They determine if a student-athlete has played professional athletics, did they accept money to play athletics, and so forth.

- *Academic Certification:* Does the college-bound student-athlete meet the legislated minimum academic requirements? This determines if the PSA is eligible for college athletics. This is true for Division I, II, or III.

Following are the requirements the PSA must achieve to be considered eligible for college eligibility.

INITIAL ELIGIBILITY ACADEMIC REQUIREMENTS

The Mainstays

- High school graduation
- Completion of NCAA-approved core courses
- Obtain the minimum GPA required within core courses.
- Earn a required SAT or ACT sum score

The Caveats

- Academic initial eligibility requirements are different for each of the three NCAA Divisions (I, II, III).
- It is possible for a college-bound student-athlete to be eligible in one division and not in another.
- Institutional academic requirements supersede *all* other requirements.

This last point is important. If you make a respectful score on the ACT, it does not mean you can get in all colleges. Certain standards are required for different colleges, and while you may gain admission to one college, it does not mean you are going to get in another college. There are a lot of coaches who would love to offer your student-athlete a scholarship, but the student-athlete may not meet the requirements of a particular college.

CORE COURSES REQUIRED BY THE NCAA ELIGIBILITY CENTER

Definition of a Core Course

- A course that qualifies for high school graduation in one or more of the following subjects: English, math, natural/physical science, social science, foreign language or comparative religion or philosophy

- Considered four-year college preparatory
- Taught at or above the high school's regular academic level
- For math courses, at the level of Algebra I or higher
- Taught by a qualified instructor as defined by the appropriate academic authority

NONTRADITIONAL COURSES

We are starting to see a pop-up of these nontraditional courses. These are courses that do not necessarily happen on campus. There are a lot of Internet courses available today. Courses are taught through:

- Internet
- Distance learning
- Independent study

Things to Consider Before Taking These Courses

- Must include ongoing access between instructor and student
- Must have a defined time period for completion (i.e., eight weeks)
- Should be clearly defined as such on the high school transcript
- Must be comparable in length, content, and rigor to courses taught in a traditional classroom setting

You should become familiar with a worksheet and know what it looks like. We have a Division I and a Division II worksheet at the end of this lecture (Charts #3 and #4).

This is how you or your guidance counselor should be able to determine which area you would qualify for depending on your PSA. What is the requirement for each NCAA Division? You must remember each division is different. First, we will look at Division I.

NCAA DIVISION I ACADEMIC REQUIREMENTS (16 CORE COURSES)

- Four years of English
- Three years of mathematics (Algebra I or higher)

- Two years of natural/physical science (one year of lab, if offered by high school)
- One year of additional English, mathematics, or natural/physical science
- Two years of social science
- Four years of additional courses (from any area above or foreign language, nondoctrinal religion, or philosophy)

In addition to the 16 core classes, the NCAA has what is referred to as the sliding scale. This is for your GPA and your SAT and ACT test scores. See Charts #1 and #2 at the end of this lecture for the full sliding scale.

SAMPLE SLIDING SCALE

Core GPA	SAT	ACT
3.525	410	38
3.500	420	39
3.475	430	40
3.450	440	41
2.850	680	56
2.825	690	56
2.800	700	57
2.075	980	83
2.050	990	84
2.025	1000	85

This means if you had a GPA average of 3.525, and you only scored 410 on your SAT, you could still qualify for an athletic scholarship at the Division I level. On the other hand, it could go in reverse. You could have a 2.025 GPA and score 1000 on your SAT or 85 on the ACT, and still be a qualifier. Division I is the only division that has the sliding scale. If you meet the requirements, you become a qualifier.

The Qualifier

- Can practice and compete during the first year of attendance
- Can receive athletic scholarship for the first year
- Can play four seasons if eligibility is maintained year to year

The Non-Qualifier

- Cannot practice or compete during the first year of attendance
- Cannot receive an athletic scholarship for the first year.

The SAT scores are only counted for the reading and the math. For the ACT, the scores are composite scores. You get the composite score from the sub-scores. If you add up all of the ACT scores from the English, reading, science, and math, you get a composite score.

NCAA DIVISION II ACADEMIC REQUIREMENTS (*14 CORE COURSES)

- Three years of English
- Two years of mathematics (Algebra I or higher)
- Two years of natural/physical science (one year of lab, if offered by high school)
- Two* years of additional English, mathematics, or natural/physical science
- Two years of social science
- Three* years of additional courses (from any area above or foreign language, nondoctrinal religion or philosophy)
- Earn a 2.000 grade point average or better in core courses
- Earn a combined SAT score of 820 or an ACT sum score of 68

* Will change to 16 core courses in 2013 and after (three years for English/math/science and four years for additional courses).

The Qualifier

- Can practice and compete during the first year of attendance
- Can receive athletic scholarship for the first year
- Can play four seasons if the eligibility is maintained year to year

After 2013, the core requirements will go up to 16 for Division II. That is why we have the asterisk for the number of core courses.

Division II has a partial qualifier rule. If you do not have either one score or the other, you can be a partial qualifier. If you have a score of a 2.0 GPA but do not score 820, you can still be a partial qualifier. It works the other way as well. If you have the 820 but do not have a 2.0 GPA, you can still be a partial qualifier. They cannot play, but they do not lose a year of eligibility.

The Partial Qualifier

- Can practice, but cannot compete during the first year of attendance
- Can receive athletic scholarship for the first year

There is no sliding scale for Division II. It is only for Division I. If you do not meet the requirements, you become a non-qualifier.

The Non-Qualifier

- Cannot practice or compete during the first year of attendance
- Cannot receive an athletic scholarship for the first year

NCAA DIVISION III ACADEMIC REQUIREMENTS

- Division III has no initial eligibility requirements
- College-bound student-athletes are not required to register with the NCAA Eligibility Center
- Eligibility for admission, financial aid, practice, and competition is determined by the college or university
- Contact the institution directly for details.

If the students are not interested in playing college sports at Division I or II, I would suggest that the student not register with the NCAA. They do not need to spend the money to sign up if they are not going to a Division I, or Division II school.

TIPS AND REMINDERS

Division I

A PSA can get early certification. By the end of your junior year in high school, you can become a qualifier. Early academic certifications for college-bound student-athletes who meet the following criteria after six semesters will be certified as qualifiers:

- Minimum SAT (math and critical reading) of 1000 or minimum sum score of 85 on the ACT
- For Division I: core-course GPA of 3.000 or higher in a minimum of 13 core courses:
  - ✓ Three English
  - ✓ Two math
  - ✓ Two science
  - ✓ Six additional core courses
- Score a 3.00 or higher GPA in the 13 core courses.

Division II

- Core-course GPA of 3.000 or higher in a minimum of 12 core courses:
  - ✓ Three English
  - ✓ Two math
  - ✓ Two science
  - ✓ Five additional core courses
- Score 1000 or over on the SAT

It is possible to become eligible for a scholarship at the end of your junior year if you meet those requirements. It is possible.

Division I

Division I has a core-course time limitation:

- From the time a student enters the ninth grade, he/she has four years (or eight semesters) to complete his/her core-course requirement. If the student fails to complete high school "on time" in eight semesters, core courses taken after the eighth semester will not be counted toward his/her NCAA academic eligibility requirements.
- "On time" also means that if the student's high school graduation takes place June 1, he/she must graduate June 1. If the student does not graduate June 1 with the rest of his/her school class, the student's academic requirements have not been completed "on time."

If you do not graduate with your class by June 1, you are not eligible for Division I. The other point people get confused about is the fact that the ninth grade courses count on the eligibility issue. Elementary school does not count on the eligibility plan.

Division II

- A student is permitted to use all core courses completed from his/her ninth grade year until the time he/she enrolls full time at a college or university.

WAYS THAT YOU CAN HELP

Oftentimes, I see coaches that come to my office and place the high school student-athlete's transcript on my desk and ask me, "Is this kid eligible?" Also, I find that a lot of high school counselors do not know how to figure the scores and do not understand the rules. It does not take a genius to figure out the eligibility rules. So I encourage the coaches and counselors to learn as much as possible on the rules and regulations. Please see Chart #5 for a quick reference guide.

- Know the initial eligibility requirements.
- Remind PSA to register with the NCAA Eligibility Center by the beginning of their junior year (www.eligibilitycenter.org).
- Encourage PSA to take standardized tests early and more than once, if needed.
- Emphasize the importance of academic performance at every step of the student's high school career.
- Help students identify colleges that fit their criteria (e.g., academics, size, distance from home, location).
- Encourage PSA, parents, and counselors to educate themselves on initial eligibility standards and recruiting rules.

Contact the NCAA Eligibility Center with questions: 1-877-622-2321

Sliding Scale A Use for Division I prior to August 1, 2015		
NCAA Division I Sliding Scale		
Core GPA	SAT Verbal and Math ONLY	ACT
3.550 & above	400	37
3.525	410	38
3.500	420	39
3.475	430	40
3.450	440	41
3.425	450	41
3.400	460	42
3.375	470	42
3.350	480	43
3.325	490	44
3.300	500	44
3.275	510	45
3.250	520	46
3.225	530	46
3.200	540	47
3.175	550	47
3.150	560	48
3.125	570	49
3.100	580	49
3.075	590	50
3.050	600	50
3.025	610	51
3.000	620	52
2.975	630	52
2.950	640	53
2.925	650	53
2.900	660	54
2.875	670	55
2.850	680	56
2.825	690	56
2.800	700	57
2.775	710	58
2.750	720	59
2.725	730	59
2.700	730	60
2.675	740-750	61
2.650	760	62
2.625	770	63
2.600	780	64
2.575	790	65
2.550	800	66
2.525	810	67
2.500	820	68
2.475	830	69
2.450	840-850	70
2.425	860	70
2.400	860	71
2.375	870	72
2.350	880	73
2.325	890	74
2.300	900	75
2.275	910	76
2.250	920	77
2.225	930	78
2.200	940	79
2.175	950	80
2.150	960	80
2.125	960	81
2.100	970	82
2.075	980	83
2.050	990	84
2.025	1000	85
2.000	1010	86

Chart #1. Division I Sliding Scale Prior to 8/1/15

Sliding Scale B Use for Division I beginning August 1, 2015			
NCAA Division I Sliding Scale			
GPA for Aid and Practice	GPA for Competition	SAT	ACT Sum
3.550	4.000	400	37
3.525	3.975	410	38
3.500	3.950	420	39
3.475	3.925	430	40
3.450	3.900	440	41
3.425	3.875	450	41
3.400	3.850	460	42
3.375	3.825	470	42
3.350	3.800	480	43
3.325	3.775	490	44
3.300	3.750	500	44
3.275	3.725	510	45
3.250	3.700	520	46
3.225	3.675	530	46
3.200	3.650	540	47
3.175	3.625	550	47
3.150	3.600	560	48
3.125	3.575	570	49
3.100	3.550	580	49
3.075	3.525	590	50
3.050	3.500	600	50
3.025	3.475	610	51
3.000	3.450	620	52
2.975	3.425	630	52
2.950	3.400	640	53
2.925	3.375	650	53
2.900	3.350	660	54
2.875	3.325	670	55
2.850	3.300	680	56
2.825	3.275	690	56
2.800	3.250	700	57
2.775	3.225	710	58
2.750	3.200	720	59
2.725	3.175	730	60
2.700	3.150	740	61
2.675	3.125	750	61
2.650	3.100	760	62
2.625	3.075	770	63
2.600	3.050	780	64
2.575	3.025	790	65
2.550	3.000	800	66
2.525	2.975	810	67
2.500	2.950	820	68
2.475	2.925	830	69
2.450	2.900	840	70
2.425	2.875	850	70
2.400	2.850	860	71
2.375	2.825	870	72
2.350	2.800	880	73
2.325	2.775	890	74
2.300	2.750	900	75
2.275	2.725	910	76
2.250	2.700	920	77
2.225	2.675	930	78
2.200	2.650	940	79
2.175	2.625	950	80
2.150	2.600	960	81
2.125	2.575	970	82
2.100	2.550	980	83
2.075	2.525	990	84
2.050	2.500	1000	85
2.025	2.475	1010	86
2.000	2.450	1020	86
	2.425	1030	87
	2.400	1040	88
	2.375	1050	89
	2.350	1060	90
	2.325	1070	91
	2.300	1080	93

Chart #2. Division I Sliding Scale Beginning 8/1/15

Division I Worksheet

This worksheet is provided to assist you in monitoring your progress in meeting NCAA initial-eligibility standards. The NCAA Eligibility Center will determine your official status after you graduate. Remember to check your high school's list of NCAA courses for the classes you have taken. Use the following scale:

A = 4 quality points; B = 3 Quality points; C = 2 quality points; D = 1 quality point.

English (4 years required)

Course Title	Credit	X	Grade	=	Quality Points (multiply credit by grade)
Example: English 9	.5		A		(.5 x 4) = 2
Total English Units					**Total Quality Points**

Mathematics (3 years required)

Course Title	Credit	X	Grade	=	Quality Points (multiply credit by grade)
Example: Algebra 1	1.0		B		(1.0 x 3) = 3
Total Mathematics Units					**Total Quality Points**

Natural/physical science (2 years required)

Course Title	Credit	X	Grade	=	Quality Points (multiply credit by grade)
Total Natural/Physical Science Units					**Total Quality Points**

Additional year in English, mathematics or natural/physical science (1 year required)

Course Title	Credit	X	Grade	=	Quality Points (multiply credit by grade)
Total Additional Units					**Total Quality Points**

Social science (2 years required)

Course Title	Credit	X	Grade	=	Quality Points (multiply credit by grade)
Total Social Science Units					**Total Quality Points**

Additional academic courses (4 years required)

Course Title	Credit	X	Grade	=	Quality Points (multiply credit by grade)
Total Additional Academic Units					**Total Quality Points**

Core-Course GPA (16 required)

Total Quality Points	Total Number of Credits	Core-Course GPA (Total Quality Points/Total Credits)

Chart #3. Division I Worksheet

Division II Worksheet

This worksheet is provided to assist you in monitoring your progress in meeting NCAA initial-eligibility standards. The NCAA Eligibility Center will determine your official status after you graduate. Remember to check your high school's list of NCAA courses for the classes you have taken. Use the following scale:

A = 4 quality points; B = 3 Quality points; C = 2 quality points; D = 1 quality point.

English (3 years required)

Course Title	Credit	X	Grade	=	Quality Points (multiply credit by grade)
Example: English 9	.5		A		(.5 x 4) = 2

Total English Units   **Total Quality Points**

Mathematics (2 years required)

Course Title	Credit	X	Grade	=	Quality Points (multiply credit by grade)
Example: Algebra 1	1.0		B		(1.0 x 3) = 3

Total Mathematics Units   **Total Quality Points**

Natural/physical science (2 years required)

Course Title	Credit	X	Grade	=	Quality Points (multiply credit by grade)

Total Natural/Physical Science Units   **Total Quality Points**

Additional years in English, math or natural/physical science (2 years required; 3 years required Aug. 1, 2013, and after)

Course Title	Credit	X	Grade	=	Quality Points (multiply credit by grade)

Total Additional Units   **Total Quality Points**

Social science (2 years required)

Course Title	Credit	X	Grade	=	Quality Points (multiply credit by grade)

Total Social Science Units   **Total Quality Points**

Additional academic courses (3 years required; 4 years required Aug. 1, 2013, and after)

Course Title	Credit	X	Grade	=	Quality Points (multiply credit by grade)

Total Additional Academic Units   **Total Quality Points**

Core-Course GPA (14 required; 16 required for students enrolling on or after Aug. 1, 2013)

Total Quality Points	Total Number of Credits	Core-Course GPA (Total Quality Points/Total Credits)

Chart #4. Division II Worksheet

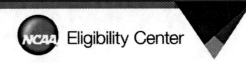

Divisions I and II Initial-Eligibility Requirements

Core Courses

- **NCAA Division I requires 16 core courses**. **NCAA Division II currently requires 14 core courses**. Division II will require 16 core courses for students enrolling on or after August 1, 2013. See the charts below.
- **NCAA Division I will require 10 core courses** to be completed **prior to the seventh semester** (seven of the 10 must be a combination of English, math or natural or physical science that meet the distribution requirements below). These 10 courses become "locked in" at the seventh semester and cannot be retaken for grade improvement.
  - *Beginning August 1, 2015, it will be possible for a Division I college-bound student-athlete to still receive athletics aid and the ability to practice with the team if he or she fails to meet the 10 course requirement, but would not be able to compete.*

Test Scores

- **Division I** uses a sliding scale to match test scores and core grade-point averages (GPA). The sliding scale for those requirements is shown on Page No. 2 of this sheet.
- **Division II** requires a minimum SAT score of 820 or an ACT sum score of 68.
- The SAT score used for NCAA purposes includes **only** the critical reading and math sections. The writing section of the SAT is not used.
- The ACT score used for NCAA purposes is a **sum** of the following four sections: English, mathematics, reading and science.
- **When you register for the SAT or ACT, use the NCAA Eligibility Center code of 9999 to ensure all SAT and ACT scores are reported directly to the NCAA Eligibility Center from the testing agency. Test scores that appear on transcripts will not be used.**

Grade-Point Average

- **Be sure** to look at your high school's List of NCAA Courses on the NCAA Eligibility Center's website (www.eligibilitycenter.org). Only courses that appear on your school's List of NCAA Courses will be used in the calculation of the core GPA. Use the list as a guide.
- **Division I** students enrolling full time **before August 1, 2015,** should use Sliding Scale A to determine eligibility to receive athletics aid, practice and competition during the first year.
- **Division I** GPA required to receive athletics aid and practice **on or after August 1, 2015,** is 2.000 (corresponding test-score requirements are listed on Sliding Scale B on Page No. 2 of this sheet).
- **Division I** GPA required to be eligible for competition **on or after August 1, 2015,** is 2.300 (corresponding test-score requirements are listed on Sliding Scale B on Page No. 2 of this sheet).
- **The Division II** core GPA requirement is a minimum of 2.000.
- Remember, the NCAA GPA is calculated using NCAA core courses only.

DIVISION I 16 Core Courses	DIVISION II 14 Core Courses	DIVISION II 16 Core Courses (2013 and After)
4 years of English.	3 years of English.	3 years of English.
3 years of mathematics (Algebra I or higher).	2 years of mathematics (Algebra I or higher).	2 years of mathematics (Algebra I or higher).
2 years of natural/physical science (1 year of lab if offered by high school).	2 years of natural/physical science (1 year of lab if offered by high school).	2 years of natural/physical science (1 year of lab if offered by high school).
1 year of additional English, mathematics or natural/physical science.	2 years of additional English, mathematics or natural/physical science.	3 years of additional English, mathematics or natural/physical science.
2 years of social science.	2 years of social science.	2 years of social science.
4 years of additional courses (from any area above, foreign language or comparative religion/philosophy).	3 years of additional courses (from any area above, foreign language or comparative religion/philosophy).	4 years of additional courses (from any area above, foreign language or comparative religion/philosophy).

Chart #5. NCAA Eligibility Center Quick Reference Guide

DEFENSIVE PHILOSOPHY: ZONE-DOG CONCEPTS

University of Pittsburgh

I am going to talk about our defensive philosophy and get into how we teach zone-dog concepts. I am going to give you some simple ways to teach zone-dog schemes and the coverages that go with them.

There are three types of coaches in here today. There are prisoners. They are the coaches the head coach mandated them to be here or were pulled here by a friend to accompany him. He cannot go unless you go with him. There is the vacationer. Those are coaches looking for a day out of the office or a night out on the town with the boys. Finally, there is the explorer. Those are coaches that want to learn new ideas and improve as a coach within the program.

When we met with our players the first day as a defensive staff, we said one thing. We told them to "Put the ball down." We want to stop the offense and drive them to the ground. We wanted them in a mindset of defensive play. We want them to play anytime, anywhere, and on any part of the field with the idea of putting the ball down. That is our attitude and how we want our defensive players to think. If there is a sudden change in the game, "Put the ball down." If we are ahead by 50 points, "Put the ball down." We want to score on defense. If there is a critical situation in the fourth quarter, "Put the ball down." We want a 60/12 state of mind. We want to play aggressively, hustle, and have a great desire to play defense. We want that for 60 minutes a game and 12 games in a season. If you want to play at Pittsburgh, you must be a player that lays it on the line.

We expect our players to be on time for everything we do. When they are at practice, we want them to have a "coach me, Coach" attitude. That does not simply mean rolling into the meeting two minutes before the scheduled starts. Being on time does not simply mean beating the clock into the room. It means being there on time, engaged, and prepared. I want them to have a notebook, pen, and their playbook out and ready to go. Part of being on time is being prepared and ready to learn.

I had the good fortune of coaching in the NFL. I told my players it is amazing to walk into one of their meetings. The good ones are in the meeting room early, with unbelievable notes, and have questions prepared from the night before. If the coach gives them a little nugget, they want more.

The players at Pittsburgh must act like champions. That does not mean practice and play like champions. They have to act like champions in everything they do. They have to go to class and sit up front. We want them to do the best they can academically. We are not dumb enough to believe that all your players can be 3.0 students. However, they can act like champions in class. They need the same mentality in the classroom as they bring to the football field. They need to have their books and notebooks ready. If they act like champions in everything they do, that will be their expectations of themselves.

The next thing they must accomplish is to "Do your job." We are a 4-3 gap control defense. When we expect runs, we expect players to be in certain positions. When we call a particular coverage, we expect certain angles to the ball. They have to do their jobs and be where they are supposed to be.

Being tough is hard to define. I look at how the players play when they are fresh and when they are tired. When a player gets tired, what kind of mental lapses is he going to have? If the player is the backside corner, is he still taking the proper angle to get into his area of responsibility? That falls into the category of mental toughness. They must not make mistakes in the secondary. Mental lapses in the secondary convert to points on the scoreboard for the other team.

We do not want the opponent to see any chinks in our armor. We want to play with great effort. We want to play to the 212th degree. That is the boiling point. At the boiling point is the way we practice. We want pursuit to the ball and everyone attacking it. We want to finish off every tackle with a gang mentality.

I have heard coaches say you cannot coach effort. I totally disagree with that. I coach this way. If I see a player make an unbelievable play on pursuit, I copy those frames and put them in a file. When I see the same player loafing on a play, I do the same thing. Then, I bring the player in and show him the two tapes. When a player sees himself on tape, he can evaluate himself. At the end of the day, if he is playing football, he is playing because he loves to play, wants to compete, wants to win, and wants to be coached.

When the player can visually see his effort, that puts the responsibility on him. You are coaching that. You are setting a standard for that player. After you set the standard, you hold him to it.

PITTS BASE DEFENSE

• Attacking 4-3 defense
• Multiple coverages
• Versatile in pressures

We are a 4-3 defense with multiple coverages. We do everything from a split safety look. Quarterbacks are getting better at reading what the defense is doing to disguise coverage. I just said that we show two-deep coverage on every snap. That is not entirely true. On occasion, we show a three-deep look and roll into a two-deep coverage. We want to give the quarterback a lot of different looks but keep it simple for our defensive backs.

We want to be versatile in pressure schemes. We will attack the offense in the run-and-pass games. We are going to be smart with our pressure schemes. We are not calling a pressure so we can run a linebacker or defensive back through a gap. We use the pressure to give the offense a negative play. We want to use that pressure from some offensive tendency based on a particular formation or down and distance.

I want to tell you how we call our front so you will know what I am talking about when I refer to

certain things. In our base front, we are an over front (Diagram #1). That lets us talk about the bubble in the defense. The bubble is the uncovered guard. We make the front call to set the bubble away from the strongside of the set. If there are two tight ends in the game, we set the bubble away from the stud tight end.

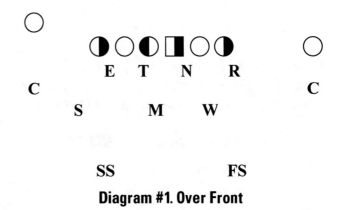

Diagram #1. Over Front

We also run the under front (Diagram #2). That puts the bubble in the defense to the strongside of the offensive set. When we build our zone pressures, we do not want to be predictable. We do not want to come from the bubble side or the three-man side in every situation. We want to have an effective way to mix up what we do to come from both sides. To have multiple blitzes, you need multiple fronts.

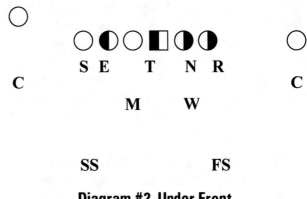

Diagram #2. Under Front

Later, you will hear me talk about the field. It is important for the defense and especially the second- and third-level players to understand field dimensions. One of the first things we ask the defensive backs to know is field dimensions. We quiz them based on that knowledge. It is critical for them to understand how we plan to divide the field in coverage. They have to understand what levels they will play in those areas.

Offenses tell you what they are doing with their splits and receiver locations. Our defensive backs know from the numbers to the sideline, it is 7 yards. They know from the top of the numbers to the sideline, it is 9 yards. They know it is 19 yards from the hash to the sideline. That is critical because it determines how we play receivers in leverage positions.

Many coaches do not see the progression of a zone-dog concept. If you are a quarters coverage team and are not using zone pressures, you are doing yourself a disservice. The same things you can do in quarters coverage can apply to zone dogs.

WHY THE ZONE-DOG CONCEPT

- Two aggressive hats in the run game
- Overload one side in passing game
- Safe
- Well disguised
- Very multiple—keeping it simple

In the zone-dog concept, we get two second-level players in the support on the run. We can overload a side in the passing game. We want to be smart as to what side we overload. We want to base it off the turn of the center in the protection scheme. It is a safe way to bring pressure and not give up a home run. The defenders play with a zone mentality. That does not mean they play with zone eyes but a zone mentality. They pass off pick routes and communicate exchanges but have a deep post safety. This is a well-disguised scheme. Once you get your base concept installed, you can be multiple in changing the pressure but keeping the same zone concepts.

The first thing you want to do when you design your package is to be quick in your alignment. In the NFL, because of the hash marks, they base everything on the middle of the field. In college, we can base our landmarks on the hash marks as well as the middle of the field. In the NFL, you call everything as an over or under look based on receiver locations. In college, we have an advantage because we can pressure and align the defense from the start. The shifting, motioning, or personnel displacement does not effective us because we are aligned based on the field or the boundary.

The first thing I want to talk about in this scheme is the coverage. We are a match, carry, and deliver team when we start talking about pressure. That means we match receivers in the coverage. That means we cover them in a man-to-man type of technique. We carry the receivers if they go vertical, and we deliver a receiver to the next defender if he runs a crossing route.

I had the opportunity to work for Steve Spagnuolo. He had a great analogy talking about zone pressures. He said, "All you do is roll out the basketball and tell the players to play three-on-three." The players will talk, communicate, and switch on the picks. We do the same thing in zone-dog coverage. We have three players in our underneath coverage.

When we count receivers, we count from strength to weakness (Diagram #3). In a 2x2 set, the outside receiver to the fieldside is the #1 receiver. The slot receiver to that side is the #2 receiver. The back in the backfield is the #3 receiver. The slot to the boundary is the #4 receiver, and the wide receiver to the boundary is the #5 receiver.

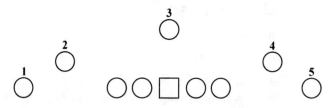

Diagram #3. Receiver Count

We have two hot players. They are seam/flat players that play match, carry, and deliver. They relate to the #2 and #4 receivers. We have a player we call the "final 3 player." He relates to the final #3 receiver. The final 3 player guides the ship when we start talking about the match-ups. He is the communicator. He is an inside linebacker—generally, the Mike linebacker. The seam/flat players will not see what goes on with the final 3 player. This is where the communication has to be good. They have to get the word from the final 3 player.

The next players in the scheme are the zone-dog third players. These players are not true cover 3 corners. They have a three-deep mentality, but they are not true deep zone cover players. They match the #1 receivers. For any upfield or outbreaking route, they are responsible for that move. They are man-to-man on those patterns. If the receiver runs a five-yard quick out, they cover it. Any inside breaking pattern, such as a shallow cross pattern, they match and carry the pattern until they can pass it off to another defender. We teach them to never pass coverage to a defensive lineman unless he calls him off. That means he tells them he has the receiver.

The middle field post player also has rules. If the formation is a 2x2 with multiple vertical threats, he plays in between the vertical routes. He reacts to the directional and delivery key of the quarterback. The directional key is the shoulders of the quarterback and the deliver key is the long arm of the quarterback. That means that one hand comes off the ball and the arm extends. In relationship to the shoulders of the quarterback, we talk about low shoulders mean short throws. If the shoulders are high, it will be a long throw.

If the formation is a 3x1, the final 3 player is primarily in the box (Diagram #4). He has to key the run first before he can react to the pass. We leave the post/safety on the #3 receiver. If the #3 receiver runs vertical, the post/safety takes him deep. The hot players are no different from the corners. They match any upfield or out patterns by their receivers. There are some gray areas in this coverage in relation to communication.

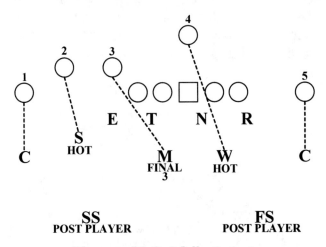

Diagram #4. 3x1 Adjustment

When you teach the seam/flat player, he has a degree of communication to understand. As he carries his receiver up the field and the receiver breaks to the post, we let the seam/flat player zone off in that area. However, there can be no other vertical pattern going up the field. If the #3 receiver is running vertical, he has to take the #2 receiver on a vertical pattern or one going to the post. On the underneath route, he flattens the route and carries it to the next underneath defender if there is one. If the next defender does not call him off, he carries the receiver across the field.

The final 3 player matches the pattern of the #3 receiver until there is an exchange to another player. He tries to carry the #3 receiver 12 yards to the post/safety player. To be honest with you, so much of that statement is clinic talk.

The final 3 player is a box player and has a run responsibility. The #3 receiver in this set is often the hot receiver. After the linebacker clears his run/pass key, he has to run a line and undercut the receiver. If the #3 receiver runs an under route, the final 3 defender flattens the route and carries it until he can pass him to the next defender. If there is no next defender, he matches the route and runs with him.

If I were a high school coach with limited time to teach, I would teach this concept in a half-line setting. That lets you concentrate on the concepts with three defenders working together. This builds the communication skills into your defenders. If the #2 receiver breaks inside, the hot players carry him and the final 3 player picks him up. The final 3 player yells "I got 'em, I got 'em, I got 'em" to the hot defender.

You will see our corners in press coverage on the #1 receivers. Their coverage is man-to-man on any vertical or outbreaking route. If the #1 receiver runs an inbreaking route, the corner carries him to the next defender and zones back. If the #1 receiver and the #2 receiver run a corner/China route, we match and deliver those routes. If the #1 receiver stemmed inside and back to the corner, the hot defender on the #2 receiver ends up taking the corner by the #1 receiver and the corner takes the China route of the #2 receiver coming to the outside.

In the 3x1 formation, the #4 receiver is in the backfield. The backside linebacker is responsible for the coverage. If he blocks, we want the linebacker to drop to the middle of the field in the underneath zone. He can help on the #3 receiver and possibly steal something with the quarterback not looking for him.

Against a bunch formation, we make a zoner call. That is one time the corner is a true deep-third corner. On the zoner call, the corner plays the upfield read. Whichever receiver broke upfield, the corner plays that route. The seam/flat defender plays off the #2 receiver, but he matches the first pattern run to the flat. The final 3 defender matches the final 3 receiver.

I have a coaching point for the dropping linemen. If they have coverage on the #4 receiver in a 3x1 formation, they must understand the progression. They are in coverage to the side of the pressure. The #4 receiver has a blitz coming in his face. He will not release on a pattern. The linemen want to run the line and try to steal the hot route from the #5 receiver. The quarterback reads the Will linebacker coming on the blitz and releases the ball to the #5 receiver on a hitch or quick slant. If the defensive lineman runs the line under that receiver, the quarterback may throw him the ball.

We want to leverage the #2 receiver with outside leverage. If the nickel back aligns inside the #2 receiver, on the snap of the ball, he works for outside leverage. If we roll the safety down on the #2 receiver, he comes down on the outside. We want to be in a low-hip position. If we have high outside leverage and the receiver runs an out cut, the defensive back is beat. We want to be on the low hip, which gives us leverage on outside breaking routes. He has help from the post safety to the inside, but he has no help to the outside.

Philosophically, I do not believe you can play the #2 receiver with inside leverage and ask the corner to play man coverage. If we talk about a tight end, we may get away with that type of leverage. However, with a #2 detached receiver, there is too much talent and speed to do that.

In our defensive alignment, the Sam linebacker is a field player. The strong safety travels with the Sam linebacker. On field south, we set the bubble to the field (Diagram #5). On this stunt, we bring the Sam linebacker off the edge from the field. The 5 technique defensive end runs a long stick to the guard. He reads the color as he goes. If the guard comes to him, he plays across the guard's face and into the A gap. If the color goes away, the 5 technique flattens and gets on the hip of the guard

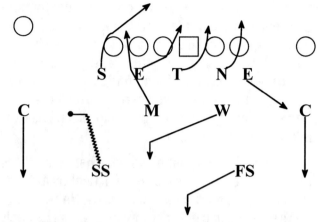

Diagram #5. Field South

and chases the run down the line. He becomes the cutback player from the outside in.

This is a 93 blue call for the defense. That tells us we are in three-deep coverage with the strong safety rolled down to the tight end side.

The next example is to bring the blitz from the boundary. You must be able to blitz off both sides of the defense. This is a field defense with the bubble to the field and a corner blitz off the boundary. We call this crush (Diagram #6). The call brings the free safety to the boundary side of the defense. The corner is coming and the field 5 technique end is dropping. If the offense has a 2x2 set, we are not going to ask the defensive end to drop on the slot receiver and match his pattern. The Will linebacker gives a hook call to the defensive end. The Will linebacker walks out and takes the #4 receiver and the drop end drops into the hook zone and plays off the #3 receiver.

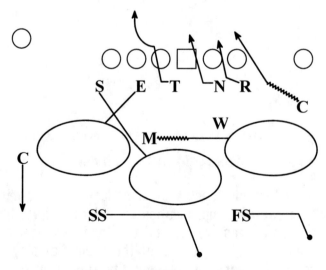

Diagram #6. Field Crush

The defensive end needs to know where the pressure is coming from so he can play his progression. He knows he drops away from the pressure. As a base rule, the end knows he is dropping for the seam/flat off the #4 receiver. He has to identify where the #4 receiver lines up. He has to know if he is in the backfield or offset strong. If the #4 receiver is not in the backfield, he has to listen for the hook call. When he gets that call, he knows someone on the second level is taking the #4 receiver and he is playing off the #3 receiver.

Once we teach the concept, we can become multiple and keep it simple for the players. We can double-call the zone blitz. The huddle call can be field-south-crush. When we do our game planning, we want to know what the offensive players will do. If they put the tight end into the boundary, they are a big toss and stretch team into the boundary. If they put the tight end to the field, they become a power team to the field. Against a team that does that, we want to bring pressure from the tight end side. We want to align the defense simple and fast but at the same time not give the drop end too much field to cover.

We make the defensive call in to the fieldside. If the wideside of the field is to the left, the linebacker makes the left. That tells us the bubble is to the field and we are in an under front. That puts the drop end into the boundary. We set the bubble to the field in our field defense. From there, we listen for the slant call; that call is lucky Ringo. If the tight end comes out and aligns to the right, the linebackers call Ringo. If we get a Ringo call, the line slants left. If we get the lucky call, the line slants to the right. The defensive end away from the call knows he is in the drop system.

The secondary knows they drop to back up the blitz pressure. If the tight end is to the field, the strong safety drops down and the free safety is into the middle. With the double call, where ever the tight end aligns, we run the zone pressure. If he aligns into the field, we run the field south. If he aligns into the boundary, we run field crush.

Against a spread team, we like to align in a split front defense (Diagram #7). That means our alignment is a two-3-technique alignment with the nose and defensive tackle. That does not tip our hand as to where we bring the blitz. The defensive

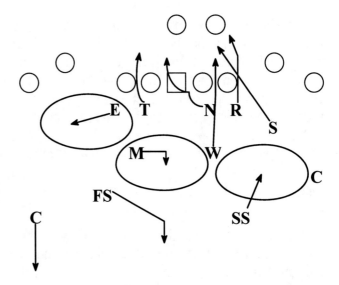

Diagram #7. Boundary Overload

end to the side of the call is an edge rusher, and he jets up the field and boxes everything back. The interior lineman to the running back aligns in a 3 technique alignment and stunts into the A gap to the opposite A gap. The interior lineman to the field aligns in a 3 technique and presses through the B gap and is the contain player to that side. We bring four rushers off the side to the running back and overload him.

The back is to the left of the quarterback. The linebacker makes a lucky call. The defensive line slants to the right. The left defensive end is away from the call and drops using his drop progression technique for his coverage. The safeties know we are bringing pressure to the side of the back and drop in that direction. We anticipate that the slide of the protection will be away from the running back. The Will linebacker mugs the A gap to force the center to give us the slide protection we want.

The defensive end to that side jets up the field to draw the offensive tackle up the field. The coaching point for the nose is not to get in a hurry. He works the A gap to the opposite A gap. He wants to threaten the A gap and not cross the face of the center too quickly. If he goes too quick, the center will turn back on the pressure. The nose wants to hold the center's block and cross face with the block. The linebacker or nickel back runs the heel line of the end jetting up the field. The Will linebacker blitzes the B gap. The blitz runners must know how to fit on the running back.

The inside blitzer comes underneath all blocks. If we guess wrong on the slide and the guard slides to the Will linebacker, he tries to work across his face. A coaching point for the inside blitzer is when the back attempts to block him. The Will linebacker wants to take the back into the quarterback. That eliminates the screen to him. If the back steps to the Will linebacker, he does not try to avoid him. He attacks him because he knows the outside blitzer will be free. The outside blitzer comes outside all blockers.

Once we declare the safeties down, they do not spin back if the formation changes due to motion. If the offense motions, we adjust with the linebackers. They walk out on the motion and give the drop end the hook call. That keeps the linebacker on the slot receiver and lets the defensive end drop into the hook area.

In our scheme, we press the corners in our normal alignment. When we want to bring the corners off the edge, they do not show. That is their normal alignment. The offense cannot see them coming. There is one thing we have to make our players understand: they should not be surprised if the offense turns them loose. That is particularly true for down linemen. When the linebackers start to mug and threaten gaps, sometimes the communication between offensive linemen is lost. The linebacker mugging the gaps creates confusion for the offensive linemen. Many times, the defenders turned loose are the 3 technique defenders. If the 3 technique comes free, he runs through the quarterback.

The last thing I want to show you is an adjustment to the empty formation. We do not drop a lineman in the drop system. We align in the split front and all the down linemen rush (Diagram #8). The interior down defenders, regardless of where they have aligned, they blitzed the A gaps. In the split front, they cheated into a head-up position and come inside. The defensive end aligns in the 5 technique and pinches off the offensive tackle's butt to the inside shoulder of the quarterback. We do not worry about rushing to the upfield shoulder. If the quarterback breaks containment, we run him out of what he was going to do anyway.

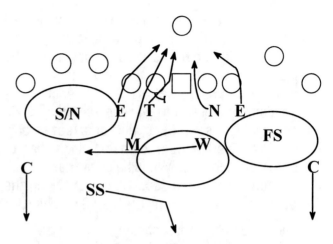

Diagram #8. Empty Set

The ball is going to come out quickly. If the ends charge up the field for two steps, they are not going to get to the quarterback. We want them coming tight off the offensive tackle's butt at a sharp angle to the quarterback. We called that technique knife.

In the secondary, the coverage is 94 coverage. That rolls the free safety down as a seam/flat defender working to the #4 receiver. The corners bail out and play outside third coverage. The Sam/nickel back has inside leverage on the #2 receiver. However, he works for outside leverage on the snap of the ball. The Mike and Will linebackers mug back and forth in their B gaps. They read the guard's slide. If the guard goes down on the A gap defender, the linebacker blitzes. If the guard turns to the linebacker, the linebacker runs a line for the #3 receiver aligned on the #3 side.

We went from the two-deep concept to the three-deep concept because the bubble screen was killing us. This coverage puts stress on the post defender, but the ball is coming out fast. They cannot hold the ball. If they do, we sack the quarterback.

The other thing we did against the empty set was to drop the tackle into the low hole in the middle of the defense. Everything else stayed the same, and we dropped the tackle into the middle short zone.

I appreciate your attention, especially this early in the day. Thank you very much.

DEFENSIVE LINE DRILLS AND TECHNIQUES

University of Louisville

I appreciate you being here and allowing me the opportunity to speak with you. My topic is defensive fundamentals and drills for defensive line play. I came to this clinic last year, and our defensive coordinator, Coach Bedford, spoke on what we like to do defensively. I thought this year I would talk about fundamentals. I also want to share some thoughts about how we develop the new players on our team.

When the freshmen get on campus, I start instructing them about what I want them to learn. We start with fundamentals. I want to show you some drills we use to develop our young players. The first thing I want to talk about is the stance.

The biggest thing I see when freshmen come to our campus is that 96 percent of them want to get in a right-handed stance. The biggest issue we have at Louisville is we designate a 3 technique defender. We do not play left and right 3 technique players. Our 3 technique players align on both sides of the ball. I tell all our defensive linemen, if they can get into a left-handed stance and play comfortably, they stand a better chance of getting on the field. Working on the stance early gives them a better chance to play.

You start with the feet in the stance. We want them to get their feet at shoulder-width apart. If they play the 3 or 1 technique positions inside, they may be slightly wider. We want them to have a good base. When we first put them down, we want them to get all their cleats in the ground. For a right-handed stance, the stagger is with the right foot back. We want the right toe aligned on the left heel in the stagger stance. That amounts to about six to eight inches in the stagger.

We want to squat and bend the knees with the elbows on the knees. We want to roll the shoulders forward and get a flat back. They take their right hand and drop it to the ground in front of their face. We want 50 percent of the weight on the down hand. That puts the weight forward in the stance. If we are in a definite passing situation, we can alter the stance. The base narrows, and we get more weight on the hand.

The off-hand placement is important to me. Some coaches teach resting the hand on the thigh board or keeping it back. I do not like that. I want the hand up and under the chin and facemask. I want it there because as soon as the offense snaps the ball, the hands come straight out in the punch on the offensive lineman.

We have to make some adjustments in the stance. Some coaches want their players to get all the cleats in the ground and be in a flat-footed stance. I do not overstress that point. Doing that has a lot to do with the player's flexibility in his hips and lower body. You may be asking the player to do something that keeps him from being a functional football player. When we put the amount of weight on the hand that I want, we may have the heels off the ground.

We are not going to play on the line of scrimmage. We play across the line of scrimmage and reestablish the line in the backfield. When we get in the left-handed stance, we progress the same way we did in the right-handed stance except it is opposite. We start by dropping the left foot back in the stagger and go from there

The important thing to remember about the stance is we do not want it to change. It does not matter if we are in an over or under front. In our defense, we stem the linemen up and down the line of scrimmage. We do not change the stance because we shift our position. I do not want to give the offensive linemen any pre-snap tips as to when we are going to move and when we are not. Too many times, when a player is going to move, he does something with his off hand to tip the fact that he is going to move.

FIVE KEYS TO DOMINANCE IN DEFENSIVE LINE PLAY

• Eyes
• Get-off
• Feet and hands
• Leverage
• Shed the block

I have five things that I believe in as far as the defensive line. The first thing is eyes. If a player is not disciplined with his eyes and does not know what he is seeing, how can he play? On first and second down, I want the players' eyes focused on the V of the offensive lineman's neck. It does not matter what technique the defender plays or where he aligns, I want the eyes focused on the V of his neck.

The second thing a defensive lineman must have is get-off. That is the biggest advantage we have with our defensive linemen. The defensive lineman has to use his quickness, athleticism, and explosion to his advantage to get off the ball. You have to stress that with your players. In most cases, they have that advantage over the offensive linemen.

The next thing is feet and hands. I tie those two things together. You will not have a player who plays with good feet if he does not have violent hands. When the lineman shoots the hands, the feet will follow. If you watch a great boxer, as he throws a punch, he steps into it with his feet. When the hands move, the feet follow.

After that, the next point is leverage. The defensive lineman must play with great pad level. Pad level is essential whether you are on the move or in a stationary position.

The last element for great defensive line play has become a lost art. That element is shedding blocks. Shedding blocks is monumental in the running game. The defensive player will never get to the passer unless he can shed a block.

I want to get into some of our drill work. Our practice field has lines all over the place for the drills we do. When we go to practice, we do not want to spend time organizing or setting up a drill. We want to get maximum reps in every drill we do. The lines are good guidelines for players to line up on so you can start the drill.

We start this drill with an offensive and defensive player on his knees. When we start the drill, we always start with a shade technique on the offensive player. We play that way on defense. We are a 4-3 defense. When we play defense, we play half a man. We do not take on the entire surface of an offensive blocker. We want to play half the man. If you draw a line down the middle of the offensive lineman, we want to play on one side of that line or the other.

This is a hand placement drill (Diagram #1). The defender is in a six-point stance. His hands, knees, and toes are in contact with the ground. The offensive lineman is on his knees. We work the drill off the whistle. On the whistle, the defender comes from the ground with his hands and punches the offensive man in the breastplate. As he contacts the breastplate, he grabs cloth with his hands. The outside hand in the shade technique is grabbing cloth on the outside tip of the shoulder pad.

Diagram #1. Hand Placement Drill

We are not trying to deliver a devastating punch. We do not worry about rolling the hips into the punch. This is a hand placement drill. We learn where the hands should go and what the target is. After we do three reps from the left shade position, they move to the middle. We do the same thing. When the defender punches the offensive man, I want the thumbs up. From the middle position, I want the fingertips in the armpit of the offensive man.

After we do three reps from the middle position, we move to the right shade on the offensive man. We repeat the drill with three more reps. Hand placement is something we do every day. We do it in the off-season, spring, pre-practice, and fall practice. Shooting the hand and hand placement to the player is like brushing his teeth in the morning.

If the player shoots his hands with the thumbs down, he may grab the jersey, but he has no control. When he locks out, tries to disengage or shed the blocker, but he cannot do it because he has no control. The defender has to manipulate the blocker, and the only way to do that is to have the thumbs up.

The next drill we do is six-point explosion. When we do a contact drill or an explosion drill, we use a ball stick, which is a football attached to a broomstick. If you do not have one, get one. Do not let your players react to a verbal sound. We want to react to the movement of the ball. I have a problem with that in drills. I have to correct myself all the time to use the ball and not a whistle or a voice command. If you use a cadence in practice, your players will start to have issues about jumping offside. Make them react to the movement of the ball.

When we do a six-point explosion, the first thing I watch is a cocking of the elbows. We work the explosion drill like the hand placement drill with an offensive and defensive player (Diagram #2). If the elbows come back before the punch, that is an error. We want the hands coming from the grass straight into the breastplate of the offensive man. The quicker the defender can get hand placement inside the offensive lineman's hand, the quicker he can lock out and disengage from the blocker.

EXPLOSION HAND PLACEMENT

HIPS ROLL TO GROUND

Diagram #2. Explosion Drill

The second thing I look for is the hip roll. I want the hips to roll forward. The hands shoot upward into the breastplate as the hips roll forward. The head is up, and the eyes are on the target. When we do the explosion drill, I want to see the hips roll and the back arch. I describe the movement as putting the hips in the dirt. As the player extends into the offensive man, the hips should end up on the ground.

When we teach the defensive lineman, you want to keep everything in a progression. We work the hand placement drills and explosion drills from the six-point. The next progression is to get them into their stance and work on their power steps. You have to start from the ground up and teach them how everything works together. When we work the power step, we work from the right- and left-handed stances. The power step is the first step coming off the ball. When the defensive lineman comes off the ball, his power step has to be in the ground before he engages the blocker.

The second step should be simultaneous with the contact. In the power step, the big question is to gauge how far to step. The best way to describe the power step coming from a right-handed stance is to step into a left-handed stance. The feet of the defensive player taking a power step from a right-handed stance should look like he lined up in a left-handed stance. Whether that step is four, six, or eight inches is up to each individual coach. I want the step to look like the player went from one stance to the other in the first step.

The thing I watch is the amount of time the foot is in the air. He may take a six-inch step, but it has to get to the ground quickly. If he does not master that movement, when you play zone teams, he will get his shoulders turned or cut down. The same thing is true of the second step. He has to get in the ground immediately. A player taking on a blocker with one foot in the air gets turned and blocked.

When the defensive lineman makes contact, we want the back flat. If I watch the drill from the rear, I do not want to see the jersey number. I want a flat back in the contact zone. Even when we play a double-team block, it is essential that the defender play with his shoulders square.

Question: What do you tell your players on the double-team block?

The first thing the player has to do is recognize the tips that the double-team block is coming. He looks at the splits of the blockers. In a normal alignment, their split is two feet. If the split reduces to one foot, he should suspect they are going to double-team him. When we get the double-team block, we want to focus on one blocker first. He has to attack one blocker, stay square, and get extension with his punch. If he gets extension and lockout, he can create air between the blockers so he can split it.

If the 3 technique defender notices the split between the offensive guard and tackle reduce, he knows what is coming. His focus is on the V in the neck of the guard. He is not concerned with the tackle. He has to attack the guard and move him to the second level. The defender has to reestablish the line of scrimmage on their side of the ball. If he stays on the line of scrimmage and the blockers stay even, 80 percent of the time he loses and gets blocked.

If the defender can reestablish the line of scrimmage, he can play the block. Even if the tackle comes down on him, he has to stay square. He stays in the crease of the blocks and fights pressure to the outside. If there is no daylight between the blockers, the defender stays in the double-team and fights the pressure. He does not try to swim or rip to escape. He stays in the block because the tackle has to get to the second level and block a linebacker. When that occurs, there is daylight and the defender works for an escape.

Question: What do you do if that player is losing ground and not reestablishing the line of scrimmage?

We use smoke and mirrors and get him right to the middle of the sidelines. This year, we had so many injuries at the defensive tackle position; I had to play an undersized player at the 3 technique position. He was 250 pounds and got overwhelmed on occasion. I taught him to grab the offensive tackle, get to the ground, and create a pile. I taught that technique for him. and I do not teach that technique with anyone else. If I have a 3 technique defender being blown up, I have to do a better job of recruiting. If that happens too often, he cannot play for us.

The next thing I want to talk about is three-step movement. This is a big part of what we do defensively. The three-step movement is a gap exchange move. This is a B-gap defender moving to the A-gap responsibility. The first step is the most important. Too many players today do not understand how to step in a lateral direction.

I had to change my coaching style with this technique. When I was at the University of Miami,

we stepped with a 45-degree angle step to execute the gap exchange. However, we had issues with defenders getting cut out of their gaps and not getting where they were supposed to be. The offensive and defensive linemen each take their first step. If the offensive lineman steps with a 45-degree angle and the defensive lineman steps at a 45-degree angle, the defensive lineman has a good chance of getting cut out of his gap.

We want to make sure we fit the front up in the run game. I want the first step in gap exchange to be a lateral step. That way, the defender makes sure he clears the helmet and shoulder pads of the offensive block and gets to where he need to get.

The first step is a lateral step. That step moves the defender into his gap responsibility. The second step gains ground into the new gap. The third step brings the body and shoulders back to balance and a square position. We teach two different techniques to use in the gap exchange.

The University of Connecticut does a good job of handling what we do. The coaches at U. Conn do a great job of coaching their linemen to handle movement. When we play them, we have to stay nice and square with our hands. We have to play hat and hands, use the gap exchange and play football after that. We play teams that are aggressive up front but do not handle movement well. Against those teams, we can slap wrist on the movement and go for penetration. Our players can use either technique they choose. They have options.

You have to give your players options to change up the technique they are using. It keeps them from getting frustrated. If what you taught them in practice is not working, they have an option they can use.

We teach the defender to refocus with his eyes. For a 3 technique defender, if he plays a straight technique, the focus of his eyes is the V in the neck of the guard. If he has to gap exchange inside, his eyes have to focus on the near foot of the center (Diagram #3). If the near foot comes at the defender, on his second step he has to get vertical through the gap. If he does not, the center will reach him, and he is overrun. If that happens, we lose a gap.

If the near foot of the center goes away, the second step of the defender is flat (Diagram #4).

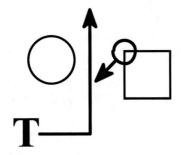

Diagram #3. Key the Foot

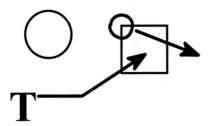

Diagram #4. Foot Away

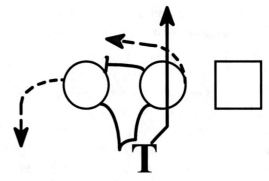

Diagram #5. Power Slip

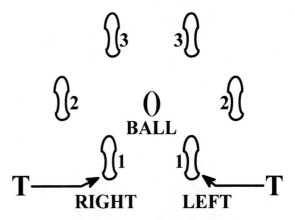

Diagram #6. Three-Step Drill

The center is working away from him to the other side, and the defender wants to pursue the ball down the line. We do not change our alignment with the three-step movement. We do not change our stance when we change position, and we do not change our stance when we move. We do not want to change or cheat the alignment to give the blocker a clue where we are going.

When the near foot of the center goes away, the 3 technique defender knows there is a scoop block from his outside. He is not trying to get into the A gap. He gets his hands on the inside and runs off the butt of the center.

If the 3 technique defender faces a power slip block between the offensive guard and tackle, I expect him to beat the guard on an inside movement play (Diagram #5). If they run the stretch play, and the 3 technique has an inside move, he does not penetrate the gap. The guard bucket-steps on the stretch play, the 3 technique makes the inside move, flattens, and runs down his gap to the outside.

When we do the three-step drill, I start them out in a right-handed stance (Diagram #6). The first movement is a right step to the right side. I move the ball, and he performs his three-step movement to the right. I turn the drill around, put them in a left-handed stance, and call left-step-left. During

this drill, I want the players to step and keep their shoulders square as they go.

In our stance, we want our inside hand down to the ball. The left 3 technique defender is in a right-handed stance. There are times we play an inside "i" technique. An example is a 7 technique or 6i technique on the tight end or a 2i technique on the guard. The 7 technique and 6i technique is the same alignment for us. That is the next set of steps we take in the three-step drill. From the right-handed stance, we call left-step-right. You have to work the footwork out of all alignments. When you do the three-step movement from in these alignments, it becomes unorthodox. You are stepping away from your down hand.

The thing that helps the defender to make that move is to reduce the stagger in the stance. We do not want to take it out completely because that changes the stance, which becomes a tip for the offensive blocker. He has to reduce the stagger, but it cannot be something so noticeable that it causes an issue later on.

There are situational times in a game, which changes the hat and hands techniques to penetration moves. If it is third-and-8 to -10 for the first down, we want to come with speed and pressure.

We call the next drill "sumo" drill (Diagram #7). This is a fit-up drill. We put the offensive and defensive players in a fitted position. I start the drill with a whistle. The offensive blocker gives pressure to one shoulder of the defender. The defender works against the pressure to get his leverage back. The offensive blocker, at sometime during the drill, flips to the other shoulder and puts pressure there.

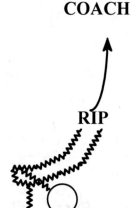

Diagram #7. Sumo Drill

The defender has to shift from one side and start to work the other way. The sumo drill teaches the defender how to fight pressure. There are situations in a game, where the defender gets off the ball late. He is late off the ball, and his helmet is on the wrong side of the blocker. He does not need to panic. The defender has to work vertically up the field and not side-to-side. When we reestablish the line of scrimmage, we force the ball back inside, and it gives the defensive linemen a chance to fall back inside and make a play on the ball.

What the offensive and defensive players do in the drill resembles a sumo-wrestling match. If the 3 technique defender is late coming off the ball and the offensive guard gets his hat to the outside armpit, the defender cannot panic. He cannot give up the position, run around the block, and try to get back outside. The defensive man wants to work vertically and against the pressure of the offensive blocker. He can work back to his gap by working

against the pressure. On the second whistle, the defender has to disengage and shed the blocker using some kind of escape move.

In defensive line play, we work with the same arm and same leg in everything we do. When you rush the passer or play the run game, the same arm and leg must tie together. When the defender feels the pressure, he has to lock out his arm to that side. He uses a push/pull move to torque the pads of the offensive block so he can get to where he needs to go. When the defender locks out with his arm, he has to bring the near leg with him so he can get his hip through passed the blocker.

When we shed, we want to use a violent pull on the offensive blocker's shoulder. We want to pull so hard he feels he is going to pull the offensive player's shoulder out of the socket. We want to punch out on the release or rip through. The key to the shed is the position of the hips. The defender's hips must clear the hips of the blocker. If the hips are clear of the blocker, they turn to the inside. That way, the defender can shed and go make a play. If the hips are not clear, when the defender makes his shed move, the offense blocker recaptures his block.

When the defender is fighting in a drill, he has to keep his elbows tucked inside and not let them flare. In these drills, we want to teach our players to play upfield. We do not want to play at the line of scrimmage. We want to reestablish the line of scrimmage on their side of the ball. In the shed drill, we work on block escapes. We work on punch-and-rip moves. The coaching point in this drill is to watch the player's body position. We do not want the defender to hop or turn his butt to the sideline when he tries to shed. The emphasis in the shed drill is extension, pull, punch, and escape.

We talk about staying square on the blocker, but you do not want to overemphasize it. The thing you should keep reminding them is not to get their butts turned to the sideline. Players are so worried about the reach block, they run outside and get their rear end turned. If the defender does not turn his rear to the sideline or expand running lanes or creases in the defense, he will be okay.

We base the escape techniques we use off the skills of our players. If I have a 6'1" defensive tackle,

I will not be happy if he tries to do many swim moves. He is built low to the ground and should stay underneath people's pads. That is his natural leverage. We fit the escape moves to what fits the physical size of the player.

When I first came to Louisville, we had a lot of teaching to do. After the first spring practice, Coach Bedford and I were not sure we would win a game. However, we stayed with the same drill each day and repetitively did the same thing. If you use a drill that is different but teaches the same thing, you can use it as a change-up. The secret is to rep your drill repeatedly. Eventually, the players will get it and figure it out. When they start to have success and buy into what you do, that is when the big improvements occur.

I want to show you some drills that deal with screens and draws. These are great conditioning drills for defensive linemen. It shows the importance of defensive linemen attacking a screen. We are a high-pressure defense. The way to attack high pressure is to screen and draw. I make sure I work on these things. I usually do them on Thursday of game week (Diagram #8). This drill is like all the drills you have seen or done. We set dummies at the line of scrimmage and make the defenders attack them with a pass rush move. They attack the passer, and he throws the outside screen.

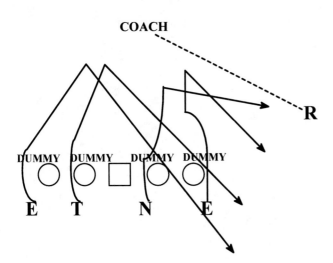

Diagram #8. Outside Screen

We throw the ball one way or the other, and they react. We do not want them to round off their turns. When they recognize the screen, they plant, open up at 45 degrees, and attack to the outside.

They burst run to a finish. The biggest thing you want them to understand is the ball can never cut back or behind them.

The next drill we rep is the draw drill. We start the linemen at the line of scrimmage like the screen drill. They attack upfield until they recognize the draw. They retrace their footwork back to the line of scrimmage. They want to take a quick peek to the inside. If the ball has crossed the line of scrimmage, they chase the ball. If it is in the area, we get in the proper pursuit angles and attack.

We do tackling drills. Many teams do not tackle with the defensive front personnel. We do tackling drills because we play a zone pressure scheme, which puts our players into secondary coverage. They play in space, must react, and make tackles. When our personnel have to chase the football, we want them to know what they have to do.

I am a footwork coach. I do a lot of bag work with the front. When we do tackling drills, I use drills that include stepping over the bags and moving in and out of them. I want to train their feet. When we do bag drills, I do not want to see players dropping their eyes or turning their heads to the side.

We run the linemen over some low bags on the ground (Diagram #9). I want the defensive linemen crossing the bag and not crossing over with their feet. At the end of the bags is a dummy holder. The linemen come out of the last bag and make a form tackle on the dummy.

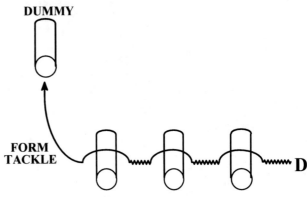

Diagram #9. Bags and Tackle

In the tackling drills, we do them against bag in the off-season programs. We can do them even if we are not in pads. When we tackle, I do not want to see players dropping the crown of their helmet or turning their head to the side. They keep the elbows in, punch up with the arms, cinch the elbows, and grab cloth. If the ballcarrier tries to spin out, we have a hold on the cloth. The feet are an important part of the tackle. We emphasize driving the feet and legs through the ballcarrier. We want to run the feet and drive the dummy back five yards. In these types of drills, we do not take anyone to the ground and focus on the fundamentals.

We do another bag drill with a form tackle at the end (Diagram #10). We line the bags up so the players go in a downhill direction. When they reach the last bag, I tell them to cut back. I add three more bags in a lateral direction. They run downhill over the bags, plant, and run laterally across three more bags. The drill works downhill with a change of direction and three more bags before they get to the tackle. When they make the tackle, they buzz their feet, work into the dummy, hit, wrap up, lift, and drive the dummy back.

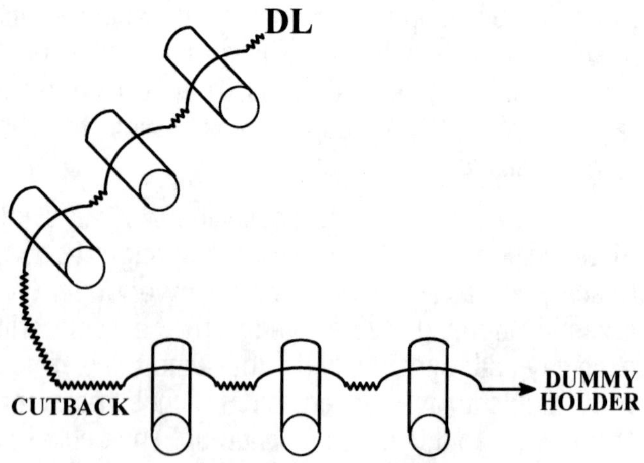

Diagram #10. Downhill Drill

We are working hard at the University of Louisville, and we are getting better. We need some more quality athletes. We would like to see you at Louisville. You are always welcome. I appreciate your attention and the opportunity to be here. Thank you for your time.

DEFENSIVE CONCEPTS AND PHILOSOPHY

University of Southern Mississippi

The lecture I am presenting today is not a lot about X's and O's. It is more about philosophy, quality control, and concepts that I think you must have defensively in order to be successful today.

I will present some other ideas that I feel are musts for a defensive unit to be successful. As we go through the lecture, you will be able to see the flipside, where you may apply these concepts and principles to the offense as well. I hope I can give you something you can take back to your program to use with your team to make them a better football team.

We are one of the most unusual professions in sports. We try to kill each other and to cut each other's throat for six months. After the season is over, we all get together and get some spare ribs and beer and then we try to tell each other how we accomplished our goals during the season. They we steal the ideas from each other.

Someone help me here. Do we have any Fellowship of Christian Athletes members here today? Which of the 10 Commandments reads "Thou shall not steal"? I know it is one of the 10 Commandments, but I am not sure which one it is. Is it the 8th Commandment? Yes! The point is, football coaches break that commandment all of the time. All we do as coaches is to steal from each other. I am not an original coach, as I am always borrowing from others.

One thing I have been blessed with is the fact I have been around a lot of great coaches in my 36 years of coaching. I have always tried to learn from them and take things from them that I think will help me in this profession. Hopefully, we will cover some things today you can use in your program. This is what it is all about.

I am looking forward to sharing some ideas with you. When we start putting our defense together, there are some general things we look at when building the defense. You can apply some of these same ideas to offense as well and to your whole football program. Until I took the job at Southern Miss, I was working with the defense, so that is what we will cover in this lecture.

OUR MISSION

Our objective is to be the college defense that becomes the standard by which other programs will begin to measure themselves. We want to be the benchmark in areas of:

- On-the-field accomplishments
- Fan base energizing
- Player/human development

If you can win on the field, that is the team. If you can energize your fans, we know you must have that support to build a big-time program with any degree of success. And we must make sure we are developing the players and that there is an element of human development. Be sure you are what you say you are!

In 36 years of coaching, the biggest change that has happened to me is not what defense we should run or what we should run on offense and those concerns. When I was a 24-year-old high school coach, I cared too much about winning and did not treat some of the young people that were entrusted to me the way I should have treated them. Now I realize I was not the best example for them all of the time. I am talking about little things, such as language, certain habits, or putting winning before recognizing that teenagers need a guiding hand at times. This is something I have learned over my career. I would rather have a former player walk up to me or come to my office today and talk with me and know that he enjoyed being around me as a person than I would to win another championship ring. As you get older, you begin to realize what is most important in life. That relationship is important. You need to make sure you are being successful in the areas of human development. Be considerate of and take care of the young men who you have been entrusted to with their lives and football careers. At the bottom of our mission, we have a quote that expresses our feelings in this area: "Be sure you are what you say you are!" Don't just give lip service to these principles.

Next, I want to talk about the guideposts of a strong staff/player/team unit:

• Mutual respect
• Mutual confidence
• One common vision
• One decision
• One voice

There is nothing wrong with a lot of moving parts as long as they are hooked to the one power train. You have a staff because you need input. You do not need a bunch of second-guessers and a bunch of complainers. Success has a thousand parents, and failure is an orphan. We do not want a group of guys who come in on Monday and all they want to talk about is what we did wrong. Don't be that guy! Once the coaches leave that meeting, it is one decision, one voice, and one common vision. Don't be the staff leak. I am talking about the guy that goes out on the street and tells the public something to make them look important. You must have trust to have a successful program!

I want to spend a moment to talk about philosophy. This is from the standpoint of what you are trying to do with the X's and O's. This is our philosophy. It is a general statement:

Never allow the opponent to move the ball consistently or effectively. Defense is all about making critical stops at critical points in the game.

The days of completely smothering the offense and shutting teams down on defense at the college level is pretty well over. Most all teams are taking a more wide-open approach to offense. They take more chances with the ball, they spread out their formations, and they are throwing the ball around.

The old deal where the defense would be unsuccessful if the offense gained over three yards on first down is not true anymore. It is unusual for a team to smother another team in football today. We did it two times last year. We held Kentucky and Vanderbilt to fewer than 100 yards in our games. That is unheard of in the game today. The common thread here is that both teams were struggling at the quarterback position at the time. It did not help them that they were playing in the Southeastern Conference. The way the offense operates today, it is going to be difficult to say the defense is going to shut the offense down. This just does not happen. So, it is about making that critical stop at a critical time and getting the ball back.

Stats can tell a story, but you can pad the stats. A team may have a lot of yards gained at the end of the year, but they ran the stats up on two or three different opponents. They could not make the big stop in the big game. To me, that is not good defense.

I have a simple axiom. The first time I heard this was from Gene Stallings. You may say this is genius, but you already knew this: you win football games with football players making plays.

Sometimes, the problem is that we get caught up with our pencils, our PowerPoints, and all of our schemes, and we pick up ideas from other coaches. We think we are going to use the plays. We have to be careful not to put the plays in front of the players. Make sure you put the players in front of the plays. The priority should be to get your best players on the field and put them in a position where they can make plays.

The quote may sound simple and you would think coaches would not have to be told this, but I have to be told this every two or three weeks. We have to back off, take some of the blitzes out of the package, and eliminate one of the new fronts we just invented. Take some of those things out of the game plan and let players make plays. As we said, winning football games is with players making plays. Put the players before the plays.

The scheme and system are certainly important. You must have an answer when your players are in trouble on the field. You must have adjustments in your package. It is not that those things are not important, but they are overrated if you do not put your players in positions where they can make plays. If you do not do that, then the X's and O's do not matter.

I am guilty of breaking the 8th Commandment when it comes to this point. Most of the ideas I have come from someone else. One thing I have always done in my career is to listen, and I have been willing to learn. I have been a sponge when I have been around good coaches. I knew I could learn from the good coaches I have associated with over the years.

There is an old saying that goes something like this: it is what you learn after you think you know everything that separates you from others. This makes you a better coach, person, or businessman or whatever you are doing.

Diagrams do not win games—players do. While we will be flexible and multiple in our system, we will always build on our scheme on the premise that puts the best players and the most speed on the field and allows them to play.

You must be sound through the center of the defense. I read a book by Tony Dungy when he was the defensive coordinator at Minnesota. It had to be back in the mid-1990s. These are the points he stressed:

• Never allow the opponent to effectively run inside.
• Do not allow throws downfield between the hashes.
    ✓ Make the opponent throw a low-percentage pass outside and or deep.
    ✓ Make the opponent throw short underneath throws.
• We will punish the receiver.
• We allow no long gainers. (No yards after the catch.)

If a team is effectively running the ball between tackles and you can't stop them, you have problems. You can say we need to be more specific than just staying effective. You know what I am talking about. If a team is moving the football on you between the tackles, you cannot draw your way out of it. You have serious problems if that happens. You want to always prepare your defense to prevent the offense from effectively running the ball inside. They may hit one or two plays in between the tackles; however, they cannot consistently move the ball in that area.

We want to take away the high percentage pass completions. We want to make the offense earn the yardage the hard way. We will punish the receivers when the pass is thrown underneath, and we will not allow a long pass play. YAC stands for yards after the catch. We also talk about yards after contact.

I served two terms as an assistant coach at Alabama, and I heard one quote all of the time. I am sure this came from Coach Paul "Bear" Bryant: "Be sure we coach their eyes." We coach all of those agility drills for their feet, and we do all of those hand drills. We teach them how to tackle and how to position their head. We teach the wrap-up, the drive-through, and all of the techniques in playing defense. All of this is extremely important. We must remind the defensive coaches of that quote I got from Alabama. Do not forget to coach their eyes.

Every snap on defense is basically made up of three aspects:
• Sight
• Reaction
• Contact

Each player must be coached, and it starts with sight. This is true even if it is an interception. It all starts with sight. If you are coaching the linebackers, you go over on the other side of the line and get where you can see the eyes of the linebacker. If he is not looking at what you told him to look at before the snap of the ball, he better be a great player to make the stop on the play. It does not matter how old they are. Get your eyes on what I told you to look at before the ball is snapped. Get where you can see the player's eyes so you can check to see if he is looking at what you have coached him to look for.

We are still not ready to get into the X's and O's. There are a lot of people who are successful running different schemes. In formulating all of your schemes and concepts, we talk about three musts. If you do not do these three things, you will not be successful as a coach:
• *Be able to teach it completely and thoroughly.* It does no good if you have a great scheme if you cannot teach it to the players.
• *Be able to adjust it quickly and to any situation.* The players will look to the coaches for adjustments.

That is the job of the coaches. You must be ready to help the players.

- *The scheme must put the players in position to make plays.* Don't force the play on the players. You must utilize the best players in the right place. The axiom shows up from Coach Gene Stallings: you win football games by players making plays.

Balance keeps coming back in this equation. You must have a good system, and you must know what you are doing. You have to be able to help the players when the system is not working. The player is the most important element. Somehow, you must hit that happy medium as a coach. You must get the right players in the right places so they can make plays for you. This is one of the great challenges of coaching. You have to be able to hit that happy medium in that you are not taking too many plays or defenses into the game and you have an answer for everything that may happen, and your team is well prepared.

Be sure you are what you say you are. To be a great defense, we must:

- Be physical.
- Be relentless.
- Tackle well.
- Have great effort to the ball.
- Have proper angles.
- Play within the scheme.
- Trust the teammates.
- Never ever never give in!

If you say you are going to be the best conditioned team on your schedule, you must back it up. Be sure you are what you say you are. I think what you say you are is important. I used to think the words were a little overrated. The older I get, I realize what you say is very important. Make sure you are not just giving a bunch of clichés or just talking to be talking. You must back it up. You must think before you talk. What you say must be exactly what you mean. You have to back it up.

The thing about our list of musts is this. Those are not things that are God-given. This is what you choose to be. You can choose to play within the scheme or you can choose not to. This has to do what you are willing to do as a player and as a coach to get all of your players to commit to the must

so you can be on the same page. To me, trust is an important word. Those are points you must develop within the team, including the coaches and players.

If you are a group of players getting ready to go out and play a game for me and I look around and I see two players who took Wednesday off and did not get ready for the game, then I know the other players will not trust them when we go out on the field. If a player did not study the film on Wednesday to get ready, you are not going to trust him on Saturday in a game. It comes down to everyone committing to do the same thing and everyone buying into the program to make it a group effort.

"Be known for something." This is a quote I heard Mike DuBose make when he was the coach at Alabama in the late 1990s. Find your identity. This can apply to the entire team, special teams, or any group. It does not matter. Be known for something! The identity of our defense will be:

- Physical
- Fast
- Flexible

The first two items are self-explanatory. What we mean by flexible is for our defense to develop an attitude that we can adjust to any offense and our defense will still be successful. We want them to have confidence, and it does not matter what the opponents do—we will adapt to them. We must be able to dictate to the opponent and be able to counter the opponent.

We want to force our opponents to do what they do not want to do. When they do have success, you must be able to counter what they do and you must react to it immediately.

When we look at things this way, we know we must practice the same way. All of these things sound good at a clinic, but if you put these things on paper and you want to talk with your players about them, you must demand these points on the practice field. You must make them demand it from each other. If you do that, these points will begin to show up on Saturday.

The next play is the only play. There is only one play in the game that the player can do anything about: the next play! Remember, focus each play on the 4A club:

- Assignment
- Alignment
- Adjustment
- Aggressiveness

When you play defense in college football today, you are going to give up some big plays. If a defensive back gets beat on one play, he must come back and play the next play. It is the same for a defensive lineman. He may get pancaked on one play, but he has to come back and be ready for the next play. He has to put the last play in the past and play the next play. The next play is the only play you can control. You can't control the last play. You could have before it started, but once it is over, you cannot do anything about it. You have to control the next play. In the book by Tony Dungy, he used the quote "The next play is the only play."

You must be careful in demanding perfection, and if you are on the players to play the next play, you must not be too critical. Then, when they make a mistake, in the back of their minds, they are thinking "Coach is down on me now!" They have a hard time putting it behind them. You have to find ways to pick them back up. You must teach them that when they make a mistake or screw up that they have to learn to put it behind them. If you play in a good league, you are going to have players that make mistakes and get beat on some plays. There is only one play in the game that you can do anything about—and that is the next play.

When you are in a tight situation and there is pressure in the game as you come down to the last two minutes of the game and the offense is in the red zone and a touchdown would cost you the game, all of the components of the 4A club come into play. When you go to the next play and get your assignment, alignment, and adjustment and can play aggressive, you have a good chance to be successful. Refocus on each snap; good or bad, you must move on to the next play.

How a defense performs in these five situations tells the true character of the unit. These are what we refer to as critical situations:

- The first possession in each half
- The last possession in each half
- The red zone (score zone)

- When the offense is backed up
- Sudden changes—turnover and kick returns

How are you going to handle those situations? We want to emphasize these five situations. "Guys, let's win these five situations. The rest of the game will take care of itself." These five points will tell you what your players are made of.

Next, we are going to get statistical. I stole this from Mickey Andrews when he was the defensive coordinator at Florida State University. He and his staff looked at a lot of film and came up with some interesting stats.

QUALITY CONTROL EVALUATION POSTGAME

- Possessions = 12
- Punts = 6
- Takeaways = 3
- Touchdowns = 2
- Field goal = 1

Teams go on offense or defense about 12 times per game. This will vary in some games depending on different styles of offense and other factors. Florida State wanted to see if it could reach these goals for each game. If it could reach the goals, it was going to be successful.

Out of the 12 possessions, the defense wanted to force 6 punts and get 3 takeaways. That is two-thirds of the possessions. If it could achieve those first two goals, it could accept the fact it gave up two touchdowns and one field goal.

With the way the game has changed today, we cannot be upset if we give up more than two-and-a-half yards on first down. It is the same with teams that have a goal of having a shutout every game. I am not sure if this is realistic anymore. If you can achieve the possession goals, the shutouts will come.

It is like the old saying "Try to achieve perfection, and on the way, you will find excellence." If you expect perfection every day, you are going to be a disappointed coach. This will be reflected by the team as well.

You may want to get 20 high school games and chart the possessions, punts, takeaways, touchdowns, and field goals to see what it would be at that level. It may come out different for you.

When I was coaching at Mississippi State University, Coach Sylvester Croom got my attention on breakout plays. Also, he is the one that got me to quit wanting to commit suicide every time a team gained four yards on first down. Some people call breakout plays "explosion plays."

Breakout plays to us are as follows: runs 12+/ passes 18+. Offensively, you have to work to achieve those plays. Defensively, you have to work to limit those plays and keep them at a minimum. If they only accomplished two of each and we want to make sure one of them is not a 60- to 70-yard gainer, we are going to be in good shape. You can go back and chart this and see if this is true.

After the game, I get the play-by-play chart and study it. When the offense takes the ball from their side of the middle field position and scored a touchdown, there is at least one breakout play in the series. One explosive play! With the wide-open offensives today, it is still hard for the offense to move the ball 70 to 80 yards to score a touchdown if it cannot produce an explosive play or two. If you can minimize these plays, you are going to be successful in keeping people off the scoreboard.

I had to learn this the hard way because I did not want to believe it. It is truer today with the spread offenses. So, we wanted to limit them to no more than two each, and we never wanted them to score a touchdown. You do not want the opponents to run the ball into the end zone outside of the 10-yard line and you do not want them to throw the ball in the end zone from outside the 15-yard line. Make the offense earn the points. If they can't score from there, what are they going to do?

If the offense gets a first down inside the 10-yard line, it is restricted to the depth of the field with the back of the end zone. The defense wins most of the battles with the field restricted because it does not have to cover as much ground, and it can break to the football better.

We charted the number of and yardage gained on breakout plays. We go over this with the players. Once the players understood the concept we were using, they started doing a better job of playing their techniques, pursuing to the football, and working on their pursuit angles. We could show them what caused the breakout plays. We

convinced them that if they would stop missing tackles, the breakout plays would be eliminated. We did our quality control on the subject, and what we found was that the most frequent cause was tackling. It was not about the defenses or the pursuit angles, although those sometimes created bad tackling. It is not the genius game plan you came out with a week before the game. It is poor tackling. We get caught up in all of the other aspects, but it all comes down to the fact we did not tackle very well.

I feel tackling starts with pursuit and pursuit angles. With the athletes we have today, if we can get the players in the right place, we can get them on the ground. We tend to overrun the play or they take plays off on you. It was not a missed assignment, and it was not a bad defensive call, and it was not a great offensive play. Most times, the problem was poor tackling.

A grad assistant compiles these charts and gives them to me. This became one of our guideposts on whether we had a good football team or not. After we started squeezing those breakout plays down, the total yardage came down, the total points came down, the number of stops we made and gave the ball back to our offense improved, and field position improved. Everything comes off this area.

When Larry Fedora first went to Southern Mississippi, we would visit with each other on the phone. He did a great job there. He called me a couple of years ago and asked me this question: "How do you evaluate a good defensive coordinator?" We had a good round-robin about it. I told him it was getting more difficult to stop the offenses today because the rules are helping the hurry-up offenses. It is hurting the defenses in that it is a wide-open offense that we have to adjust our defenses to. It runs in cycles. The defense catches up and then the rules change that helps the offense, and they come up with another innovation, and we are playing catchup again. It has been tough in the last few years. Statistics are proving that it is more difficult to stop the offense today. You must take away their offensive philosophy. You cannot just cold-stop an offense anymore. I told him there are three areas the defense must concentrate on to be effective today. They are the most important to me:

- Breakouts
- Takeaways
- Red zone

That first point is what I just covered: breakout plays. If your defense gives up a lot of those, you have problems. That is what the offense today is trying to create: explosive plays.

The second point is takeaways. You must get the takeaways. If the offense takes a wide-open approach to the game and is not conservative, then you better make it take care of the football. The more wide open the offense becomes, the harder it is to take care of the football.

The third point I stated was to make sure you are winning the red zone. If you can do that, you force the offense to kick field goals. If the offense has to kick field goals, it gets impatient. It gets away from what it does well. It starts throwing the ball too much and forgets about the running game. These three things have become more important to me with the changes in the game today.

Ralph Friedgen, the former coach at the University of Maryland, came to speak at our clinic last year. He talked about play killers. The play killers can work for you on offense, and they can work for you on defense. The offense wants to prevent them from happing. The defense wants to force the offense into these mistakes.

PLAY KILLERS

- Fumbles
- Interceptions
- Drops
- Sacks
- Penalties
- 12 percent of snaps

He went on to say that if the offense can get this down to less than 12 percent of the number of snaps the offense has, they would be successful on offense.

On defense, the more poise we play, and the more calm and collective we are, and the more aggressive we are, and the more we make the offense drive the ball the long way, soon or later,

we are going to get some play killers. I am not sure if we can make the offense have penalties. You can force the first four of these points by the way you play on defense.

This is big for me now that I am a head coach. I am going to get with my offensive coordinator and make sure he is aware of these points. If you can eliminate those things on offense, you have a chance to have a good day.

Here is another thing we did on quality control. Anytime we had a live 11-on-11 drill, practice, scrimmage, or game, we charted certain aspects of the game. These items were recorded by each position coach by positions and by individual players. I had a summary sheet that I filled out for all positions and all players.

In addition, a coach or grad assistant would record the total yards gained after these things happened to us on defense:

- *Missed tackles*—Also, compile the total YAC after missed tackles.
- *Missed assignments*—results
- *Finish*—effort or loaf
- *Penalties*—pre-snap and post-whistle

After all the info was compiled, we would go over it as a defensive unit. You would be surprised the number of yards a missed assignment or a missed tackle can cost your team.

We went beyond the missed tackles and missed assignments and counted the number of loafs and certain penalties. We did not count grabbing the face mask. We did record jumping offside and hitting after the whistle and personal fouls. We wanted to know the total number of yards the team cost us for its lack of discipline on defense.

For the finish and the penalties, we gave out a certain number of up/downs for the next practice. If it were in a game, it would be on Monday.

We used to call the plays where players may not have given their very best effort "loafs," but we decided it would be better if we called them "finishing." If a player goes hard for 20 straight plays, he may not be able to go all out every play. So, we changed the name from loafs to finish.

FINISH

- Not sprinting to the football
- Change of speed in pursuit
- Rush defender not turning and running to the ball
- Getting passed up by another player
- Not finishing aggressively at the end of a play (put your body on the ball)
- Turning down a hit
- Staying on the ground

Loafs will cost you specific "payments": grass drills. You can decide what you want to do for the payments. We did grass drills or up/downs. You need to do these as a staff and not just by one position or you may have problems with some of the players.

REWARDS

- +4 shutout
- +4 outscore
- +2 less than 15 points
- +2 score
- +1 less than 300 yards
- +1 red zone stop (inside 25)

START WITH NEGATIVE REWARDS: -4

- Zero rewards means no payments.
- Positive rewards means rewards.
- Negative rewards means a payment for each half-gasser.

All of these topics I have covered leads me to the last point—and that is this: you must have a system. You need to have a system, and you need to have a reason for running that system. Instead of talking about the 4-3 or the 3-3 defense, we develop the concept of a system methods.

SYSTEM METHODS

Our system will be built on the following elements:
- We will base out of a 4-2 scheme.
- In our perimeter, we will base with man and marry a zone:
  ✓ Man coverage adjusts easier.
  ✓ Zone cuts off the man-beater scheme.
  ✓ Consistent run fits carry over in both.
- We will employ several junk packages to complement our base.
- We will use both man and zone pressure schemes:
  ✓ Some quarterbacks handle one better than the other.
  ✓ Some coaches handle one better than the other.

You can learn this from the scouting report, especially for the quarterback. You may find some quarterbacks or coaches that are good against one type of man or zone coverage. We do not want to help the quarterbacks by playing what they can handle best.

You must not get involved in going to a clinic and come back and try to install another defense because you saw something you liked at a clinic. You must make sure your players can handle the scheme before you sell out and make a lot of changes. You must fit the plays to the player. Don't fit the player to the plays.

I hope you can take some of these points back and apply them to your situation. Some of the information is very general, but the more I am in this business, the more I realize you must do what you say you are doing. You may think you are doing the things you say you are doing, but you have to be careful and not get away from the fundamentals and great effort, and those things that make a player a great player are the same things that make a team a great team. It is not the system and the X's and O's as much as you must be doing the little things and special things that are going to make sure you are going to have a good defense.

Thanks for your time. I enjoyed being here.

PRACTICE ORGANIZATION: THE KEY TO SUCCESS

University of Oregon

Thank you. It is a pleasure to be here, especially since the military is here. I want to relate a short story about our tour overseas with our troops in Pakistan. We were on the *USS Eisenhower* about 80 miles off the coast of Pakistan. The temperature on the flight deck was 137 degrees. The personnel responsible for the takeoffs and landings of the aircraft were 18-, 19-, and 20-year-old kids. These people are the same age as the players I am coaching in college. These young kids were running millions of dollars' worth of machinery. Not once did you hear any of them complain about being hot or how bad the weather was.

I made a promise to myself. I promised I would never complain about the weather again. I watched people who had a tremendous amount of responsibility go about their jobs with a great degree of professionalism. They did their jobs with great enthusiasm. Understanding what they do for this country was humbling.

I made up my mind that if I ever got the chance to speak to a group about football or another topic, I would publicly acknowledge the men and women that service this country. I want to thank them for what they do for this country, and I want you to give them a round of applause. There are many common themes in what we do and what they do. The big difference is we are playing a game and they are dealing with life and death situations. If you get a chance to thank one of these fine men or women, do it. Give them a thank-you and let them know you appreciate what they are doing.

I appreciate being here. Anytime you get a chance to talk football after the recruiting season has ended, it is good. We are starting to look at our tapes of last season and self-scout ourselves. We are looking at what we did well and what was not so good. You cannot keep patting yourself on the back for a good season or kicking yourself in the butt for a bad season. You have to move forward. That is the good thing about our program. We are forward thinking and trying to find out how we can make ourselves better. Coaches here today are here to make your programs better and make yourselves better.

I want to share some thoughts about what we do. I think what we do is unique. I am going to tell you how we got to what we do and how we do it. Like everything we do, it comes from how you practice. That is one thing coaches have an effect on more than anything they do. If you do not take that very seriously, you are not going to be very good. Sometimes, the other team has better players than you do, and you cannot control that. What you can control is how you practice.

PREPARE TO PLAY

The unique thing is how we prepare to play on Saturday:

- Define your role as a coach
- Define what you ask your players to do
- Trust
- Communication
- Level of commitment

The first thing you have to do is define your role as the coach. That is important to ask coaches what they consider their job is as a coach. When I took over two years ago, I sat down with the staff. I told them we wanted to create an environment where our players had the opportunity to be successful and to get out of their way. I have seen too many coaches who overcoach players during a game. The players end up thinking too much about what the coach told them to do instead of playing.

We have an outstanding defensive line coach at our school by the name of Jerry Azzinaro. I think he is one of the best coaches I have ever known. He had the opportunity to coach Dwight Freeney when he was at Syracuse. He recruited him and coached him for four years. He tells this story about Freeney. Dwight came off the field and Jerry got him on the bench and was giving him all kinds of advice and techniques to play. Freeney told him, "You have had all week to coach me; now shut up and let me play." Coach Azzinaro did not take that as Freeney being confrontational; he took it as being a great point.

Why would you overcoach a player during the game and make him play slower than he normally would? The coach has to be great during the week as a coach. Therefore, when they have the opportunity to go perform, the coach lets them perform without thinking about it. None of the coaches are stepping over the sideline and playing the game. The players are the ones playing the game. It is not what the coach knows; it is what the players know.

There are some coaches who are amazing when you talk football with them. They have an answer for every situation and everything that goes on within the game. When you watch his players perform, they do not perform as well as he talked. The coach is not playing the game; the players are playing. The coach is calling the game and going through the scenarios and situations. That is what his job is. If he is trying to coach up individual things in the middle of the game, he is confusing the players.

It does not matter which level you coach on— you are working with young players. Define for them what you expect. When you ask them to do something, it is very hard for them. The first time you ask a player to do something, no one does it perfectly. If they do, they were lucky. When they do it the second time, they will fail. Then, they have to try it again while people are watching they. I do not think there is any player on your teams who wants to screw something up on purpose. Sometimes, the coach takes it that way.

You have to put yourself in their shoes. You are asking them to do a skill that they are going to fail. They have to recover quickly and forget about it. Then, they have to try it again while people are watching them. It is like a coach giving his first clinic talk. You may be nervous up on the stage in front of many people, even though you know your subject matter well. It is no different for the 15-year-old player the first time he has to go out there. The key to doing that is the player has to trust and respect the coach who is asking him to do that.

Trust is a huge word for us. When players trust the coaches and the coaches trust their players, it goes a lot further in the coaching process. The player has to believe the coach is not going to ask him to do something that he is not capable of doing. The player must believe that the coach believes the player can do the skill more than the player believes it. There is no difference in the players in high school and the players in college. The only difference is ours are a little bigger.

Their egos are the same. They are fragile, and their self-esteem is the same. The player may have the appearance of confidence and talks smack, but deep down, he is the same as everyone else. Every person is nervous the first time he has to do something new that takes him outside his comfort zone. The coach has to see things that maybe the player does not see himself. The coach has to make sure the player knows he can be successful, but there are going to be missteps along the way. The coach's job is to pick them up, dust them off, and let them go at it again.

Coaches have ruined too many players. They think coaching is yelling, screaming, being tough, and showing them what he knows instead of putting them in an environment where they can be successful. That environment depends on the culture of your team. It depends upon the makeup of the players in your program. The coach has to be aware of what he is asking his players to do.

The quicker you build trust between the players and coaches, the quicker the lines of communication will open. If someone is asking you to do something and you do not trust him, you will not listen. The player thinks the coach is trying to screw him. That makes for an adversarial operation. When the player and coach are adversaries, the player and coach will not be successful. If that situation exists, the team will not be successful.

One of the biggest things in your program is the level of commitment your players have to the program. When you can get 100 percent of your players committed to the program and not to them, that is when the program can be successful.

Football is a team sport, and there is no one above the team. There is no one above the program. The players must understand that commitment to a common goal with a group of people is bigger than what it is for individuals.

I tell our player all the time, if the reason they are in this is for the individual, they need to go down the hall to the golf or tennis office. Those are individual sports. When they made a decision to join our team, they made a decision to be a member of the team. If individual statistics are what is on the player's mind, he will hurt your football team.

They have to sacrifice for the good of the team. When you sacrifice for the team, the ultimate success of the team is bigger than any success the player could gain individually. If they cannot understand that, they need to go play an individual sport. Tony Dungy's son Eric is on our team. Two years ago, Tony came to speak to our team in preseason camp. It was somewhat eerie. He said he had one message to get across. "The ultimate teams have one thing in common. They have players on their team that are willing to sacrifice." He asked the team if they wanted to be in Glendale, Arizona, on January 10, 2011, playing for the national championship. All the players raised their hands. All our receivers sat in the same area. He asked them to hold up their hands if that was their goal. They all held up their hands. Then, he asked them if they would want to be there in the championship game if it meant not catching a ball all season. Some of the players took their hands down.

He told them he appreciated them being honest with him, but that that was what a team is all about. The individual has to sacrifice his individual accolades for a team accolade. That is the ultimate sacrifice for a wide receiver. He has to be willing to do that.

It is interesting that the wide receivers have to think about the question when the offensive line does that all game long. No one asked them what they were willing to sacrifice because they do it all year long. That group is a unique group in their own right. They shop for clothes at True Value Hardware. The only thing they want is to change the snap count occasionally. Besides that, they do not gripe and do not want anything.

The first level of commitment is not really a commitment. They are out for the team because some of their friends got them to go out for the team, but they do not really care. They do not know why they on the team, but they will see what it is like. They will not last long.

The second group is what most of your young players are like. They simply say, "Okay, if that is what it takes." They do not really believe it, but they do not want to buck the system.

The third group is the worst. The coach has to work hard to find out who they are and work hard to change their attitudes. These are the conditional committed players. I will do it if it benefits me. If it does not benefit me, I am not in for it. Those players are cancers to your program. You have to identify them early and explain to them that their mind-set is not in concert with what is going on in the program. You have two choices with those players. You can train them or trade them. We tell our players that we have a standard of what we are about and a vision of what it is supposed to look like.

Either the player agrees with that vision and is all in or he does not agree. If that is the conditional player, we love him, but we will miss him because he is not going to be in the program. If he makes me choose between the standards of this football team and an individual, there is no choice. An old coach once told me, if you have 25 players and 24 of them are good with one jackass, you would be all right. If you have two jackasses, they will meet and you will have a jackass farm. You cannot let situations of conditional commitments continue to fester. If it does, it becomes worse.

We have a "Yea, Buddy" rule on our team. If a player is complaining about anything to another player, that player's response is, "Have you talked to the coach about it?" If they say, no, the player's response is "Shut up."

If the player gives the complainer a "Yea, Buddy," the complainer thinks he is right about his gripe because his "buddy" said he was. If the "buddy" agrees with him, you have two complainers, and it builds from there. It is the coach's job to keep his door open and talk to the players about their complaints. Players want to make their friends feel good. Your job as a coach is not necessarily to make the players feel good. You have to be frank, straightforward, and honest with them.

If he wants to know why he is not playing, we can show him. We can show him the number of dropped balls, missed assignments, the number of times he loafed, and all the other factors that determine playing time. You have many players who do not want to do that because the coach will not say "Yea, Buddy."

At the University of Oregon, we have no individual goal at all. If individual recognition comes, that is great. LeMichael James, the best running back in Pacific-12 Conference history, never had a Heisman Trophy campaign. If you are going to win the Heisman Trophy, you should win it on your merits alone. I told people that if we send out a flier to tell people that he is a good player, they should not have a vote. He is the ultimate team player and ultimate for our team chemistry. He knows he would not gain a yard if it were not for the offensive line blocking, the receivers blocking, or the quarterback did not carry out the fake. He would never put himself above the program.

He played a game against a I-AA school. He had 14 carries for 227 yards and three touchdowns. They asked him after the game what he thought of the game. He told them he played terrible and let the team down. He told them he missed two blocks and a blitz pickup. When I hear a player talk like that, I know our program is going in the right direction. That player is in the program for the right reasons. He has put the program above himself.

PHILOSOPHY

Every coach has to ask himself the same question: "What do you want to be?" That is the great thing about football. You can be anything you want. You can be a spread team, I-formation team, power team, wing-T team, option team, or wishbone team. You can be anything you want, but you have to define it. Too many teams we watch on tape do not know what kind of offense they want to be. That is a big problem. The offense is an inch deep and a mile wide. Their offense is a series of disjointed plays with no system.

When you decide what you are going to be, it should show up in your practices. If you say "We are all about respect." However, in practice, you see players that cheap-shot their teammates and coaches who do not say anything to them about it.

I should be able to go to your practice and tell what you defined for your players. It does not matter what you pick, but you should see that in the way you play and practice.

TEAM DEFINITIONS

- Fast
- Hard
- Finish

We are going to be fast in everything we do. We practice fast, move fast, talk fast, ask questions fast, we recruit fast players, we develop fast players, and run everything at a fast tempo. I ask every player who comes into our program "How fast are you?" If he tells me he is 4.4, that is how fast he should be every times he runs. If he is 4.8, that is what we expect from him every time. The football team at Oregon is fast on defense, fast on special teams, and fast at how we practice.

The second thing is hard. The ultimate compliment you can get from the opposing coach is when the coach tells me we played hard. We emphasize that in practice all the time by putting them in hard situations. You do not just show up and play hard. You have to practice that way. It has to be part of what you do. It has to carry over into everything you do.

The last thing we stand for is finish. Our team in the fourth quarter has a calm demeanor about it. There is no panic. We understand what finishing is all about. The coaching staff has put them in so many situations in preparation that they understand what finish is all about. We are fantastic in the fourth quarter, and we are fantastic in overtimes. We are 34-6 in the last three years. When we come to the fourth quarter, it is our time. We out-practice faster than anyone, we out-practice harder than anyone, and we always finish. We finish every drill we do.

We take the same analogy over to the academic side. Be fast and early to class. Be hard and challenge yourself in what you take academically. Finish and make sure you get your degree. It is around our stadium. That is the only signs we have. We are not a slogan operation and all that other bull. Every year in those programs, there is a new theme and the motto changes. We stand for the same thing we have always stood for. We are going to be fast, going to be hard, and going to finish. That is it, and we have defined ourselves.

You have to decide, but my advice to you is not to pick too many. If you have too many things, you have trouble figuring what is important. We settled on three, and every unit on our team knows what they are. At Oregon, our older players coach our younger players. We do not have a lot of time in the off-season, but the older players can coach the younger players because they know what we stand for. They understand when a player is not practicing fast. They know when a player is not playing hard and giving maximum effort. They understand it when a player is pulling up in a drill and not finishing through the cone.

The point is, when you decide what you define yourself as, someone can come to your practice and see it in five minutes. If you came to our practices and the coaches were standing around talking to one another and they were not saying anything to anyone about finishing, it makes you wonder. Was all that clinic talk or do they believe that is what they are doing?

When I got our players together, I told them we were going to practice better than one has ever practiced. The great thing about practice is the coach controls it. You have coach and player control. That is up to you as a group. If you do not have a good practice, you cannot blame anyone else but yourself.

As an individual, if he did not practice well, his mind was somewhere else. That is up to each individual player. You have to challenge the players and coaches every day to have the best practice they can. The coaches are role models. The players take their lead from what they see. If the coach is lollygagging with the other coaches, that is what he can expect from his drills. If the player is practicing fast, hard, and finishing, tell him he is practicing harder than anyone else. The key is we control what goes on in practice.

TEACHING PHILOSOPHY

- I see and I forget.
- I hear and I forget.
- I see and I remember.
- I do and I understand.

When you teach this first point is huge. I am speaking to you, but I am showing it to you. How many times have you said "I do not know why he did that because I told him to do it this way"? That is the second statement: "I hear and I forget." We think because we said it once that it registers with them. It does not. I will leave here today, and tomorrow, you will remember about 5 percent of what I said. That is common with verbal instruction.

The third part of that is "I see and I remember." We are going to tell our players how we want things done and then we are going to show them. That makes them audio learners first and then visual learners. If you teach a route, you tell them how to run it first. Then, you show them how to run it the right way. I will have a video clip of it and have one of the older players show them. We tell them we run five steps on the outside leg, plant the outside leg on the fifth step, and break at a 45-degree angle 1 yard inside the corner.

What he hears at a 45-degree angle may not be exactly what you want. You have to show it to him. Some players get it when they hear it and some get it when they see it. We told them what to do, we showed them what to do, and then we put them in a situation where they actually did it.

Do not every ask them to do something on a Friday night in a game that you have never put them in that situation before. I do not understand that philosophy or that mind-set. In a critical situation, you cannot call a play that you never work on in practice. When it does not work, you cannot explain it. I know why it did not work.

There is a phenomenon in basketball that I have never understood. There is five seconds to go in the game. It is sideline out of bounds and you are down one point. The coach calls a time-out, the team comes over, and he gets out a whiteboard and designs a play. In basketball, that is commonplace for that to happen. What do you think would happen if Bill Belichick in the Super Bowl did the same thing? When you draw up those plays, very seldom does it work. Why not call a play that you work on all the time?

We practice the two-point play every week. When we have that situation in a game, all the players know the formation and play we run. In a critical situation, you go back to your teaching philosophy. If you did all those things, they will execute the play. We practice the play all the time, we do it all the time, and when they get in that situation, they execute it.

PRACTICE

When you go to practice, you must have a pre-practice routine. If practice starts at 3:15 p.m., every group has a pre-practice route. I do not care what it is, but I want them doing something. I do not want the coaches to run them into the ground. However, when they arrive at the practice field, I want them doing something organized. Every group we have is out for pre-practice. Having a routine keeps the players from fooling around and not being organized. It sets the tone for what goes on in practice. If the players are sloppy before they get into practice, that trend will continue into the practice. We make sure we work on an individual skill that is beneficial to them, and it is a consistent thing for us.

We call the first period of the day "zero period." It is a three-minute period. It is before we stretch. For the defense, we use a turnover circuit. For the offense, we run a thing called "county fair." In this period, we run a deep-ball drill, a curl drill, and a stick route. It is a way for us to warm them up. These are not full-speed drills. They work at 50–75 percent speed.

We follow the zero period with a walk-through, which amounts to a meeting on the field. In the meeting room, we show them the play, which is "I see and I forget." You show them a video of what you showed them, which is "I see and I remember." In the walk-through, we walk-through the play on the field. We do all this at a teaching tempo. This is the "I do and I understand" part of teaching. We never do teaching tempo at full speed. You crawl before you walk, and you walk before you run. If this is red zone day, we get the chance to walk-through the red zone offense before practice starts. It is a 5–10 minute period.

I will say one more thing about walk-through. When you call for a scout team to give you a look, it should not take long if you organize it. We designate our look team. Our second offensive line is the four down defenders and the Mike linebacker. The quarterback is the free safety. The wide receivers are the corners. The slot receiver and running back are the strong safety and Will linebacker, respectively. The tight end is the Sam linebacker. That keeps us from having 9 or 14 on defense. On the defensive side, it is just the opposite for them. The second Sam linebacker is the tight end, and everything else falls into place.

Whatever system you choose, find a way to do it quickly. We have the zero period, walk-through, and stretch, and no one is ever late for practice. When we go to our stretch period, we use a dynamic-moving stretch. We emphasize what we stand for. When we stretch, all the coaches are involved with the stretch period. We want the players to know this is an important period. Do not let the coaches stand around and not be involved. That sends a message to your players that stretch is not important. If you do not think stretch is important, do not do it.

The players cannot be selective participants. They cannot choose the drills they want to do. That goes for the coaching staff also. If the coaches are not excited about stretch as they are about the tackling period, the players take the lead from them.

If you as the head coach accept it, you should expect it. If the player does not touch the line in a stretch period, expect him to not do it in the game. If the player lines up two yards over the start line in sprints and you do not correct him, do not jump his butt when he does it in the game. It is about the little things. If you do not correct the offensive lineman in practice for holding, do not bitch at the official for calling it in the game. If you accept it, you should expect it in the games, and that is on the coach.

You have to correct those things in practice. In the games, they are SIWs (self-inflected wounds), and on occasion, we cannot recover from them.

We have two speeds in practice. The first speed is teaching speed. The second speed is game speed. If you practice at any other speeds, you are wrong. Either you are at game speed or you are teaching. You cannot go game speed the entire practice and you cannot teach the entire practice. We have to consider carefully the practice organization to accommodate the speed we want.

You cannot allow a team to do something at three-quarter speed. Nothing in the games happens at three-quarter speed. Make all the groups go at the same speed. When we do a pat and go drill, I want the quarterback taking a full-speed drop. If you have the offensive line busting their butts in a full-speed line drill and the linebacker involved in a tackling drill, it will not hurt the quarterback to go full speed in a pat-and-go drill. If we are in game speed, we go full speed.

This past year, we had 1,064 plays. We listed all the situations we had on those plays. You need to look at what you actually face in a game and practice those situations. It used to blow my mind when we did goal line for 20 minutes. We may be in a goal line situation three plays or fewer in a game. We are going to be a great third-down team. We had 197 third-down plays, which is 18 percent of the snaps. We spend Tuesday, Wednesday, and Thursday working on our third-down package.

Your practice has to match what happens in a game. We practice the last play of the half. We practice what to do with no time-outs. Your organization for practice has to hit everything you have to cover. We were in second-and-long as much as we were in third-down situations. You have to work on the four-minute offense when leading and when behind. The game of football is about situations. You need to practice them. Do not put the ball in the middle of the field and say we are going to scrimmage for 20 minutes. If you do, you shortchange your players.

When you set your practice schedule, set it to the amount of time you need to accomplish what you need. In some periods, 5 minutes is too short and 10 minutes is too long. Make the time fit what you need. As the season moves along, you do not need the same amount of time to work on a repetitive drill. When we are getting ready for the bowl game, we do not need to spend the time working handoff drills for four minutes.

We use multiple huddles in our practices to maximum reps. We work the defense with multiple reps. Even though we are a spread team, we can give our defense a good look of conventional teams; however, the tempo does not slow down. We practice the same tempo on offense and defense.

You cannot ask your players to practice at the speed we do for the whole practice. We alternate a teaching period into the work period to give them a break. If you try to go at that pace for an entire practice, the players learn how to coast during some part of the practice. We do not want that. If we work a 7-on-7 drill, we come back to a teaching period before we go to a team period. 7-on-7 is a team period for the wideouts.

We change our practice as the season goes along, and we learn what we are good at and what we are bad at doing. We have to figure out how to practice and adjust the time because of injuries. Our practice will run 1 hour and 45 minutes. We do not condition at the end of practice. We condition during practice. In a 12-minute period, we get 36 repetitions. Our first team is in for 4 plays, the second team is in for 3 plays, and we start over. We play in bursts.

Coaches cannot talk to their players during a drill. If you want to talk to a player, you coach him on the run or sub for him. Do not stop a drill to talk to one player. The coach has to learn time-on-task. Everyone must be moving. We want players getting repetitions. We do not want a coach talking on the field. If you talk to him, he will forget it. He needs to do it to remember. Our coaches do an unbelievable job of coaching the players who are not in the drill. We call that giving mental reps to the players not in the drill.

You must have code words and phrases that mean things to the players. Our coaches are always running around on the field. You can coach a player on the run, but you have to move with him. We want to play the next play.

If you are in a no-huddle scheme, you need to communicate. Even if you are not a no-huddle team, you should practice in no-huddle. That allows you to practice faster. If you want to play fast, you cannot be a huge motion or shifting team. There is a give-and-take in every system. Motioning is not wrong, but you must decide how you want to play. There is no perfect system. You must live with what you want to do.

Time of possession is not a good indicator of winning in college. We were dead last in time of possession and third in scoring.

The way we practice, the games are slower for our players. The game is a piece of cake for our players because you have to wait for the officials and the chain gang.

There is not one way to communicate. Your needs drive the type of communication you want. Education is the transportation of knowledge. You have to transport the knowledge to the players. The first way to communicate is by wristbands. The problem with the wristband is speed and flexibility. They have to look at the band, and changes in formation are difficult. How many plays can you get on a wristband?

Boards and flip cards are an option. You control them, but they lack flexibility and they are awkward. Pictures are a method. One picture is worth a thousand words. The problem is they must be big enough, and how many boards can you have? It takes people to use them, and it is awkward.

At the University of Missouri, the entire coaching staff signals their position players. All the signals are different and mean different things. They are hard to steal. The problem is practicing them in practice. All the coaches have to be on the sideline when you practice signals. It is an interesting way to do it, and we have studied them all, trying to find what is best for us.

Our players make up our calls and codes. They choose things that make sense to them. The coaches may be totally out of touch with what they know and associate to their situations. You want them to choose things they can remember. What makes sense to you as the coach may not make sense to them. Information is the reduction of uncertainty. The players must all speak the same language and understand it. You want all your players on the same page.

"Red light" tempo for us is slowing the play down. It is checks and audibles. We run the clock and run the ball. In this tempo, it is where the quarterback looks to the sideline and changes the play or takes time off the clock. The coach totally controls the red light tempo from the sideline.

The "yellow light" tempo is a check and audible system for the quarterback. We may want to run the play to the 3 technique. It is a "check with me" type of play. He calls the play and figures out where the 3 technique is and calls the audible. We may want to run toward a safety or away from a certain defensive player. This tempo is slower, but the quarterback controls it on the field.

The "green light" tempo is as fast as possible. When you run at this tempo, you must be willing to give up some plays. There will be plays you call with a green light tempo that the defense has the answer. You are snapping the ball, and they have not lined up. You may be running a sprint to the field, and they have 10 defenders to the field. You must have the culture of playing the next snap and not the last one. If we knew they had 10 men to that side, we would not have run it. Play selection is limited when you play fast. There are only certain plays you can run. It is tough to run a man-blocking scheme when you do not know who the men are.

One of the things we talk about all the time is that our preparation is the key to our success. That is what we control. When I took over as head coach, I made that a huge point of emphasis in our program. Our players take a lot of pride in it. It does not matter how talented the other operation is if you spend your time on your preparation and get your players to understand what the game plan is. Then, you have a chance every Friday night. Thank you very much. I appreciate it.

ONE ASPECT OF THE MULTIPLE 4-2-5 DEFENSE

The University of North Carolina

Thank you. I appreciate that introduction, and it is a pleasure to be here. This is the third time for me speaking at a Nike clinic. I see many familiar faces, and it looks like you coaches are getting younger. Every time I look in the mirror, it seems I am getting older. I am new to North Carolina, but I have been in college coaching for some time.

The last two years, I was the defensive coordinator at Illinois. We ended up with the seventh-best total defense in the country. Two years ago, we were 38th in the nation. The year before I got there, they were 93rd in the nation on total defense. We made some strides in the years we were there. I was at Kansas State for one year. That is my alma mater. Coach Bill Snyder had just come out of retirement, and that was an attractive situation to me. I was at Clemson with Coach Tommy Bowden for four years. When I left Clemson, we were eighth in the country in total defense. We also led the Atlantic Coast Conference in total defense.

I have coached at Memphis, Wyoming, and Troy State along the way. I have been around some great coaches and had some great experiences. I have coached my share of good players.

What I talk about today may not be what we run at North Carolina. We may start in this scheme, but it will depend on what our players can do. Last year at Illinois, we did some things we had not done before because of the personnel we had.

Next week, we are going to start our off-season program with the coaches involved. That will tell us what we have. From there, we will design a package around the talent we have.

If we do not have the personnel to play man coverage, we may be a big zone team. Charlie Bailey told me a long time ago that you get your bad and average players to use up the blockers and get the good players to make the tackles. We will see what we have and build the system around what they can do.

When I was at Clemson, they criticized me for not blitzing enough. In the scheme I like to use, we bring pressure about 40 percent of the time. At Illinois last year, we brought someone about 57 percent of the time. We will do many different things and give many different looks to the offense. Schematically, we are a cross between a 4-2-5 and a 4-3 defense. As I go through this presentation, I will alert you to the different schemes we run.

Dallas is the first thing I want to show you. When we put our system in, we use city calls for our defensive schemes. We named this defense after a bandit linebacker position. When I was at Troy, I had a linebacker by the name of DeMarcus Ware. He was a good linebacker. We were blitzing the linebackers and dropping DeMarcus Ware out in pass coverage. I thought we should do something different with him instead of drop him into coverage. Shortly after that, we started with the city calls on defense to tell the bandit what to do.

On the Dallas call, against the spread offense, we are in a 4-2 type of front (Diagram #1). We are in the nickel package. To the two-receiver side, we are in a 3 technique, with the tackle and a bandit defender aligned in a wide alignment on the slot receiver to his side. There is no tight end, and the bandit aligns almost head-up the slot receiver to that side. The nose shades the center to the other side of the formation, and the backside defensive end aligns in a 5 technique on the offensive tackle.

In our system, we call this bench Dallas. We bring the Mike or Will linebacker on the blitz into the fieldside A gap. The nose loops into the fieldside B gap. By looping the nose into the B gap, we create a double eagle front. If the flow of the ball is to the

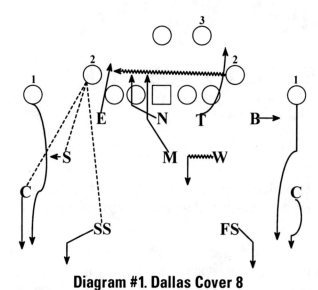

Diagram #1. Dallas Cover 8

boundary side, the linebacker that did not blitz plays the boundary side A gap. In my first coaching job, I was the defensive end coach for Joe Lee Dunn. It was a great opportunity for me, and I am indebted to him for getting me going.

We want to play zone coverage behind this scheme. We double call the coverage. In this case, we call 8 sink. If the offense comes out in a 2x2 formation, we play cover 8. Cover 8 is the same things as cover 4, which is quarters coverage. In the quarter scheme, when we play cover 4, the bandit blitzes and the Will linebacker drops into his coverage. Cover 8 tells the secondary that the bandit drops and the Mike or Will linebackers blitz. That is the only difference. We play the same rules in the coverage. There are some differences when we play robber against a pro set into the boundary.

We play this defense to help us against the run. However, it is not a helpful defense against the pass unless you can gauge the protection scheme in the passing game. We create a double eagle front, but we rush only four defenders on a pass. The bandit on this call is taking the first threat to the flat to his side. Against the 2x2 formation, we play three defenders over two receivers on both sides.

In the diagram, the Mike linebacker blitzes and the Will linebacker replaces him in his pass coverage. The bandit replaces the Will linebacker is his coverage. The 3 technique defender becomes the contain man into the boundary. We tell him he has to contain through the B gap. The 5 technique end to the field plays a box technique. He keeps everything

inside of him and contains the quarterback on the pass.

The strong safety reads the #2 receiver to his side. The safety's rule tells him he reads from the #2 receiver to the #1 receiver. With no #2 receiver, he double-covers the #1 receiver down the field. The Sam linebacker has the first threat to the flat.

This is a good example of how we adjust to the 3x1 formation (Diagram #2). We play 8 sink in the secondary. It is a double call. The cover 8 was what we played against the 2x2 formation I showed you before. Against the 3x1, we play the sink coverage. Sink coverage to us is a three-deep coverage. In this coverage, the Sam linebacker walks out on the #2 receiver and plays from #2 to #1 receiver in his coverage. He keys the #2 receiver for his run key. If the #2 receiver releases on a pass, the Sam linebacker drops under the #1 receiver. The alignment of the down linemen is the same as the previous diagram.

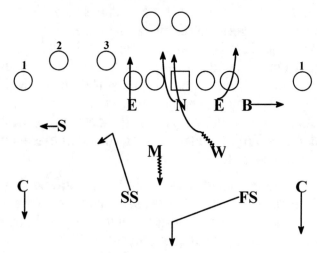

Diagram #2. Dallas Sink

The sink player is the strong safety. On the snap, he rolls down and plays the #3 receiver, who is the inside winged slot in the triple set. He plays the #3 to #2 receiver. That means he reads the #3 receiver for his run key. If the #3 receiver blocks for the run, he supports on the run. If the #3 receiver releases on a pass, the safety drops in coverage on the #2 receiver.

The free safety rotates back and runs to the middle of the field. The bandit is aligned in a loose 5 technique to the #1 receiver side of the formation. He is in a three-point stance, but he drops into coverage under the #1 receiver to his side. He plays the #2 to #1 receiver. Since he is on the backside of the trips set with no #2 receiver, he buzzes out under the #1 receiver.

One of the inside linebackers will blitz according to the backfield alignment. The linebacker that does not blitz is the seam runner under the #3 receiver to the trips side. Anytime we play a three-deep coverage, we must have a seam runner inside the third receiver. The seam runner takes the #3 receiver on a vertical route. He has to protect the free safety against four verticals.

We feel like we are strong at stopping the run with this adjustment. The problem you have with the spread is the running game. The spread offense will throw the ball, but if it can run the ball, it can beat you. Typically, if you cannot stop the run, you do not stand a chance in defensive football. In this defense, we are solid against the run. If they pass, we have to rally to it.

We use stem techniques to confuse the offense. In a 2x2 set, we align our down linemen the same as before (Diagram #3). With the quarterback in the shotgun and the running back set into the boundary, the boundary defensive end aligns in the 3 technique. The shade nose aligns to the field and loops into the fieldside B gap. The defensive end into the field aligns in a 5 technique and plays the box technique. The Mike linebacker is to the fieldside and the Will linebacker stems outside and aligns outside the offensive tackle. The bandit aligns inside the slot receiver into the boundary.

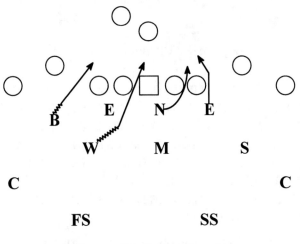

Diagram #3. Dallas Read 2

The Will linebacker cheats to the inside and blitzes through the fieldside A gap. The bandit is in a position to be a free defender on runs his way.

In the secondary, we play read 2 coverage. If the bandit and Sam linebacker are inside the #2 receiver, we play read 2 with the safeties and corners. The corners and safeties read the #2 receiver to their side. If he releases outside, the corner holds off the #1 receiver on his release and rolls to the flat. The safety plays over the top of the corner. If the #2 receiver releases inside, the safety and underneath coverage have coverage on him. The corner locks on the #1 receiver and plays him. If the #2 receiver releases up the field, the safety takes him.

If the bandit and Sam linebacker align even with or outside the #2 receiver, we play robber coverage (Diagram #4). The corner locks up on the #1 receiver. The safeties read the #2 receiver. If the #2 receiver releases to the outside, the bandit or Sam linebacker takes him and the safeties rob the pattern of the #1 receiver. If the #2 receiver releases up the field, the safety has him. This is nothing revolutionary because many coaches play this coverage.

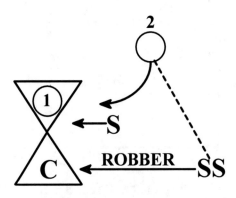

Diagram #4. Robber

If a team aligns in a 2x2 formation and start short motion just before the snap of the ball, it is difficult for the secondary to change the coverage. We have to play what we call. Our three-deep coverage is not exactly what people might think three deep is. Our three deep is more pattern read coverage instead of spot drop coverage. We do not drop to landmarks in a zone. We play pattern reads and it is more man-in-the-zone coverage that a spot drop.

When we assign players #3 to #2 reads, they have a double-read. They read the #3 player to see if he run-blocks or releases on a pass. If the receiver blocks for a running play, the safety gets into his run fit and supports on the run. If the player releases on a pass, the safety finds the #2 receiver and covers him in his zone. The quarterbacks are too good to drop to a spot and react to a throw. We read the patterns the receivers run and try to pick those receivers up within our zones and play man coverage in a zone.

If we want to change up the coverage on the 3x1 formation and stay in the quarter scheme, we call fish (Diagram #5). The fish call means free safety inside. We still play cover 8, but instead of sinking the strong safety down on the #3 receiver, we use the free safety. We do not play 8 sink; we play 8 fish. We play the wide receiver and the middle slot receiver in a three defenders over two receivers quarters scheme. We play normal quarter coverage on those two receivers. The free safety cheats over and takes the #3 receiver or inside slot receiver.

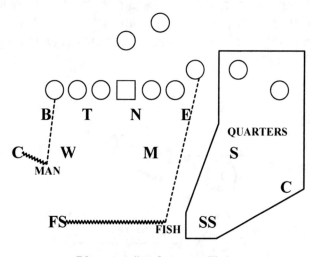

Diagram #5. Cover 8 Fish

Instead of playing three deep, we play a quarters man scheme. We play the quarters scheme on the #1 and #2 receivers to the trips side. We play the backside corner in a lockup man-to-man coverage on the single receiver side. The free safety cheats from the boundary side into the strongside and drops down on the #3 receiver to that side. If the #3 receiver runs deep, he belongs to the free safety.

We blitz one of the inside linebackers and everything else is the same. Typically, we blitz the linebacker away from the running back set. In this diagram, the back sets to the left of the

quarterback and we blitz the Will linebacker. We do that because they can run the speed option toward the back and we want the Mike linebacker in position to get into that play.

The play we must defend from this formation is the zone read. Every time we run a scheme, we must have someone in the B gap to the backs side. The end or linebacker, depending on the call, outside of the offensive tackle has to play a sitdown technique. We call the technique taking the air out. He has to sit down and squeeze down so there is no room between him and the B gap defender. He is responsible for an inside/out position on the quarterback if he pulls the ball on the option. He is a half-man defender on the quarterback.

On a dive option, you must have two defenders on the dive and two defenders on the load of the option. You must have someone who takes the inside half and someone to take the outside half of the ballcarrier (Diagram #6). On this play, the defensive end is the half man outside on the give inside to the running back. If the quarterback pulls the ball and runs outside, the defensive end is the inside half on the quarterback. The Sam linebacker is the outside half of the quarterback.

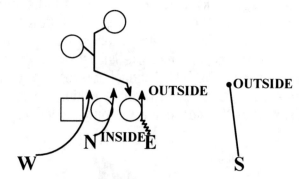

Diagram #6. Option Responsibility

If the #3 receiver blocks the Sam linebacker, the free safety replaces the Sam linebacker as the outside half on the quarterback. In our schemes, we have replacement schemes for all the support players. The offense has to use somebody to block a defender. When that blocker comes off on a defender, the player in the read on him becomes the replacement player.

The difference in playing zone and man is where the eyes focus. In the zone coverage, the defenders can support more on the run. They do not have their entire focus on a receiver. They can see the run patterns developing and react accordingly. In man coverage, the receivers can run the defenders out of the play. However, the quarter schemes I showed you are a basic man scheme.

When you play a team that runs the zone read, the defense has to be a nine-man surface. That amounts to quarter schemes or zero-man schemes. You must play that type of scheme if the quarterback is a runner. If you do not, the offense can pull someone around and get more blockers than the defense has defenders.

We did something this year at Illinois that was unique. This goes with the 3x1 adjustments. We call it switch (Diagram #7). Teams that use the trips set like to put their best receiver into the boundary as the single receiver. They feel that the corner to that side is on an island and playing soft. The good thing about this scheme is it is multiple and allows you to do many things. We play the quarters scheme with the Sam, corner, and strong safety. Instead of the free safety coming over in the fish adjustment, we use the Mike linebacker to carry the #3 receiver.

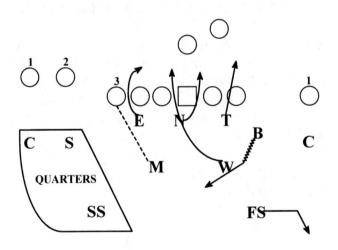

Diagram #7. Switch/Pitt

We refer to the blitz adjustment as Pitt. The nose goes to the boundary side A gap and the Will linebacker blitzes the fieldside A gap. This is not a good run defense, but we can get away with the coverage. We can scheme it better and put a dime back into the game to carry the #3 receiver. We blitz the Will linebacker even though he is to the side of the back. The bandit replaces the Will linebacker.

To the boundary side, we play two defenders over the single receiver. That gives us a hard corner and protection over the top. It allows the corner to take away the quick throws without worry about the deep patterns.

This next coverage comes from one of the subpackages in our scheme. This is a zone read stopper (Diagram #8). We want to play quarters but stop the zone read. This is a zone blitz package. We moved the bandit to the field into a 5 technique on the offensive tackle. The Will linebacker moves over the tight end to the boundary. We walk the Mike linebacker up to the line of scrimmage and show a pressure look. On the snap of the ball, the bandit and the nose pinch to the inside. The Mike linebacker becomes the flasher and loops to the C gap into the field.

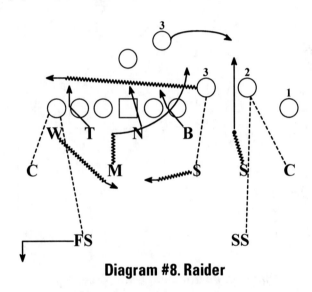

Diagram #8. Raider

When we play the wide slot formation, we take away the bubble screen by alignment. On occasion, we take the Sam linebacker and align him in a robber (head-up) alignment on the slot receiver. Before the snap of the ball, he adjusts to an inside alignment. We want to give the receivers many different looks from the overhang players. The corner and safety read the #2 receiver. The Sam linebacker does not have that receiver, but he has to get his hands on him to protect himself. However, his focus is on the #3 receiver. He widens the #2 receiver and holds the curl area in his zone. If the #3 receiver releases, he takes him.

In the diagram, I show a bubble screen to the outside. On this play, the #3 receiver goes in motion to the other side. When that occurs, the running back becomes the #3 receiver for the Sam linebacker. The technique played by the Sam linebacker is the same technique the bandit plays to the other side. In our subpackages, we have nickel and dime receivers in these schemes. The personnel may change, but the techniques do not. This scheme is good if the offense tries to throw the ball. If they have any type of man-blocking scheme, the Mike linebacker looping to the outside could become a free rusher.

The problem with this coverage is the running back in the backfield as a pass receiver (Diagram #9). The problem we have is with containment. If the back releases to the trips side as the fourth receiver, the Mike linebacker has to pick him up. However, you cannot have your cake and eat it too. You have to give up something to cover that back.

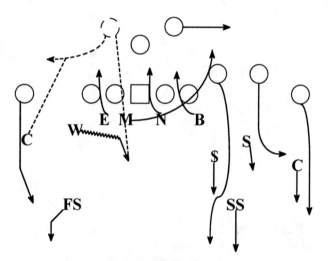

Diagram #9. Running Back Coverage

The corner playing under the #1 receiver into the boundary has the #2 receiver from the backfield. If the back aligns to his side, he rides the receiver, but his eyes have to go to the back in the backfield. If the back releases, the corner has the coverage on him. The free safety has the wide receiver in an inside/out man coverage. If the back releases into the middle, the folding Will linebacker has him that way. The Will linebacker drops into the middle of the defense and plays.

At Kansas State, we played a sluff technique. I never perfected it at Illinois. It is an advanced technique to confuse the receivers. We aligned the corners hard and bailed them as if they were going to the deep third. We watched the receivers on tape.

We wanted to know with which step the receivers determined the leverage of the defensive backs. If the receiver thought the corner was playing soft, he ran a certain route. If he thought the corner was playing hard, he ran a different route. We do the same thing they expect, but we do it at a different depth. It confused receivers, and they ran route into us.

In our subpackage, we have the storm package. When we play this package, we have a bunch of defensive backs on the field. If we call anything with a weather system, the defense is a blitz from the field. We want to bring four defenders from the field. If we call lightning, thunder, tornado, storm, twister, or something like that, it is our call for the field blitzes. In this package, we play with the nickel and dime package on the field. In the weather package, we always played hard coverage to the field and quarters to the boundary. We might change what we do up front, but we did not have to change the coverage.

We played the bandit in a 5 technique to the field (Diagram #10). The nose played his shade to the tight end into the boundary. He can also align in a 0 technique on the center. The defensive end plays a 5 technique into the boundary. The Will linebacker plays a loose 90 alignment with the tight end. The nickel back plays in a six-yard stack behind the defensive end and locks on the tight end. The Mike linebacker plays his normal position to the field. The dime back plays into the wideside of the field one yard outside the offensive tackle and five yards deep. The Sam linebacker aligns inside the #2 receiver to the field.

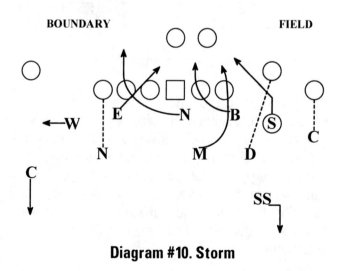

Diagram #10. Storm

The Will linebacker did the same thing each time on this package. The storm blitz was the Sam linebacker blitzing off the edge. The Mike linebacker locks up on the running back if he releases on a pattern. He is an add-on blitzer if the back blocks the Sam linebacker. The only thing that can hurt on this blitz is the slow screen to the running back. That is why we assign the Mike linebacker to him. We want the Mike to blitz, but he has to be aware of what the running back is trying to do.

The thing we want to do is play a hard underneath coverage on the receivers to the side we bring the blitz. If the offensive coach sees the blitz coming from the field, they want to work that side. We play a three-over-two scheme to the field. In the diagram, we twist the bandit and defensive end into the A gaps. The nose goes behind the defensive end and into the B gap, working for containment through that gap.

We can use twist stunt involving the bandit and Mike linebacker. In that twist stunt, the nose slant across the guards face into the A gap. The Mike linebacker presses the line of scrimmage and attacks the offensive tackle to the outside. The bandit comes off the Mike linebacker's tail into the B gap. We call that stunt a pick and roll. We can also slant the defensive front one way or the other. The movement in the front can change to take advantage of what the protection scheme is.

There are times when you do not want to bring the blitz runner from a wide position. However, when you bring the blitzer off the #2 receiver, not many teams will pick him up. The thing you want to do is smother any quick-breaking patterns to that side.

There were many games during the season when we told the Mike linebacker to go ahead and blitz in this package. If the team did not run the slow screen or have some scheme with the running back, we turned the Mike linebacker loose in this package. In the storm package, we can change the blitz runner and play the scheme. Those are the other blitzes in the scheme.

All the experts picked the Illinois defensive front to be 12th in the conference. They picked our linebackers as the most unproductive group in the conference. In the bowl game, we had the game

won. All we were trying to do was get the game over. We gave up a 30-yard gain. If it were not for that run, we were six yards short of being the #1 team in the conference in total defense. These players played the entire year with a chip on their shoulders.

We can zone blitz using the same concept but bring it from the boundary. These are our viper blitzes. This has snake terms to describe the blitz. The interior linemen slant to the fieldside (Diagram #11). The Will linebacker blitzes off the edge of the formation. The nickel back blitzes inside the offensive tackle. To the field, the Sam linebacker, corner, and strong safety make the coverage look like a three-over-two quarter zone. Actually, they play man-to-man coverage. The corner takes the #1 receiver and the safety has the #2 receiver. The Sam linebacker has the #3 receiver in the backfield.

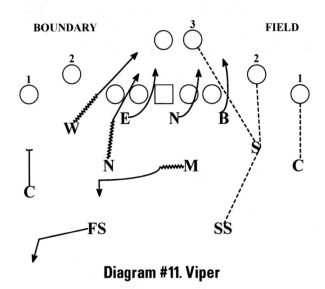

Diagram #11. Viper

To the boundary side, the corner rolls up into the flat zone and the free safety plays over the top of the corner. The Mike linebacker cheats to the boundary side and picks up the #2 receiver to the boundary if he tries to get deep down the middle. If he runs shallow to the inside, the Mike linebacker takes him if he comes into the middle of the field.

If we have a 3x1 set, we can run the viper blitz (Diagram #12). Everything in the alignment of the defensive is the same. The difference is that the Sam linebacker has a detached receiver to play man-to-man. The Mike linebacker has no #2 receiver to the boundary side of the formation. He turns the tight end over to the corner and drops to the trips

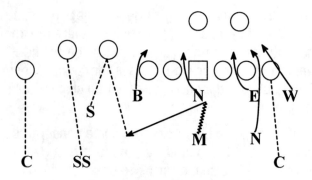

Diagram #12. Viper vs. 3x1

side of the formation. He gets inside leverage on the #3 receiver and helps the Sam linebacker on his coverage.

We play many different players in our coverage schemes. We want to get the best players on the field. We play them in different positions on the field. What I am trying to emphasize is to find your best players and find out what they can do. That is the thing our system has allows us to do. We can get into a defense and have our best players on the field.

I want to tell you what is going on at North Carolina, and this comes straight from the heart. We are going to make our players tough and hard nosed. Our situation is like the old saying "A leopard does not change his spots." That may be a true statement, but players turn out to be what you train them to be. We have some things we have to do. Our players are going to learn, they are going to hit, and they are going to win. We are not going to put players in positions where they cannot be successful. It is not fair to your players to ask them to do things they cannot do. That is what this package does. It put players in positions to make plays.

Coach Larry Fedora has an open door policy, and we would like you to visit. The thing you want to do is call before you come. Trying to start the program and organize all the things we need to do, we may not be available when you want to come to visit. However, we will do everything in our power to accommodate you. Thank you very much for your time and attention.

SPECIAL TEAMS ORGANIZATION AND DRILLS

Ball State University

It is good to be back talking football now that the season is over. I am entering my 12th year as a head coach. The job becomes increasing difficult, especially when you are taking over a program that needs rebuilding. There are so many things besides the X's and O's that you need to fix.

It is difficult to be the offensive coordinator and head coach. I do not know how some coaches are able to do that. Special teams with me have become a bigger part of what I do on the field and with the players every year. It gives me a chance to reach out and touch those players who play special teams. We all know that, with the exception of some offensive and defensive linemen, all our players play special teams. With the responsibility of the head coach, I cannot sit in every offensive or defensive meeting. Coaching the special teams allows me to stay connected to the X's and O's of the football team.

The first thing I want to talk about is selling the special teams program to your players. Special teams have to be important to your players, and they need to understand why that part of the game is so important. You have to show your players the impact of field position in the game.

The kicking game gains importance when you understand scoring percentages. It may sound simple, but the numbers do not lie. The more field you make the offense earn, the less likely they are to score points. Special teams impacts field position more than any other aspect of the game. Special teams plays can result in points or large chunks of yardage. The average play on special teams is over 30 yards. The average offensive play is five or six yards. We must make our opponents play on a long field and give our offense the best chance to score with a short field.

The players need to understand that the punt return and kickoff return can account for huge changes in field position as well as momentum in a game (Diagram #1). In our first special teams meeting in the fall and spring, we want our players to understand how field position affects our ability to score or our opponent's ability to score. We show them the impact chart in regards to field position. The chart shows where offensive drives start. It also shows the chances of scoring points from those positions.

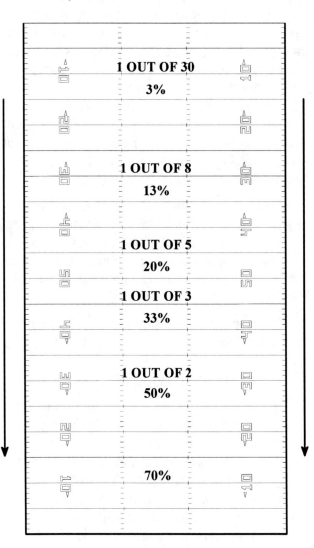

Diagram #1. Field Position Impact

HOW WE EMPHASIZE SPECIAL TEAMS

- Practice—time commitment
- Meetings
- Special teams pledge
- Weekly goal chart
- Point production chart
- Player of the week
- "Trinkets" (be creative)
- Nicknames for units ("Assault")
- Buzz words ("hit the beach")
- Notes in lockers (corrections)
- Head coach involvement

Another way to show your players the importance of special teams is to practice them. If you have a practice schedule that spends 10 to 15 minutes on special teams, it is not important to you. If you have a two-hour-and-15-minute practice session where you spend 40 minutes on special teams, your players will know it is important. If you throw, the special teams work at the end of practice when the players are tired, you will not get much out of that. If you mix special teams work in the time allotted for offense and defense, your players will know it is important. At Ball State, we commit the time to special teams.

We spend meeting time on special teams every day. We have a 20-minute meeting session daily. The A- and B-team linemen and quarterback go with their position coaches, but everyone else is in the special teams meeting. We meet on Tuesday, Wednesday, Thursday, and Sunday.

We have our players sign a special teams pledge. This gives them a sense of ownership in the team.

SPECIAL TEAMS PLEDGE

This document is my pledge to be special and to make a difference. I will find a way to contribute to the success of my unit, our special teams, and the 2011 Cardinals. My opponent may be bigger than me, he may be faster than me, he may be stronger than me, but he cannot match my will, and he will never match my intensity. Momentum and field position are my focus. I thrive on the opportunity to make big plays and positively affect the outcome of the game.

I understand that offense and defense begins with special teams. Our return and block units will have an offensive mentality. We will secure the ball at all times, as possession is our first priority. If we do not score a touchdown, we must set one up by giving our offense a "short field." Our coverage units will have a defensive mentality, as field position is our first priority. We will look to create momentum and cause turnovers.

I will be coachable. I may not be perfect, but I will not make the same mistake twice. I will be accountable for my responsibilities and win the 1-on-1 battles. I will study my opponent and know my assignments. I will believe in our mission, and I will follow through physically and mentally.

Whether I am a starter or a backup, a senior or a freshman, I will never underestimate my value as a special teams player. Above all, I will outhustle and outhit my opponent.

You can count on me.

Signature:

Date:

We have a weekly goal chart for reaching goals for all the units you have. We keep a point production chart for every player who participates on special teams. We post it every week so the players know it is competitive. We want them to come into the locker room and look at the chart to see who is at the top. We want the players on these teams to want to get to the top of that board and become the most productive player on the team.

We have a special teams player of the week just as we do an offensive, defensive, and scout team player of the week. I think trinkets are great ways to motivate players. When I was at Elon University, I watched the special teams tape. The first player who crossed the 30-yard line on every kickoff, I gave him a Milky Way® candy bar. I did so in front of the team, which gave the player special recognition. Our special teams coach, Justin Lustig, puts all kinds of gadgets in the players' lockers as part of our player recognition program.

If you give your teams nicknames to particular units, it adds to the players' excitement of being on the teams. We call our kickoff coverage team the "Assault Unit." When they assemble on the sidelines before they go onto the field, Coach Lustig tells them to "hit the beach." It gives them the feeling of going into battle. The players get excited about it.

We put notes in the players' lockers daily. After we watch the films from practice, we have a little red card on which we write notes to the players. It is like a pink slip notice you get from work. However, it is about something a player did well in practice or a correction we want to see the player make.

The head coach wants to send the right message to his team. If he stands to the side and watches as the special teams work, that sends the wrong message. If the head coach is directly involved, this makes it important to everyone else. Coaching special teams gives the head coach a chance to interact on the field with almost every player on the roster. If the head coach is intimately involved in special teams, he can make decisions during the week and on game day to tie the entire game plan together.

If the head coach is actively involved in special teams and understands the importance of winning the game on Saturday, it helps him manage and oversee the offensive and defensive coordinators as well. At the end of the day, the job of the head coach is to keep everyone on the same page. All three of the coordinators know going into game what it is going to take to win the game. We all have to be on the same page.

In a particular game, our offensive coordinator may want to throw the ball. However, the overall plan has to minimize the risks because the opponent is extremely effective on offense. That puts more pressure on the defense, if we turn the ball over. That has to enter into the total scheme and game plan. This keeps all the coordinators on the same page.

We have weekly objectives on special teams just like the offensive and defensive teams. One of the huge items is "no penalties." That plays such a big role in field position. Having a long return

called back because of a holding or block in the back penalty can be devastating.

WEEKLY OBJECTIVES

- Win—make a meaningful contribution
- No penalties
- Score or set up a score
- Turnovers—create one, allow none
- Protection—allow no blocks or shanks
- Explosive plays (KOR>40, PR>20, blocks, fakes +1)
- Returners—field all kicks cleanly
- Punt protection—35 yard net
- Punt pressure—10 yards/return, opp. net < 30
- Kickoff coverage—deep inside 25 / sky inside 30
- Kickoff return—average drive start > 31
- PAT/Field Goal—100% inside 30, 75% outside 30

We have a production chart for our players. We grade each phase of the kicking game and assign a score for each player on those teams. In addition to the players receiving points, they can amass negative points. They receive minus point for missed assignments, loafs, and penalties. We post the results weekly, declare a special teams player of the year, and honor him at the banquet. Following is an example of one of our production sheets for the kickoff team. We have charts for each team and score each of them.

KICKOFF TEAM PRODUCTION SHEET

Play	Points
Outstanding team or individual play	10
Kickoff into end zone and downed	5
Forced fumble	5
Recovered fumble	5
Kickoff into end zone	3
Kickoff inside five-yard line	1
Great effort	3
Tackle	2
Grade 100 percent	3
Loaf	-5
Penalty	-5
Missed assignment	-3

There are qualities we look for in special teams players. We want as many safeties, outside linebackers, wide receivers, fullbacks, corners, and those types of athletes on these teams. We want players who can *run* and *hit* on these units. The more players of that type you have in the program, the more you can incorporate them into these units. We want players who pay *attention to detail*. We will spend time with them, but we are not going to spend as much time as we do with their offensive and defensive positions. We want players who can see the big picture and are coachable.

The players on these teams, especially the ones who return the ball, must be *reliable* and *trustworthy*. Your punt returner cannot field the ball inside the five-yard line. He has to make good decisions and be trusted to catch the ball. Mistakes in the kicking game can break a game wide open. Players on these teams must have *courage*. They must play with reckless abandon. Covering kickoffs is something that is not right for all players. There are players who want to do it. It takes a special breed to cover the kickoff.

In spring practice, we find our special teams players. We consistently evaluate our personnel in the spring. We work the fundamentals and evaluate the people who can perform the fundamentals.

Each year, we do a quality control sheet. We take the year's statistics and put them in a final tally. It allows us to see the areas where we need to improve and give more attention to those areas in the spring and fall workouts. We did a study at Elon when I was there. We compared the statistics in a four-year period. It pointed out some trends for us. In the years of 2008 and 2009, we had a great offensive team. That meant we kicked the ball off more. We needed to spend more time on the kickoff coverage team.

In 2009, we did not return many kickoffs. The reason for that was the defense was extremely good. Our opponents did not score many times against us. These types of studies can help you concentrate on the things you need to work on in practice. I think it is important to know what you are actually doing each year in the kicking game. That lets you organize the practice time more accurately. Personally, I feel you should spend more time on punting the football than any other phase.

You do that more than the other phases of the game. The blocked kick is a tremendous momentum changer. These types of studies and scouting lead you into practice time allocations. This gives you an idea of how we decide how to allot practice time.

PRACTICE TIME ALLOCATION

- What do you see from opponents in each phase?
  ✓ Example: Shield punt versus pro (spread) punt.
- At least 75 percent of opponents used the shield punt.
- What type of team do you want to be (personality)?
  ✓ Example: Blocking punts versus returning punts (percent).
- What limitations do you have (personnel, meeting time)?
  ✓ Example: Pro punt versus shield punt—Complex versus simple.

If you want to be a team that blocks punts and kicks, you have to invest the time in those areas. That is why we went to the shield type of punt. It simplified the punt-blocking scheme for us. We did not have to spend as much time teaching the scheme and adjustments. We now spend the time in reps and execution instead of teaching. We are committed in the special teams program. I want to share with the amount of time we spend during the week with special teams practice.

SPECIAL TEAMS QUALITY CONTROL

- *Sunday (helmets only)*
  ✓ 30 min. (meeting), 10 min. (kickoff cover drills), 5 min. (punt)
- *Tuesday (full pads)*
  ✓ 20 min. (meeting), 5 min. (specialists), 10 min. (punt pressure), 8 min. (punt), 7 min. (kickoff return or kickoff)
- *Wednesday (uppers)*
  ✓ 20 min. (meeting), 5 min. (specialists), 5 min. (PAT/field goal), 10 min. (kickoff return), 10 min. (kickoff cover), 5 min. (punt)
- *Thursday (uppers)*
  ✓ 20 min. (meeting), 5 min. (specialists—kickoff return), 5 min. (PAT/field goal), 10 min. (punt return), 10 min. (punt), 7 min. (kickoff cover), 8 min. (kickoff return), 5 min. (special situations)

- *Friday (helmets, walk-through)*
  - ✓ 40 min. (meeting), 10 min. (review on field, personnel call-ups)

We play our game on Saturday; however, in the MAC conference, we do have mid-week games. If we were to play on a Tuesday, the next day would be the Sunday practice. On Sunday, we are on the field for 45 minutes. Of that time, we spend 15 minutes on special teams. The linemen and quarterbacks work with their position coaches during this time.

Thursday is a polish day for the kicking game. We work special kickoff return teams against air. A coach stands next to the kickoff man and instructs him on where to kick the ball. He kicks it to the right and left corners. He uses a high pooch kick to both sides. He kicks the ball onside to both side and the dribbled onside kick down the middle. We want to cover all aspects of trickery in the kickoff. We want to make sure all 11 players on the kickoff return team plug into those types of exotic kicks. We must cover these types of kicks even though they may occur only once or twice a year. During this time, we also cover the special situations that occur in a game. We have the hands team align to receive an onside kick. We cover the kick after a safety and receiving after a safety.

On Friday, we have a special teams walk-through. It may not include every unit, but we concentrate on the teams we feel a need to cover. After that, we go through a mock game. We do different personnel call-ups. We practice the substitution patterns during this time. We call each unit as if we would in the game.

When we have our five-minute special period during practice, we assign a place for everyone to be. The punters, long snappers, and punt return personnel go into one area of the field. The place kickers, short snappers, holders, and kick returners go to another section of the field. In one corner of the field, we have the team of the day. They will work on some kind of fundamentals, which is specific to that unit. For example, it might be the punt pressure unit working on punt-blocking techniques. It is not full speed, but we are working on takeoff, block positioning, and fundamentals. The coaches are spread out with their units and working with the players.

LITTLE THINGS

- *Pressure field goal at the end of practice*
  - ✓ Spring
  - ✓ Pre-season
  - ✓ Tuesday in season
- *Coming out drill (-1) plus "danger punt"*
  - ✓ Spring (1 time)
  - ✓ Pre-season (2 times)
- *Punt fakes*
  - ✓ Install in spring
  - ✓ Pre-season and every Wednesday/Thursday in season
  - ✓ Consistent throughout year (like special plays)

We have 105 players during this time, and every one of them has something to do. I have some little nuggets I want to share with you. We do these things, and I think it has helped us. We do a pressure field goal at the end of practice. This would occur on a Tuesday or Wednesday for us.

You do it at the end of practice with the whole team participating. We get the first field goal unit and first block unit in the drill. If it is during the season, you might not want to go full tempo and get someone hurt. We take all 100 players and surround the kicker. They yell at him, talk about the last one he missed, talk about his girlfriend, or anything that could unnerve him. The kicker has to block all that out and kick the field goal.

The second situation is the backed up punt. It does not happen too many times during the season, but we want to work on it in the spring to be ready for it. We put the ball on the -1 yard line. The offense has three plays to drive the ball out. If the defense stops them, the punt team has to come out and punt the ball in that situation. This forces the punter to punt under direst.

The fake punt is something that cannot happen in the course of a week. You cannot draw it up on Monday, work on it on Tuesday and Wednesday, and expect it to work on Saturday. What I do believe is: you can install the fakes in the spring, and work on them in the spring, pre-season practice, and weekly during the season. If you do that, you will have the confidence to use them when you need them during the season.

I want to get into the drill section of the lecture. I do not expect you to change what you do in your kicking game because I show you a scheme, however, these drill can go with any type of scheme. When we teach our drills, we do them from the hash marks moving toward the sidelines. When we use the finish drill in the punt return, we use the entire field.

KICKOFF COVERAGE: THREE-DRILL CIRCUIT

- Avoid a frontline block (whip/flash)
- Two-gap a backline block
- Takeoff drill

On every kickoff, the coverage team has to avoid a frontline block by the front blocking unit. When they get close to the ball, they have to use a two-gap technique on a backline blocker. When they get in the area of the ball, they cannot avoid the blockers and take a side. Every kickoff coverage team has to get great takeoff in their coverage. It does not matter what scheme you use; these drills can help you.

The first thing I watch when we start to break down an opponent is their kickoff coverage team. If all ten of their players hit the line at the same time, I know we probably have a quality opponent. If they are scattered in their run up to the ball, we will have success against them.

The first drill is an avoid drill. There are two parts to this drill. We have two techniques called "stem and whip" and "stem and flash." I want the coverage team to understand the position of the blocker as they come down. If the blocker's butt is to the sidelines, that is the way the ball will come. If his butt is to the middle of the field, the ball will come up the middle. The coverage team wants to avoid the block to the butt side of the blocker.

The difference between the whip and flash is the path the coverage team takes. On the whip, we come across the face of the blocker to his butt side (Diagram #2). With the flash, there is space between the blocker and coverage man (Diagram #3). The coverage defender beats the blocker with speed and gets to his butt side.

We use the two-gap technique with a backline block on the kickoff (Diagram #4). When the

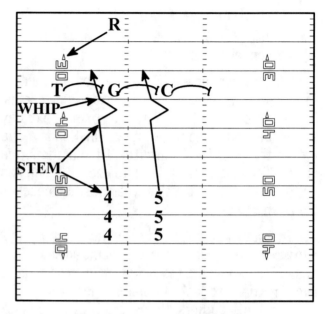

Diagram #2. Stem and Whip

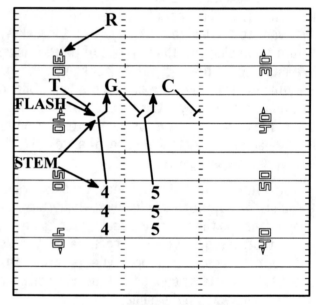

Diagram #3. Stem and Flash

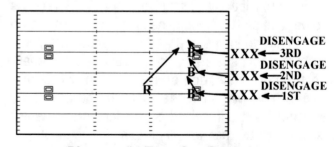

Diagram #4 Two-Gap Technique

coverage gets within 15 yards of the football, they cannot avoid blocks. They have to take on the blocker. They attack the blocker down the middle and stun him with their hands. They have to stun with their eyes. They must see the target and attack. They have to get their pads under the blocker's pads and shoot the hands. I want the elbows in and the hands tight with the thumbs up. The coverage wants to drive the opponent back into the ballcarrier. When we get to the ballcarrier, we want to disengage when the opponent threatens our leverage.

The next drill is the takeoff drill (Diagram #5). The coverage team straddles a line 10 yards from ball as a general alignment rule. They move based on their speed and vision of the kicker. They will have to find their start point so they hit the line at the same time as everyone else. They always hit the line one half yard behind the kicker. They want to see the ball kicked ("peripheral") and then get their eyes downfield. All 10 men should hit the line at the same time. We refer to that as "birds on a wire."

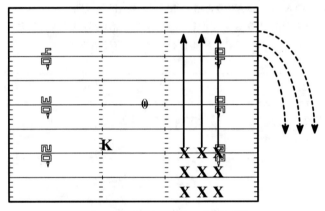

Diagram #5. Takeoff Drill

PUNT RETURN: THREE-DRILL CIRCUIT

- Get-off (at line of scrimmage)
- Harass (maintain)
- Finish (block or screen)

The next circuit is a punt return circuit. The get-off phase is attacking the coverage defenders at the line of scrimmage. The harass phase is the middle part of the return, when the blocker runs back with the defender. The defender escapes the line of scrimmage, and the blocker tries to maintain a position on him to block him. The finish phase is the moment of truth for the blocker. He has to decide if he can legally block the defender. If he can block him, he has to know how to do it.

This drill is the get-off phase of the circuit (Diagram #6). The defender gets into a three-point stance when facing a pro punt. If it is a shield punt, we align in a two-point stance. We key the man if we are in a return mode. If we are in a rush mode, we watch the ball. Against the shield punt, we want to mirror the release of the coverage at the line of scrimmage. As we come off the line of scrimmage, we use the off hand to widen the path of the coverage man.

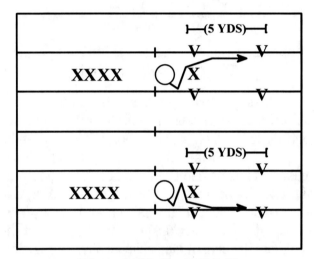

Diagram #6. Get-Off Drill

Against the pro punt, we explode off the ball at movement and stun the opponent with the hands at the top of his numbers. We want to maintain a 90-degree flexion at the elbows and step on his toes. We ride the coverage along the line of scrimmage and run with him after he escapes. The get-off drill is a mirror drill at the line of scrimmage.

The next part of the circuit is the harass phase (Diagram #7). After the coverage gets off the line of scrimmage, he gets into the transition stage. As the defender begins to cover downfield, we must stay in contact with him. We can buy additional grass for the returner in this phase. The blockers have to maintain leverage on the coverage as he runs down the field. We put the fingers on the defender's hip, eyes on the hip, run with him, and widen him. We want the coverage to be aware of us as we run down the field. This drill does not have to be a full-speed drill. We watch the hands and eyes of the blockers. We want to widen opponents and allow no space between the blocker and the cover man ("Reel up the slack").

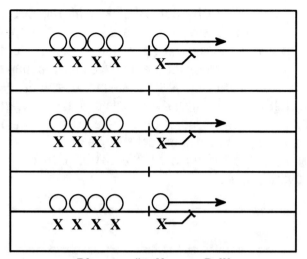

Diagram #7. Harass Drill

The last phase in this circuit is the finish (Diagram #8). Three things happen in this phase. We can use a high shield block on the coverage. When a defender attempts to tackle without coming to balance, we must bend as he bends and get our body between him and the ballcarrier. We are not blocking; we are shielding him from the ballcarrier. We may have to pull off. If the blocker gets stacked behind the opponent, he cannot block him legally. He peels off and looks downfield for late coverage players (e.g., shield or punter). If the defender breaks down to make the tackle, we mirror his movement, engage, and block.

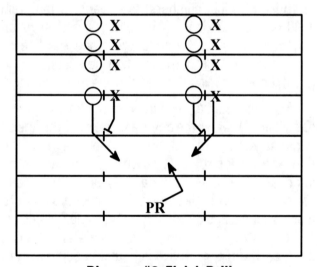

Diagram #8. Finish Drill

The coaching point on this drill is not to get a penalty trying to block someone. Pull off and find someone else. The penalty is not worth the attempt. If you cannot high-shield or block the defender, pull off.

KICKOFF RETURN: FRONTLINE

- Drop-to-fit
- Angle drop-to-fit
- Strike and shuffle square

In this part of the game, we talk about snap keys. The blocker cannot run very fast if he looks at the ball in the air. If the blockers watch the return man, they will know where the ball goes. We want the frontline blockers to snap their heads around to the returner to find out where they should run. That is the snap key. The coverage team will funnel to the place where they kick the ball.

When we teach the drop-to-fit, we teach it in two phases. We teach a drop-to-fit with a vertical drop and an angle drop. We open to both the left and right as we drill the vertical drops on air (Diagram #9). In this drill, the blocker uses the vertical drop with second man in line acting as the cover man. Working down a yard line tells us if the blocker is running in a straight line. The fastest way to get from point A to point B is a straight line.

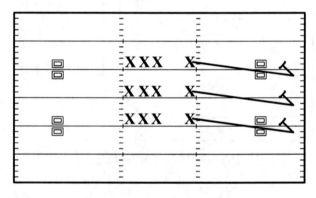

Diagram #9. Vertical Fit

The second drop-to-fit is an angle drop (Diagram #10). We angle drop on air, working on opening both to the left and right. When we angle drop, the second man in line acts as cover man. This is where the snap key fits into his drop. When we do the drill, we use three whistles. The first whistle starts the drop. The second whistle starts the coverage man, and the third whistle stops the drill.

The strike and shuffle drill is similar to the mirror drill (Diagram #11). Strike with a good base and proper leverage based on the return called. This is the point of contact. The face mask will be involved initially because the defender has run 40

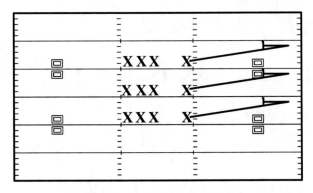

Diagram #10. Angle Fit

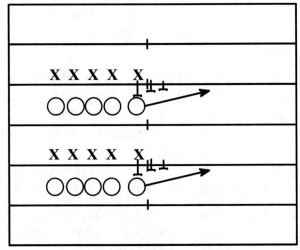

Diagram #11. Strike and Shuffle

yards. The first thing we have to do is get the head out of the block. If the blocker buries his head into the defender, the defender can easily disengage. We strike the breastplate, cover up the defender, and get into a square position.

After we get a square position on the defender, we shuffle with the block. We maintain the block without crossing our feet over. We steer the defender. The blocker can shuffle before contact to get into position to cover up the defender.

One of the big arguments in special teams coaching is the tempo of the drills. During spring practice, we are more inclined to do some live drills. In the fall, the drill tempo is full speed through contact, but it is relaxed very quickly. We want to avoid the violent collisions, which can occur. We use great judgment when we run a kickoff or kickoff return drill. We will cover a couple of kicks live in the pre-season scrimmages, but we are very careful. You can do the drills in half-pads and helmets. You can teach the techniques and fundamentals. One coaching point I can give you to make the drills better is to coach the dummy and bag holders so there is resistance on the target.

Thank you for your attention. We welcome you and your staff to visit us. Our doors are open. Thank you for your time.

INVOLVING THE TIGHT END IN THE PASSING GAME

The University of Georgia

I appreciate the opportunity to be here. It is especially exciting to be here on the last day of this clinic. I know the coaches sitting here love football. It is great to be here with this particular group. On behalf of Coach Richt, our offensive coordinator, Mike Bobo, and the rest of our offensive staff, I appreciate the opportunity to be here.

I am going to talk about the Georgia passing game. I want to mention a couple of other things first. We must have a belief in the way to win football games. I hope some of the things we talk about will have some carryover to what you do and you can get something from this lecture. I hope that you can use some of the concepts we use. Our concepts are simple. We are not complicated. I do not know if other teams find our passing game complicated to prepare for, but we do not want to complicate things for our players.

Many of our young players are successful, and I think it is because of the simplicity of our system. They are successful because they buy into what we do. There are things in this system that can help them be successful early in their career. However, we do a good job of recruiting. Many times, it is not the plays but the players that make a successful program. We present some things to our players that help them along the way to success.

I want to take you through one of our typical Tuesday in-season practice schedules. During the week, this is our biggest workday. Sunday is our players' day off. We give them Sunday because we feel like they should rest the day after the game. There are no classes, and we felt it was the best day to take off. We tried Monday, but it was not good for our players. The coaches liked it better because it gave us more time to work on the practice preparation and game planning. However, Sunday made more sense because it was like a true day off with nothing for them to do.

When you set up a practice schedule, you can tell what Coach Richt wants to emphasize by the way things are set up. During last season, we ran the ball 580 times and threw it 470 times. That amounts to 56 percent run and 44 percent passing the ball.

In our league, you must have a physical offense. There are times when you have to exert your will physically on the opponents. In games that are close, you have to make first downs in the fourth quarter. To finish the game, you must be able to line up and run the football. We are not a spread offense that throws the ball a high percentage of the time.

On Tuesday, we start the session with individual meetings with the position coaches. When we come on the field, one of the first things we do is a brief 10-minute walk-through with our offense on things we want to cover during that week. It may be sight adjustments or blitz pickups. It may be the script of plays and protections for that day's practice. This is a calm tempo in which to teach and get ready for the day's practice. This is a 10-minute set, but you do not have to fight the clock. When we get into the regular practice session, you continually fight the clock to get everything done.

We start the practice with a kicking and specialty period. We follow that with a three-minute ball security period. When we do this period, everyone participates. The offensive and defensive personnel do these drills. For the tight end, it may be a strip drill or some kind of ball distraction drill.

We do some things that have been very successful for us, but it is hard to get the quarterback to do it. You get frustrated with your quarterback because he does not check the ball down, follow his progression, or throw to a certain receiver when he should. He wants to throw vertical patterns, but they are hard balls to catch, and the receivers drop many of them. He cannot find receivers because the defense covers everyone in the immediate or deep areas. Everyone clears the zones, and there stands a lone running back. The quarterback can throw a five-yard pass and we could get 25 yards out of the play.

We feel if we are going to be good, our quarterbacks have to understand their progression and make the throws to all the receivers. We have individual time built into our practice for the quarterback to work with each group of receivers on an individual basis. The quarterback works individually with the running back, tight ends, and wide receivers. The receivers like that because that is what they signed up to do. The rest of the time they spend in doing the things that help the offense go. If the wide receiver wants to get on the field at Georgia, he must block. When we have the individual drills, we work on catching.

In those drills, we concentrate on catching the ball, and we put pressure on them when they do not. The tight ends and running back sometimes feel forgotten in the passing progression. These individual drills with the quarterback give the receiver confidence, and it lets the quarterback work with those positions. The more he throws to them and learns who can catch, the more confidence and comfortable he is with the tight end and running backs.

When I coach the tight ends, I tell them where they stand in the progression the quarterback uses on a play. They may be the fourth receiver in the progression, but they know they have a chance to catch the ball. In the 5- or 10-minute passing period, the quarterback may throw him the ball on occasion. That gives him hope that on Saturday, the quarterback may look his way.

On Saturday, the quarterback knows the tight end will be where he is supposed to be. If the defense takes away his primary receiver, he can come to the tight end and have confidence that the tight end will be in the right place and catch the ball. That holds true with the backs as well.

That is the reason our tight end has led us in receiving or been one of the top three receivers that last seven years. This past year, we had a running back who led us in receiving. The passes he caught were not all screen passes. Our quarterbacks are beginning to check the ball down to the running backs and the tight ends. When the quarterback does not have his primary receiver, he is getting the ball to someone who will save the sack. That receiver may get one yard, but he also may get 20 yards.

In practice, we do a 2-on-2 drill, where we work on our bubble screens and quick screens. We work on our passing game in the 7-on-7 drill. A large percentage of the schedule is devoted to the passing game. You have to do that to be successful in the passing game.

In our practices, we try to do drills that have carryovers to the game situations. I have done it myself. I do what I think is a great five-minute drill. However, when I step back and look at the drill, I have no idea how that helps us in a game situation. If you do a drill that is unrelated to something that will make your players better, you are wasting your time. We want the drills to apply to what they have to do that week or for the rest of the season.

One of the things we work on in practice is a release drill. The tight end aligns and release through a dummy holder and runs his route on air. We work the release we think we will see in the game on Saturday. We work drills with dummies representing the 5 technique tackle, Sam linebackers, and Mike linebackers. Most of the releases the tight end takes involve avoiding or fighting through one of those defenders.

The tight end in our offense is not always in a tight formation. In some of our 3x1 formations, the tight end is in a flex position, working against nickel back personnel. He has to work on getting inside on a defensive back when he runs his dig routes. We work a six-yard drill against the curl/flat defenders.

When we work ball drills, we want something going on around the tight end. Very seldom does a tight end catch a ball where there is no traffic. We work many distraction drills and drills where the quarterback throws the ball outside of the framework of the body. The spot-up patterns we run off linebackers are generally patterns where the quarterback delivers the ball away from the linebacker. For the tight end to catch the ball, he has to extend his arms away from the linebacker and catch it outside the framework.

We expect the tight end to catch the ball. He has to make the average catch and the ones where the conditions are not ideal. The quarterback cannot always throw the ball that is easy to catch. That is the difference in average tight ends and the good ones. They can go get the ball when the quarterback does not throw it with a great deal of accuracy.

We run a dig drill with the linebackers (Diagram #1). The tight end releases through a dummy holder at the line of scrimmage. This drill simulates the defender coming from inside and getting into a hip position on the inside of the tight end. The tight end has to run the pattern where the linebacker has leverage on him. We have a dummy holder at six yards down the field. The tight end approaches the dummy, plants his outside foot, and fights across the dummy to the inside.

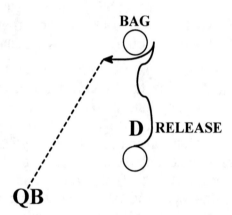

Diagram #1. Dig Drill

We work the box drill to work on their cutting skills. We set up four cones in a 10-yard square. The tight end works a release off a dummy at the first cone. He works the perimeter of the cones making 90-degree cuts at each cone. You can put a catch at the end of the drill if you choose.

We work a slant drill with a dummy holder at the line of scrimmage. We set the cone at five yards and the tight end comes off the ball through the dummy, breaks at five yards, and receivers the ball in the window between the outside defender and the inside receiver. The thing we want to concentrate in this drill is catching the ball clean. Anytime you run a short breaking pattern to the inside, you have to absorb some contact. If you do not catch the ball clean, the chances of holding on are slim.

I just wanted to give you some of examples of drills we do in practice daily. In all the drills, we work on getting off the line of scrimmage and catching the ball in traffic with many distractions.

What I want to do now is give you some of the patterns we work in our scheme and talk about the concepts and our thinking in the play. Our base formation is a pro type of offense with two backs, one tight end, and two wide receivers. We are going to be in some kind of I-formation scheme. Our game plan always starts with some form of I-formation football.

We call the first concept our bench concept. We do not number our routes. We provide a name for the pass routes we run. The numbers in our offense are the protection scheme. The tags get long at times, but we consolidate most of the calls to keep them manageable. The tags help the receivers because it tells them what to do. The bench concept works for all the sets we may run because the patterns are the same for each formation.

In the bench split, the wide receivers are one yard above the numbers into the boundary and four yards from the hash mark into the field (Diagram #2). The Z-receiver is the #1 receiver to the strongside of the formation. He runs a six-step speed-out. We do not plant and square off the cut. We want him to roll off the inside foot and work back to the sidelines. The tight end is the #2 receiver to the strongside. He runs what we call a broken arrow pattern down the seam. He comes off the ball, stems to the outside, and keys the middle of the

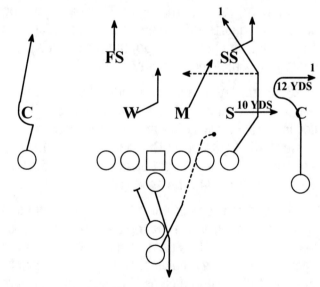

Diagram #2. Bench Split

field. If there is a two-high safety look in the middle, he runs up the seam, angling for the far goalpost upright. He makes his cut at 10 yards. He is the number-one read on this play.

If the middle of the field is closed with a middle safety, the tight end shuts his pattern down. He bends the pattern to the inside under the angle of the deep safety. It is almost a dig pattern into the windows behind the linebackers and in front of the middle field safety. The quarterback comes off that read and works the Z-receiver to the checkdown of the running back. If the coverage is a cover 3 or quarters look, the quarterback is not thinking of throwing into the middle of the field.

The X-receiver to the boundary works on the corner to that side. He has a go pattern, but we want him to work on the leverage of the defensive back. If we get press coverage, the X-receiver could be the primary receiver. The pattern converts from a go to a fade route. If the corner has outside leverage on the receiver, the receiver wants to attack the corner's leverage. He wants to stem to the outside and make the corner widen to keep the leverage. The receiver does not want to run up the field and let the corner have the leverage.

The Z-receiver runs the six-step speed-out. That puts him at a depth of 10 to 12 yards. He is into the wideside of the field and has room to the outside to work the pattern. The coaching point for the receiver on this play is to explode out of the break. If he eases out of the break, it becomes an easier pattern break for the defensive back. We want the receiver to threaten the defensive back deep. He has to break the cushion of the defensive back, make him turn, and break behind his tilt. If the quarterback throws the ball to the Z-receiver, it will be on the way before the receiver comes out of the break. The receiver has to locate the ball when he snaps his head around.

Even though we have room to the outside, the underthrown ball is not what the quarterback wants to do. If the quarterback throws the route, he has to deliver the ball on time and to the outside. We always want the ball thrown up and to the outside so the receiver can make the catch and continue to run. Against press coverage, we can tag "takeoff" to the call and both outside receiver run a takeoff pattern. We do not run that particular tag much.

The quarterback progression against a two-high look is tight end, Z-receiver, to the running back. Against the single-high look, the Z-back is the first choice, and then the running back. The tight end could come open in the middle behind the linebackers.

The protection on this play is 144 sprint draw protection (Diagram #3). The quarterback has a five-step drop on this play. He fakes the sprint draw. The center identifies the Mike linebacker for the protection scheme. The five offensive linemen are responsible for the four down defenders and the Mike linebacker. We work a trio scheme on the Mike linebacker, 3 technique defender, and the 1 technique defender. The tackles take the rushers coming off the edge and the center and two guards zone on the inside defender and the Mike linebacker. If the Mike linebacker does not blitz, the center is the free blocker.

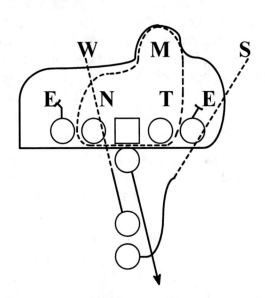

Diagram #3. Protection Scheme

The demon concept is a double post concept (Diagram #4). This concept has many of the same elements and thought processes of the bench concept. The #2 receiver strong (tight end) runs the broken arrow pattern as he did on the bench. This takes advantage of the middle-of-the-field safety. The #1 receiver strong (Z-back) runs the second post cut. The progression for the quarterback is the same. He looks for the inside post, the outside post, and down to the back.

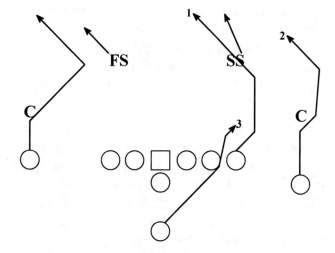

Diagram #4. Demon

The Z-receiver sticks his foot in the ground 12 to 14 yards and runs a post cut. He aims for the near upright of the goalpost. He has a lot of field to run into. The X-receiver is not in the progression or thought process of the quarterback. However, what he does is tremendously important to the play. Our X-receiver was the second leading receiver and would have been first but he missed three games with an injury. He caught many balls for us this year. He runs a corner route, but we want him to take up two defenders against any two-deep coverage.

He stems his pattern into the seam and sets a high angle on the corner route to pull the free safety to his pattern. We do not want the weakside safety to be a factor on the strongside patterns.

We want the tight end to try to get a pre-snap read on the secondary. If the tight end reads a single-high safety, his thinking is to bend the broken arrow pattern under the drop of the safety. The quarterback reads the single-high look and knows he is reading inside, outside, and down to the back. He wants to see how deep the safety is going to drop. If the drop of the safety is too deep, the quarterback can hit the tight end if he does not run his pattern too shallow. If he is too shallow, the Mike linebacker can be a factor in the play.

If the safety jumps the tight end on the broken arrow, the Z-receiver is running a post pattern behind him. The running back runs the checkdown pattern. He has a blocking assignment on the Sam linebacker before he can release. If the Sam linebacker blitzes, the running back cannot release

on a pattern. There is a sprint draw fake on this play. However, if the back sees the Sam linebacker coming on the blitz, he does not waste time coming over the ball for the fake. We do not want to block the linebacker one yard in front of the quarterback. When the back sees the blitz, he has to go take it on.

Against the single safety, the tight end drives at the middle safety and takes him to the far upright with his pattern. When the safety follows the tight end across his zone, the post cut from the Z-receiver is on the backside seam, heading to the near upright. The quarterback reads from inside post to outside post. If he does not like either of those patterns, he drops the ball to the back.

Against two-high safeties, the important route is the X-receiver to the backside of the pattern. He has to get the attention of the weakside safety and make sure he is a treat to him. He stems his pattern to the inside to get in the eyesight of the safety. When he runs the corner route, he wants to keep it high and not so much into the sideline until the safety bites on the threat and moves toward the sidelines and off the hash. The double post puts a stretch on the field safety. If the safety does not respect the tight end, that is the quarterback's first choice. If he jumps the tight end, the quarterback takes his second choice and throws the second post.

We played a true freshman at quarterback last year. In the fifth game of the season, he still did not know what city he was in. It is hard for a young quarterback to deal with all the things a defense can throw at him. The zone blitz schemes that teams run are hard to see for the young quarterback. It fools the experienced ones at times. Against perimeter blitzes by secondary players, we sight adjust into hot patterns. We do that by game plan.

At times, we use slants as the sight adjustment hot patterns. When you get to a situation like this, there is no right answer. There is no perfect way to handle those things. We plan for it to work out and hope we can execute it when the situation arises. If everything fails, we throw the ball to the coach.

If we get man coverage, the tight end wants to bend the broken arrow route more and work away from the strong safety. He runs the pattern like a true dig route across the middle.

We can run the same concept from a 2x2 set (Diagram #5). We use six-man protection with this type of pattern. In the six-man protection, we slide the offensive line one way or the other, depending on the scouting report, and block the back opposite the slide. In this formation, we flex the #2 receiver to the strongside. The backside tight end runs a drag across the middle. Instead of releasing the back into the middle on the checkdown pattern, he runs a scat pattern.

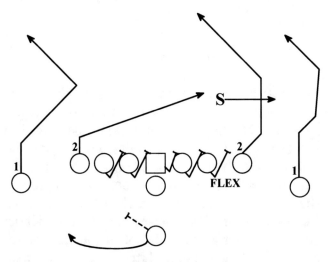

Diagram #5. Demon 2x2

The flexed #2 receiver to the strongside wants to stem his pattern to the outside to get the strong safety or the curl/flat defender to react to the flat. He wants to work inside that defender up the field on the broken arrow route. The Z-receiver does the same thing he did on the previous route. With the second tight end on the backside, we run him on a drag route under the linebackers. The X-receiver runs his same pattern. The running back does not check down in the middle. Since the second tight end works the short middle, we run the back on a scat pattern. In six-man protection, he has a blocking assignment to the side away from the slide. If there is no outside threat, he runs the scat (wheel) route out of the backfield. If we want to seven-man protect, we do not release the tight end and put the back to the other side, and he runs his normal checkdown route if no blitz comes.

Offensive pass routes are like defensive zone blitzes. When the defense runs a zone blitz, they can bring anyone they choose. It does not matter who comes or who drops because it is the same scheme behind the blitz. They play three-deep in the thirds and three defenders underneath.

It is the same thing with a pass offense. You build the plays into every formation you run. The personnel groupings you use do not matter. The patterns are the same for whoever runs them. The quarterback progression is the same in a 3x1 formation as it is in a two-tight-end set. What we are trying to do is run something that looks different to the defense but is the same for the offense.

We built the race route for a quarter coverage scheme or a two-high look (Diagram #6). The tight end (#2 strong) may have to flex slightly to get to where we want him. He runs a deep cross route called race. At 10 yards, he wants to be over the ball. There a number of ways he can get there. He may be over the ball at four or five yards, push vertical to 10 yards, and roll out of the pattern to a crossing route. In the playbook, the pattern is 16 yards deep, but he may not get that deep. If he can get to 12 to 16 yards, that is an acceptable depth. He runs to the open area in the middle of the field, working for the far sideline.

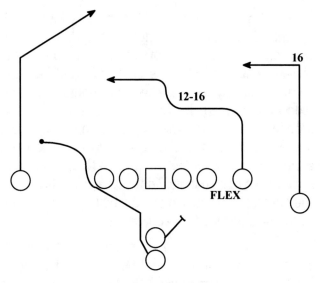

Diagram #6. Race

The running back checks his pass protection and works into the weak flat area. The X-receiver runs a read post. If he reads quarter, two deep, or a two-high safety look, he runs a post cut for the near upright. If he reads a single safety in the middle, he runs the 9 route, which is a takeoff go pattern. This pattern puts the safety in a bind. He cannot be right with his reaction.

In the quarter coverage or two-high look, the safety cannot be right. If he takes the post from the X-receiver, the race route is 12 to 16 yards in front of him. If he jumps the tight end on the race route, we throw the post behind him. If the corner tries to fall in on the race route, we have the back working in front of him. That gives us a high/low read to that side.

The #1 receiver strong has a 16-yard dig route. If the defense tries to run robber coverage of some kind, we end up with our body in front of the safety to that side. That is the last option of the progression. I do not know if we have every made it back to that progression.

Against the single-high safety, the X-receiver runs the corner out of the play with a takeoff pattern. The 16-yard cross is coming right under that pattern. The quarterback reads single-high or two-high. If he reads single, he knows he is working to his tight end. If he reads two-high, he has to key the weakside safety. If he takes the post, he throws the cross. If he comes down on the race, he throws the post over the top.

Our tight end at the NFL combines last week benched 225 pounds 35 times. He was the type of tight end who could get off the line of scrimmage. He was physical when he came off the line, and he used his hands well. The coaching point on the read post pattern is the angle of the post. The X-receiver may set the angle at the near post; however, there is lots of green grass behind the safety. If he is clear, he can flatten the pattern and run into the open middle. That is an easier throw for the quarterback. He can put the ball into the middle of the field and let the receiver go get it.

The last pattern I want to talk about is what we call Dino (Diagram #7). I have been at Georgia for four years and never asked why we call that pattern Dino. I thought about it on the plane coming out here. What I take from the name is "double-ins," relating to "D-In." That is the way I remember the pattern. We want to put the two-deep side in a bind in some way, shape, or form. The strong #1 and #2 receivers run mirror routes. They run a six-yard in pattern. The tight end has to stem and get inside the curl/flat defender when he gets to six yards.

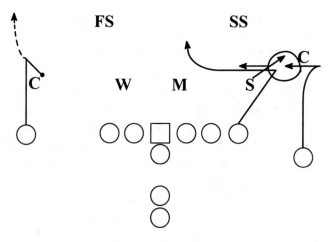

Diagram #7. Dino

When he reaches six yards, he sticks his foot in the ground and comes inside at a 90-degree angle. He wants to stay on the move in his pattern. The Z-receiver runs the same route, but he has the ability to stop his route and sit down in the zone. He does not want to run away from the coverage by the corner into the coverage of the curl player. To the backside, the X-receiver runs a five-yard hitch pattern against a two-high look. If the coverage is a single-high coverage, the hitch converts to a fade route.

This is an easy read for the quarterback and an easy throw and catch. We threw this pattern seven times in one game. We completed six of them, and five were for first downs or touchdowns. If the tight end continues to run, he can get up the middle of the field in the crease between the linebackers. The pattern that comes open all the time is the second in pattern.

Into the X-receiver side, the thing the quarterback must see is the rolled down corner. If he thinks that is what he is seeing, he works the fieldside of the pattern.

On the pattern, we can tag individual routes to take care of the heroes in the defense. We can call Dino bang. That pattern is a hitch and goes for the X-receiver. If the corner tries to jump the route with no help over the top, we call this pattern.

Before I go, I want to tell you how much I respect what you coaches do. I appreciate you being in here today. That tells me you want to be good at what you do. Thank you.

THE 3-3-5 MULTIPLE FRONT DEFENSE

San Diego State University

I appreciate you coaches being here. I go to many clinics, and I like to listen to other coaches talk. I go to listen to assistant coaches on offense and defense, and I learn something every time I go. There is a completely different attitude between offensive coaches and defensive coaches. The offensive coaches come up with a nice little PowerPoint presentation. One coach said it does not matter where the receivers align because the first receiver runs a 7 route, the second receiver runs a 4 route, the third receiver runs a 5 route, and the backside receiver runs a complementary pattern. He said it was simple, and I got confused after the first pattern.

They are extremely organized, but he said something in there that got to me as a defensive coach. I wrote it down so I would not forget it. He was talking about throwing a bubble screen. They have two players in the bubble screen. One of them catches it and the other blocks the defender. Offensive coaches are a hell of lot smarter than defensive coaches are. All you have to do is ask them something. He said the offensive player blocks the meat eater and not the lettuce eater. According to his diagram, the safety was the meat eater and the corner was the lettuce eater. Anybody in here that ever played corner should take personal offense to that.

After hearing the offensive coach, I went in and listened to the defensive coach talk. He was showing them how to blitz, run through gaps, and all that stuff. A coach asked him how he covered a particular adjustment. He told him they did not do that.

I catch myself doing this all the time. You come up with a great idea and you start to install it. One of the coaches working with you asks what we do if they do this. The next question is what if they do that. The first thing you know, you cannot do anything with your great idea. The biggest mistake defensive coaches make is they react to the offense. If the offense goes to a particular formation, the defense checks the coverage. That is what most defensive coaches do. Several defensive coaches say, "The hell with that!"

They want the offense to react to what they do. Make the offensive coaches in their room make adjustments in their scheme because of what we do. Make the quarterback read what you do. Make them react to what you do.

If you make them react to what you do, they end up with one or two protection schemes, and by halftime, you know what those schemes are. If you have a multiple scheme that allows you to do things, at halftime, you can come up with something that will kill their butts.

Every offensive coach alive knows how to block a shade defender and a 3 technique defender. If they know how to block it, do not line up in it. Get into something the offense does not know is a shade defender and a 3 technique defender. You can still play the defense; just do not align in something they recognize. We do not get any traps anymore, unless you count the long trap or the counter play. We see two blocking schemes today. We see the zone scheme and the gap scheme. We get no isolation plays anymore. If you can make the offense react to what you do, you can make it a simple game for your defense.

We give the offense multiple looks. I want to show you our base front. We have a base front called a 30 stack (Diagram #1). I will talk about all the fronts later. The coverages can make these fronts 4-3, 4-2, over, under, 5-2, or anything else. You can become a 4-3 defense by coverages or stunts. We have three defensive linemen in this defense. We use movement to change their alignment and the front.

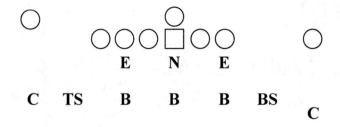

Diagram #1. 30 Stack

We can adjust to other fronts from this base look. If we want to get into what we call a solid look (Diagram #2). If there is one tight end, we can break the stack to that side and step the linebacker down to the line of scrimmage. If there are two tight ends, we step both outside linebackers into shade on the tight end. With one tight end, we are in a 4-2 look with the tight end stack on the line of scrimmage. If we want to create an over look from this alignment, we can move the defensive end into a 3 technique and nose the nose into a 1 technique. The other defensive end moves into a 5 technique to that side and we have an over look.

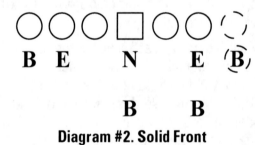

Diagram #2. Solid Front

We can also get into an eagle look (Diagram #3). To get into the eagle front, the defensive ends move into 3 techniques on each side. We can move the outside linebackers to the line of scrimmage or play them in some combinations of alignment based on the offensive alignments.

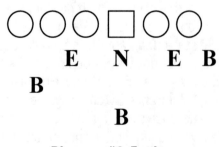

Diagram #3. Eagle

There are two reasons for having multiple fronts. Every year, we get different players. The coach from Florida State University talked yesterday about rushing the passer. It has such a recruiting base it can recruit to a scheme. The University of Alabama can stay in a 3-4 every year because it recruits players that can play that defense. If the players they recruit were in California, they would be 6-6 and 225 pounds playing basketball. In Alabama, they are 6-6 and 290 pounds and play football. Most of the colleges in America today are just like high schools. You recruit the best players you can find and they will not necessarily fit into your scheme.

Last year, our noseguard was 6-2 and 285 pounds. We started a defensive end that was 5-11 and 234 pounds. The other defensive end was 6-3 and 240 pounds. That is not what Alabama or the University of Southern California's defensive line looks like. The assumption that everybody recruits and they all have great players is wrong. In high school, it seems to go in cycles. In some years, you have good players, and some years, you do not. In some years, you have little players, and in some years, you have big players.

We develop our defense based on who our best players are. If our best players are little defensive linemen, we stunt. We slant, twist, and turn them in all different directions. The linebackers do not align in a shade technique; they blitz into a shade technique. If we have big, athletic linemen, you would see more of the solid, over, and under fronts with the linebackers roaming.

There was a time when the hybrid players playing down safeties were strong safety types. Now they are nickel backs because of the spread teams we are seeing. That means they are big corners. There was a time coaches looked down on and frowned on this defense. In the NFL today, when they go to their nickel and dime schemes, they align in this defense.

Ninety percent of the high school teams are in the spread offense. About 50 percent of the teams we play are in the spread, and 90 percent of them have a spread package. We see the spread more than any other offense. I have changed my mind on who the best players on the defense must be. The best players in this scheme have to be the two nickel backs, the two outside linebackers, and the safety. That is because of all the bubble screens and having to rush the quarterback.

They are the ones who have to play the backs coming out of the backfield and the bubble screens. The defenders in the middle of the defense are old 50 defense type football players. They have to plug the A gaps and stop the run. The middle linebacker and noseguard take up blocks when they play. Everyone else around them has to be great athletes.

Forty years ago, an old coach told me a fundamental of defensive football. He told me the number one fundamental of defensive football is balance. If you draw a line down the middle of the offense and they have five and a half players on each side of that line, the defense had better have five and a half defenders on each side of that line. There is one way to do that and always be right. You must play man coverage.

I see some coaches already shaking their heads because they cannot play man coverage. That has nothing to do with it. Any coach in here can play man coverage if you can get enough pressure on the quarterback. If you are scared, play stack defense and let them run up and down the field. The score will be 67-56, and I hope you have the 67 points. That was Baylor University and the University of Washington in the Alamo Bowl. Have you ever seen a game like that?

In the past when we played a triple option team, that was real football. You have to be a tough sucker to play against the wishbone. You do not have to be tough to play against the spread. Teams that run the spread offense have trouble with their defense when they play running teams. When that defense practices against the spread all the time, it has trouble against someone that runs the ball at it.

When we call our defense, the first thing the middle linebacker calls is tight end position. If there is one tight end, the linebacker calls the direction to the tight end. If there are two tight ends, he calls the directions to the strength of the formation. If it is a balanced formation, he calls to the field. If the ball is in middle of the field, he calls it to the quarterback's arm.

When we call the stunts, we run them toward or away from the call. We call our stunts with a tight or open call. The same thing holds true with the secondary. You will have to make an adjustment as to who your best players are. That could determine what coverage you play. If you have a real dumb team, which we do at times, the thing your defense will never mess up is a field call. If we have a dumb team, we tell the linebacker to call the tight side to the field. It does not matter whether they align the tight end to the field. That makes all the stunts field stunts or boundary stunts. We base everything we do on a tight or field call.

The three down linemen move as a group on some stunt calls. We call this movement slant, angle, loop, pinch, or go. The linebackers have games. When we run the games and the stunts together, that is a combo.

We run our stunt off the direction calls from the linebackers. If we want to slant the ends and nose to the tight end, we call tight. If we want to run the slant away from the tight end, we call open. If we call tight, open, field, or boundary, the defensive line slants those calls. The pinch and loop calls are for the defensive ends (Diagram #4). On the pinch, the defensive ends run their slant techniques to the inside. They become B gap defenders. When they loop, they go to the outside from the 5 technique into the C gap. On the pinch and loop, the nose plays football and the middle linebackers play their normal defense.

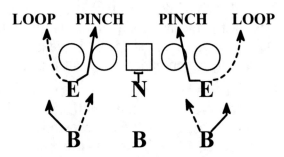

Diagram #4. Pinch/Loop

We can run stunts involving two defensive linemen. When you run the tac with the end coming down to the inside, he can start from anywhere (Diagram #5). We can run the tac stunt from a 9, 8, 5, or 3 technique. That stunt is the end closing into an inside A gap and the nose going around to the outside. We run the stunt the other way, with the nose going out and the tackle coming behind, and we

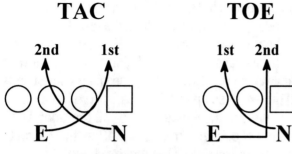

TAC   TOE

Diagram #5. Tac and Toe

call that a toe. However, the defensive end cannot come from the 9 technique on a toe stunt. Some of these stunts are for pass rushing and some are for zone read teams.

From this defense, the games the linebackers can run are numerous. It is what the coaching staff wants to do with them. They must know their gap responsibilities on the stunts run by the defensive line, and their fits come off the movement of the line. You can blitz the linebackers in any combination and number of linebackers that you choose. You can blitz one at a time, two at a time, or all three if you chose.

When we slant and stunt, we give the defensive players aiming points as to where we want them to go. We give them aiming points by down and distance. We give them aiming point by formations. We give them aiming points by where the offense's best players are. Sometimes, the aiming points are the face of the guards. Sometimes, it is the inside shoulder of the tackle. To say that a player blitzes through the B gap is too simple an explanation. By game planning, our defenders have aiming points.

If I want to play an under front, I can do it with a single linebacker blitz. If the direction call is tight right and if the boundary linebacker blitzes the B gap, it causes the defensive end to loop to the outside. The nose goes away, which puts him into the tight A gap. The tight defensive end loops into the C gap, and the linebacker steps to the outside. Using the movement of one defender, we end up aligned as if we were in an under front defense.

We can get into these movements and drop the free safety down to seven yards and we have a 4-3 alignment. We did that with Brain Urlacher at New Mexico University. We played the same adjustment out of our two-deep secondary. We rolled him down

to seven yards and played him inside outside on the ball. He made about 170 tackles in 11 games. You can get into any defensive front you want by moving your linemen with stunts and getting in to gaps. If your good players are the linebackers, you hit those gaps with the linebackers.

People want to know why we play with 195-pound linebackers. I want to talk about the linebackers we played this year. One of them will be in the NFL. He was 6-2 and 240 pounds and played the right linebacker. The middle linebacker was 5-10 and 195 pounds. The left linebacker was 6-3 and 195 pounds.

The best 3 technique we have on our team is 5-10 and weighs 195 pounds. The best 3 technique on our team is the middle linebacker. He went to the right aiming point, and he was too short for the big offensive linemen to block. He played with leverage and they did not knock him back. He was always in the backfield making something good happen.

I love to watch the linebackers playing downhill at a power play. I never know what coverage it is, but they are aggressive and playing with a lot of toughness. They are hitting the gaps and recovering nicely if the play turns into a counter. It does not matter what the coverage is because it is a power play and we are playing the run.

Everyone we play wants to slide or half-slide pass protect against us. We can get to the quarterback if we put two defenders through the same gap. If you put two defenders through the same gap, that is not fundamentally sound. However, if one defender can pick the offensive blocker, the second defender coming through that gap is a free rusher. We do that with our edge blitzes.

You must play man coverage. If you play a soft zone, the quarterback will complete the ball. If you play the soft zone, the offense will dink and dunk you down the field and score. If you get after their butts, you will stop them and your offense will get back on the field. We are going to play that way. We are not going to take the offense picking and choosing where they want to throw.

The offense always wants the ball back. They hate playing against a wishbone team because wishbone teams run the ball and control the time of possession. They hold the ball for 14 out of the 15 minutes. The offense has to sit on the sideline, it plays crappy when it gets back into the game, and it blames the defense because it is cold. You have to get after the offensive players and make them turn the ball back to your offense.

In the secondary, we play cover 3 and cover 2. When we play cover 2, it is Tampa 2. We put the free safety at the middle linebacker position. The middle linebacker has a hard time running with the seam pattern down the middle of the field. Middle linebackers have a certain mentality that safeties do not. The middle linebackers overreact to the run. Safeties do not. The free safety has to be a good tackler, but his nose will not be up the noseguard's butt.

The middle linebacker stands next to the noseguard. If the offense runs a play-action pass, with the #3 receiver running down the middle, the middle linebacker will never cover him. The free safety will be nowhere near the line of scrimmage until he is sure it is a run. If you want to play Tampa 2, do not do it with the free safety at the middle linebacker.

One of our man-free coverages is gold. If you cannot play man coverage, you must get to the quarterback. I have shown you some five-man pressures. In a five-man pressure, someone on the offensive line is blocking one-on-one. Let me regress here a minute. The offenses are progressing faster than the defense. What they are doing on offense now is unbelievable. They are doing things today I never expected them to do.

If you cannot play man coverage, do not give up on that scheme. Figure out more ways to tackle the quarterback for losses. The smart coaches on offense will keep extra blockers in to block. Most of the teams we play in the spread offense have three wide receivers in a slot formation. They have two players in the backfield with the quarterback. One of the backs in the backfield is another wide receiver. He keys to see if the blitz is coming. If there is no blitz, he releases and runs a pattern. He runs his normal patterns as if he aligned in the slot.

When you blitz and take on the wide receiver that is not used to blocking linebackers or a big defender, your scheme can affect what they do.

What they do is replace the wide receiver with a tight end or fullback. The tight end is coming back into the spread set. The spread teams are never under the center because if you go under the center, you are not a smart coach.

Offensive coaches know the defense keys the positioning of the running back as to the slide of the offensive line. The smart coaches set the running back to one side of the quarterback and blocked him on the other side to screw up the blitz scheme of the defense. If you watch enough film, you can get a feel for the slide by watching the offensive linemen. One of the offensive linemen will tip the slide every time by his stance, weight on his hand, or shoulder lean.

The smart linebacker that sets your defense can spot that from the offensive line. When he sees the slide direction of the offensive line, he calls the pressure from the opposite side. To counter that move, the offensive puts in a tight end and keeps him in to block. They put the tight end on one side and the running back to the other side. That gives them seven-man protection. The defense has to have a way to outnumber the offensive blockers to a side.

That is where the combo coverages come into play. Gold coverage is our man-free scheme. In the gold coverage, we can get into a multiple blitz scheme (Diagram #6). This can give you six or seven blitzers. We cover the back coming out of the backfield with a back at the line of scrimmage. If the offensive tackles are not exceptional, the defenders coming off the edge will get to the

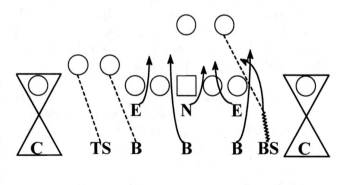

Diagram #6. Combo Blitz Gold Coverage

quarterback. We bring two rushers off the edge and challenge the athletic ability of the offensive tackle. You have to bring more defenders than the offense can block.

The boundary safety on his play is in the blitz pattern if the running back blocks. If he swings on a hot route, the boundary safety has coverage on him. He cannot try to sack the quarterback and let the back release.

If you do that, you cannot be scared of what happens in the secondary because it is one-on-one coverage back there. The defensive backs fall down sometimes, and other times, they get beat. Nevertheless, you are dictating to the offense what type of pass route it can run. It can only throw two passes. It can throw the slant and the fade. It can throw a hot to the back who swings out of the backfield. However, there is coverage from the boundary safety on the swing hot route.

The biggest problem we have with this scheme is the wide receiver screen. The tunnel or alley screen is the thing that gives us the most trouble. The reason we have trouble is we are going to the quarterback and all the action of the pass goes the other way. If we are not good at turning and retracing our steps, we get hurt.

Another problem we have is a team that identifies our overload blitz. If they know which side it comes from, they run the speed option away from it. If they do that, we are screwed. That is the only place we have had trouble, although sometimes we play teams with better talent. When we played Michigan, we should have sacked the quarterback six times. We did not lay a hand on him on five of those occasions and he scored two touchdowns. We had two defenders come free on the blitz six times and only sacked him once.

You cannot play for them, but you have to give them a chance to win. If you put a player in a 3 technique or a two-gap noseguard, he may be a tough player, but he will get the snot beat out of him. The linebackers face the same thing if the lineman cannot keep the blockers off the linebackers. That happens because you are not aggressive.

We believe in this defense. If we had the best players in the country, we would play this defense.

If we had good players, we would play with Alabama. The two best teams we played last year were Boise State University and Texas Christian University. We would never tell our players this, but they were so much better than we were physically. They were bigger, stronger, and faster.

Against Boise State, we fumbled the opening kickoff and the next two punts. We were down 21-0 with less than four minutes gone in the game. The score was 35-28 going into the fourth quarter. Against TCU, the score was 27-21 going into the fourth quarter. What we have are tough players who like to play football. We are a talented team.

I thought Boise State was the best team we played last year, and we played 0 coverage 43 percent of the time. You can align exactly right every time in man coverage if you do it by the numbers. When we play teams that play with 12 personnel, one of the tight ends is a blocker and the other is a pass receiver. One of them is less a threat to block someone. We know that, and we slant off that fact. We do not worry about him blocking, so we slant to him.

When you play man-to-man coverage, you never worry about being outflanked by the offense. If they try to change the strength of the formation with motion, we balance with a defender coming with the motion. We will always have the same number of defenders as the offense has blockers. The defensive back will make the adjustments.

We do not have a 190-pound defensive back in our secondary. Their play is all about attitude. I was upset about the coach who talked about lettuce eaters at the corner. I think Kellen Moore is the best quarterback in college football. We pressured him and gave him fits throwing the football. He missed receiver after receiver because of the pressure we put on him.

This defense keeps the offensive blocker off balance; they are never sure whom to block. It makes them slow down. It makes them uncomfortable with who they are supposed to block.

I want to give a brief explanation about one of our zone coverages. If we run a thunder blitz, we bring five defenders on the rush (Diagram #7). With five blitzers, we have six defenders in the secondary. The defensive line slants to the right

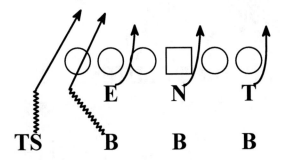

Diagram #7. Thunder Blitz

side of the offense. The left outside linebacker cheats to the line and blitzes through the inside shoulder of the tight end. The tight safety comes off the edge. If we ran the blitz to the boundary, we call it lightning. It is the opposite stunt bringing the boundary safety.

If the offensive formation is a 2x2 formation, we play three under and three deep (Diagram #8). We call that coverage 33. The corners fake a press coverage and bail out into the deep thirds. The free safety plays the middle third. The middle linebacker plays the curl/flat to the strongside, and the right linebacker plays the middle hook area. The boundary safety plays the backside curl/flat area.

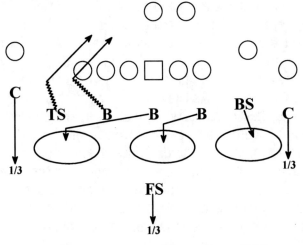

Diagram #8. 2x2 Three Deep (33)

In a 3x1 or 2x1, we play four under and two deep (Diagram #9). Twenty-two is four under and two deep. In this coverage, we roll the corners down into the flat area. The middle linebacker is the hook-to-curl player. The right linebacker plays the hook to the curl area to the backside. The backside corner rolls down and plays the backside flat area. The boundary safety drops up the seam and plays half-field coverage. The free safety rolls to the strongside and plays half coverage to that side.

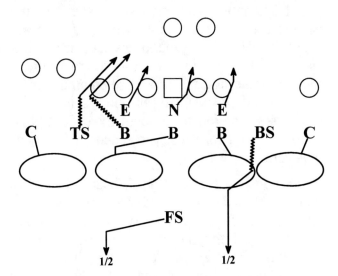

Diagram #9. 3x1 or 2x1 Two Deep

In the secondary, we try to make everything look like man coverage. I am out of time. I am sorry about all the technical difficulty. I hope you got something from this. I appreciate your being here and your attention.

RECEIVER DRILLS AND RUNNING ROUTES

Duke University

Thank you for that introduction, and I appreciate your being here. I am going to go fast but do not be afraid to slow me down. I want you to ask questions. What I am going to talk about is receiver play and the drill we use to train the receivers. If you find something you like, I will be around after this is over if you want to talk about some aspect of it. One thing I found out about the coaches that come to listen to a receiver coach: he has good receivers.

In the off-season, we go through a 20-minute fundamental individual period every day. We work on our stance and start. After we work that aspect of getting off the line of scrimmage, we go to ball drills. Then, we work on route breaks and how we attack press coverage. The last thing is blocking. However, that should be the first thing in importance. The most important thing is the hardest thing to do. I will try to give you as much information as I can and you can take what you want.

Stance and start are important to the receiver because the faster he gets off the ball, the more effective the route is. With a good stance and start, a 4.7 player can play like a 4.5 player by perfecting his start off the ball. It works the other way too. Players that run 4.4 in the 40, play like 4.7 players because they do not get off the ball in the most efficient manner.

The faster the receiver can come off the ball, the better his routes are. It makes every route he runs better. Every practice, the thing we harp on is lining up correctly and having a good stance.

In the stance, we want the player's shoulders over his knee. We want the knees over the toes, with the inside foot aligned on the ball, forward in the stance. Most of our receivers ran track in high school. I try to relate the start at the wide receiver to the starting blocks in track. I find that the lower the chest is in the stance, the more explosive the receiver is coming off the line. If they are too tall in their stance, the first thing they do as they come off the ball is to drop or dip in the hips to get lower. When we come off the ball, we want to drive off the back foot and roll off the front foot, with no false-stepping or false movement.

We want 75 percent of the weight on the front foot and a small amount on the back foot. If the receiver does not have most of his weight on his front foot, his first step is back. We want the shoulders and chest down in the stance and most of the weight on the front foot. In every drill we do, we want a good start and a definite finish. We try to define every finish in the drill.

We do our stance and start drill from the hash marks on the field, running toward the sideline. I want the receivers to come off the ball and sprint as if they were running a 100-meter dash. They sprint through the numbers on the field and coast into the sideline. As they sprint, I want their heads up and their eyes forward, looking at the sideline. I do not want their eyes directed to the ground. A receiver must see the defender to know what he is doing. In the stance and start, every pattern the receiver runs has to look the same coming off the line of scrimmage. The go pattern and the hitch must have the same appearance to the defender.

When I teach stance and starts, I show my players cutups of pro players performing what we try to do. The one I show them is Andre Johnson from the Houston Texans. If the great ones do these drills, you should not have any trouble getting your players to do them. They have the same stance every snap. The first five yards of the route are the most important part of any route. We want to use models of the good receivers to show our players what they should look like.

I have a 4.7 wide receiver who beats all the other receivers to the five-yard mark. He does it because he has an explosive start, which comes from great fundamentals. The stance has to be a habit, and it has to look the same way every time you line up. The start has to look the same every time you release off the line of scrimmage.

One of the biggest things we do is catching the ball with the arm extended. We want the receiver to catch the ball with his arms extended in front of the body. We refer to the skill as stopping the ball with the eyes. When you extend the arms in front of the body, it allows you to focus on the ball better. The second thing the arms extend does is make the receiver catch the ball in his hands. With his arms extended, he cannot trap the ball against his body.

We drill this skill with the receiver running forward toward the coach. The receiver runs toward the coach, and the coach throws the ball to the receiver. The receiver extends his arms, catches the ball in his hands, and looks it away into his chest for ball security. We want the players catching the ball with their thumbs together, as if they were taking a picture of the ball with a camera. They frame the ball in the framework of their hands and catch the ball softly. If you can hear the ball hit their hands, they are not catching it right. We want them to catch the ball in the fingers and focus on the tip.

There is a time differential between a receiver who catches the ball against his chest and a receiver who catches the ball in his extended hands. The receiver that catches the ball in his hands stands a chance to make a defender miss on a tackle. He gets the ball in his possession a fraction of a second faster. That may be all the time he needs to make a defensive back miss the tackle.

The receiver that catches the ball against his body does not have a chance to make a move in tight coverage. You need to get the receivers to buy into that idea. If the defensive back is tight to the receiver, the receiver can still catch the ball if he extends his arms away from his body. If the receiver catches the ball in his hands, he can maintain his speed. If he catches it against his body, it slows his speed. Keeping his feet on the ground allows the receiver to speed through each catch.

We work a drill to teach that arms extend away from a defender (Diagram #1). We work the drill in pairs. The defender and receiver work side by side in the drill. The drill starts with the defender's inside arm under the receiver arm. They start together with the defender's arm in between the receiver's arms. As they run toward the coach, the coach delivers the ball. The receiver extends his arms and catches the ball. The defender does not try to knock the ball down. He is only there as a distraction. The receiver extends his arms and catches the ball with the defender's arm in between his arms.

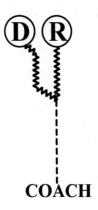

Diagram #1. Extend The Arms

We can change the drill slightly. The defender runs behind the receiver. In this part of the drill, the defender puts his inside hand on the hip of the receiver and reaches with his outside hand toward the ball. The receiver has to extend his arms to catch the ball. The receiver extends his arms to catch the ball so the receiver cannot reach the ball. This is a drill to make the receiver frame the ball with his eyes, ignore the defender, and catch the ball with the arms extended.

We teach the receivers to focus on the tip of the ball. We feel that if the receiver zeros in on a small area, it helps him to focus more. We want the receiver to see the tip of the ball instead of the entire ball. We think that sharpens his focus. The smaller the object is, the sharper the focus. They asked San Francisco great Ronnie Lott why he was such a good tackler. He told them he focused on one particular part of the ballcarrier's jersey number. He did not see the ballcarrier. He only saw that small part of the number. We teach the same thing to our receivers.

All the throws in these drills are toward the shoulders of the receivers. We want the receiver to frame the ball and catch it with his thumbs together. If the receiver catches the ball with his thumbs apart, he is not seeing the ball. With the thumbs together, the receiver frames the ball in that window and he can see it. We work on low throws with the little fingers together in another way. Jump ball situations on deep throws are the same type of situation. You have to frame and see the ball to catch it.

This next drill is the combine drill. The pro scouts do this drill at the NFL combines in Indianapolis (Diagram #2). We align our receivers on the sideline. There are two quarterbacks in the drill. The course is 20 yards long. The receiver starts at the first marker. We want him to run straight down the sideline. He runs five yards down the sideline and the first quarterback throws the ball at the 5-yard marker. The receiver catches the ball and immediately drops it to the ground. He continues to run down the sideline.

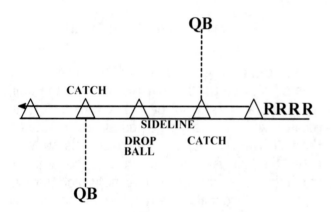

Diagram #2. Combine Drill

The second quarterback is on the opposite side of the first quarterback. After the receiver drops the first ball, he snaps his head around to see the second quarterback. The second quarterback throws at the 15-yard mark. We catch the balls at 5 yards and 15 yards. The receiver must get his head around quickly to see the quarterback. This is a speed drill and the balls come out quickly. If you do this drill, make sure you have plenty of balls as well as managers to chase the dropped balls. That way you can have a rapid drill without people waiting around to round up the balls.

In this drill, we want the receiver to relax and catch the ball in his hands. We do not want him to fight the ball. The coaching point is for the receiver to put his face at the point he catches the ball. If the ball is low, the receiver's face is low. If the ball is high, the face is there.

When I do ball drills, I want the receiver to find the ball. I do not want the ball still in the quarterback's hand when the receiver turns to catch it. I want the ball on the way so he has to find the ball and position himself to catch it.

To drill that part of the throw, we use two tall stand-up dummies (Diagram #3). We have two quarterbacks throwing in this drill. The dummies are spaced eight yards apart. The receiver runs down the sideline on the opposite side of the dummies and the quarterback. As the receiver approaches the dummy, the quarterback throws the ball. We want to time the throw so the receiver catches the ball just as he passes the dummy. That means part of the flight of the ball will not be visible to the receiver. He has to find the ball and catch it.

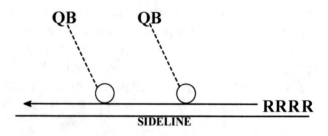

Diagram #3. Find the Ball

The receiver catches the ball, drops it immediately, and continues to run to the second dummy. At the second dummy, the second quarterback delivers the ball with the same timing. We use the same techniques and mechanics in this drill as we did in the combine drill. However, in this drill, both quarterbacks are on the same side. We emphasize catching the ball in the hands and keeping the speed constant. I do not want them to catch the ball against the chest.

The next thing we do is combine the two dummies drill and add a blaster (Diagram #4). Instead of dummies, we use extra players. Immediately past the distraction defender is a dummy holder. He has a shield dummy. When the receiver catches the ball, he swings the dummy and hits him across

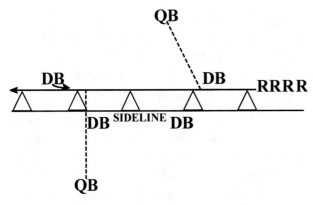

Diagram #4. Distraction Blaster

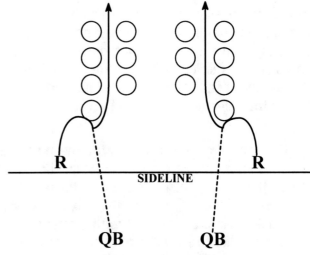

Diagram #5. Vertical Drill

the shoulder. The receiver drops the ball and flips his head around to the second quarterback. The same situation occurs at the next throw. There is a distraction defender and a dummy blaster to hit the receiver as he catches the ball.

We want to teach the receiver to focus on the ball. He cannot worry about the hit from the blaster with the dummy. He has to find the ball and focus on catching it. In the drill, you must coach the blasters. We do not want to get anyone hurt. The object of hitting the receiver with the dummy is to make him concentrate on catching the ball. The object is not to knock him down with the dummy or deliver a hard blow. We want the dummy swung to do what we want it to do. We want to distract and break the focus of the receiver.

We want the receiver to catch the ball and get north and south with it. The vertical drill teaches that skill (Diagram #5). We use seven small dish markers on the ground. You could use cones. We align them in an alley going up the field. We do the drill off the sideline, with the markers three yards into the field. The receiver breaks to the tip of the first marker and hooks up, facing the quarterback. The quarterback is five yards behind the sideline. The quarterback throws the ball and the receiver catches it. Immediately on catching the ball, he turns and sprints up the alley of markers.

When the receiver catches the ball, I want him to drop his shoulder to the side of the alley and get upfield immediately. I do not want a receiver to catch the ball for a first down, try to elude a tackler, and run away from the first down. I want him to catch the ball, turn, and get north and south up the field. We want him to drop the shoulder, drop step, do a 180-degree turn, and get up the field.

If you are going to throw the ball deep, you must drill it in practice. The key to catching a deep ball is the vision of the receiver. The receiver cannot run a deep pattern looking back to the quarterback. He has to get his head straight down the field, run to clear the defender, and get deep. Receivers that look for the ball when we snap it cannot get open or deep. We tell our receivers not to look for the ball until they get 20 yards deep.

The other thing we tell them is to hold the line (Diagram #6). We coach the quarterback to throw the deep football from the numbers to the sideline. The receiver has to hold the line and keep the defenders out of that area. They want to stay down the numbers. If the defender tries to push them to the sideline, they want to hold the line and give the quarterback an area of the field to put the

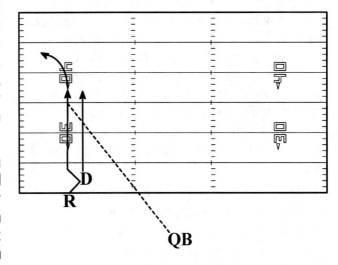

Diagram #6. Hold the Line

ball. If the receiver gets off the numbers and into the sideline, the quarterback has no margin of error. He has to throw a perfect ball and the receiver has to make a perfect catch for us to get a completion. If the receiver can hold the line, the quarterback can throw the ball into an area and the receiver can go get it.

If we are into the boundary of the field, the area becomes two yards outside the numbers. The longer the receiver can hold the line, the less time the defender has to react to the ball. In the NFL, they line their practice field with a vertical line running parallel to the sideline at four yards. That area belongs to the quarterback. The receiver holds the line and does not get any closer than four yards from the sideline. If he gets against the sideline, the quarterback probably throws the ball out of bounds.

When we run the deep-ball drills, the receiver must learn how to high-point the ball. We run drills to make the receiver perform that skill. I like the quarterback to use the underthrown ball on a fade route. If the receiver is under tight coverage on the deep ball, he stands a better chance of stopping and high-pointing the throw than the defender. The defender does not see the ball as soon as the receiver, and his momentum will carry him past the receiver if the ball is underthrown.

The secret for the quarterback is to throw a catchable ball. In this situation, two good things will happen. The receiver will catch the ball or we will get an interference call. When the receiver slows down to go back for the ball, he has to attack the ball above his head. He has to high-point the ball. The second thing that can happen is the pass interference [PI] call. If the receiver has good position on the defender, as he slows, he turns and goes through the defender for the ball. That can lead to the PI if he does not catch the ball. We do not want to put our hands on the defensive back, but we want to jump through him to high-point the ball.

We tell the receiver to hold his line until the ball is on the downward arc. The best receivers are the ones that can catch the ball over the opposite shoulder. They end up in that situation because they can hold the line down the field. If they catch the ball over the opposite shoulder, their body is between the defender and the ball. If they try to catch it over the outside shoulder, the defensive back has a good break on the ball. The opposite shoulder catch uses the receiver's body as a shield, which keeps the defender away from the ball.

The receiver may break outside the numbers on his initial release from the line of scrimmage, but we want him to get back on the numbers and stay that course. If the defender tries to force him off the line, he leans into the defender and continues to run on that line.

If the receivers can hold the line, they give the quarterback a huge area to throw the ball. The throw from the quarterback does not need to be that accurate. If the receiver is aggressive and attacks the ball, we should get a completion. The receiver must be able to adjust to the ball's flight. He may have to alter his path to get to the ball, but he has the first chance to get there if he holds the defender into the field.

The worst thing the receiver can do when he high-points the ball is to wait for the ball to come to him. When he breaks stride and slows down, he has to come back to the ball and use his vertical leap to get up to the ball. He has to get the ball at the point closest to the quarterback. He cannot be moving away from the throw. He has to come back, jump, and attack the ball. He has to take the ball away from the defensive back. The defensive back coach tells the defensive back the same thing. It becomes a contest to see who wants the ball more.

In these contested situations, the receiver does not want to jump straight up to try to catch the ball. He wants to have contact with the defensive back. He wants to create contact on these types of throws if the defensive back is contesting the catch.

SPEED CUT

I want to get into some route breaks. The first one is a speed cut. We use that cut on digs and out patterns. When we do a speed cut, we want to maintain the speed through the break. We do not want to break stride during the break. The secret to the speed cut is to make the corner as tight as possible. We want to maintain the speed and at the same time keep the corner from being too rounded.

When we drill the speed cut, we want to do it off yard lines (Diagram #7). We start the receivers running down the sideline. At the first cone, they speed cut and run to the numbers on the field. At the numbers, they make the second speed cut and run 10 yards. After they run 10 yards, they make the third speed cut and run to the sideline. There are no ball throws in this drill. We simply run the cuts, focusing on sticking the outside foot and staying tight on the turns. That is why we run down the lines.

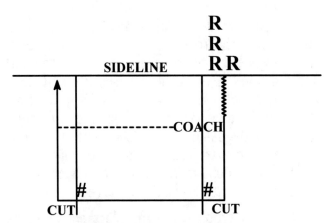

Diagram #8. Square Drill

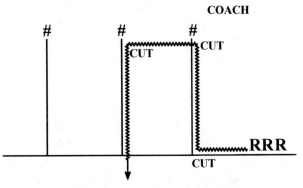

Diagram #7. Speed-Cut Drill

When the receiver does a speed cut, you should see a slight increase in speed as he gets to the breakpoint. When he gets to the breaking point, I want a power step and explosion with the outside foot. When he explodes, I want the receiver to keep the tight corner.

We do another simple square drill off the sideline (Diagram #8). We break the receiver off the sideline, running to the numbers. At the numbers, he makes a speed cut and runs for 10 yards to the next cone. He makes the speed cut back to the sideline and receives a thrown ball from the coach standing at the start line.

When I do these drills, I want to get to a place where I can see the eyes of the receivers. Defensive backs look for body clues in the receivers. Those are indicators as to the pattern the receiver will run. We want the eyes straight ahead. When the receiver sticks his outside foot, the last thing that comes around in the cut is the head. The other thing I look for is the body posture going into the break. If the receiver starts to lift or to drop to get into the cut, that gives the defensive back an edge.

The running profile should be the same all the way through the cut.

If the receiver's eyes go down, the defender knows he is reaching the breakpoint. We want the eyes straight down the field, watching the defensive back. The receiver has to use his stance, start, and eyes to sell the defensive back on the deep pattern. The defensive back must believe the receiver is going deep when we use the speed cut.

We run the quick out on steps. The quick out for us is a 4-step pattern. The deep out for us is a 6-step pattern. If we run a speed-out cut at 8 yards, the throw will probably be a 10- to 12-yard out. If the receiver can speed-cut and get back down to 10 yards, that is a tight corner.

HITCH/CURL PROFILE

The next break I want to talk about is the hitch/curl pattern. The key to this pattern is how fast the receiver can get into the break and out of the break without slowing down. When we start teaching these breaks, we do them at half speed, emphasizing body clues that the defensive back sees. We run the hitches into the boundary on three steps and into the field on five yards. Into the field, we run five-yard hitches. We run our curl patterns on depth.

On the hitch, we run the pattern on two steps. We plant the outside foot and get out of the move with the inside foot or second step. When we tap the outside foot, we accelerate the arms. To stop the movement down the field and run the hitch, the chest has to be over the knee when we plant the foot.

To stop, we plant the instep of the plant foot. That allows the receiver to turn and step at a sharp angle back to the quarterback. On the curl and the hitch, the receiver works straight back to the quarterback. The receiver must get off his toes and plant the instep in the ground. If he tries to plant on the ball of his foot, his next step is not back to the quarterback. His next step is outside, and that takes one more step to turn back to the quarterback. He has rounded off his route.

The next problem the receivers encounter is looking for the ball before they stops. We want them to stop, keep their eyes downfield, keep the chest loose, and break back with a sharp angle to the quarterback. We drill the cut with a sideline W drill (Diagram #9). The receivers align at the sideline and run at 45-degree angles to the inside for three steps. That puts them on the next yard line. They plant their outside foot and drive back to the sideline, which is the next yard line, and repeat this for three repetitions.

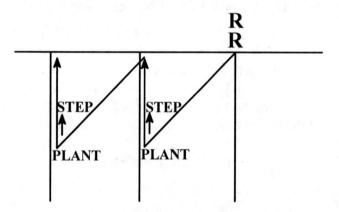

Diagram #9. Hitch W Drill

We can do the drill and add balls to the drill. We have the receiver do the repetition on the hitch and have two quarterbacks throw at two places in the drill. That covers pattern running, catching fundamentals, and timing. If there is a threat of a flat defender on the hitch, the receiver runs the hitch and slides away from the flat defender.

When we run the curl, we run them at depth. A 10-yard curl goes to 12 yards deep. The first 10 yards are like a 10-yard sprint. When we hit 10 yards, the chest comes over the knee; we plant the instep at 12 yards and run the sharp angle back to the quarterback. The thing we do not want to do is give the defensive back an indicator of which way the receiver will turn. His head and eyes are the last thing to move. The eyes must stay downfield on the defender until the last second.

Timing is so important in throwing the curl route. The ball has to come out at the right time or we have no shot. The sooner the receiver comes open, the quicker the defense covers him if the ball is not there. If the receiver does not run the proper depth, he comes open, but as the ball arrives, the defense covers him. The indicator for the quarterback in the curl route is the chest coming over the knee in the plant step. When the chest comes over the knee, the quarterback delivers the ball.

In the receiver runs a slant, the break comes off an outside plant of the foot. On this break, the receiver cuts off the ball of his foot. The slant cut is a 90-degree angle, which does not require a sharp cut. The quarterback indicator is the outside lean that goes with the inside break. When the quarterback reads the outside lean, he delivers the ball.

When we drill in practice, I set all the drills up in circuits to get maximum participation for our entire team. We go at a rapid pace in everything we do in practice—not only in drill work but all the team and group drills. Coach David Cutcliffe is big on up-tempo practices. He does not want a dissertation on the practice field. He wants repetition in everything we do. We script our drills and explain them in the individual meetings. That makes your practice time highly efficient. With the hourly requirements of the NCAA, if you are not prepared and go fast, you will not get it taught.

Any time you want to talk receiver play or anything that has to do with our offense, get in touch with us. Our football staff is very accessible to high school coaches. You can sit in our meetings and look at anything we have. You coaches are always welcome. Just give us a call, and we can work something out. I appreciate the opportunity to speak. Thank you for your attention.

NAVAL ACADEMY FOOTBALL AND THE OPTION GAME

United States Naval Academy

It is definitely a great honor for me to be here today. I appreciate your sticking around to hear me today. Hopefully, there is something I can give you that you can learn from.

I would like to start with something one of my coaches gave to me a while back. He just handed it to me. I think it is one of the greatest compliments I have ever received as a coach. It is a quote by Abraham Lincoln.

Nearly all men can stand adversity, but if you want to test a man's character, give him power.

—Abraham Lincoln

Sometimes, as coaches, we are looked upon as being bigger than life. We are human beings just like anyone else. We are just men. This is just a great reminder for me to never forget that. We as coaches are in a great profession. We are in the profession of developing people.

I have been at the United States Naval Academy since 1995. It is a great institution, and I am proud to be there. It is gratifying to go to work every day and see the men and women that are there. They are there because they want to serve our country. We live in the greatest country in the world. Sure, things could be better for everyone, but nonetheless, we live in the greatest country in the world. Those men and women are there to give the ultimate sacrifice for us and those of us who live in our country. This always comes to my mind as I coach these young men. From the beginning of our academy, people come there to learn how to lead. What I have found out in the 14 years I have been at the Naval Academy is you cannot learn how to lead until you learn how to serve.

My dad was a cook in the Coast Guard for 23 years. When he got out, he was the manager of a restaurant. When I was young, every time I would go look for my dad in his office, he was never there.

I would ask if anybody had seen my dad, and they would say yes, he is in the kitchen. When I went into the kitchen, there was my dad cooking with the cooks. I saw how those men and women, the bakers and the cooks, had such great respect for my dad because he was not an office type of guy. He served. It was amazing to me to see how they followed my dad as he learned how to lead them by serving them. For us as coaches, that is a great thing for us to learn.

I like to use an acronym: **LEAD**

L = Love

E = Example

A = Appreciate

D = Develop

You can be a coach who has the greatest knowledge in the world, but if your players or the people who work for you do not know you love them, they will shut you off. Coaching is not just about yelling at people and getting after them. Do not get me wrong—I like to coach hard too. You have to be able to pick up a guy when you go to the locker room and ask a guy how he is doing and how things are going in his life for him to see you as a leader. You have to make sure you love those you lead.

We have to be an example. We always want our players to be on time. You cannot expect your players to be on time if you do not start your meetings and your practices on time. Get out there early and make sure everything is set up before practice starts. When your players come to practice, be out there waiting on them. This is not a time to be cool as a coach; this is the time to set an example. If you want your players to be early for team meetings, you need to be there early. Our players are going to hear what we say, but what we do speaks volumes.

It is important to appreciate what these guys go through. What their background is, what they have to overcome, and all the things that go on in their lives.

The biggest part to me about winning football is development. At the Naval Academy, we are typically not going to get the four- and five-star athletes. We do not get the big, strong, and fast athletes some of the major schools are getting. We might get a taller skinny kid we have to play at defensive end. We are going to develop these people. There is a lot of patience involved with that.

To be a great coach, you have to be a great teacher. Some people teach differently than other people. The good coaches get their message across. First and foremost in this is good communication. As a sender of a message, you may think the message is pretty clear, but the receiver has to receive that same message, and it has to be clear. As coaches, you have to look at how you are communicating your ideas and are they getting through. If the receiver of the message is not as clear as the sender, it can cost you a game.

A good teacher will make sure his pupils are prepared and organized when they go to class or meetings. When our players walk into one of our meetings, I want to make sure it is a conducive learning environment. If we want them to write something, we provide a pen and paper. If your players come in and see you are organized in a classroom setting, it makes it easier for them to learn. It is the same thing with practice.

I let my assistant coaches coach, and the one thing I make sure they do is to be prepared for practice. Everything has to be detailed. Everything they need for a drill must be there before everyone else. If certain players need more reps during a drill, my coaches need to have that spelled out beforehand. We do not have very long with our players, so we have to make the most of our time. Every second is precious, so we have to be prepared. This transfers to the games.

Setting clear goals is important for a program. The goals for our entire program are: first, to win the Commander-in-Chief trophy, which means we have to beat the Air Force Academy and Army; our second goal is to win a bowl game. When I

go visit schools across the country, sometimes I notice schools have a separate set of goals for offense and defense. Sometimes, their goals are not clear and precise. If that is the case, it is hard to accomplish them. Your program has to have clear goals established.

SEVEN STEPS TO OUR SUCCESS

In order to reach our goals, we have a clear plan.

1. Run the ball on offense (option).
2. Run to the ball on defense (50/3-4).
3. Be good at what we do! Never forget who we are!
4. Be sound in special teams.
5. Be tougher than all of our opponents.
6. Play harder than all of our opponents.
7. Don't beat ourselves (penalties, turnovers, missed assignments).

We talk about this plan every year. First, we are going to run the football. That is who we are. We are going to limit the number of times our opponent's offense is going to have the ball. If our opponent is used to having the ball 13 times, we are going to give it to them 9. If our opponent is used to getting the ball 12 times, we are going to give it to them 8. We run the football because we are an option football team. For us, that gives us an opportunity to be successful. We feel like running the ball and keeping the clock running gives us the best opportunity to win football games. We feel the option gives us the best opportunity to do that. If we had to line up and run power and isolation plays, we would get killed.

We want to be known as a team that runs to the football. All our drills are predicated on running to the football. We are not the biggest team in the world. If we do not have 11 guys running to the ball, we are not going to be a successful defense. We may not have the best call or be in the best position, but we are going to make sure we run to the football on every single snap. In the practice drills we have, we make sure we finish with all 11 guys running to the football.

We want to make sure we are good at what we do. We are not going to worry about what everyone else is doing. We are going to work on what we do. There are a lot of different great ideas out there, but we have to remember we have to be good at what we do. Our biggest offensive linemen are about 6-3 and 280 pounds. They are not the biggest guys in the game. For us to line up and try to throw the football every day and every down would be very hard for us.

We want to make sure we are sound in the kicking game. A lot of teams will have a philosophy that they are going to be aggressive and go after every kick, but our philosophy is to be sound.

Being tougher than our opponents and playing harder than our opponents have been very important for our program. We have to be tougher and play harder than all of our opponents. If we do not accomplish #5 and #6, we are in trouble. We emphasize this to our players every time we can.

It is important to make sure we do not beat ourselves. This year marks the third year in a row we have had the least amount of penalties in the country. We are always in the top 20 in preventing turnovers. Even if we are not having penalties, turnovers, and missed assignments, we are not the biggest team out there, so we are going to struggle. If we cannot accomplish items 5, 6, and 7, we might as well hit the showers. We have to do those things just to give us a chance of winning football games. If someone is to ask what our culture is, it is items 5, 6, and 7. Be tougher than everyone else, play harder than everyone else, and do not beat ourselves.

Skills are very important part of the football game. I think this quote by Bill Walsh encompasses what I feel about skills.

We talk about skills. Skills are the very essence of playing the game of football.

The best coaches select the skills that are related to their program, their philosophy, or their system of football. They isolate those skills and then they develop drills to teach those skills. The very essence of coaching or teaching is to isolate skills and then find an efficient way to teach them that's practical—that can be applied to playing a game of football. That's the toughest job.

So, a staff member should take full advantage of developing a full knowledge of the skills that he must teach his players. Then, he should develop drills and establish drills that players totally understand—that are an efficient way to impart those drills and those skills to the players. That is an absolute critical part of coaching.

—Bill Walsh

The key is finding the skill for a given position. Finally, when you have identified those skills, come up with drills that will accentuate the skills that are needed to win. When we look at each position, we determine what types of skills are needed for that position. Once we have identified those skills, we ask what are we doing to develop and improve those skills.

This is how we organize our practices. We start practice with a team get-off. This is where we do our stretching and calisthenics. The thing I focus on is at the end of this part of the practice. I want our players ready to go. I do not want them to need another 5 or 10 minutes in order to get ready to practice. Whether it is 12 or 15 minutes, whatever it takes, our players need to be ready to go at the end of this period. We have a team get-off session where we are trying to build our intensity and breaking the huddle and getting off on the snap count.

Sometimes, I will have a score period rather than a team get-off period. Every defense has the pursuit drill, so I wanted to have something we could do offensively. In the score drill, we are going to start on the 20- or 25-yard line and we are going to score. We are going to be excited when we score. It allows us to do two things. It is a way to start off practice and get some momentum going, and it will get our condition going. I guarantee you our offensive linemen hate this drill.

This is what we start off with every day. We are going to make sure everyone is involved. I do not want guys standing around. We will either start out with our score period or our team get-off period. While we are doing this, the defense is either doing pursuit drills or they are doing tackling drills. Right from the get-go, we are getting after it.

The next phase of our practice is ball security. I want all of our skilled guys to start off with ball security. We want to make sure we emphasize taking care of the ball. If we do not take care of the football, we are done. We want to make sure we have the ball tucked high and tight. We want four points of pressure. We emphasize they must keep the ball secure up until the time they give the ball to the manager. I do not ever want to see anybody carrying the ball loosely at any time.

Right after that, we go into our individual fundamental drills. We are going to have individual drills every day of practice from day one until the end when we play Army. Just like Bill Walsh said, we are going to make sure our skill set is strong in what we are doing. We work on that through our fundamentals in our individual period every day. This period will last 20 to 30 minutes each day.

The quarterbacks and the running backs might work on their mesh during this period. The number one skill set for our A backs is arc blocking the perimeter. This is where they would be working on that. They are going to drop-step with their outside foot and cross over. Their aiming point is to the outside thigh.

Our wide receivers do not see a football for the first 10 minutes of practice. That is the culture we are trying to create. We practice our blocking first. We want them to have the mentality that they can be the person that makes the block to spring a big play. If they need to catch the ball during the course of the game, they can do that too. Their first priority is to block. This is the culture we are creating. One that is very unselfish and of tireless workers working hard. Our wide receivers will practice their stock block as well. This is a very high priority for our receivers. We start off with drills where they can work on their feet.

Our offensive linemen will work with the chute in their drills. The first step our linemen take in drills is our zone step. We really exaggerate the backside knee to push the hips over. We want to make sure we are north and south and our shoulder pads are over our thighs. Our knees should be leading our toes so we always have angles in our knees. We want to keep a flat back. These are just some of the drills that we might run during this period.

Fundamental group work comes next for about 15 minutes. We work on this every day. For us, it might include a three-on-three drill versus a 50 look or an odd front. It does not have to be long. Later on, we may have the receivers involved so they can

practice their perimeter block. It does not have to be complicated.

The next part of our practice is our team option period. It goes for 20 minutes and is live. We get a lot done during this part of our practice. We get as many reps as we can. We have two huddles versus one scout team. We usually get 40 snaps during this time frame. Our plays are scripted, and we have a lot of energy on the field for this.

We have three-foot interior splits across the board. Our basic formation is the spread formation (Diagram #1).

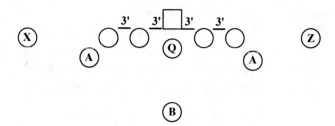

Diagram #1. Spread Formation

We have had to tighten up our Abacks because of NCAA rules concerning cut blocking. Our A backs are basically behind our tackles. The heels of the fullback are five yards from the nose of the football.

This is a look at our double flex formation (Diagram #2). It has been a good formation for us because our basic rules stay in place. With the double flex formation, we can do different things with our wideouts. It makes the defense adjust down, so when we do pitch the ball, we have more grass on the edges.

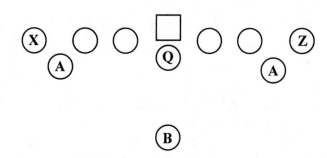

Diagram #2. Double Flex

Our trips formation gives us this look (Diagram #3). We are moving our A back over. We like to start out in our spread and then move our A back over to

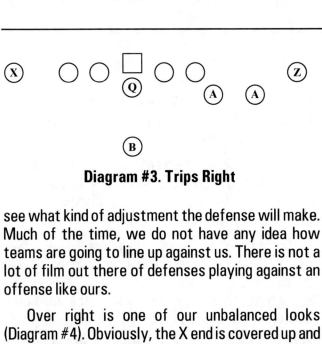

Diagram #3. Trips Right

see what kind of adjustment the defense will make. Much of the time, we do not have any idea how teams are going to line up against us. There is not a lot of film out there of defenses playing against an offense like ours.

Over right is one of our unbalanced looks (Diagram #4). Obviously, the X end is covered up and is ineligible. This gives us another formation. If the defense does not adjust, we have better angles, and it gives us an advantage.

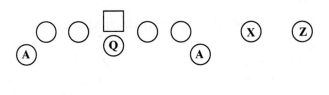

Diagram #4. Over Right

If the defense does make an adjustment, we want to know what they did. Once we know their adjustments, we attack from there. If the defense makes an adjustment by playing our X up tight because it knows he is ineligible, we move to our over right green formation (Diagram #5).

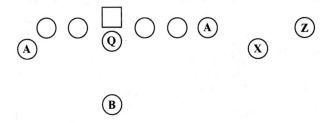

Diagram #5. Over Right Green

Now the X is eligible and the A is ineligible. If the defense wants to play us up tight, we throw our very sophisticated curl/out combination route or our very sophisticated smash combination route.

We can run a trips look with the tight end as the third receiver (Diagram #6).

Diagram #6. Over Right Brown

Our heavy formations have been very good to us (Diagram #7). We bring our heavy tackle to the right side.

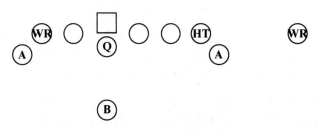

Diagram #7. Heavy Right

We still have two eligible receivers on the left side. Everybody knows we are going to run the veer. If teams cheat over too much, we can hurt them on the backside with either a run or a pass. If we know we want to run to the backside, we have a third tackle on the left side and run jumbo (Diagram #8).

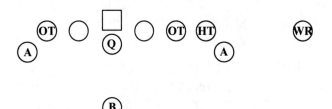

Diagram #8. Jumbo Right

The last formation I have is our heavy right over (Diagram #9).

None of this is rocket science. These are our rules for running the triple option. We have nothing to hide. It is nothing complicated. Every defensive coordinator we go up against knows what we are going to do. What we do, we do. If we have a problem, we know how to fix it.

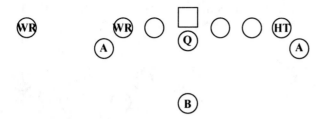

Diagram #9. Heavy Right Over

We are going to see what the defense does and we are going to run our offense and make adjustments based on how our opponents try to defend us. If we cannot beat you running our offense, we are in trouble because we are not going to be able to beat you doing anything else.

TRIPLE OPTION RULES

PSWR—Near deep defender: This allows the wideout to come off the ball. The number one skill for him is stalk blocking. We work on it every day.

PSA—Run support (whomever that may be): Normally with three deep, it is the free safety. If #3 is in the middle of the field, we will end up load-blocking him. This basically means the playside tackle and the playside A back block the playside linebacker and free safety, however it unfolds. Anytime the run support defender is outside the tackle, we are not going to load-block.

PST—PSLB: The playside tackle has the playside linebacker. The rule for him to determine who that is is the first guy from his outside hip and in. He is making that call so everyone knows who he is blocking. His rule for the veer is simple.

If the playside guard is uncovered he runs an outside release and loops because the playside guard can protect for a run-through. If the guard is covered, he is going to veer inside to protect the B gap if there is a B gap threat. The number one skill of our playside tackle is veer releasing. We want to make sure he steps, dips, and rips.

PSG—Base: If he is covered by a down lineman, he is going to block him. If he is uncovered, he has the Will linebacker. Where the playside linebacker is lined up will determine if we try to help the guard with a combo block if we have a 3 technique lineman. If the playside linebacker is lined up right on top of the tackle, we are solo. We go into it with the idea that we are going to help the guard with a 3 technique, but it depends on how the playside linebacker lines up and how he plays.

From a rules standpoint, the guard is blocking for the dive. The tackle is blocking the quarterback to pitch. Our blocking rules can change based on how the defense lines up and what it likes to do.

C—Scoop: If he is covered with a 0 technique, he will T-board right. His second step is going to be right on the ball. Then, he runs his track. If the nose fights through his hip, he will block him. If the nose goes backside, he works up to the next level.

BSG—Scoop: Run their track and block whomever shows.

BST—Scoop: Run their track and block whomever shows.

BSA—Tail motion/pitch path: His first step is right at the rear end of the fullback, and he is at a full sprint. We do not want a half jog. Once he reaches the rear end of the fullback, he is going to take three steps and then mirror the quarterback. The fullback is lined up at five yards. We can use different types of motion packages to get him there.

BSWR—Cut off

B Back—Veer track: The read for the fullback is the first guy inside the tackle. The fullback has to listen for the call of the playside tackle so he knows what is happening ahead of him. If there is a combo call, he will start on his track, but he knows he may have to cut it back. He still has to read it.

QB—Veer footwork/option reads: The pitch read key is going to be the first guy touching the tackle on an out. The quarterback is going to read #1 on the dive. The next guy out is going to be the pitch key. Even though he is reading #1, if #2 comes hard, he is thinking quick pitch. He will read his angle; if #2 is covering the pitch, the quarterback will tuck it up inside. Over the years, we have had different types of keys for the quarterback to decide whether to give the ball to the fullback. We have come down to can someone tackle the fullback? If no one can tackle the fullback, give him the ball.

PENN STATE FOOTBALL: TEAM ESSENTIALS

Penn State

First of all, it is really great to come to the Pennsylvania area and not be booed. The last time I was here with the New England Patriots, we had a good day. I am really glad to be here. This is the fourth clinic I have done since coming to Penn State. People have been really great, and they have come up to me afterward and thanked me so much for coming to their clinic. I have to tell you, I love doing clinics.

I would much rather talk about football all day long than to talk to someone about nonfootball issues. I know I have to talk to other people. but I love talking football. I think you will find that I am approachable and our staff is approachable. We love to talk football, and we love teaching our players how to play football. That is important to me.

There are a couple of other things that are very important to me that I would like to touch on here. I have been coaching for 20 years. When I started coaching, I went to Brown University. One thing coaching at Brown University taught me was to take a good look at each situation. It taught me how to ask "why." It taught me to not just take something somebody gave me and just go use it. When I left Brown I went back to my high school, just north of Boston. I helped my high school coach with his team. That experience was the springboard for me to go into coaching and showed me that I would love to be a coach. I love to teach a kid how to play football and tell him why he should do certain things and to watch players improve. High school football is a huge part of a young man's development.

When I was coaching with the Patriots, when we would leave the hotel, I would get on the bus and sit next to Tom Brady. We would go over the call sheet of our game plan for the 15th time that week. We went over and over and over it before kickoff because we were that detailed.

Heading into Pittsburgh as we were coming through the tunnels and coming up to the stadium, it is a pretty neat deal. We saw the houses along the road and Tom Brady said to me, "Wouldn't you have loved to play high school football here in Pittsburgh or in Pennsylvania?" To me, that was a huge statement from a guy who had a great high school experience but pointed that out to us as we were driving from our hotel to the Pittsburgh stadium. This is where football is really important. It is in the fabric of people's lives here in Pennsylvania.

One of the things I learned from Bill Belichick was how to prepare a team. One thing Bill is great at is preparing a team to play each and every week. Before we left for the Super Bowl, he put a video together with a Kenny Chesney song called "The Boys of Fall." On the video, for each guy on our roster, he had a highlight of them in high school, a highlight of them in college, and then a highlight of them with the New England Patriots. It was a great motivational technique. As soon as those pros saw their high school highlight, there was not a dry eye in the room. It was because of what the high school coaches meant to those guys. It is where they learned how to play football. It is where they learned how to throw and catch the ball, tackle, play special teams, and play as a team. I had already accepted the Penn State job, and it just really struck me what high school football meant to all those guys on the New England Patriots team.

I had about a week to prepare for my second interview with Penn State. What I learned from my research was that at Penn State, you can run a program the right way. You can have excellence on the football field with smart and hard-nosed football players and you can do it right in the classroom. I titled my presentation for my job interview "A Championship Program On and Off the Field." A lot of that is what I am going to go over with you today. Now, the interview was a six-hour interview. This is going to be about an hour-long talk. As I researched Penn State, I knew personally this was the place for me to do things the right way on and off the field.

There are four things we are going to talk about today. This is what makes up the foundation of our program:

- Academics
- Football
- Respect
- Integrity

When you are setting up a high school football program, I hope you will take a few of these points and use them to set up your program because they can help your program. That is the goal I have for you today.

The first thing is academics. We have already had some early morning runs for guys who did not go to class. If you cut class and we catch you, you are going to run at 5 a.m. on Monday. That is the way we are going to do it. I have always said that if you show up to class, you are well on your way to getting your education and graduating.

The second aspect we are going to talk about in building the foundation of our program is going to be about football. When we talk about football with our players, our players have to understand how detailed we are going to be as a staff and how detailed we are going to be when we approached them in preparing them as a player.

We are already talking to our quarterbacks about coverages. Before you can even talk to your quarterback about what we are going to be doing offensively, you have to teach them about defenses. If your quarterback does not understand anything about defense, how in the world is he going to play quarterback for you? There is a lot to learn about defense. They have to know about fronts, coverages, pressures, techniques, inside leverage or outside leverage, linebackers outside on tight ends equals man-to-man coverage, corners outside on tight ends equals zone coverage.

All the little tips I have learned over the years, we have to teach to our quarterbacks so they can understand how we are going to attack the defense. We have just spent two or three days with our quarterbacks on how to understand the defense. We are going to talk to our guys constantly about recognizing formations. When they break the huddle, there is only a few things the defense can do out of a certain personnel group and formation. We learn this from studying film and preparing how we want to go against a certain team.

We are going to talk to our team constantly about special teams. We use the term complementary football a lot. Complementary football means if the kickoff team goes down and does a great job of pinning the return team inside the 10- or 15-yard line, our defense needs to go out there and keep them there. Get a three-and-out so we can play on a short field. We talk about that constantly.

If our punt return team does a great job of returning the ball 50 yards to the 15-yard line, we have to turn that into six points and not three. If our defense recovers a fumble, we have to turn that into points. That is complementary football. When our offense goes down and scores a touchdown, our defense has to hold the opponent to a three-and-out or get a turnover and get the ball right back to the offense and understand the momentum you are building when you are doing that. Those are all examples of complementary football.

Situational football is important as well. I learned a lot from Bill Belichick, and one of the things he taught me was the game is broken down into three segments. You may agree or disagree with this, but I agree with it. You have the first quarter of the game where both teams are going at it and trying to figure out what each other is doing. We learn what types of coverages they are going to use in certain situations.

Also, we get an idea on what personnel groups they like to use against our personnel groups. We determine how the game is going. You cannot wait until halftime to make an adjustment. You have to make that adjustment during the first quarter or just after the first quarter. Maybe our game plan is perfect for what we are doing, but maybe it is not. During halftime, you have to think about opening up the second half a different way.

The halftime is the second part of the game. We want to make sure we open up the second half differently than anything we have shown before.

Sometimes, we would go out and line up with no huddle and in an empty formation, which we had not been in during the whole game. The third part of the game is the fourth quarter. Are you behind or are you ahead? What are your best third-down calls? What are your best running and passing calls? That is all the fourth quarter is. This is our vision for Penn State football, and we are going to teach our players how to play our way.

The next thing we have to discuss is respect. A couple of guys came into my office the other day to talk about future schedules. All I am thinking about, in my mind, is how are we going to handle the first spring practice. As a coach, sometimes you have to look forward for certain things. The guys I am talking with are good people, but they are not football people.

In pro football, you usually meet the team on Wednesday morning and go over the game plan with the players. Every Wednesday, for the five years I was coaching in New England, after that meeting, Tom Brady would turn to me and say, "There it is again. We are playing the '85 Bears." We had the utmost respect for that team, for their physical skills, for their coaching staff, how they would prepare, and everything about that team for that week. Every game was a dogfight for the most part, regardless of who we were playing. To coach in the NFL, that is one thing you learn. In every game, you have the ultimate respect for your opponent.

At Penn State, we are going to have respect for our opponents, but we are also going to have respect for our program. Our program is not going to be a lovey-dovey program. Football is not a lovey-dovey sport. Football is a violent sport. It is two guys knocking the stuffing out of each other to move the ball forward or to move the ball backward. On our football team, I am not going to have 120 guys that love each other. They will respect each other. That has to be the way we do things at Penn State. We have to have respect for each other in our program and understand what that word means, and we have to see it every day. We will have respect for opponents, and we will have respect for coaches. Respect is a huge word in our program

Integrity is the fourth point to discuss. I have said from day one, we are going have an open program. With Tom Brady, we did not run the ride-and-decide type of offense. With the guy making $18 million a year, you do not run that stuff. I know what I know, and I know I don't know the ride-and-decide stuff. If you come in and talk to me about what I know about football, I may ask you what you know about football and have you get up front and draw it up on the board for me so I understand it.

As it relates to integrity, we have nothing to hide. We want you to come into our program and see what it is all about. I am personally proud of the staff we have put together. These are great men—and men of character, family men, and coaches that know what it is to be demanding of kids in teaching them and preparing them. We think it is really important to have people see our program and see what we are all about. It is one thing to talk about integrity. We want to be able to show our integrity when we show you our program.

When we talk about staff, we talk about four points:
• We want to have a unique blend
• Family
• Knowing your role
• Loyalty

I want to focus on the last two points. The first thing you have to do when you get a job as a head coach is to get a list of the coaches reporting to you. You also need to know what job responsibilities they had prior to coaching with you. You have to set up your own organizational structure. I developed a flowchart with everybody's name on it, and I meet with them individually. I discuss with each person what his role is and what his responsibilities are.

After that, I brought them into my office. I went into more detail about what they were responsible for. You have to go from the janitor to the receptionist to any one of the coaches and let them know they have a vital role in your program. You have to define it for each and every one of them.

One of the things we constantly talk about at Penn State is loyalty. We are going to be loyal to each other. We go into a room with our fellow coaches and fight like cats and dogs about how we are going to attack our opponent. If someone tells me they want to run a certain play in a certain situation, I will ask him why. I will ask him to show me. When we leave the room and present it to the players, no matter where you coach at—whether it is college, pros, or high school—everyone has to be on the same page. Everyone has to believe in the mission and how we are going to accomplish that mission. That is where you start to have loyalty on your staff. You really do not know about loyalty until you are in a game when the bullets are flying. This is where you see loyalty. When you go to war with the right tackle who is playing next to you or you are coaching your butt off with the coach next to you, that is where you see loyalty.

I had a team meeting the day I got the job. I went into the team meeting and I told the players I am going to put two signs up. The sign on the way in to our facility said this:

Know Your Role
Work Hard
Be Attentive
Always Put the Team First

Our players are going to see this sign every day when they walk in the building. The number one thing is to know your role. We talk to the players in our program about what their roles are.

An example of this would be with one of our tight ends. He is a great kid and is a great student and works his butt off. He's 6 feet 5 inches tall, and I knew he was more of a tackle. I asked him what position he played, and he said he played tight end. I watched him in winter conditioning and then I brought him in for a talk just after that. I told him we had some good tight ends coming back this year and that some good tight ends were coming in as freshmen. I told him I did not know how much he was going to play as a tight end. I told him that after I watched him move, he could be a great tackle for us. He did not want to be a tackle. The first time I timed him running his routes, I had to use a sundial to get his time, and I knew he would not be a tight end anymore.

I told him where I had come from in evaluating talent—that I saw him as more of a tackle. I let him know I did not want to move him just to be moving him. I told him by moving him, it would help the overall team.

He asked me to show him how. We put together a tape of guys who came to college as tight ends and then developed and filled out their bodies more

and moved to tackle and then became draft picks. We showed him how he could help the team, and he came back a couple of days later and had agreed to move to tackle. Now he is one of the happiest kids in the world. He is doing well at tackle and is on the two-deep rotation going into spring practice. He is a guy we spent time on to explain what his role is and how his role would help the football team.

Every guy on your team has to understand his role. The role of a player as a long snapper is important. He cannot have a bad snap. Tell him how you see him. Show him what you see on tape if you have the means to do that. Make sure when the player leaves your room he understands his role and then put him in that role. Do not have him do something else in practice that is not part of his role.

The second item is to work hard. Everyone says work hard. Bill Belichick, during training camp, would bring the team up after practice and say that was a good day of practice and we can put that in the bank. He would then go on to say that there is no light at the end of the tunnel—just keep working.

There is no substitute for hard work. No one will ever outwork us. We have an extremely hard-working staff. This has already worn off on our players. We ask our players to get up on Tuesdays and Fridays at 5:30 a.m. in the morning and work extremely hard on our winter conditioning. Our players are putting in the time and then they are going to class. Some of them have 14- to 16-hour days. That is the way it is going to be. If we want to win the way we say we want to win, there is no substitute for hard work.

We want our guys to be attentive. In New England, our team meetings were divided down the middle of the room, with the offense on one side and the defense on the other. Tom Brady was our leader, and he would sit in the very front row and on the aisle. Everyone in our meeting could see Tom up front. In every meeting, I noticed that he had brought with him a notebook and something to write with. In every single meeting, he would stare up at Coach Bill Belichick and take notes on what Bill was saying. That had a great effect on our team. Tom was being attentive, and everyone in the room would watch Tom Brady write something in his notebook and then they would write something in their notebook.

In team meetings, you have to be attentive as a player. If our players are sleeping, we are not going to kick them out of the meeting. We are going make them stand up. We may bring them up to the front of the room, where they have to be attentive. Being attentive is the only way they are going to learn the details and learn the game plan and learn the technique that you want them to play with.

"Always put the team first" is huge for us. What does that mean? You cannot just look at a player and say you have to put the team first, no matter what. Again, you have to show your players that you want them to do something and this is why. "You have to play this way so we can beat this team this way. We have to play this way to give us the best chance to beat our opponent. No matter what you do, even outside of football, when you see something that is not right and is not a great situation, you have to get out of that situation because you have to put the team first. You have to understand how you would hurt the team if you get into trouble. You have to understand how your position move is going to help the team. Always put the team first."

A sign on the way out of our facility reads like this:

Prioritize Academics and
Community Involvement
Manage Expectations
Don't Believe or
Fuel the Hype
Speak for
Yourself
Ignore
Noise

This is the last thing they look at when they leave our facility. They have to go to class, and they have to do well in school. State College in Pennsylvania is a great place. You have about 40,000 students and 50,000 residents. It is about half and half. We have to get out in the community. We are involved in Habitat for Humanity, Make-A-Wish Foundation, and the Special Olympics.

I have appointed a guy by the name of Elijah Robinson to work with our athletes in community services. He played at Penn State and was injured. He was a good football player, got a scholarship, but then got hurt. He is a guy that gets it. He understands what Penn State is all about and also knows that is important to get our guys invested in the community. We are going to make sure this is a part of our program.

We have to manage expectations. We do not know how it is going to go for us next season. We are just taking it day by day. We have a lot of confidence in our staff and in our team. It looks like we will have a big physical team and a couple of guys that can run. When we win, we have to be able to manage expectations. I tell our players when they go outside the building that that is where they are going to have to manage expectations. When everyone is slapping you on the butt and telling you what a great player you are after you have won, that is where it gets hard. We have to move on to the next game. Each game presents a huge challenge to us. We tell our team we have 12 one-game seasons. When we win or play one game, then and only then are we going to look toward the next game. We are going to take them one game at a time.

Don't believe or fuel the hype. This is really important to me. I am going to say it wherever we go. What went on in the past at Penn State, I have to address at times. We now, as a staff and as a team, have to move forward. We have to take a huge amount of pride in being Penn State players and coaches. There are a lot of players out there over the years that have developed a great reputation for Penn State. It is an honor and a point of pride to be able to continue that great reputation and represent Penn State football.

We coach our players up on how to speak to the media. We do not tell them what to say; we tell them to speak for themselves. If a reporter asks how Johnny's knee is, you do not know how Johnny's knee is; tell them to go ask Johnny. The only thing you can talk about is what is happening with you. You can talk about how you are doing academically, how much you love being at Penn State, what you are doing in the community, or things that affect you.

Ignore the noise goes back to and is similar to do not believe or fuel the hype. There are two things that matter as it relates to the football player. Number one is his family. There is one group in this world that will love you unconditionally, and that is your family. No matter what happens, they will love you. The next most important group of people are the guys that are on your team and the guys that coach you. Those are the only guys that matter when it comes to football.

When we get into the team meeting room, all that matters is the guys on your team. We tell them not to waste their time for one second about what somebody outside of the family of the football program says. We tell them to just worry about doing the best they can in the meeting room, on the practice field, or on the game field.

This is the type of football program we are going to build. It starts with our recruiting system, and our coaches are learning how to use it. Recruiting is an inexact science, but we try to apply science to it. There are a lot of ways to do it, and people have done it different ways.

BUILDING A FOOTBALL TEAM

- Tough, smart, physical
- Be able to play in all kinds of weather
- Situationally smart
- Complementary football

The number one thing we want to do is to be a tough, smart, physical football team. We want good-size lineman. We want the type of running backs who are big first-down and second-down backs. We want third-down backs who can catch the football. We want good-size defensive lineman. We want big linebackers. We want big corners who can possibly play as a safety. We want to be big, physical, and smart about things. We do the best we can to try to judge that when we recruit our players.

We have a great indoor facility. I do not know how much we are going to be in there because we are going to practice outside. If it snows, we have to play in it. It is going to rain, and we have to play in it. There is extreme heat in August, and we have to play in that. We have to play all four seasons, and we have to be a team that is ready to play in all kinds of weather. We are going to practice outdoors. In New England, we knew how to play in the snow because we practiced in the snow. We did not go inside to practice.

I have already talked about being situationally smart and about a complementary football team. Coach Belichick would talk to our team every day about the situations. First-and-10 is a situation. Second-and-11-plus is a situation. Third-and-one is a situation. The two-minute drill is a situation. You do not have to teach it all at once, but you have to teach players about situations every day.

What do you do on second-and-long? The offense is trying to get halfway to first down, so screens and draws might be something you look at. The defense wants to keep them in a long-distance situation. They only have so many options. You have to be prepared for all of them. Some teams will change how they play in a given situation. Some teams will play max coverage in the field, but when they get into the red zone, they will play max blitz. You have to be prepared to handle those things.

After every game, we list all the situations where we did good and bad in playing complementary and situational football. We list each and every one of them individually.

I really want to thank everyone for listening. It is like I said when I got the job: I think if you can meet our staff, you will like what you see. We will be honest with you about how we treat our players and how we evaluate them. We are going to strive every year and every day to build relationships with you. We want you to feel that your kids are going to be treated right and be coached right if you send them to Penn State to play football. Thank you.

STRESSING THE THIRD DOWN DEFENSE

University of Central Florida

Before I get started, I would like to make one thing clear. Before you leave here today, make sure you have one thing you can take back to your program. Do not let me leave here today without giving you at least one positive thing that you can use.

The topic they asked me to speak about today is third-down defense. Let me just clue you in. If you want to have good third-down defense, you have to do it on first and second down. This is my 44th year in coaching. Our goal for first down is 57 percent of the time, to have second-and-seven (or more) so we can dictate to the offense what they are going to do. In college and high school, if the offense does not make four yards or more on first down, they are going to throw the ball on second down. That is just what they do. First-down defense is critical. If you are going to keep a stat, we use 57 percent as our goal, to put the offense second and plus seven.

This time of year, everyone is talking about what their stats were. Let me just tell you, stats are for losers. If someone is looking at stats, they are probably trying to justify why they lost, or it is some offensive guy trying to get a job. That is how it works. There are only four stats that I have kept throughout all of my coaching. I have kept these stats for five years to prove to my own coaching staff that these have meaning.

We are 31-6 when we are leading in the first quarter over the last five years. Why is that important? It is important because players and coaches are front runners. I have found when most kids are not successful early; you have to become a cheerleader as a coach on the sidelines. It is important to get off to a good start early. How does that affect coaches? Most coaches will start to second-guess their game plan if they are not successful early. Coaches start to panic and start making adjustments. You should not have to do those things. The only reason you are doing it

FOUR IMPORTANT STATS

Stats	2006–2011	2011
Lead first quarter	31-6	4-2
Trail first quarter	7-24	0-3
Less turnovers	31-4	3-2
More turnovers	6-24	2-3
Rush > 150 yards	32-8	5-1
Rush < 150 yards	10-26	0-6
Possession time +	32-18	4-4
Possession time -	9-15	1-1

is because you are behind. I have found this holds up throughout the years. Watch your kids, and you will see it is true. Kids today have that Little League syndrome. If they are not successful, they are looking for their mother or father.

The second stat is for turnovers. When we have fewer turnovers than our opponent, we are 31-4. If we have more turnovers, we are 6-24. Turnovers get you beat. They get you beat field position-wise and scoring-wise. When I look deeper at this stat, I look at whether it was forced turnovers or technique turnovers.

We like to run the ball. I believe that you have to run the ball and stop the run in order to win championships. I do not care what level it is. Whether it is high school, college, or the pros, you have to run the ball, stop the run, and have good specialty teams in order to win championships. That is how you get that done. Yes, you do have to throw the ball some. It has been proven that teams that throw for a living do not usually make the big games. They put people in the seats, but that is all they do. If you are a good throwing team, people are going to eventually make you run the ball. We were 32-8 when rushing for 150+ yards. We were 10-26 when we had less than 150 yards rushing.

Possession time is also critical. The offense cannot score if they do not have the ball. If you have possession time in your favor, that equates to field position. These are the only four stats that I look at. I believe they make the difference between winning and losing. Let me go over our third-down objectives.

THIRD-DOWN OBJECTIVES

- Prevent long runs and passes.
- Allow no missed assignments.
- Allow no foolish penalties.
- Have a great short yardage defense.
- Stay focused on turnovers.

If you cannot prevent the long run and pass, you are going to get beat. This is especially true on third down. I do not want to see any missed assignments. I call missed assignments, MAs. My definition of an MA is something that has happened after the snap. If I say ME, that is a mental error. A mental error happens before the snap of the ball. An example of this is if our split is not right, or our depth is not right. A mental error is on the coach. If the player you are coaching is not lined up right, that is on you. MEs are coaching issues. MAs could be the coach, but usually it is the player. If you have a lot of MEs, you are wrong even before the snap.

There is no reason for a foolish penalty. Jumping offside is a foolish penalty. When you go back and track those, it is usually the same people. When I look at a room, I look at ants and roaches. If you go into a room you see ants lined up in a straight line. When you walk into a room and see roaches, they scatter all over the place and are pointing their finger at everyone else. You want to get rid of the roaches off on your team. You want a team of ants that get in line and follow orders. You will find the roaches are the penalty guys. They are always blaming somebody else for what happened.

You have to have great short yardage defense. Why? You have to get off the field. I want to be three-and-out all of the time. If we are not three-and-out, I want to know why. What happened?

Was it a mental error? Three-and-out controls field position and it controls momentum.

We must stay focused on turnovers. When I talk about defense, I am talking about takeaways. When I talk about takeaway techniques, I talk about CPR. CPR stands for club, punch, and rip. On offense, they are called turnovers. Every day in practice, we talk about and practice takeaways and turnovers. Every day in our scripts for practice, I will randomly circle two or three CPR plays, and the ball had better come out. It does not matter to me if it is a pass or a run. I will circle them as a CPR play, and they know the ball has to come out defensively. If not, we are going to run them after practice. It drives me nuts when I hear coaches yell to take the ball away, yet they do not spend time on it in practice. I want our players to understand what it means when we say to take the ball away. That means get the ball.

When people say somebody is loafing, what does that mean? It means something different to everyone. I decided to define it for my football team. A loaf is:

- Not being in a proper stance.
- A change of speed. When I see someone going after the ball, I better see a five-yard burst to get there. Do not let them jog. It creates bad habits.
- Getting passed by player at your position.
- No five-yard burst when the ball is thrown.
- Staying on the ground. I grade what people do when they get knocked to the ground. That is going to happen and is part of the game. I give them a G- if I do not see them snap their head up. When I see a player on the ground, I want to see his head snap up. If his head snaps up, he is getting up. He wants to see what is going on, and that gets him moving. Make them snap their head up every time. You can become a better defense just by doing that.
- Turning down a hit. That is not just a loaf; I will have his scalp. That is the old olé play. That will get you beat.
- Taking the path of least resistance.
- Once the tackle is secured, not attempting to get the ball.

Because so many offenses run the no-huddle, we teach the hanging huddle on defense (Diagram #1). We never huddle on defense. I have defined it to make sure everyone understands the procedure.

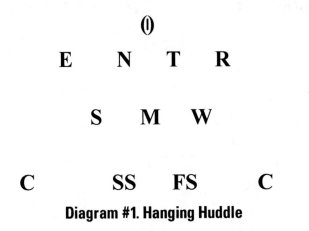

Diagram #1. Hanging Huddle

- Alignment in three levels.
- The nose man sets the first level three yards away from the ball.
- The linebackers are at the second level.
- The secondary is the third level.
- All eyes are to the sideline to get the call. I make everyone get the call. Once we start practicing getting the call in the spring, I do not let anyone repeat the call. I will then ask them at random what the call is. They better know the call. It is not just one guy looking over to get the call and another not knowing what the call is. Everyone looks over and gets the call, and we go from there. It is usually the linemen who are asking, "What is the call?"
- Mike will echo the call.
- The strong safety will give the down-and-distance.
- The free safety gives the offensive personnel.

That is the communication for the hanging huddle. Everyone knows what to expect and what their responsibilities are.

Let us take a look at why the ball was moved on your defense. This is just a way to make sure everybody is on the same page in your defense.

- Defensive error
  ✓ Poor adjustments
  ✓ Poor call
- Individual error
  ✓ Responsibility
  ✓ Poor technique
  ✓ Out of position (He lined up wrong—ME.)
- Lack of contact
  ✓ Initially, I want to see our players make contact at full speed. I do not want them to slow down or come to a stop to make the tackle. I also want them to lead with their chest and shoulder pads. I do not want to see them lead with their hands. Your hands come from separation and lockup. The guys who put their hands up are stopping and grabbing. Contact speed means going through people. The arms come to secure the tackle.
  ✓ Control of line of scrimmage
- Missed tackles
  ✓ Poor pursuit

Do you all see a lot of one-back sets? You are only as good as your base defense. When you install your base defense, you have to be able to defend against the one back. It may not be the best in terms of alignment, but your players must know what their responsibilities are.

- You must have answers to adjustments. All defensive packages. Alignment-motion-shift.
- Flexibility in front and coverage. It is not just important to run a two or three deep coverage. What is important is what you do underneath it. The underneath coverage is what helps with one back offenses. The middle of the field is either open or closed. You play a version on cover 2 or cover 3. Pay attention to what you do with the underneath coverage. This is where people that play really good third-down defense really excel. You have to do things that take away those five-yard dead zone routes. I will give you some ideas on that in a minute.
- Ability to pressure. Make the offense execute.
- The key to defending one back. Know what they are attempting to do. Are they spreading you out to run the ball or are they spreading you out to pass the ball. Know what they are doing. When they run the ball, they are counting hats. You need to have one more guy in the box then they have

people to block. That is the key to good third-down defense.

✓ Run—where and how

✓ Pass—protection

• How many ways do they get to a one-back formation? Draw them all up along with the adjustments you make to it. Are they balanced or unbalanced? How are you going to defend that?

I try to make it real simple with our kids. Either they are in a 2x2 set, or they are in a 3x1 set. That encompasses everything. What are our adjustments from there? Are we going to run a six-man box or a seven-man box? I am not going to let you run the ball from a one-back formation. You can book that. I am going to have another guy in the box, and you are not going to be able to run the ball. I am going to make the quarterback throw the ball. We are going to change it up for him by running stunts and other things. I am not going to let you run the dive for four or five yards.

Before we go any further, let us talk about our personnel categories. Our personnel identification starts with the first digit being the number of running backs and the second digit being the number of tight ends.

PERSONNEL IDENTIFICATION

A	20	2RB – 0TE – 3WR
B	21	2RB – 1TE – 2WR
C	22	2RB – 2TE – 1WR
D	23	2RB – 3TE – 0WR
E	10	1RB – 0TE – 4WR
F	11	1RB – 1TE – 3WR
G	12	1RB – 2TE – 2WR
H	13	1RB – 3TE – 1WR
I	30	3RB – 0TE – 2WR
J	31	3RB – 1TE – 1WR
K	32	3RB – 2TE – 0WR
L	00	0RB – 0TE – 5WR
M	01	0RB – 1TE – 4WR
N	02	0RB – 2TE – 3WR

Every personnel group has its own run and passes tendencies and down and distance tendencies. How are we going to defend those?

When we call 21, we know there are two backs and one tight end, which leaves two wide receivers on the field. We are going to know who is on the field. We know how to align up to that. If we call a 10, we know that there is one running back and four wide.

2X2 SHIFT

• Hash and field

• Back

• Middle of the field left

• M.O.F. —open

• M.O.F. —closed

• 5-6-7 man box

• Line games

• Level disguise

These are the mechanics on how we line up the fronts and our shifts for a 2x2 formation. In a third-down situation, if they have a tight end in the game, it is pretty easy. We are going to kick the 3 technique down to the tight end side. When they do not have a tight end in the game, as in 00 (Diagram #2) or 10 personnel, where do you shift the front? If I have not seen you before and do not know what you are going to do, I will play hash and field. If the ball is on the hash, I am going to bubble the front toward the field.

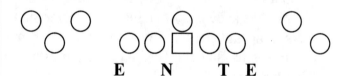

Diagram #2. Front Mechanics vs. 00—Hash Field

If the back is offset, I am going to kick the front that way (Diagram #3). If they are in the middle of the field and there is no tight end in the game, we will go middle of the field left (Diagram #4).

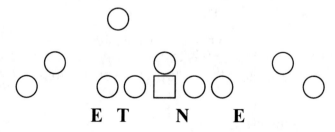

Diagram #3. Front Mechanics vs. 10—Back

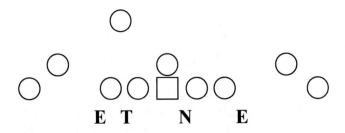

Diagram #4. Front Mechanics vs. 10— Middle of Field Left

What am I looking for? This is important. When I face one-back teams, it is not just about coverage. When I face a one-back team I am looking for mismatches in the front line. When I line up, I am going to keep the 3 technique to the side of the field. I do not like using the bubble to the field because it makes it too easy to protect against. The next thing I am going to do is find out who the weak lineman is. They have five linemen, but there is going to be one that is not as good as the others. Believe me; I am going to put my best rusher on the guy who is most susceptible to getting beat. I am going to have somebody in his face. I am going to make their best blocker block air. Make him help somebody. Do not cover up their Stud. Make him help someone else. You have to study that through tape. We have led the conference in sacks quite a few years, and that is because I make sure that we understand what we are supposed to do. We isolate and attack the weak and circumnavigate the strong.

The other thing I am very aware of is when to play five, six, or seven men in the box. The down-and-distance and their tendencies will determine how many we have in the box. You have to understand when you are facing one back, what is taking place.

SUCCESSFUL PASS RUSH

These are the points I like to stress concerning a successful pass rush with our defensive line.

- Sack the quarterback for a loss. That is not the end-all in itself. There are a lot of components that make up a good rush. What I see today is too many high rushers on the outside and the two inside guys are not getting it done.

In a four-man front, if you are rushing the quarterback, it is real simple. Your ends, if they are rushing in their correct lanes, should be fronting the curl zones. The passing lanes are on the outside. The two inside guys should be fronting up the hook zones. Here is where you have to be smart coaches. If the defensive end takes a speed rush and gets real wide outside, he opens up the passing lane. Do not always just look at sacks; you have to look at pass rush lanes (Diagram #5). They cause more problems than anything else. That is why the Giants knocked so many passes down.

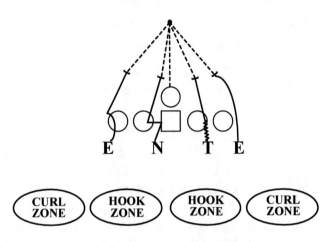

Diagram #5. Pass Rush

The nose does not work the center; he works the guard to block the passing lane. Your guys are going to say they cannot get to the quarterback. They do not have to get to the quarterback every time. We are half-man charge guys. I am coming through your outside half as a defensive end, and I am walking you back into the quarterback. When the quarterback's arm, or indicator, comes up, that is when the defensive player's hands come up. It is not just about sacks. Pass rush lanes are critical.

- Squeeze or limit his area of operation.
- Force him closer to another rusher.
- Do not give him time to look at his second-choice receivers. We want a quick takeoff when the ball is snapped. We work on that in practice with the ball on a stick. When practicing defense, do not go on a cadence. Always go on ball movement. Coaches wonder why they are always jumping offside on the cadence when that is all they practice with during the week. You are teaching them to jump offside. Watch the ball.
- Force him out of his designed throwing area.

- Force him to throw on the run.
- Divide his concentration because you have been all over him all day.
- Cause him to fumble.
- Cause him to lose confidence in his teammates or offensive system.
- Limit his vision, and force a bad throw.
- Bat the ball down.
- Tip it, and cause an interception.
- Force elevation of the throw, and give the secondary more time to break on the ball.

It is not just about sacks. All of these things are critical for the defensive lineman on third down.

This is how we run Lex and Rex. If I want to run a Lex to the tight end, the end and tackle are free rushers (Diagram #6). It is a two-way go. If I said Rex to the tight end, the right defensive end and the nose tackle are free rushers. The free rushers come hard and go over the top or step underneath. The other two guys have to maintain their pass lane responsibilities. I have gotten more sacks using this than just about anything else.

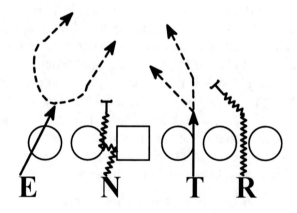

Diagram #6. LEX to the Tight End

You can run Lex and Rex to the bubble or however you want to run it. It helps to know who the weak linemen are when making this call. You have to know what their third down protection scheme is in order to have a good pass rush on third down. The two guys that are not the free rushers know to play off the two free rushers. They know which two are going hard and know what to expect the quarterback to do. Our kids love to run this.

Let me go over something with you concerning cover 3 or three-deep pass defense. With every formation we see, I draw up the progressions with the five eligible receivers and number them. I number them from passing strength over (Diagram #7). In every coverage, we have someone who is responsible for those numbers for our man-in-zone concept. It is not straight man coverage. My guys know where the hook zones and curl zones are, but to be honest with you, I do not even teach it. Everything that we do, we relate to numbers. We play straight cover 3. The strong safety has the progression from the #2 receiver to the #1 receiver. In most people's terminology, he would be the curl/flat player. In my terminology, he is receiver #2 to #1. That is good coverage.

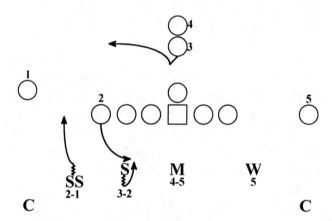

Diagram #7. Cover 3—Coverage Progression

What I do that is different is our mini-packages. You have to have this. When you have the quarterback drop back, you are telling your linebackers to drop 10 yards. The problem is you create a dead zone. If it is third-and-four, what are you going to play? The offense is going to drop back and throw a little curl to the back for a first down. If I say 3 jump, I am going to jump the #3 if he goes weak and the #4 and #5, who are always weak (Diagram #8). We will zone off #2 and #1. This way, I can take care of our dead zone drops.

Normally, the Will has to take the curl and then jump the flat route. Now, we are jumping right away. The quarterback has to hesitate. That is what gives you pressure and gets you sacks. If they line up in a shotgun, it may look like this (Diagram #9). We are jumping #4 and #5, which are always

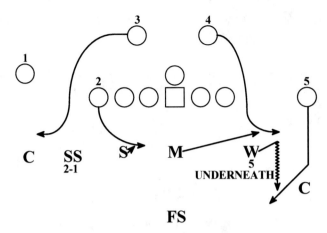

Diagram #8. 3 Jump With Two Backs

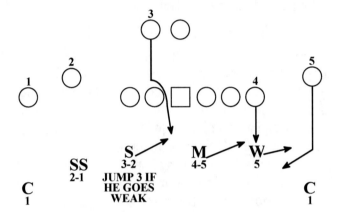

Diagram #9. Jump With Shotgun

weak, and #3 if he goes weak. If #3 stays to the strongside, we are going to zone it off. This takes care of the five-yard dead zone. The only thing that gives us problems with this is if they have a tight end who can run.

If they have a tight end who can run, we will run an alley check (Diagram #10). If the tight end is a Stud, it can give our Will problems on the jump. If we are worried about that tight end, we will run alley

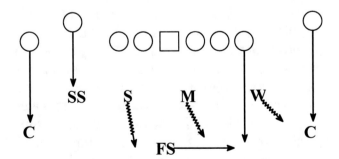

Diagram #10. Alley Check Weak

check right. The strong safety will then carry any two vertical. This tells the free safety to cover the tight end going vertical. The same thing can happen on a 2x2 formation.

The whole idea is to make the quarterback hesitate. This will give our rushers time to get to him and make the quarterback throw out of sync. We can do the same thing to the strongside. These are just some of the calls that we have for three deep. It is what you do underneath that can really help you. That is how you win games. Make the quarterback hesitate and look to see what is going on.

The last thing I will cover with you today is qualities of a coach. This is what I use when I interview people.

QUALITIES OF A COACH

Learn the trade, not the tricks of the trade. I will tell you something right now. Those of you, who came tonight are a lot better coaches than those that did not come tonight.

- Know the business.
- Have the capacity to motivate.
- Have the capacity to think systematically.
- Have the ability to make quick decisions.
- Possess character and integrity in tough times. I judge pressure in people when the pressure is on. I do not judge people after a win; I judge them after a loss.
- Create an atmosphere of positive self-expectancy and positive self-motivation.
- Be a great competitor.

    I say this to my players and coaches every year:
- I am proud of you.
- I believe in you.
- I need you.

    If I cannot say those things about an individual on my team, I bring them in. I want to find out what is going on.

    Thank you for your time, gentlemen. You are welcome to come down and visit us in Florida. We have great facilities now. Thank you!

WIDE RECEIVER BLOCKING DRILLS AND TECHNIQUES

Marshall University

Everything I will tell you and show you today is something someone else has done. I am not a guru by any means. Everything I know comes from coaches such as Joker Phillips and others. What I am covering today is what he taught me. Here, the exception is that our jerseys are a different color. What I am doing is what coaches do. They take the ideas of someone else, put their terminology to it, add what they are successful with, and make it a coaching strategy.

The most important thing we do as wideouts is to block first. Once we get our players to buy into that point, we know we have them on our side. Once we get the receivers to buy into being tough, we know they are going to be able to play.

The catchword for offense today is the spread. I am not sure I know what a spread offense is anymore. We play with three or four wide receivers and five offensive linemen. With the ball on the perimeter as much as it is, the wide receivers have to buy into blocking as much as the offensive linemen block. The difference between wide receiver blocking and O-linemen blocking is space.

The wide receiver has to block in space, which is tougher for the player. When we block, we teach it in a progression. I am going to take you through that progression and show you what we do in the blocking game. From there, I will show you some of the release work we do. I did not want to come here and talk about catching the football.

That is not to mean we do not catch footballs at Marshall. We go out every day, spend 10 minutes on a ball machine, and go through an entire progression of catching the ball. It is an important skill for all wide receivers, but I do not think you came in here to hear how to catch the ball.

Everything we do starts with our four base blocking rules. The progression starts from there and ends up with somebody's bloody chin.

BLOCKING RULES

- Your feet stop when the defender's feet stop.
- If the defender is low, the receiver is slow.
- Shuffle-shuffle and do not cross over.
- Step, punch, drive.

I learned that when I played at Kentucky. When the wide receiver got in trouble with blocking, it was because they played too fast when they did not need to play fast. The receiver has to understand when to change his feet demeanor and start blocking. When we coach our receivers, we treat them as if they are in elementary school. They learn the rules and repeat it back to us. I make them repeat it back to me three to five times during the drills.

HE STOPS–YOU STOP

If the receiver has a cover 3 corner aligned on him, the corner is responsible for the deep third. He will bail out and retreat to his coverage when we threaten him. The corner starts to backpedal as the receiver releases off the line of scrimmage. As long as the corner backpedals, the receiver pushes him down the field. As soon as the corner transitions his feet and sinks his hip to support the run, the receiver sits down and gets ready to block.

The first drill we do daily is a simple reaction drill. We start with two receivers aligned on the sideline, running down a yard line (Diagram #1). We place two defenders four yards in front of the receivers. The coach stands in the middle behind the receiver and gives directions to the defenders. The receiver move off the sideline and the defenders backpedal. The coach gives the defenders a direction to react back toward the sideline. When the receivers see the defenders' feet stop and their hips sink, their feet become active. They stop and get the feet moving.

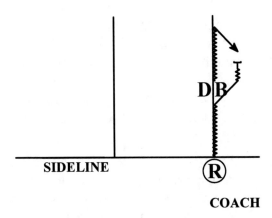

SIDELINE

COACH

Diagram #1. Reaction Drill

The coaching point to this drill is the footwork. You do not want the receiver to get into an elongated step. We want short, choppy steps with the feet close to the ground. If they overextend with their stride, they have trouble. They cannot have slow feet. That is a cardinal sin with our blocking schemes.

The receiver wants to leverage the defender according to the play. The defender will not run straight downhill at the receiver all the time. He works inside of or outside of the receiver depending on his responsibility. The receiver has to chop his feet and maintain leverage on the defender. They have to learn how to pop their feet and sit down.

HE'S LOW—GO SLOW

If the defender is low in his alignment, the receiver is slow. That is the second rule for blocking. If the defender works toward the line of scrimmage, the receiver has to set his base and slow down his movement toward the defender. In cover 2, the slot receivers have to deal with linebackers and a strong safety rolled down in coverage. Those defenders have no deep coverage most of the time. The receiver cannot drive them out of the area. The receiver has to move off the line of scrimmage and maintain his leverage on his blocking assignment.

As the receiver comes off the ball, the worst thing that can happen to him is to come out with a foot-over-foot movement. The problem is that the receiver loses his base and ability to change direction. The second thing that can happen is the linebacker runs right past the receiver, and he ends up flagging him to the ballcarrier. The first thing the receiver has to do is come out of his stance and set his base. He gets his feet popping and starts to gain ground for contact on the linebacker. After the contact, the receiver tries to maintain the contact on the block.

The receiver has to keep his leverage on the defender. When we run the bubble screen, the wide receiver targets the defender's outside shoulder pad. We want to work to the outside and control the defender. We design the bubble screen to get four yards. If we do a good job of blocking, we can get a big play out of a short pass.

SHUFFLE-SHUFFLE AND DO NOT CROSS

The third rule for blocking is shuffle-shuffle and do not cross over. The most important thing in this rule occurs with the feet on contact. When we get to this rule on contact, the blocker must change his feet. When receivers hear the term shuffle, they get into defensive back shuffle mode. When they do that, they end up with one of their feet off the ground. That means the blocker is trying to block with one foot on the ground. If he tries to block anyone with one leg, he is finished.

As soon as the defender does anything different from what I am expecting him to do, the receiver is beat. If a linebacker has two feet in the ground and the blocker has one, there is no contest. The coaching terminology is shuffle-shuffle and do not cross over, but there has to be a change in the foot action. They have to pop the feet on the ground and keep them with ground traction all the time. They have to buzz their feet and tread water. We want to make sure we keep leverage and do that.

When we work this drill, we work it off the sideline. We get the defensive back going in all different directions. We have him coming downhill straight toward the receiver. We have him working on a 45-degree angle, which is more believable. To get them to go on the diagonal, we give them a direction call. The receiver has to pop his feet, keep his base, and gain ground in the direction of the target. This is hard to teach, and we have to work at it.

Another way to do the same drill is to work in the buddy system off the sideline (Diagram #2). We align five or six sets of receivers on the sideline. One is the defender and the other is the blocker.

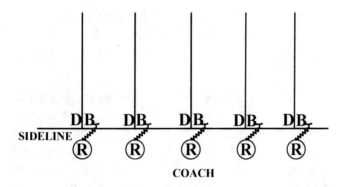

Diagram #2. Buddy Drill

The coach gives the direction the defenders move and the receivers react to that movement. They align two yards apart. The receiver gets his base, pops his feet, the defender moves right or left, and the receiver blocks. As he pops his feet, he gets leverage to the outside of the defender, continues to pop the feet, and gains ground to the outside of the defender.

At Marshall, Monday is our off day. On Tuesday, we refer to it as bloody Tuesday. All our players know that. All the drills we do concentrate on the same thing. We want them to pop the feet on contact. When they pop the feet, it is essential for them to not cross their feet and get caught on one leg.

STEP-PUNCH-DRIVE

This is the last of the blocking rules. Our receivers did an average job this year of this skill, but we will be better next year. I tell the receivers that the best part of the rules is when contact comes to the receiver. When the contact comes, we want to step, punch, and drive. If all 12 of my receivers came in here today and I asked them what type of step to we take, they would all say positive.

The biggest problem that young receivers have with blocking starts with the step. When contact comes to the receivers, all of them want to turn their heads or take a step backward. That is the cardinal sin in my opinion. We never want to drop our feet and step backward on contact. We want to pop the feet and get a positive step in the ground on contact.

We do blocking drills in a progression of skills. The first thing we do is get them in a fitted position with the receiver's hands in the defender's

chest. The receiver buzzes his feet and moves the defender down the line backward. The coach stands behind the receiver and pats him on the hip to the side of the step. We want to see a positive step forward down the field as he moves ahead. We work stepping with the right foot and the left foot.

When we teach the punch, the receiver punches with the heels of the palms of his hands. We want to deliver the punch into the chest of the defender while rolling the hips and driving in an upward direction. We want to arc the back with the head up. The elbows are in tight and the thumbs up. The punch is no different from an offensive lineman driving his punch home.

The second progression is to back the defender up to three yards. The receiver breaks off the ball for two steps, gathers his base, and repeats the first progression. The step in the drill is the point at which the receiver sets his base and steps with a positive step into the defender. The receiver delivers his punch and buzzes his feet in the drive phase of the block.

The third progression of the drill is to keep the defenders off and let them move to one side or the other (Diagram #3). The drill is the same for the receiver except he has to work for leverage on the defender.

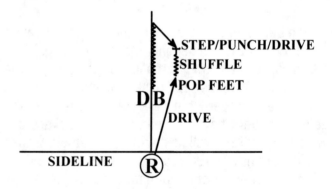

Diagram #3. Drive for Leverage

The coaching point in each of these progressions is the same. We want a positive step before the contact. The punch has to stun the defender and the feet must pop or buzz through the drive. In every one of these drills, the receiver must exaggerate his foot movement. We emphasize the movement of the feet and make them concentrate on that movement by overexaggerating it.

The big mistakes the receiver often commits are hopping instead of shuffling or failing to drive at the defender as the corner retreats. As long as the defender will run deep, the further the receiver wants to drive him. If he does not need to block him to keep him out of the play, that is to our advantage.

When I got to Marshall a year ago, the receivers were soft. For us to be a perimeter blocking team and run the spread, we had to change the whole demeanor of what we did in our room. To toughen up the mentality, we started to use drills like the one I am going to show you. When we started doing these drills, they did not want to do them. They wanted to catch the ball and not think much about blocking. I knew that when the receivers stopped complaining about the blocking drills that they had bought into what we wanted them to do.

We work a three-on-one drill (Diagram #4). The blocker aligns with his feet on the sideline. The coach stands behind him. The three defenders align in a line two yards from the blocker. The defenders on the side are two yards outside the blocker, with one defender head-up the blocker. On a command, the blocker buzzes his feet. The coach points to one of the three defenders. That defender attacks the blocker. The blocker has to step, punch, and drive on the defender. On the whistle, the blocker resets in his original position and the coach points to one of the remaining defenders. The drill repeats through all three defenders. We get three repetitions each time the blocker goes into the drill.

toes and get the feet on the ground to hit. The secret is not to receive the contact but deliver it. They should punch and drive through the defenders and not the other way around.

When we talk about the chin shot, we refer to the helmet into the chin. We want to put the two screws holding his face mask to his helmet into the chin of the defender. When we do this drill, everyone has their mouthpiece in with their chin tucked low. We want the blocker to run through the defender. We teach them to put the helmet in the chin, walk up the defender, and get belly to belly.

When we drill these skills, I align the blockers on the sideline and give them a direction of the ball. The coach stands behind the blockers. The defenders are five yards off the blockers. I tell the blockers that the ball is to their left. That gives them a leverage point. I give the defenders a direction to attack and snap the ball. The receivers come off the line and apply their blocking rules.

One of the best drills we did last year was the hoop drill (Diagram #5). We did this drill for two reasons. We wanted our receivers to be tough. This was a toughness drill from them. The second reason was to make sure we sent the right message about what we wanted them to do. The hoop drill is a two-yard diameter circle. We put the circle down over a yard marker number, with the yard line running through the center of the circle. We take two receivers and put them on either side of the yard line inside the circle. On a command, one receiver tries to drive the other player out of the circle.

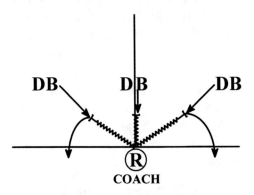

Diagram #4. Three-on-One

Diagram #5. Hoop Drill

The coaching points are to stay low, buzz the feet, and get the chin shot in with the headgear. They have to keep the feet on the ground or the defenders whip them. They have to get off their

When we installed the drill, the players did not like it. They began to brother-in-law each other in the drill. One receiver would let the other receiver drive him out of the ring with almost no effort. We corrected that behavior with several after practice sessions. What they gave up in practice, they paid for after practice. They learned very quickly that they have to fight each other in the hoop or fight each other after practice—with my help.

We continued to put them in the hoop and they started buying into it. The hits and the sound of the excitement of our group spread over the practice field. We got excited about the hits and collisions. The excitement was so great that the defensive backs wanted to come into our drill and participate. We started having the defensive backs versus the receivers in the hoop. It created a healthy competition. It also achieved what we were looking for.

We turned the hoop drill into a street fight. I told the receivers that they could not lie in the hoop. You had to perform or get crow. When they continue to talk after their turn in the ring, I love that. There were no excuses, and you had to man up to stay in the drill. We did not discriminate one from the other. It did not matter if it was senior on freshman or big on little. We wanted them to get tough and compete. That is what this drill accomplished.

They hated this drill when we started, but they love it now. When you get your players believing in what you are doing and get them blocking, they begin to take pride in their blocking in the game. I tell them that if they get a knockdown in the game, it is a steak on me. With the money I make and my wife getting ready to have a baby, we may have to buy cheap steaks. They come to my house and we feed them steak. At the beginning of the year, there were no steaks. However, by the middle of the year, I was buying some steaks. When it happened in the game, they could not wait to come to the sideline and say "Steak." That was a small thing to get us going in the right direction.

We use that progression in practice every day. It is constant drill work and repetition to get the job done. If you come to our practices, you will see the same thing I just showed you. I think we have improved our toughness, and it will continue to get better next year. I want to go forward and talk about releases.

RELEASES

When we teach releases, we use the K.I.S.S. (keep it simple, stupid) method. There are coaches that teach 12 different releases. I do not agree with that, and we do not do it. We do not want to name a bunch of releases that the players cannot remember when they try to get off the line of scrimmage. We count steps. The releases we do are on half or full steps.

If a defensive back presses a receiver at the line of scrimmage, the receiver knows he will use half steps in his release. Using the half steps means the receiver gets his feet in the ground quicker. Because the defender is on top of him, the receiver wants to keep his feet on the ground. If the receiver wants to take an outside release, that is a two-half-step release. We align our receivers with their outside foot back in their stance. The receiver takes a half-step movement with the outside foot and a half-step movement with the inside foot in the release.

The two pop steps are not the only thing the receiver must do. He has to hide his shoulder, get rid of the arms of the defender, and all the other stuff you hear at clinics. I do not care how they do it. They must get their shoulders back to square and run. I do not want them to think about the techniques it takes to release through a defensive back. The only thing I want them to concentrate on is getting their shoulders square and start running vertical like a track athlete.

If the defensive back uses his outside arm to disrupt the receiver, we want to punch across and rip with the inside arm. More and more defensive backs are using the backside arm. We tell our receivers to win the leverage and play basketball. We cross over as a basketball move and win the battle. We want the hands up as if we were in a fighting stance. We club through the inside arm and run off the line of scrimmage. That gets rid of the inside arm. We have to get the shoulders square and run. If the receiver can get his shoulder past the defensive back, he wins. It does not matter how fast the defender is.

In all of our release drills, we tell our receivers to keep wiggling and stay loose. When I played, I had to be a technician because I was slow. If I did not win at the line, my game was over. The players we have are more talented than I was. The receivers we have do not have to be too technical to get a release off the line. I tell my players to make up the ground, wiggle on the defender, and get going down the field. The big receivers have to know leverage, but they can get off the line.

If the defender bails from the press, the receiver uses his full steps to close the distance and the half steps to get by the defender. We try to convince the receivers it is like dancing. In practice, we work with a partner drill (Diagram #6). We work from the sideline to the hash marks. We like to work down the sideline because we want the receiver to release past the defender and get back on the line to run vertical. We drill all our releases in a partner drill. We use two-half-step releases to begin the drill.

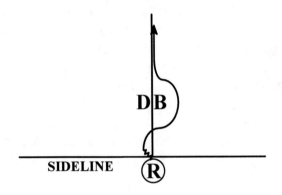

Diagram #6. Partner Release

The next drill we do is a lean drill (Diagram #7). The defender aligns to the inside of the receiver. On the snap of the ball, the receiver releases to the outside of the defender. The defender runs with the receiver and wants to force the receiver off the line. The receiver has to get his shoulder past the defender and get back to the line. If he gets even with the defender, he leans into him and pulls his shoulder past the defender.

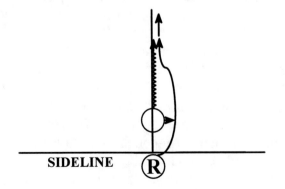

Diagram #7. Lean Drill

We progress forward and combine the two drills (Diagram #8). We put a coach at the line to make the receiver use his two-half-step release from the line. The second defender is behind the first one and simulates the lean drill. The receiver has to perform both movements to get back to the line and lean into the defender.

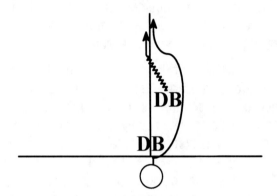

Diagram #8. Combination Drill

The drills have to change when the defense changes from man coverage to zone coverage. These releases are tough for slot receivers or outside receivers against a cover 2 look. You have to teach landmarks in the vertical patterns when the receivers are squeezed by the defenders. The secret for the receivers in a zone cover is to beat the disruptions by the defenders. They have to get their foot in the ground and get by the bumps and disruptions to get vertical as quickly as possible.

When I refer to a stem of the receiver's pattern, I mean the path he runs off the line of scrimmage. He may run his pattern at the outside shoulder of the defender to gain leverage. If he stems his pattern inside the receiver that is the path, he takes off the line of scrimmage. When he stems his pattern at the core of the defender, that means he runs straight at the defender, which is seldom the thing you want to do.

When we stem, we want to keep our leverage off of what we already have. If the receiver runs a six-step speed-out and he already has inside leverage, there is no stem. If the receivers already have the leverage they need to run the route, they keep it. If he does not have the leverage he needs, he wants to get into a two-way go position on the defender.

The receiver versus a cover 2 corner has some problems. If the receiver stems down the core of the defender and pops their feet to get past him, he has a problem. The problem is the defender gets his hands all over the receiver and disrupts his pattern. We tell our receivers not to stem at the core of the defender but a yard or two outside of the defender. By stemming the receiver to the outside of the defender, the defender has to move to maintain the leverage he wants on the defender.

One of the best drills we have for this problem is the cone-hand release drill (Diagram #9). The coach puts a small cone on his outside hand and extends his arm. The receiver aims at the cone on his release. The cone will widen with the movement of the receiver or does not move. If the cone widens, the receiver pushes the cone wider, pops his feet, crosses over inside the defender, and gets back to his pattern. If the cone stays stationary, the receiver continues outside, pops his feet, gets ready for contact, and gets his shoulders square down the field.

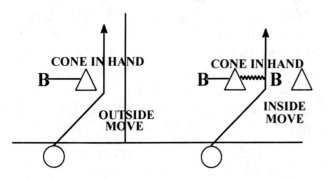

Diagram #9. Cone-Hand Drill

The coaching point is to pop the feet whether you go inside or outside the defender. If they try to stick one foot in the ground and make the cut, there is a problem. The receiver is on one leg. If there is any contact by the defender, the receiver is knocked off his balance, loses his base, and the pattern is done. We want the receiver to get to the break point and pop the feet. If the defense is good at collision on the receivers, we can use a two-half-step release.

Let me go back and make some remarks before I stop. I think the most important thing we do at Marshall occurs in our drill work. The drills we do apply to what we do on the field. We vary the

drills daily. We must make sure that our room is on point with what we have to block on the perimeter. The biggest compliment a coach can get from his players is when the players comes off the field and tell you, "That was a good drill. I really like it."

I ask the players all the time what they think about a particular drill. If I think it is a great drill, but the players do not think they get anything from it, I wash out the drill. I make sure I talk to my players and get their input into what we do on the practice field. You must be aware of what your players are doing and what they need to work on to improve.

We mix up our drill and vary them every day. The worst thing you can do is spend practice time on something you can do in some other drills. If you go out each day and do a ladder agility drill, you are wasting your time. You work on footwork every day in your release drills. You have to understand the difference between a pre-practice drill and an individual drill. Work in practice on what you do in the game. Let the weight and conditioning coach do the ladder drills.

We do not run over bags and do bag drills. The wide outs feet are never off the ground as you see in the bag drills. We want balls in our hands or balls thrown to us in the drills. We want footwork drills that help us get off the line of scrimmage and to get open. I want to make sure our players are doing what we have to do to have success. I listened to Urban Meyer this morning, and it fired me up more about being a coach. The reason it fired me up was my head coach, Doc Holliday, is the same type of coach.

When my players do something wrong, you cannot blame the player. You cannot say he is not very smart. If he did something wrong, that mistake is on me. If he fails a test, that is my fault. If he gets in trouble off campus, it becomes from my shortcoming. I could have done something that would prevent those things from happening. I did not talk to him enough about doing the right thing or did not work him hard enough on the field to perform to our expectations. Making excuses is easy for a young coach. It is easy to say he is not very smart or he does not have what it takes.

The three freshman receivers we brought in last year were not very tough. They are now. You have to learn what the head coach wants and do it. If you do not, it exposes you as a coach. Understanding that has made me a better coach. One of the big pluses in my life was teaching school for a year. When you are in the classroom seven periods a day teaching all different types of students, you learn about accountability.

That is what we do in coaching. In our position room, we have to teach the players. Not all players can learn the same way. You cannot teach all the players the same way. I have an X-receiver who I would never tell to run a seven-step glance. There is no way he can get to seven on the field. He cannot count to seven on the run. We worked with him on the field and not on the count. He now knows that seven steps gets him to 12 yards deep on his pattern.

The best receiver on our team could be the coach in our room. He could get up in front of the group and say everything that I would say verbatim. I do not do all the talking in our room. I depend on him for some of the instruction. However, I never sit down in the meeting room. I think if the coach sits down in the meeting room, the players' eyes get heavy. I am up and challenging them all the time. If I have to go to someone else, I have a player in the room do it. Their eyes are on the player a lot more than they are on me.

There are things that my father told me, and he still tells me these things. However, they do not sound the same as when they come from a coach. If it comes from a coach you respect, the message comes through differently. I want to touch all areas of teaching. I use the whiteboard. I give the players the remote control for the video machine. When they say the things you would say, you know you are reaching them with your teaching.

On the field, if the players correct one another and are doing it the right way, I do not interrupt. That is part of the leadership within the team. That is what we want to happen. We want our players to take ownership and responsibility for their teammates. If you give your players that kind of ownership in the team, they will go to the wall for you.

If you bring your players into your home, feed them, and let them meet your wife, they will start to understand. If they know you genuinely care for them, they will play for you. That is why I wanted to coach high school and college football. I have no desire to coach on the pro level. In high school and college, you can make a difference in your players' lives. When things go wrong in your players' lives, you have a chance to straighten them out and make it better for them.

You have to know your players. You need to know their parents' names, where they live, and what they do for a living. I think you have to invite them into your home and make them feel like one of the family. You need to become a part of their lives. If something happens, they will feel guilty about it. Not because they feel threaten by you but because they feel they have disappointed you. It works the same way on the field. If you correct them on the field, you know they will respond in a positive way because they know you care. As a coach, you have to continue to grow and have the answers for your players. Thank you for the attention.

CONCEPTS WITHIN THE PASSING GAME

University of Arkansas

It is good to back in Louisville. I see some of my former players here. The military is here today, and I cannot say enough about what they do. They allow us to coach football. They give me the freedom to do what I love to do. I am here to talk football today.

One thing I truly believe in is the concepts within the passing game. I believe in working hard on execution, drill work, and getting good at what we do. My father had a definition for execution. As a coaching staff, we live by it.

Execution is created by the constant repetition, which establishes sound habit formation that creates a conditioned reflex to any given situation.

That definition means to rep everything, over and over. Do it repeatedly. If you are going to do something, do it repeatedly against all the different looks from all the formations until it becomes a reflex. It will become a habit, and they will not have to think about it. That allows them to go out and play fast. To be able to execute, you have to play fast and understand what you are doing.

It is always nice to speak at events like this. In 1983, in Great Falls, Montana, I attended my first coaching clinic. I finished my playing days and was a student coach for my dad. I was working on finishing my degree. An old-line coach from the Michigan State University staff spoke that night. His name was Buck Nystrom. He would holler, yell, and swear a bit, but he gave a good talk. No one sat in the front row because he got so excited he would spit when he talked.

There was one thing I took from that clinic that I have never forgotten. He was talking about being a coach. He said that coaching was the ability to "confront and demand." That was something I took and used throughout my career. To be a coach, you have to confront your players when they are not doing their techniques, not being a good teammate, not performing their fundamentals, or not playing hard. You cannot let things slide and think you are going to be a great team.

You have to confront your players and then demand they do things right. Obviously, from 1983 to 2011, the way you demand has changed. When my father coached me, he used to grab me by the facemask, rattle my cage, and demand that I do it right. You cannot do that anymore. However, it is the same thing; you just have to find another way to go about it. You have to make sure that you confront and demand so players do things the way you want them done.

What I am going to talk about today is the passing game. I am going to talk about some of the concepts we use. It is nothing fancy, but they are good base plays. One thing I do believe in is throwing the ball. I like to throw it on first and second downs. I believe if you are good at throwing the ball when you do not have to, that will make you better when you do have to throw it.

At Texas A&M University this year, we were down 18 points at halftime. For us to get back in the game, we had to throw the ball. We had to spread the ball around and get back in the game. We did that and made some stops on defense. We found some confidence, came back, and won the game. Also, we had to do that in the next two games. We had to come back to win those next two games.

PASSING GAME

- Quick game
- Dropback game
- Curl
- Out and corner
- Control
- Seam

- Combo
- High/low
- Crossers
- Empties
- Play-action

The first thing we start with is the quick game. If we are under the center, the quarterback takes a three-step drop. If we are in the shotgun, he takes a two-step drop. We want to get the ball out of the quarterback's hand quickly. At the beginning of the year, we were not very good at running the football. The quick passing game was our answer to running the ball. We started the season with three running backs injured. We kept working on the running game and finally got some backs healthy. We threw the quick passing game more in the beginning of the season than at the end.

The second part of our passing game is the dropback passing game. We break that down into categories. The number-one category is our curl routes. We love to throw the curl. We believe when you insert that play, you need to do a lot of good teaching. You teach your receivers how to read coverages. You teach the quarterback how to key and read. You teach him how to go from one side to the other against one high safety or a two-high safety look. In the Super Bowl, the Giants hit two big curl patterns on their winning touchdown drive. You always want to go to what you are good at in crunch time. We like the curl.

The next category for us is the out and corner routes. If the defense gives you those routes, you take them. However, when they take them away, we have something else to run. We have concepts within routes.

The next category is what we call control routes. These are 8- to 10-yard patterns. They are third-and-medium situations. We like to throw them to get the sticks moving. I personally like to throw the third-down passes on first down. If you do that, you get better at it.

We build hot routes into the control patterns. That allows you to get the ball out of the quarterback's hand quickly. He does not have to worry about changing protection, and he knows where he can go with the ball.

We ran the control category more this year than we did with Ryan Mallett. We ran the ball so much better when he played quarterback and got the opportunity to throw the ball deep off play-action. Ryan was more adept at changing the pass protection schemes. This year, Tyler Wilson was more of a dump-the-ball-quickly type of quarterback. He did not change the protections much and used the hot reads to get rid of the ball.

The next category is seams. We do not run the four vertical patterns as we used to. We still run the seams down the middle of the field, but the boundary seams are convert patterns. That means we run patterns to the outside that can convert to a go route against a two-deep secondary. We still want to run the inside seams against a single-high safety look. You must have the ability to hit the inside seams from a 2x2, 3x1, or a 3x2 set. You have to threaten the seams so the defense has to cover them. When they do, you have somewhere to go.

We like the combo category. This category has combinations of two concept patterns built into the formation. If we come to the line of scrimmage and the secondary is a two-deep coverage, we have one side of the formation built for that coverage. The quarterback works that side. If the coverage is a single-high safety, the quarterback works the other side of the formation with patterns built for a single safety.

The quarterback knows his progression and where to throw the ball based on those reads. We may build the patterns to the right to beat cover 2 or quarter coverage. We build the patterns to the left to beat cover 3 or man-free coverage. You always have something built into a combo route when the defense plays cover zero and brings the blitz.

The high/low read is the number-one thing we do in our quarterback progression of reads. We isolate a linebacker, run a high/low route, and make it a simple read for the quarterback. We do that many times in a game. However, we do it with the crossing routes more than any other routes. When we run crossing routes, we always have a high/low read involved with the play. Those are the areas we will work extremely hard at and make sure our players understand the concept of the play. We want them to know the philosophy and make sure the quarterback knows why we built the concept.

It is important for the quarterback to know why he is running a particular route. He has to know the philosophy that goes with each play we run. We have an empty scheme in our concepts. The big question we have to answer each week is what type of personnel we are going to use with the empty set. We will run the same basic package each week, but the personnel groupings change from week to week.

If a defense stays in their base defense no matter what the formations are, we want to use a five-wide-receiver set. That allows us to find and exploit the mismatches in the defense. We want to get wide receivers on linebackers and safeties.

If the defense is going to match personnel, we find ways to empty out of our two tight ends and normal groupings. We want to mismatch with our receiver personnel on their linebackers and safeties. That is what we try to do when we go to our empty set. We think it is as important to use it on first down as it is to use it on third down.

We are a great play-action team. The number-one reason you can be a good play-action team is you run the ball well. If you can run the ball well, you will be a good play-action team.

We base the movement areas within the play-action pass. When you play-action pass, you have to move the quarterback. You have to get him outside the pocket or move him over the tackle. That gives you a different launch point in which to throw the ball. By doing this, we hope to avoid the sack. If you have a quarterback who can throw the ball on the run, this type of pass will be good for you. There were a few games last year where the opponent's defensive line was better than our offensive line. We could not use the five-step drop or the three-step drop. We had to move him to other launch points to throw the ball.

Screens are part of our dropback passing game. Last year, we were maybe the worst screen team in America. We were laterally terrible in that part of the game. We quit throwing it and stopped working on them in practice. We did not do a good job of coaching it or executing it. I will guarantee: we will be better at it next year.

The quick game for us is the 90 series. The first thing in the quick game is a play we call "90 double hook" (Diagram #1). The wide receivers align with their outside foot back. They are going to run a five-step hitch route. The receiver runs the pattern with three long steps and two short steps. He must get to the depth of six yards, whether he starts on the line of scrimmage or off the line. If he gets a press or J-corner, the pattern converts to a fade route. We ask the receiver to tell us what he does on our 90 route. He repeats for us that he runs a five-step hitch and, if pressed, he runs a fade for a touchdown.

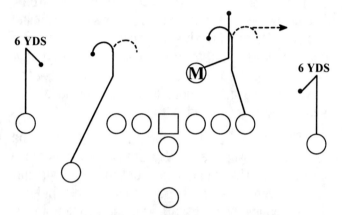

Diagram #1. 90 Double Hook

We want him to say those exact words. We want him to get the idea of telling the defensive back, "Come on up here and press me so I can run the fade for the touchdown." We ask the quarterback the same question, and we expect the same answer. We want to put in both players' minds what we are looking for. As coaches, we want the player to speak the language we speak. We make them say the same things that we say and diagram the play the same way as we do. The coach wants to be particular as to what the players say back to him. The reason we do that is the communication factor. In a game, when we say something to the player, we want a picture to appear in the player's brain.

We want the quarterback coming to the sidelines and telling us the receiver has a jam corner. If we can hold the safety, we can throw the ball down the sidelines. We want that communication from the quarterback. The inside receivers run a hook route. The hook route we use is a hook in, hook out, or breakout off the nearest defender. We want the receiver to stem into the defender. We stem in at the linebacker, push up the field, and give the receiver a two-way go. We do not want the linebacker to run out to the receiver; we run to him and make our break off him.

On this pass, the quarterback has some simple rules. If they allow us to take the hitch, we throw that pattern. If they roll the corner down or press the receiver, we throw the hook route off the most tucked-in linebacker. In this case, we want to throw the hook off the Mike linebacker. A tucked-in linebacker is the one playing in the box.

If the coverage is a two-high look, we must know what the Mike linebacker is doing. If he locks on the running back, we send him opposite the tight end. That pulls the Mike linebacker that way and opens up the tight end running the hook. He may spot drop or drop straight back.

This is a good play to run with tempo. If you make a first down, you hustle to the line and run it again. It does not matter what the defense does and we should get a completion on the play. If we get the hitch pattern, we want a catch and run for at least 10 yards on the play. The receiver has to know something about the defender's leverage. If the defender played him with inside leverage, the receiver wants to catch the ball and spin to his outside. He should have a plan to beat the defender after he catches the ball.

With these types of plays, the quarterback has to make a decision. He has to decide whether to take the sure completion or go after the big play. It is up to you as the coach to give him some guidance on what it is you want. There are certain defenders we want to go after, and we plan that into the reads. Another thing the quarterback has to consider is whether he is hot. If he has just completed four or five passes, we go after the defender and try to throw a touchdown. If he is not hot, he takes the easy completion.

If the quarterback is struggling, it is up to you as the play caller to get him some easy completions. Get him four or five easy throws in a row so he can get his confidence going. After you get the confidence in check, we can start throwing the patterns we want to work.

With this pattern, we can add an option route to slot side (Diagram #2). The tight end and flanker run the hitch-and-hook pattern. The slot and split end run the option combination. The flanker runs

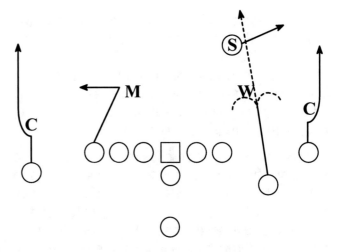

Diagram #2. 90 Hook Option

the hitch or the fade if pressed. The tight end runs the hook route off the Mike linebacker. To the split side, the split end runs a fade pattern on the option route. The slot has an option route. He releases off the ball, runs six yards, and has an option to go in, out, or over the top.

The thing that tells the slot to go over the top is the safety in a two-high look. If the safety is inside of him on his alignment, he wants to go in or out. If the safety gets off the hash and toward the split end, he takes it over the top. If the safety stays inside, the quarterback wants to take the split end fade in the hole between the two-deep safety and the rolled-up corner. After we make the catch, we want to get vertical and down the field.

We call the next play "97 blue-Y/X-hitch" (Diagram #3). The tight end runs a six-yard out pattern. We like to run this play into the boundary.

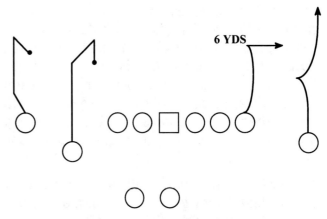

Diagram #3. 97 Blue-Y/X-Hitch

The flanker into the boundary runs a fade route. The split end runs a hitch route and converts to a fade if he gets press coverage. The slot receiver runs what we call a seam hitch. If the receiver has a linebacker or safety over him, he comes off the ball. At three yards, if the defender is still sitting there, he runs through his inside shoulder.

When the receiver goes through the inside shoulder, the defender has to open his hips to the receiver to get his hands on him. When he does that, we get more yards after the catch of the X-receiver running the hitch. When the defender goes inside with the seam hitch, the quarterback throws the ball behind him to the Z-hitch route. The slot receiver opened the inside, and the X-receiver will have space to run.

If the defender buzzes to the flat, the slot receiver goes up the seam and hitches at five yards. We used to take him up the seam, but the throw was too hard to time out, and given the time you needed to practice, it did not justify the number of times it happened in the game.

If we have a two-high safety look, we work the hitch side of the pattern. If we get a single-high safety, we are thinking the tight end side of the pattern. The quarterback, when he reads one high safety, knows he is going to the tight end side. The flanker runs the fade route. The quarterback wants to throw the ball to the tight end, but he must read the corner. If they break the coverage and the corner rolls up, the quarterback looks for the hole past the rolled-up corner. A big part of the quick game is the run after the catch.

I like to coach the receivers because they only have to do four things. The first thing they have to do is get open. That starts with the stance and get-off, how you beat the jam, and how you run your route. The second thing is to catch the ball. You teach catching with ball drills. The third thing is the run after the catch. We work on getting north and south and making people miss. The fourth thing a receiver must do is maintain possession of the ball after the catch.

When we have a hitch in the pattern, we want to take that if they give it to us. On the 97 pass, we want to throw the tight end pattern. This is one pattern where we do not take the hitch if it is available. This is a great pattern if the defense blitzes off the tight end side. The tight end sees the blitz and shortens his route slightly so the quarterback can get the ball out of his hands.

When we recruit a wide receiver, tight end, or running back, we want to see if he can pass the sideline test. If the player runs up the sidelines, we want to see what he does. We want to see if he runs out-of-bounds. We want to see if he stays upright on the sideline. We want to know if he has the ability to get off the sidelines and back into the field.

The quarterback on a two-high look has a simple rule for the 97 cut of the tight end. We make him say it repeatedly. The rule is: "Hold the safety; key the corner."

If the corner gives the wide receiver a free release to the outside, we throw the ball to the flanker in the hole between the corner and free safety. If the corner shuffles and gets his hands on the flanker, we throw the six-yard out to the tight end immediately. That is an eight-yard gain, and it is second down and two yards for the first down if you get no yards after the catch.

When the quarterback decides to go for the home run, the only question we have for him is: "Why?" He generally decides he is going for broke before he snaps the ball. He can get in trouble for doing that, but he also comes up with some big plays. The only thing I can tell you about a route like that is to recruit more track players. The fast ones can outrun the half safety. If the quarterback throws the ball perfectly, we can score a touchdown. When the receiver catches the ball against the sideline running deep, he has to lean into the field. If he leans to the sidelines, he cannot stay inbounds.

The receiver hugs the sidelines when he tries to beat a cover 2 safety. We want as much width from the safety as possible. That does not give the quarterback much room. It has to be a great throw. If we have press coverage, the receiver runs what we call the red line, which is six yards from the sidelines. That gives the quarterback more room. He can use any of the six yards to place the ball.

I want to show you one of our base dropback plays (Diagram #4). The outside receivers have mirror step routes. The outside receiver to the openside runs a 5-4 curl route. He runs up the field for five steps. He plants and runs to the post for four steps, then plants and comes back to the quarterback on a 45-degree angle. The receiver counts the steps as he runs. He counts, "One, two, three, four, five," plants, "One, two, three, four," and breaks to the quarterback. The outside receiver on the tight end side has a 4-5 curl pattern. He stems inside for four steps, takes it vertical for five steps, and comes back to the quarterback at a 45-degree angle.

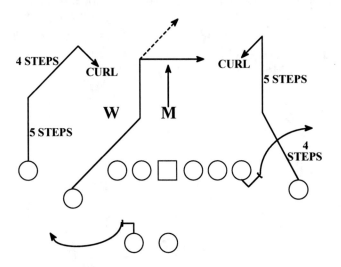

Diagram #4. 80 Dropback Pass

The slot receiver runs a streak read. There are three things involved in the read. The first thing he does is stem inside of the apex linebacker. After he gets inside the Will linebacker, he pushes vertical and takes the Mike linebacker, who we call the middle of three, away from the curl. If there is a single safety in the middle, he sits down and finds the window in the coverage. If there are two high safeties and they split, he takes his pattern through the middle of the safeties.

If the Mike linebacker does not carry the slot receiver, you can get an easy touchdown. If it is zero-man coverage, he is going to run a post for a touchdown. He runs at the defender, steps on his toes, and runs the post for a touchdown. He catches the ball over the inside shoulder. If we ask the receiver what he does on the play, he can recite his pattern by the coverage. Against man, he runs a post for a touchdown. Against a single high safety,

he pushes vertical and works the middle. Against cover 2, he runs through.

The tight end has a pass blocking assignment on this play. If his assignment drops, he runs a six-yard diagonal pattern. This pattern is not an arrow or an out. It is more of a bend pattern to the outside. If he ran out-of-bounds, he would be six yards deep. When he gets three yards from the sideline, he turns and shows his numbers to the quarterback. He is an outlet pattern on the play. The quarterback does not look at him until things start to break down on the inside routes. He is usually open.

The back runs a check stretch. He flares to the outside and gets to a point, splitting the numbers and the opposite hash mark. If he catches the ball, he will be three yards behind the line of scrimmage. If the ball is in the middle of the field, he checks and runs to the top of the numbers. If he runs into the boundary, he splits the difference between the numbers and the sideline. On the boundary side, he has to get more depth as he releases. When you practice the play, you must practice it from all three positions.

This pattern fits into our combo category. If we have a two-high safety look, we key the openside patterns. We call that the control side of the pattern. The slot receiver controls the two high safeties. With the single high safety, the quarterback holds the Mike linebacker with his eyes and keys the curl/flat defender to the tight end side. We want the linebacker to take three steps to his drop and square back up. If he does that, we win. If the quarterback stares at the curl, the linebacker will not square his shoulders and continue to drop under the curl.

When we talk to our quarterback, we tell them three counts to hold and three counts to key. We never tell them to look off the defenders. We tell them to look past zero, which is into the other side of the field. I never liked the term "look off the defender."

We tell our quarterback, if the defense is playing zone and a defender comes free at the line of scrimmage, throw the ball to the back, and let him make a play. We cannot do that in a man-coverage situation. In man coverage, there is a defender assigned to the back. The quarterback knows the linebacker he is supposed to hold is the linebacker covering the back. If he drops, he can give the ball to the back.

If there is man coverage and someone comes free, the quarterback has to throw to the curl. If the curl receiver cannot beat single man coverage, he cannot play for us. When we throw the ball, we want the quarterback to target the face mask of the receivers. All the receiver has to do is get his hands up and catch the ball.

The next play is very similar, except the tight end has an option route. We call the play "80 Y-option" (Diagram #5). We run this from a trips set. The outside receivers run their 5-4 curl and 4-5 curl patterns. The slot receiver runs the diagonal route to the sidelines, and the back check stretches to the single-receiver side. The quarterback reads the key to give him the primary receiver. We call the back and curl as both being the primary receiver based on the read. We describe that read as a 1-1 read. We do not describe the receiver as first read and second read. They are both first choices off the key read. The tight end is always the third read. On the slot side, the diagonal and curl routes are the 1-1 read with the tight end as the third read to that side.

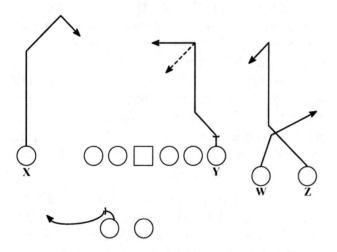

Diagram #5. 80 Y-Option

However, we remind the quarterback that the tight end can become the number-one read. A coaching point for the diagonal route is not to get in a hurry to reach the sidelines. He wants to slow down. If he does not, he will hit the sidelines before the quarterback is ready to throw.

When we drill our quarterbacks in the red zone, we concentrate on keeping two hands on the ball and pressing the line of scrimmage at a 45-degree angle. When he steps up in the pocket, he steps up at 45 degrees. When we drill it, we put a receiver down the field. As the quarterback steps up, he holds up one hand or the other. The quarterback throws to the hand. If he puts up no hands, the quarterback tucks the ball and gets five yards.

The 80 midget Z-post comes from the trips set also (Diagram #6). If you see many two-deep looks, this is a good play for that. The tight end has a check release. He is checking for a blitz from the field. We can call the play "480" and give the tight end a free release. He checks and releases down the middle of the field between the uprights.

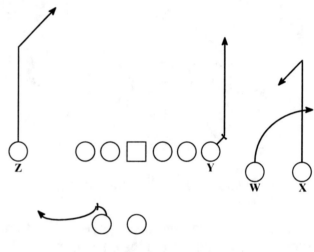

Diagram #6. 80 Midget

The boundary single Z-receiver runs a 9-post cut. The midget call comes from the reduction of splits into the field. The slot receiver in the trips set splits the difference between the tight end and the field hash mark. The outside receiver splits the hash mark and numbers. His pattern is point-to-point curl route.

A point-to-point curl has no stem in the route. We like the pattern because it gets the ball out of the quarterback's hand quicker. It also sets up the post play for a touchdown. The 9-post is not a glance or skinny post. We think that pattern is an NFL pattern and does not fit in our game. That is because of the difference of the hash marks in the pro game. You do not get the same pattern in the college game.

One thing we teach the quarterback when he studies the safety is to look for the width and depth of the safety. He has to know both things. Against Texas A&M, their safety aligned at 20 yards deep. The width of that safety was never a factor to our patterns. We had the #2 receiver all day long because of the safety's depth. On this pattern, the quarterback holds the Mike linebacker and keys the flat defender. If the defender takes the diagonal, there was no way the safety could be a factor on the curl because of his depth.

The receiver has a triangle read. He reads the defender over him, the linebacker inside of him, and the safety. He has to know how the defensive back is covering him. He has to be aware of the linebacker's alignment. If he is in a blitz alignment, that could affect his pattern. Keying the safety will tell if we can score a touchdown. If he sees the blitz alignment, he yells to the quarterback to alert him.

This pattern goes with the category "outs and corners." This is 81 C-wasp (Diagram #7). The boundary wide receiver runs a corner route off a snug split. If he were in a normal split, he would stem the pattern inside. On this split, he goes right at the defender and breaks to the corner. The breaking point is 12 yards deep. However, when we coach them, we tell them to run past two yard lines. That makes them more consistent in their pattern, and they are never too short on the pattern. The tight end runs the check diagonal.

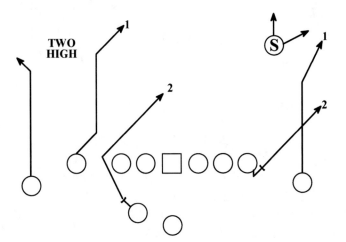

Diagram #7. 81 C-Wasp

The inside receiver to the field stems inside, pushes deep, and crosses the safety's face. The outside receiver runs a corner route. The back has an angle route. He checks, comes outside the tackle's alignment, and runs an angle read to the inside over the ball.

In a two-high look, the quarterback reads the boundary safety. If the safety works for depth, the quarterback works the boundary side. He looks for the corner route to the diagonal of the tight end. If the safety gets width to the boundary, the quarterback works the field side of the formation. He works from the post cut from the inside receiver to the field to the angle cut by the back.

The 71 C-Tiger is the same progression for the quarterback (Diagram #8). It is the same play from a different formation. The formation is a trips set into the field with the tight end set into the boundary. The outside receiver to the field has the angle cut, which looks like a shallow cross. The #2 receiver runs the corner and the #3 receiver runs the post to the middle. On the backside, the tight end runs the corner, and the back runs the diagonal route. The quarterback keys the field safety. If he gets width, the slot receiver has the touchdown. He only has to beat the Mike linebacker to the post.

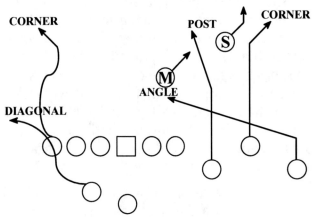

Diagram #8. 71 C-Tiger

This play comes from the control category. We call this play Scat 73 Miami (Diagram #9). The play comes from a trips set to the field. On this pattern, we want 8 to 10 yards. We build in hot patterns to this play. The route run by the running back is a bend route. It is not a diagonal. He takes an arc release so he gets away from the offensive tackle. He pushes to two yards and bends to the sidelines. We bend the route so he does not run into the offensive

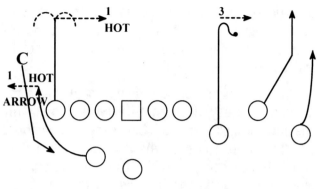

Diagram #9. Scat 73 Miami

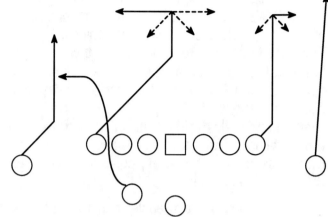

Diagram #10. 483 Miami

tackle trying to block the outside. The release also buys the quarterback some time. He does not want to come open too soon. The tight end has the middle and runs an option route. He stems in, pushes up, and hooks in or out. He can also break inside or outside.

The inside receiver to the formation side has an option route, but he cannot come to the middle. The middle belongs to the tight end. He can hook over his alignment or work to the outside. To the fieldside, the #1 and #2 receivers must take an outside releases to protect the inside patterns. They run vertical routes.

The built-in hot patterns depend on the protection scheme. We run the hot release off the corner (#1) or inside linebacker (#2). If the corner blitzes, the running back yells, "Hot, hot, and hot!" He stops the scat route and converts to an arrow route to the outside away from the coverage. He yells it three times. The tight end reads the same thing and yells, "Hot, hot, and hot!" He wants to break away from the defender. The protection scheme tells them if they are hot off #1 or #2.

The progression of the quarterback is to work to the scat back and tight end as the primary reads. We consider them both number-one choices based on the read. The number-three read is the second option route run by the inside receiver in the trips set.

We can align in a two tight ends set and run the same thing. We call it "483 Miami" (Diagram #10). This is a control pass, and all we work on is getting the completion for the first down or putting us in a short-yardage situation. The progression is the same.

The last play we want to talk about is scat 73 cub (Diagram #11). We run the Miami scheme to the tight end side of the formation. On the split side, we run a trade route by the outside receiver to the alignment of the inside receiver at six yards. The inside receiver runs a swing stop at six yards. The read and progression is the same for the Miami route. We welcome a blitz on this play. This is a good tempo play. We use this with the hurry-up no-huddle scheme.

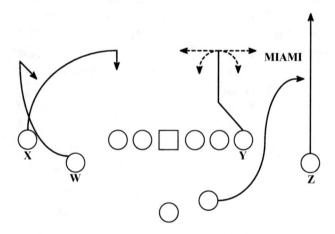

Diagram #11. Scat 73 Cub

This is a good control pattern, which gets the ball out of the quarterback's hand quickly. He does not have to worry about the blitz because we build the hot reads into the pattern.

I appreciate your attention. Thank you very much.

TRANSITION FROM THE 4-2-5 DEFENSE

East Texas Baptist University

I want to start off with this short, one-minute film clip. The reason I am showing you this clip is so you can see the different offensive formations defensive coaches have to face today. We have a dilemma going on in America. The offenses have gone wild in recent years. If we take the first segment of the film clip, we can see the number of different formations and plays used. The offense has gone ballistic now.

This is our offense at East Texas Baptist University in the film clip. The first play they ran was the midline veer for a 50-yard touchdown. If we watched Baylor University in their bowl game, we saw that play against University of Washington. On the second play, they ran a jail screen pass to the right side. They came back with a bubble screen to the left side.

I listened to Bobby Petrino at our Dallas Nike Clinic recently. He was talking about the fact that a lot of teams are running the zone read play. The quarterback keeps the ball, and then he has the option to the bubble screen pass out to the right. They have added to their arsenal the zone read play. The quarterback reads the play, and if the bubble screen is not there, he continues the option and pitches the ball to the trailing back to the backside. People who run the zone option are good at it. Offenses are going hog wild at every level of football.

It can be frustrating trying to defend the many facets of offenses today. I feel the offensive teams are out to get me, and I feel we must fight back. The offense is out to get me and humiliate me and to embarrass me. They are trying to take me to the cleaners with the sophisticated offense teams run today.

We have a defensive package that we have been using for some time now. The bottom line is that we are going to be an attacking defense.

Several coaches have said that when you go to a clinic, you just want to gain one thing, and that makes it worthwhile.

We are going to start our premise with our base 4-2-6 defense. The point you may get out of this lecture is how we transition from the 4-2-5 defense to the 4-3-2, the 3-4 look, or an odd stack defense. I will cover our terminology. I realize you have your own terminology, and that will work.

People often ask why we do certain things in football. Why do you do what you do? There is a reason for that. It has to do with the people who influenced you and taught you what you know about the game of football. Coaches help each other in many ways.

I am covering the paths of my coaching career so you can see how many people taught me the game of football. It is not about me, but the way I learned football and how I progressed to where I am today. I grew up in Texas, where football is important. It is not a matter of life and death as many people think it is. It is a lot more important than life or death in Texas. I grew up in one of those Friday Night Lights—type high schools. I graduated from North Mesquite High School in Mesquite, Texas, located in the outskirts of Dallas. Back then, the Dallas Cowboys played a 4-4 flex defense with the defensive ends and tackles pulled back off the line a little. They ran a lot of stunts on the defense. That is the same defense we used at our high school.

I played defensive end in the 4-4 flex defense. Ends were the little guys who could move and get upfield from the end position. We were taught to play with tenacity. I was out of position because of my size. I was also a running back.

I went to Cisco Junior College and was a running back from 1981 to 1982. We played the numbers defense. The numbers told the defensive tackles where to line up. Everyone worked off the alignment of the tackles. Examples of the calls on the numbers would be: 31, 13, 11, 22, or 33. Bum Phillips ran that defense first in Texas, and it was a popular defense.

From there, I went to Tennessee Tech University as a running back from 1983 to 1984. They ran the 50 defense. Later, I became a graduate assistant at Tennessee Tech. I worked with the running backs in 1985. The defensive end coach at Tennessee Tech was Gary Patterson, who is the head coach at Texas Christian University now. The defensive coordinator was Dick Bumpas, and now he is the defensive coordinator at TCU. It is funny how things have changed around.

We played Murray State University each year. The head coach at Murray State was Frank Beamer. Murray State, under Beamer, ran the old wide tackle-6 defense. Frank got the defense from Jerry Claiborne, who coached him at Virginia Tech. Claiborne started running the wide tackle-6 when he coached at University of Maryland. He moved from Maryland to Virginia Tech, and then to the University of Kentucky.

They lined up six men across the defensive line. They had two guards, two tackles, and two outside defensive ends. They had two linebackers lined up on the offensive tackles. We had a terrible team then, but it did not have anything to do with the coaches.

At Tennessee Tech, the head coach for three years was Gary Darnell. Our defensive end coach was Gary Patterson. The defensive coordinator was Dick Bumpas. The offensive coordinator was Dennis Franchione. Most of you know about Dennis coaching at the University of Alabama, TCU, and Texas A&M University. He is coaching at Texas State University now. We had good coaches, and still we were horrible. We ran the 50 defense that year.

I became a graduate assistant at Tennessee Tech after graduating in 1985. After one year, I was the defensive end coach in 1986, and we were still bad. We had several coaching changes, but we were still a bad football team. In 1987, I coached the outside linebackers. That year, we ran the wide tackle-6 defense. We did win five games that

year. We got our package from Frank Beamer from Murray State. Frank left and went to Virginia Tech as the head coach by that time.

I left after that season and went to coach defensive ends at Middle Tennessee State University in 1988 and 1989. We took the wide tackle-6 defense with us. I want you to know where we came up with the wide tackle-6 defense. At that time, we were the best defense in Division I-AA football for 10 years running. At the time, Georgia Southern University was a great team in the division. They ran the handoff from the double slot. We managed to beat them with our defense.

I left Middle Tennessee and became the defensive coordinator at Trinity Valley Community College. I did not want to call our defense a six-man defense. The reason for the change was to keep the good prospect on defense. We did not want to tell the defensive prospects they would be playing a defensive end position if they were cornerback-type players. As a result, I changed the name of the defense to a 4-4 defense. All of the spacing was the same, and we played it the same as before. You can play this defense with lesser athletes.

In 1993, I became the head coach at Trinity Valley. We were good enough to win the national championship in 1994. That was a great experience. We ran the same basic defense.

I returned to Tennessee Tech as the offensive coordinator in 1996. We still had the same defensive coordinator, so I moved to offense. I was really a defensive coordinator in disguise. We had a lot of low scoring games during that time, from 1996 to 1997. We ran the 31, 13 alignments on defense.

From there, I went to Middle Georgia College as the head coach in 1998. The defensive coordinator was a 3-4 defensive coach. There was always a struggle between the old odd front coaches and the even front new staff members. I just sat back and learned a lot about both defenses. We ended up running a 3-4 defense. We had the best record in the history of junior college football. We were pretty good, and we won the championship.

I went to the University of West Alabama as the head coach in 2001. It was a Division II school. We had moderate success there, and we used the eight-man front.

Next, I went to Mobile, Alabama in 2001 to become the dean, athletic director, and head football coach. We ran a 3-3 odd stack defense (Diagram #1). Cottage Hill Christian Academy was a private Christian school. We had started using the 3-3 stack defense some when we were at the University of North Alabama. I learned a great deal about the defense and decide to use it at Cottage Hill.

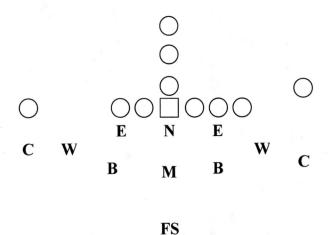

Diagram #1. 3-3 Odd Stack

From there, I went to Northwest Mississippi Community College for the 2005 season. We used the 4-4 defense. When Katrina came through the Southeast, we had a short season. I had a defensive coordinator who was a 4-4 defensive coach. I let him run the defense. We had a rough year the first year, so he left our program.

Two weeks before the second year, we went back to the 3-4 defense. I recruited a player from Galveston, Texas, who was 6'5" and 350 pounds. I have a picture of him on the front page of the New York Times. They had a few photos of him lifting weights, and doing a backflip. He ran a 4.8 40-yard-dash and could run. I knew he could play my two-gap nose man. We had some good players there. We had the best team of the four junior college teams in Mississippi.

We based our defense out of the 3-4 look. The issue we always got into was this: "We need to get four hands down in the dirt" in certain situations. It was the odd front versus the even front. So I decided we would base out of a 4-3 look, and we would spend most of our time in the 3-4 set. By doing this, we would not have to try to figure out how we could get four down lineman when we needed to rush four men.

I made a brilliant decision the next year. In 2007, I went to Houston, Texas, and started a professional league called the All-American Football League. We were going to play in Europe and the USA. We went through the draft and selected Eric Crouch as our quarterback. Our personnel looked good, and it appeared we would make some money. We went out of business before the league could get started.

I was out of a job. I had four girls at home, and I was on the street looking for a job. I was fortunate in that I got a job working with a national football clinic based out of Colorado Springs, Colorado. For the last three years, I have been studying football and running coaching clinics around the country.

A local high school in Colorado Springs asked me to coach, and we ran our 3-4 defense. We finished 12th in the state one year.

Here is where I am now. We are a multiple defense based out of the 4-2-5 look. We are a private Christian university in Marshall, Texas. We have been playing football for 10 years now. We call our defense a chaos defense. As we engage in this discussion, let's not forget what makes any sound scheme work. What we do is not as important as how we do it and who we do it with.

The first thing we teach on this defense is the position names (Diagram #2). Also, we teach them how to get to the huddle. This is how we label the players.

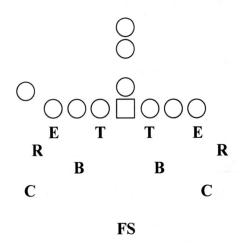

Diagram #2. Position Names

The Players

- E: Defensive ends
- T: Defensive tackles
- B: Linebackers
- R: Rovers (strong safeties)
- C: Corners
- FS: Free safety

I do not know why teams do not get in the huddle anymore. There is esprit de corps, teamwork, and camaraderie in getting in the huddle. The first thing we teach is how to get into a regular huddle (Diagram #3).

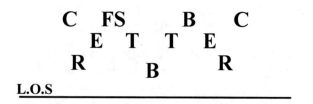

Diagram #3. Regular Huddle

Huddle Procedure

- Right tackle sets the huddle 3.5 yards from the ball.
- Backers make the front call.
- Free safety makes the coverage call.

The next thing we teach them is how to use the no-huddle against alignment (Diagram #4). We want to make sure we have a plan for this and that we are not milling around out on the field. You must have a communication plan.

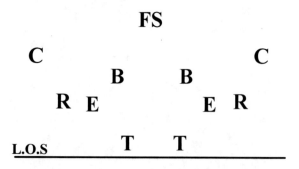

Diagram #4. No-Huddle Alignment

No-Huddle Rules

- Align normal awaiting call.
- Defensive tackles are three yards from the ball.
- Defensive ends are five yards from ball.
- Make sure you can see the call.
- Call out the front and coverage loud.

Following is how we call our defensive alignments and gaps. Basically, we are defining our techniques and gaps (Diagram #5).

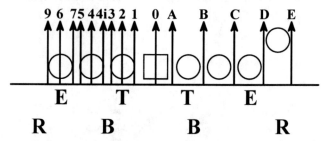

Diagram #5. Defensive Alignment and Gap Nomenclature

Techniques

- We use the college numbering system.
- Odd numbers are an inside or outside eye of the offensive player.
- Even numbers are head-up or nose-to-nose on the offensive player (including zero).
- Shade is a shade on the center (left or right eye).

Gaps

- The gaps are A through D with the inside gap closest to the center.
- The E gap is located outside of a wing player.

One important coaching point I want to make here is to be sure to count the E gap. We all know where the A, B, and C gaps are, but we need to include the E gap when a team lines up with a wing on that side of the end. The offense puts that man there to create a gap, and we must account for him.

I want to talk about the aspects of defensive performance. This is one sheet I would make sure you had if I were passing out two forms to you today. It is important to follow these aspects in the order they are listed.

THE 10 ASPECTS OF DEFENSIVE PERFORMANCE: 10 COMMANDMENTS OF DEFENSE

- *Alignment*
  1. Listen

2. Communicate
3. Understand
4. Align
5. Stance
- *Assignment*
6. Step
7. Keys
- *Assessment*
8. Reads
9. Reaction
- *Attack*
10. Perform

You must become good on 10 aspects in relationship to your individual position. If all 11 players do this, we will be a great defense. All mistakes are a result of a breakdown in one of these areas.

- *Listen in meetings*
  ✓ To your coaches
  ✓ To the huddle call
  ✓ To your teammates
- *Communicate*—to your teammates and to your coaches
- *Understand*—your responsibility in the defense called.
- *Alignment*—You must be perfect every play. Proper alignment gives you the opportunity to win the physical battle.
- *Stance*
- *Step*
- *Key*—Key the proper details with your eyes to decipher the offensive play as quickly as possible.
- *Read*—Run or pass
- *React*—and secure your assignment
- *Perform*

There are three things that really matter. What does it really boil down to on defense?

- *Read*—run or pass
- *React*—escape and pursuit
- *Respond*—tackles and takeaways

#1: LISTENING

- Huddle call
  ✓ Technique (Example: Torch, Jet, Go = Torch/40/A/Cover 3)
  ✓ Front (Examples: 30, 40, 50, 60)
  ✓ Stunt/Blitz (Examples: A, AC, CA, Able, Baker, Charlie)
  ✓ Coverage (Examples: 3, 1, 0)
- Down-and-distance (Example: third down and 12)
- Right or left call (Example: right, right)
- Receiver strength (Example: pro right/split left; secondary)
- On or off call
- Check (Example: on, on; hand pat on hip)

#2: COMMUNICATION

- Down-and-distance: defensive end
- Huddle call: linebacker
- Right or left call: linebacker
- Receiver strength: 1) Rover and Will tell each other and 2) safety tells everyone
- Formations: corners tell safety, and safety echoes the call
- Checks
  ✓ Linebacker: front
  ✓ Safety: coverage

#3: UNDERSTAND—RESPONSIBILITY

Fronts/Technique

The first word you hear in the huddle will be the technique or front. In theory, we are a gap control defense. Our basic fronts will make each individual responsible for a particular gap. The technique call for a base front is simply called "base." This is where the defense begins. Stunts and blitz will change responsibilities.

Stunts and Blitzes

The second part of the huddle call, stunts, and/ or blitzes determine your steps and area of responsibility. This is what makes our defense multiple and exciting. Know the following techniques, and get excited about executing them.

- Techniques
  - ✓ Base
  - ✓ Torch
  - ✓ Jet
  - ✓ Go
- Stunts
  - ✓ A
  - ✓ C
  - ✓ AC
  - ✓ CA
  - ✓ Slant
  - ✓ Bingo
  - ✓ Strong
  - ✓ Weak
- Inside Linebacker
  - ✓ Able
  - ✓ Baker
  - ✓ Charlie
  - ✓ Blast
- Rover
  - ✓ Cat
  - ✓ Dog
  - ✓ Cyclone
- Assassin
  - ✓ Attack
  - ✓ Crunch
- General
  - ✓ Goal Line
  - ✓ Goal Line Tight

Technique—Base

Front	Stunts	Blitz	Cover
1. 40	1. A	1. Able	3
	2. C	2. Baker	1

Technique—Torch

Front	Stunts	Blitz	Cover
2. 60	3. AC	3. Charlie	Zreo
	4. CA	4. Cat	2 man
		5. Dog	2
		6. Cyclone	4

Technique—Jet

Front	Stunts	Blitz	Cover
		5. Dog	2
		6. Cyclone	4

Technique—Go

Front	Stunts	Blitz	Cover
3. 50	1. Slant	1. Able	3
	2. Bing2. Baker	1	
		3. Charlie	Zero
		4. Cat	2 man
		5. Dog	2
		6. Cyclone	4

Front	Stunts	Blitz	Cover
4. 30	1. Strong	1. Able	-
	2. Weak	2. Baker	3
		3. Charlie	1
		4. Cat	Zero
		5. Dog	2 man
		6. Cyclone	2
		7. Attack	4
		8. Crunch	-

COVERAGE

Our basic rules for pass coverage are simple. Do not let the offense catch the ball. If they do catch the ball, punch the ball and cause a fumble. Hold off the long ball, and break on the short pass.

Zone

The key to zone coverage is to know what the quarterback is thinking. Focus on the football, and attack it.

- *Cover 3:* four under, three deep
- *Cover 4:* three under, four deep
- *Robber:* four under, two deep with a robber

Man

The key to man coverage is to know what the receiver is thinking. Never let him inside of you and stick on him like glue.

- *Cover zero:* True man-on-man, six-man pressure

Combination Man-Zone

- *Cover 1:* Man-on-man with a free safety, five-man pressure
- *Cover 2 man:* Five under man-on-man, two deep with four-man pressure

#4: ALIGNMENT

Proper alignment is critical to our success. Learn where you begin on every front and coverage. If the word slide is added to a front call, the weak inside backers slide to responsibility prior to snap.

#5: STANCE

Our stances are designed to put your body in the most efficient position possible to be successful at your particular position. Take pride in a perfect stance every snap.

#6: STEP

Proper steps give you an advantage at the snap of the ball. Improper steps give the offense the advantage. Each position will only have a few different steps to learn. We will work hard on taking proper, intense steps to ensure the most productive initial movement.

#7: KEYS

A key is who or what you are looking at in order to learn what the offense is trying to do. The keys that your player looks at will determine run or pass, ball action to or away, and fast or slow flow. Very seldom will he be locked in on one person but will have primary keys and secondary keys that will enable him to read the big picture and understand the intent of the offense.

The faster your player can do this and be right, the better football player he will be. The front people will key the near lineman to the near back to the ball triangle. Most of the time, front men will not focus on the near lineman (primary key), but will feel him while looking to the near back-ball-triangle (secondary key).

The defensive secondary players' keys will be dictated by man or zone coverage concept. If it is man, then they will key the man that their coverage rules dictate. If it is zone, then they will line up according to particular coverage alignment rules while capturing their receiver in their peripheral vision but reading through the near lineman to the quarterback. In zone, the quarterback is the key. In man, the man is the key. Many coaches lose track of that simple rule. So, if confusion is present, go back to that simple rule.

#8: READS

Reads are the actual interpretation of the offensive schemes. Actions of the keys determine your reads, and your reads dictate how you fit into the scheme. The faster your player diagnoses the problem, then the faster he can fix the problem. Each position has specific reads that must be learned. To be great, your player must perfect the reads he receives from his keys and the techniques associated with those reads.

All of this starts and finishes with training the eyes and instilling the interpretation. This goes back to the language piece. Everyone needs to speak the same language and fit in where they belong as quickly as possible.

#9: REACTION

Reaction is what you do in response to the offensive scheme and how you fit into the defensive solution. Your reaction starts with doing your job with excellence, locating and attacking the football, then securing the tackle while attempting to create the turnover. The faster reaction time your players have, then the better defenders and defense you will have. This may sound elementary, but training reaction and response is a key to defensive success.

#10: PERFORMANCE

Performance of course is the bottom line. The athlete who performs consistently better than his competitor is the one who wins. These 10 aspects of defensive performance can serve as a logical progression for locating and attacking the football, and then securing the tackle while creating turnovers.

THE ETBU BASE 4-2-5 MULTIPLE DEFENSE

- *Who we are:* Selfless soldiers in the army of the living God.

- *What we do:* The base 4-2-5 multiple defense implemented with the A4 teaching process.
- *Where we do it from:* Stemming from a 4-2-5, we seamlessly transition to a 4-3-4, 3-4-4, and a 3-3-5 alignment.
- *How we do it:*
  ✓ Fundamentals: taught through the A4 process
  ✓ Conditioning:
    ⇨ Agility
    ⇨ Speed
    ⇨ Strength
    ⇨ Power
    ⇨ Flexibility
    ⇨ Aerobic
  ✓ Decision-making: abiding by the 10 Commandments

THE A4 DEFENSIVE TEACHING PROCESS

The A4 defensive teaching process is a concept designed to teach effectively non–negotiable aspects of defense. By using alliteration, we will be better equipped to understand how to play football from a defensive perspective. Since football is a reactionary game and not a thinking game, with the A4 Process we will use a systematic approach to teach players how to react more quickly and be more fundamentally sound, resulting in better efficiency. The A4 defensive concept will allow a player to be more efficient as a football player while playing within the parameters of our scheme.

The Non–Negotiable Aspects of Defense

- *Alignment:* No matter what scheme you run on defense, players are required to line up each down in a specific alignment which is paramount to success in each play.
- *Assignment:* No matter what scheme you run on defense, each player is given a specific assignment to be carried out for each play.
- *Assessment:* Before and after the ball is snapped, each player must process through keys and reads to make an accurate determination of what they need to do. This is what makes defensive football a game of reactions.
- *Attack:* The number-one mission of a defensive player is to attack the football, whether it is in the hands of a ballcarrier, in the air, or on the ground. Pursuit, escapes, tackling, turnovers, and recoveries are the components of the attack mode.

What are the basic differences in schemes? Defenses are referred to by the number of defensive linemen used and then by the number of linebackers deployed. Following are four basic defenses and how they align:

- *4-2-5:* 4 defensive linemen, 2 linebackers and 5 perimeter players
- *4-3-4:* 4 defensive lineman, 3 linebackers and 4 perimeter players
- *3-4-4:* 3 defensive lineman, 4 linebackers and 4 perimeter players
- *3-5-3:* 3 defensive lineman, 3 linebackers and 5 perimeter players

I want to show you the basic defensive alignments of the four defenses. First is the 4-2-5 look (Diagram #6).

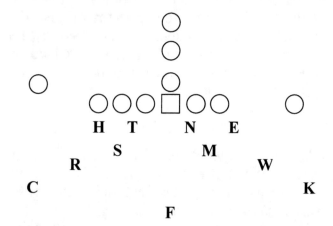

Diagram #6. Basic 4-2-5 Defense

You can call the players by different names and use different terminology on all of the defenses. I am showing the basic alignments. This is the 4-3-4 look (Diagram #7). We have added a linebacker and taken out a defensive back.

Next is the 3-4-4 look (Diagram #8). We have taken out a down lineman and added another linebacker.

This is the way we line up on the 3-5-3 basic defensive alignment (Diagram #9). We have our three down lineman, and we have five linebackers and three deep defenders.

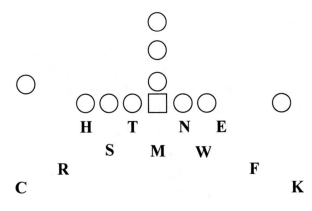

Diagram #7. 4-3-4 Base Defense

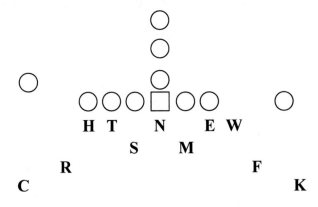

Diagram #8. 3-4-4 Base Defense

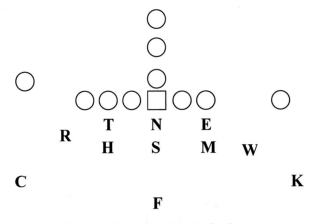

Diagram #9. 3-5-3 Basic Defense

Once we have the defensive alignment, we must know what to do as we line up. There are four points related to what we need to be concentrating on in our alignment:

- *See:* Must see the formation, how many receivers on the left/right, how many backs in the backfield, is the quarterback under center, or in the shotgun.

- *Settle:* Once we have identified the formation, we settle into the proper alignment.
- *Stance:* According to your position, use the stance that will allow you to gain the most leverage over the offensive player in front of you.
- *Step:* Once the ball has been snapped, the proper step will need to be taken to gain leverage over the offensive man as we progress through our reads.

Your assignment involves the following four points:

- *Find:* Locate the primary read on each and every set.
- *Fit:* According to the read given to you by your primary read (each fit action is predicated by position and assignment)
- *Flow:* Takes you from a primary to a secondary read and will involve working through multiple keys or from one key to another based on the information gained by reacting to your primary read.
- *Fill:* The gap or physical space you will need to occupy as a result of find, fit, and flow. Flow takes you from a primary to a secondary read and will involve working through multiple keys or from one key to another based on the information gained by reacting to your primary read.

I want to leave you with our team pursuit drill (Diagram #10). We use our cover 3 rules on the drill.

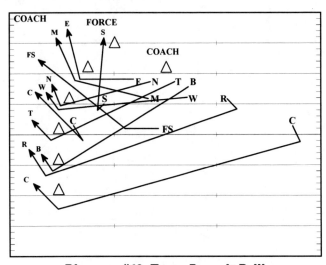

Diagram #10. Team Pursuit Drill

Pursuit Drill Guidelines

- *Defensive lineman:* Once the ball is snapped, all defensive linemen hit the ground and then get up and get into a pursuit angle.
- *Playside end:* Go down the line of scrimmage and turn up the field, looking inside for the ball.
- *Mike and Will linebackers:* Read the play and go to their assigned cones. The playside backer takes the alley (cone 2). The Mike backer sets up in the alley next to the end.

Cover 3 Rules

- *Sam and Rover backers:* They should take a read step and then go to their assigned cones. The playside man is the force player. In the diagram the Sam backer on the force.
- *Defensive backs:* Use proper footwork, and then go to the assigned cones.
- *Playside cornerback:* Slow support (cone 3).
- *Free safety:* Alley (Cone 2).

If you are interested in any of the material I have covered, just let me know. Send us your Best of the Rest Senior Prospects. Thank you.

INSIGHTS OF THE NO-HUDDLE SHOTGUN SCHEME

The University of Arizona

I sat in the back earlier listening to the lecture by Chip Kelly. You can see why they are successful. They have a plan, they have players, and they do a good job with their program.

Most of the things I am going to talk about today are going to be about our offense. But I want to give you a chance to ask some questions. When there is interaction between coaches and coaches, and coaches and players, and players and players, that is when you learn.

My first 10 years of coaching were at the small college ranks. I do not want to hire a member of my staff unless he has been a high school coach or a small college coach or a junior college coach at one time in his career. If you only hire those that have only coached at the big schools, sometimes they get spoiled. They are used to having a manager for each position. They have a water boy for every position, team doctors, and five video staff members.

At the small schools, you have to do a little bit of everything. I did that when I was the coach at Glenville State College. We had five coaches and three or four volunteer coaches. We lined the field, taped the athletes, cleaned up the locker rooms, and did a little bit of everything. I think this can give coaches a better appreciation of the coaching profession.

I have spoken at a ton of clinics in my coaching days. Several times after my lecture, I have had coaches come up to talk with me. "Coach, I am just a junior high coach!" I say, "Whoa! Wait a minute. Before you say anything, don't ever say that." It may be "I am a Pop Warner Coach." Are you kidding me? A lot of time, those coaches have more impact and influence on kids in their neighborhoods and schools than I do in my situation.

In college, we can still develop kids. In high school, there is no question coaches can develop kids. In junior high, you are developing kids. Don't ever look at yourself as just a junior high school coach. Because the kids are still young, you have a chance to make an impact on those kids.

Everyone wants to know about our system. When we first started running the fast no-huddle offense was back in 1990 back at Glenville State. We did not know any other teams that were running this offense that we knew of. What we did see what a version of the run and shoot offense that June Jones ran when he coached the Houston Oilers and Detroit Lions, where they scored all of those points. I had a quarterback that was 5-10 and he weighed 220 pounds. He was not a runner, but he could throw the ball, he was smart, and he was tough.

I was a defensive coach before I became a head coach. To me, the tough thing to defend was the two-minute drill. Have you ever seen a team that does nothing for the first part of the game? Then, when there are two minutes left in the game, they go up and down the field.

I wanted to know why they did not do this the whole game. So, that is what we tried to do. We were going to run the two-minute drill the whole game. It did not make a lot of difference at that time because we only had 500 people in the stands, and if they got upset, who cared?

Running the run-and-shoot offense, Warren Moon set the record for the NFL for the number of times he got sacked. He would open up with the 5 o'clock step, then take the 6 o'clock step. Defenses blitzed him from the backside because he never did see them coming. That was because he was under the center with his head turned. I decided I could take my quarterback and put him in the shotgun and get five fat players to line up in front of the defense. They got run over, but it slowed the defense down. Now our quarterback will have a chance to see what is coming.

Once thing that Coach Kelly mentioned in his lecture—and I wanted to talk about it earlier—once the ball is snapped, it is out of the hands of the coach. Right—once the ball is snapped, it is those kids making plays, tackles, and doing everything. Up and until the ball is snapped, you have some control. All coaches are control freaks—every one of us. So, why not get as much control as you can until the ball is snapped?

One thing you can control the most is conditioning. Chip Kelly mentioned it earlier: the single most overlooked factor in football is conditioning. Nothing else is even close. Everyone works on the fundamentals, but conditioning is the most important factor in football.

You may say "I do not want to coach a cross-country team." You are not just going to run sprints of 40 yards or 100 yards or run miles in practice. How do you get in your conditioning? You get your conditioning in how you practice. It is the same way that the University of Oregon does it—by the way you practice. We do the same thing as well. We are going to get in our conditioning in the way we practice.

We hear coaches talk about the kid that runs a 4.6 or 4.7 for the 40-yard sprint. Does he run that same time for seven or eight times in a row? Can he run those times back-to-back? You can control conditioning by the way you practice. You control it by how your kids train in the summer. In the old days, we never worked out in the summer. We did to some extent, but now kids do work out in the summer. If they are competitive, they want to play. Coaches will say they have a voluntary workout. What the heck is a voluntary workout? If they are going to play, they are going to work out.

Back a few years ago, we would call our players in and talk with them at the end of the spring session. We would ask them what they were going to do for the summer. Now we do not even ask them what they are going to do for the summer. We know they are going to work out because they want to start and they want to play in the fall.

The two greatest motivators are money and playing time. We are not paying them, but they want to play. What are they going to do to make sure they play? They are going to work out in the summer and they are going to do conditioning drills. The point I am making is this: don't overlook the conditioning factor.

This is especially true when you start playing the games. When you start the season and are playing games, you run the fine line of determining if the players need rest more than conditioning. You want their legs fresh on game day. If you practice with conditioning at the forefront of your mind, your players will always be in shape.

When you start playing games and the starters are playing 75 to 80 plays per game, you must remember the backups and subs are not getting the same conditioning. They may need to get more reps so they will be in condition when they get their chance. At times, you will see a starter get hurt and the sub comes in and is not as effective because he is not in very good shape.

GOALS OF OUR OFFENSE

Create mismatches and get the ball in the hands of the playmakers from the shotgun. Why the shotgun formation? I do not care what you run. Whatever formation you run, you must have the answers. You must know what you are doing. Don't just grab-bag and pick something at random. You must know how to fix your problems, and it does not matter what offense of defense you use.

Here are the reasons I like the shotgun. You remember when I told you we had a 5-10 quarterback when I first started coaching the spread offense? Think about it, if I am a quarterback and I am up at the line of scrimmage under the center, it is hard to see everything. One of the most important things for a quarterback beside his accuracy, and footwork is his vision. I am talking about the quarterback's eyes.

For our quarterback, he must be able to see the entire field before the snap and after the snap. When the quarterback under center looks right and left, he is fine. He may not see everything very clear. If he backs up five yards, he can see things much clearer. It is a lot better vision for the quarterback. His vision is better in the shotgun.

In a game, the quarterback throws a pick and then comes over to the bench. The first thing the coach does is to jump his butt. "Why did you throw the ball to them?" What is the first thing the quarterback is going to tell his coach? "I did not see that man." No kidding! The truth is, he probably did not see the man. It may be because his eyes were not in the right spot.

The first thing you want to know if you are running the shotgun or spread offense is this: Where are his eyes focused? We have this neat little camera that is something that can help you with quarterbacks. We started doing this about five years ago. Our video staff bought a small video camera and taped it to the helmet of our quarterback. You can get these cameras for $99 now. You tape the camera to his head with duct tape. We would turn on the camera before the snap and after the snap to find out where the quarterback's eyes were focused. Was he looking down at the ground, were his eyes up, or was he looking at something different? You can see where his eyes are focused at all times.

After practice, we would have the video staff incorporate it into the video system. When we showed them a play, we would run a tight copy, a wide copy, and then the quarterback cam copy. This was only for the quarterbacks' meeting room. The quarterback can see what he is looking at during each play.

If it were me and I was just starting out coaching, I would get a small camera and tape it to his head so you can see where he is looking. He could watch the film as well. He can see where his eyes are focused. The most important aspect is his vision. When he can see where his eyes are focused, he can make a better read.

How many of you in here run the spread offense? Quite a few run the spread. Back in the days, there were only a few teams that ran the spread. It was really fun for 10 years when we were at Glenville State. There was only a handful of teams running the spread that we knew of. We did not see a lot of sophisticated defense back then. Nowadays, it seems that over half of the teams run some type of spread offense. The difference in the spread that we run is the fact that the quarterback has to make a decision before the snap. They have to see the field before the snap. Most times, they have to make a decision after the snap on just about every play. This is true on run and on the pass. If it is a run, does he keep the ball, or does he hand the ball off,

or does he throw a bubble screen pass, and does he throw the ball to the right receiver?

The spread offense forces the defense to defend all skill players. If the offense lines up a player wide in the formation, the defense is going to line someone outside with him, right? How many of you out there coach defense? What is the first thing you do on Monday or on Sunday night if you meet then? The first thing you do is to line your defense up on the formations you will face that week. You want to make sure you have the offensive players all covered.

As a defensive coach, the last thing you want to do as a defensive coach is to have little Johnny lined up all the way across the field with no one on him. If the offense puts a man out wide, the defense is going to have someone on him. That is the advantage of the spread offense. It spreads the offense out.

The spread defense forces the defense to play its base defense. The single hardest skill to perfect in football is to tackle in the open field. The second hardest thing to perfect is to block in the open field. At times, the slowest man on offense may be your best stalk blockers. The fast offensive men get downfield too fast and have to hold the block too long. We may have a couple of slow players, and we will tell them they are perfect for this offense. They may not be able to catch the football, but they can be great stalk blockers. You tell them, if they give All-Conference Stalk Blockers, you will be on that team. That gets them all fired up for it.

The spread offense keeps the plays simple for the offensive line. I can look at coaches today and tell if they are offensive line coaches. Most of them have pancake syrup on their shirt; they dropped a little of the stuff on their shirt, and they did not want to get up early to hear Coach Rod. No, I am just having fun.

The most fundamental position you have is the offensive line. Where are all of the offensive coaches? You have the hardest job on the staff because you have more fundamental skills to teach, which include footwork, hand placement, angles, blocking schemes, and all of the other things. You have more to teach and to perfect than any other position. I have coached quarterbacks for a long time, and I know you have more to do. We want to keep it simple for the offensive linemen.

We are going to work the offensive line, but we are going to treat them better than they have ever been treated. We want to keep things simple for the linemen because they have so much going on in such a short time and in a short amount of space.

We do not list goals for the number of points we want to score or anything like that. We want to score whatever it takes to win the game. All of those stats are clinic talk. We do not make playbooks anymore because that information gets on the Internet. I found out one of my playbooks has been on the Internet for 20 years. We have two goals. They are score and win. Those are our two goals.

Here are the basic elements of our goals. The defense will have to play us all across the field. We want to play with multiple tempos. We have two distinct advantages on offense. First, you know where you are going, and second, you know when you are going. You may count the snap count, but we do not go one, or two, or all of that stuff. This can confuse the offensive line. They have enough to think about without giving them a snap count that is confusing.

Our snap count is very simple. We used to call the "hut hut." I decided to change all of that when I was at Glenville State. When you were a tot and you played football out in the yard, how did you call the snap count? You said, "Ready, set, go!" So, our cadence is "Ready, set, go." That is what we go on, and we do not use any other terms.

The defense does not know when we are going to call the cadence. We may snap the ball as soon as the official gets out of the way or we may wait to see what the defense is lining up. We may change a play or we may act as if we are changing a play, but we are not. We never let the defense know when the cadence is going to be given.

How many of you change the tempo as to when you are snapping the football? If I were coaching the defense and played against a team that always broke the huddle with 17.5 seconds on the clock and lined up and gave a lot of signals, tucked at his jersey, and a few other moves, I would want to know this. If the quarterback went under the center and the ball is snapped in about 4.5 seconds,

it is a rhythm cadence. If I coached the defense, I would work on beating the snap count if they never changed the tempo of their cadence. I would tell the secondary they had 11.5 seconds to disguise our coverage and to move around so the offense would have no idea where we were going to line up.

If we were a team that huddles up because you do not want to give the play away, that is fine. If you do not want to signal in the play, you can still control the tempo of the game. How could you do that? You could break the huddle and line up quickly and snap the ball. I would break the huddle and wait at the line of scrimmage until the defense showed what they were playing and then snap the ball. I would mix up the system as to when we would snap the ball.

When Spike Dykes was the head coach at Texas Tech University, they would break the huddle quickly and come to the line and snap the ball immediately. This is a neat concept. They always went on the quick sound so the defense could not disguise their looks to the offense. The offensive team can control the tempo.

Here is our run philosophy. It is numbers, angles, and graphs. What does all of this mean? Our offense—run or pass—is based on this premise. It is simple. I repeat it every day to our staff.

I want to cover one important point here. How many of you in here are head coaches? Several! I have been a head coach for 18 or 19 years. I still call the plays on offense. I still help coach the quarterbacks. I still mingle in the offense. I do not do much with the defense, but I know what they are doing. I do coach one unit of the special teams. It may be the snapper or it may be the bullets or another part of the kicking game.

I still coach the offense. Other coaches ask me why I still coach the offense. One, it is because it is one part of the job that I enjoy, and second, it is how I became a head coach. It is your own personal philosophy on this matter. Sometimes, when you become a head coach, you try to oversee everything and you end up not teaching anything. One reason you became the head coach is because you were probably good at something. It could be coaching and teaching the linebackers or coordinating the offense. Then, when you become the head coach, you have lost your value in doing something you were good at doing.

I have told our offensive coaches, if I do not have time to sit in the film room and watch the films, make decisions, evaluate personnel, and work with the offense, they need to come to me and tell me I am not involved in the offense enough to know what is going on. I am going to make enough time to do all of those things because that is the value I bring to the program.

I always tell the young coaches to "provide more services than what you are paid for." When I was at Salem International University, I made $18,000 a year. Now I am making a lot more money than that, so I have to provide more services for my salary. If coaches were paid by the hour, they would make more money. Never forget this as a coach. As young coaches, do whatever it takes. No job is beneath you.

When I got on offense, I looked at the two-minute drill and decided to go with the no-huddle offense and to adjust the tempo. The second part of the philosophy was to run where the numbers are. If the defense has four men in the box on the right side and three defenders in the box on the left side, I am going to run the ball at the three-man side. If we are throwing the football, it is the same idea. If the defense has three on the right and four on the left, we are going to throw the ball on the three-man side—to the right side.

We package our offense similar to what Oregon does. We have a concept that we call go. Everyone knows what to do on the go package. We do not use a full-field read package. Who has time to teach all of this? Who has the time to throw that pass in those reads? You can full-field read before the snap. As a coach, you are going to look at the entire field. But after the ball is snapped, the quarterback is going to pick a side and work that side or pick an area and work it. How do you determine that? Where they are lined up and where the numbers are. We use the center as the midpoint.

Our big running plays are the inside and the outside zone plays. We read the defense on those plays. If we have called the zone to one side and the quarterback wants to run it to the other side, he changes the play. Why run against the numbers?

Run and throw the ball with the numbers in your favor.

The second part of the equation is the angles. Angles are like a 1 technique or a 3 technique. If we are going to run the zone play, I would prefer to run against a 1 technique and a 5 technique than I would against a 3 technique and a 5 technique. It is easier to block a 1 and a 5 than it is to block a 3 and a 5 on the zone play.

Because we have a better angle, we can run the ball in the B gap, which we call the bubble. Because we have a choice on where we are going and the defense does not know where we are going, we run the ball with the angles. If the numbers on each side are the same, we run with the best angles. If the numbers are the same and the angles are the same, we go to the wideside of the field if the ball is on the hash mark.

In practice, our guys want to spot the ball in the middle of the field. In college, 80 percent of the game is played from the hash marks. It is probable true in high school as well. We are going to practice 80 percent of the time from the hash marks. Don't put the ball in the middle of the field all of the time in practice.

If everything is equal and the ball is on the left hash, and the numbers are the same on each side of the center, and the angles are the same, then we are going to run the ball to the field or wideside. We have more grass over there. This is our philosophy, and we build our plays around this concept.

We will run a total of 50 plays this spring. We run the zone play out of four different formations. That is four plays. I think 50 plays may be too high for us. We may not get to that total.

The most important thing we put together after the spring is what we call the answer sheet. Coaches want to know what we have on our play chart that we have when we are on TV. Some coaches have it hanging on their necks, and it is a big sheet. Who could remember all of the things they have on that form in the heat of the battle.

Our play sheet has the typical information: first-and 10, red zone plays, go zone, which is inside the 10 yard line. We have our two-point plays on the form as well. Do you know how often I look at that sheet in the game? Never! I may cover my mouth when we are on TV with the sheet. I am not worried about them reading my lips on the plays I am calling. It is because sometimes I forget I am on TV and say some words that I should not say.

On the back of our game plan sheet is the thing we do look at the most. It is what I call the answer sheet. I look at that sheet during a time-out or between quarters. If you would like a copy of this answer sheet, I will send you a copy. Just write me a note at the University of Arizona. We are located in Tucson. Now the sheet will be blank because I am not going to list our plays on the sheet.

Before the players report in the fall, we list our top two or three plays against all situations and types of defenses we will face. For example, if we see cover 4 against our spread offense, it means we have the numbers to run the football. We are going to have a few runs that we like the best against defense. We have two or three passes we like to run against that look. We list the plays we like to run against the different defensive looks.

If we see the bear defense, we know there are not a lot of running plays we can run. We may only have one or two running plays when we face that particular defense. There are three or four passes that are best against cover 1 or cover zero. We list the plays we like to run against the Tampa cover 2 defense. We try to cover all the situations that we expect to see in games.

We take a look at our conference schedule and list the things they like to do on defense. We create a category down for the plays to use. We can't list but about six plays because we can't rep them all. We have that on our answer sheet before our players report in August. Those are the plays we are going to call and we are going to rep. When we get in the games, we can refer to that sheet that covers most of the things we are going to see in a game.

When I am in a game, I have a headset on and I am talking with my offensive coordinator. I do not have time to listen to all of the coaches during the game. The offensive coach up in the box tells me if a play is good or if it is not good. That is about it. You do not have a lot of time to talk in the game when you are calling the plays.

When I was at Tulane University as the offensive coordinator, I taped all of the conversations from the headsets—from the press box and including the conversation from the field. Tommy Bowden was the head coach and I was the offensive coordinator. I may do that again this year. It was fascinating in that things happen so fast. You do not have a lot of time to discuss a great deal about the play selection. I would listen to the recordings on Sunday. I learned a lot about calling plays and how to be effective during a game with the information from the press box.

We do things a little different in that we use headsets in every practice as well as in the game. It is the same thing Oregon does in that our practices are going to be quick and swift. It is not going to be long before we run the next play. We are going to coach the players on the films. Everything is fast paced. We want to run 12 or 13 plays in a 5-minute period. We communicate in practice on the headsets just as we do on game day.

We have a graduate assistant with a headset on, and he is on the sideline. Our offensive staff has their headsets on, and they are on the field. We have the battery packs for our headsets. That is the way we communicate. It is a great teaching tool.

We have three tempos. This is how we do it:
- *Jet tempo:* Fast, no huddle
- *Regular tempo:* Snap as soon as official is set
- *Indy tempo:* Fast but can change the play if necessary

We have our regular tempo, which is the no huddle, and it is quick, but the quarterback will look to our sideline. People ask me how we know if the quarterback got the signal from the bench. I can tell by the amount of time he stares at the sideline. However, the quarterback must understand our system.

You may have a problem with crowd noise on the cadence. We had problems with this at home and on the road. Our center ended up making the go call. He gets a signal from the quarterback when he is ready to go. He may use a leg kick, point a finger, or a clap of the hands. We always changed the indicator when we need to. The center looks through his legs to get the indicator.

To change things up and to stay ahead of the defense, we may have the center keep his head up and have the guard put his head down and give the go count. The defense will watch the center, and when he puts his head down, they move around. If we see that, we let the guard make the call and the center keeps his head up to see the defense. Then, he gives a signal to the center when to snap the ball.

If there is a problem with crowd noise, we have the quarterback call it out: "Ready, set, go." He can control the snap better that way. You can use the center to make the call if necessary.

Our skill players are going to look at the football. They should never be offside. The backfield is going to see the ball snapped from the center. The only people we have to worry about hearing the cadence is between the tackles.

The defense will try to key the signal and jump on the count if you just go on the same sound all of the time. We call a freeze and we do not snap the ball. If the defense jumps offside, then the center will snap the ball and we try to get a free play. In high school, if the defense jumps offside, they blow the whistle and call encroachment.

How many of you here run the zone read? The reason teams run the play is that the defense has to play all 11 offensive players. It is like the option, but you are in the shotgun and you are safer. When teams started running the zone read play, the defense would teach the frontside to fit in the gaps and the backside players were taught to run to the ball and watch for the cutback.

Now you see the defense fit the frontside one way and the backside fit another way. They have different ways to fit the frontside and different ways they fit the backside. We have to make a couple of calls and adjustments to handle those situations.

I want to spend a few minutes to talk about our profession. Coaches do not get the credit you deserve as a teacher. At heart, we are all teachers; that is what we are. We are teachers of young people, and we hope they learn more than just football. I take a lot of pride in our players in the fact they have an appreciation for what this game is all about. It is the greatest game that we have.

Every day, I think of ways we can be better as coaches. I think coaches are better today than they have ever been. Part of it is because of technology, right? Coaches are smarter because of the advancements in technology.

Here is a coaching point that we need to improve on. In practice or in a game, we see a player drop a pass. What is the first thing most coaches, or the fans say to the player? "Catch the ball." No kidding! Think about this. How is that helping that player to catch the ball? I tell my coaches not to say "Catch the ball." That player did not drop the ball on purpose. You have to determine why the player dropped the ball. "Keep your eyes on the ball. Put your thumbs together." There is a reason why the player did not catch the ball.

If you only get one point from this lecture, this is one that can help your players and team. We are not going to say "Catch the ball." Give the player a descriptive point to help him catch the ball.

This applies when a player misses a tackle. "Tackle him." Okay, how do you tackle him? "Bring your feet up under you. Bring your hip up. Explode up through the man." "Wrap your arms" is a great descriptive in tackling.

Our game is under attack and, in some respects, rightfully so. This is because players are using the top of their helmets. Back when I played, we may have had a concussion, but we did call it a concussion. They were not diagnosed as such. The point is this. Our game is under attack from a lot of people because of the concussions. They are concerned, and I understand this point. The equipment has gotten better, but it has become a weapon to some players. Do not ever let your players put their head down. I am talking about both sides of the ball.

I do not think the issue is the upper-body collisions. I think it is the crown of the helmet that is the main concern. It is when a player puts his head down that result in injuries and concussions. I think they should outlaw tackling below the knees. Anytime a player puts his head down, it scares me. I do not believe you should be able to run and make contact with your head down. When you make contact with your head down, bad things are going to happen. Teach your kids to see "what you hit and always keep the head up."

A coach should never be put into a situation where he has to make a decision if a kid plays or not. I will never get involved in that situation. You are smart enough to figure that out. If the trainer or doctor tells us the player should sit out, that is what we are going to do. No question! We do not know how long a player will have to sit out because of a concussion.

As a coach, you can never step in and tell a doctor if a kid should play or not. That is left up to the medical people. As a coach, you ask the medical staff what players we have and when can the others come back to the game and go with it. Don't let the players put their head down. There should be dirt and scrape marks on the face mask. They should not have marks on the top of their helmets. Check the helmet of the players. If they have a lot of marks on them, they are either banging their helmets against a wall to impress their girlfriends or they are doing the wrong thing in the game.

In the time I have left, I want to give you a chance to ask questions.

Question: How much single-wing offense do you run in the shotgun spread offense?

I was talking to Coach John Majors earlier. He was an All-American at Tennessee, and they ran the single-wing offense. There are a lot of principles in the single wing and the shotgun zone read. To me, the zone read is an option play from the shotgun. It is a safe option. Instead of pitching the ball back, we are just reading the end. It is a matter of running at the numbers and running at the best angles. We want to run the zone to a 1-5 techniques and not to a 3-5 techniques.

Question: How did you spend your time last year being out of coaching?

It was very interesting. When August came, I did not know what to do. I did work with TV with CBS Sports. On Tuesdays and Wednesday, I was in New York in the studio. That was different. The most valuable thing I did was to study other teams. With the modern technology out today, you can get the game films off the Internet and put them on your iPad. I got most of the games downloaded to my iPad. All week, I watched games from all over the country. The hard part was doing the games in that I had to prepare for two teams. If you are coaching, you only have to prepare against the opponents. So, when I was broadcasting, I had to study both teams.

I learned some football, and I got to see some other campuses. I had a great situation, and I enjoyed it. The best part of the deal is the Arizona job allows me to get back in coaching. I told all of my assistant coaches that we would have to take the opportunity to learn football while we were not coaching together.

The one big point I learned in doing the TV was the visits I had with the head coaches on Friday. You could see the emotion and intensity in the coaches as they were getting ready for the game the next day.

Question: Which team will you fear the most: Ohio State or Oregon?

I do not fear any team we play. I think we will be competitive. I think the Pacific-12 Conference is going to be very competitive as it can be. We have a lot of work to do in our program. I do feel I am in a great spot.

I do appreciate your attention. For what you do, regardless of the level you coach, you do a tremendous job. You are in the greatest profession in the world—bar none. I loved doing the games on TV, and it was fun. But nothing compares to coaching. It is the players you are with, the families you meet, and the coaches you work with that make this a great profession.

The last point I want to leave you with is this. The most important thing from a teaching standpoint—coach to coach, coach to player, player to player—is communication. I think the same thing is true in your family. I have two kids: a daughter who is 15 and a son who is 13. They come to practice and they know what I am doing and why I am doing it. They know the deal. Throughout the last several years, when we left West Virginia and Michigan, they knew the deal every step of the way because I always communicated with them.

This is the most advice I can give you. You must communicate. Right or wrong, good or bad, communicate so everyone is on the same page. Let's enjoy this game. Life is too short not to have a good time. We need to enjoy what we are doing. I appreciate you guys. Thank you.

TEAM CONSISTENCY AND A COVER 3 ZONE SCHEME

The University of Alabama

It is a pleasure to be here today. I would like to congratulate all the coaches here who received awards. Every coach who received an award has a great program. I think that is something we all can have. We can have a great program that helps the kids to be more successful in their life. I also appreciate the military being here, and I appreciate all they do to help us live the lifestyle we live in this country. I know there are tremendous sacrifices they make for us.

I cannot begin to tell coaches how much I appreciate what you do. You probably do not get many of the players you coach to tell you how much they appreciate what you have done for them. They do not tell you they appreciate the lessons you taught them. You have taught work ethics, discipline, the ability to overcome adversity, and all those qualities that make them better people. They will not tell you that until sometime later in their lives when they understand how much you did for them.

However, coaches have a greater responsibility now than ever before. There are fewer coaches in the school building. There is more media attention for the coach to deal with. The expectation on coaches is greater than ever before in terms of what you should or should not do.

The reason I appreciate what you do so much is because of my feelings for my high school coach. There is no one other than my parents that had a greater influence on me than my high school coach did. I had great mentors throughout my athletic career. Don James was my college coach. I coached with Jerry Glanville, who was an odd man, but I learned a lot of football from him. I work for George Perles at Michigan State University. I coached for Bill Belichick with the Cleveland Browns. I have been around many good people.

Saying all that, the coach who had the biggest influence on my life was my high school coach. He was eight times West Virginia Coach of the Year, and he never called a play. When I played for him, we lost the first game when I was a sophomore and won 33 in a row after that. His name is Earl Keener. He taught us teamwork, togetherness, execution, and all the important things in football. The story I remember was when I was 15 years old and playing quarterback. I called all of the plays as a quarterback.

Monongah High School was the center of our community. When we played on Friday night, everyone went to the games. It was a great community to grow up in because everyone had an interest in what you were doing and were involved in high school athletics. The games were important to everyone. Our entire lives centered around whether we had success on the football field.

We went up in the mountains to play a team. Where we dressed was on the other side of the graveyard from the game field. You had to walk through the graveyard to get to the field. Our entire town was there and all the fans from the other school were there in this dimly lit stadium. We had to beat them to make the playoffs. In those days, only four teams made the playoffs.

We lost the first game of the season and they were undefeated. We were behind 18-0 at halftime. In the second half, we came back and were down 18-12. We gained possession at our 20-yard line with 1:27 to go in the game. We got the ball to the 20-yard line but had a fourth-and-12 to go play. Our coach called our last timeout.

I was elated because I would not have to call that next play. The success or failure of the entire season was based on whether we made the next play. I went to the sideline, and he asked me what I thought. I told him I wanted him to call the last play. He told me, "You have the fastest player in the state playing left halfback. Your split end has made

All-State three years in a row. I do not care what play you call—just make sure one of those players gets the ball."

I called a play-action pass to the running back and threw a post/corner route to the split end. He made a circus catch and we won the game. After the game, coach told me that when you are in a tough situation, do not think of plays—think of players.

That was the right approach, and it was a long time in my coaching career before I heard that again. Bill Belichick talked about that all the time. He always talked about where to put players and how to use them. I learn that when I was 15 years old and that was the first thing I ever learned about being a coach. There are things to learn from everyone, and I have had some great mentors.

One of the things I did as a youngster was to go to Pittsburgh to see the Pirates play. My father would take me to the game. At that time, Roberto Clemente was the right fielder. When I was eight years old, I learned a lesson from my father. I was staring at an Asian person sitting in the stands. When my father asked me why I was staring at him, I told him he had funny-looking eyes. My father told me that to him, I have funny looking eyes. That is what I am going to talk a lot about tonight. Sometimes, you have to look at thing from the other person's perspective.

We need to do that with the players we coach. Today, everyone is self-absorbed. Everybody wants to think how everything will affect him. The players you coach now are not as they used to be. They do not do what you said to do just because you said do it. You have to tell them what you expect of them, and you had better define it. You have to define how to do it and spend some time telling them why it is important to do it that way. They want to understand how it affects them. You have to look at things from the other person's perspective.

It is a challenge to the coaches in terms of what we do. We have to make it about the players. We have to explore how we can make coaching about them.

Everything we do, we have to consider how the players think. There is one thing you have to get over. I do not like the media any more than the next coach does, but they do a great job of promoting our game. They are not in the business we are. Stop expecting them to promote your program. They are in the business of selling newspapers. Coaches have to accept it. That is the way it is, and we cannot do anything about it.

When you are a coach, there are two kinds of love. There is conditional love and there is unconditional love. Unconditional love is what your dog does when you come home—win or lose. Conditional love comes from all the fans and people patting you on the back. The love is conditional on one thing. You have to win the game to get the love. If you do not win the game, you are criticized, and you cannot let it bother you.

You can say all the good things about Nick Saban, but I have had my share of adversity in my career. No one remembers this now but the first year I was at Alabama, we lost to ULM. That was five years ago, and I bet most people do not know what ULM stands for. It stands for the University of Louisiana at Monroe, and they beat us in Tuscaloosa.

You have to stick with the process of what you believe is going to make you successful. Jesse Jackson spoke to our team when I was at Louisiana State University. He did a marvelous job of speaking to the team. As we walked out to the field, he told me that my team was closer to the kingdom of God than my church. He was talking about Tiger Stadium. What he said was true. In our game, we clearly define the rules. Everyone has the same goal and everybody is together. That means you have races and social economic division all rooting for the same goal. That is the importance of our game and sports in general. It gives people an opportunity to do that. I respect what you do because of the quality of what you do. However, you cannot get away from the process it takes to be successful.

You have to define your expectations for your players. I hear coaches tell their players they want them to play with intensity. The players he is talking to do not know what intensity means. You have to define it for them. You need to define the expectation as it relates to them personally, academically, and athletically. You need to talk to them about their future as to what it is and what it can be.

The players have to respect the organization and the rest of their teammates. Their actions reflect on the rest of the team. We had 38 players make the Southeastern Conference honor roll last fall while we were trying to win the national championship. That means they had a 3.0 GPA or better. We check everything a player does when he goes to school. If they do not go to school, they do not play. If you create these expectations for your players and define it, you will get what you expect.

I would never tell a player to shave his beard. We do not have any rules when it comes to those types of issues. What I tell them is I want them to be neat in their appearance. However, if I did ask them to shave their beards to be part of the team and they would not, I would not want them on the team. If I tell a player "The next time you do that," what do you do when it is the next time? We tell our children all the time, "The next time you do that, you are going to get a spanking." The next time they do it, they look at you with those "Please don't do it, Daddy" eyes. I am not spanking them; they spanked themselves.

It is like players when I was coaching in the NFL. When they come to a meeting late, they looked at me and plead for me not to fine them. I did not fine them; they did it to themselves because it was their choice to be late. If you define those things clearly, they are never late. If a player refuses to do the right thing to be a part of the team, you cannot depend on him. In a critical time in the game, the player will not do what he is supposed to do and let you down. As coaches, you must understand that.

You can have no team chemistry on your team if everyone does not buy into the same principles involved in the organization. It does not matter whether it is on or off the field. Everything we ask the player to do is in the best interest of the player. I ask the players all the time this question: "Is there anything we ask you to do that does not have your best interest in mind?"

Character is an accumulation of your thoughts, habits, and priority on a daily basis. That determines the choices you make. The choices make you who you are. It can make you a good person, bad person, hard working, lazy, responsible, or irresponsible. They are going to do the same thing on the field.

When they understand they have to do the right thing, you are helping them.

You do an athlete a terrible disservice if you make compromises for him because he is a good athlete. If he can violate the rules and not suffer any consequence, you hurt him. If the coaches think he is good and he is not going to school, that falls on the coach to make sure he goes to school. I tell my coaches it is on them because it is not going to be on me. If he is that good, help him to do the right thing or he will be gone. You call that support.

In our program, we have a pyramid of success, which is relative to focusing on the right things. We live in a result-oriented world. In the first game against LSU, we probably outplayed them. However, we kept shooting ourselves in the foot. We were inside the 25-yard line five times, outgained them, only punted twice, and scored six points. It is almost not possible. The loss was all about what we did. That is what our players saw the next time we played. The pyramid is all about being the best you can be.

It is about being the best you can be personally, academically, and athletically. When it comes to football, our theme is "Be a Champion." It does not say win a national championship or an SEC championship. We do not talk about that. The first meeting, we had three weeks before our first game. I told them that *no one* was to speak about winning the national championship. I told them not to talk about it or think about it.

I wanted them to think about and focus on the player they had to dominate in the game. They had to assume he was going to be the best player they ever had to play against. That should be the mind-set for the players to play their best football. That is what we needed to do in the beginning. We play one play at a time for 60 minutes of the game. Treat every play as if it had a life of its own. We ask our players to be a champion in everything they do and not to win championships. That starts with being a team.

Two words get to the root of team. They are respect and trust. If your players do not respect the principles and values of the organization and they do not respect each other, you cannot have a team. If there is no respect, there is no trust. The players have to trust the person he is playing with and know that he is going to do the right thing—that he will execute and do his job properly.

Everybody says there is no "I" in team. However, there is one in win. The individuals on your team make the team what it is. The character and attitude of the individuals on your team leads to what I call the "three Is." The three "Is" are Intensity, Immediacy, and Intelligence. Intensity is mental energy. Immediacy is a sense of urgency. Intelligence is to play smart. The players need to understand the game. They need to understand their role. They need to understand the situation so they are able to play smart. The individuals on your team are the most important thing.

We need to be engaged and communicate with them. We need to influence what they do. We cannot go to practice every day and think everything will work out. You must get out of the box as to how you affect players currently. We constantly show our players videos of role model athletes to get our players to think the right way about who they are and what they have to do to be successful.

It affects people when you get their role models to say and do the right things. I know Tiger Woods has had his problems, but he makes great statements about what it takes to be successful. He has won many major championships, but the first thing he says is "You never arrive." There is always the next challenge, and you are only as good as the next tournament. You are not entitled because you have had success. You have to continue to do the things you need to do to be successful. All these things are important to being a good teammate, part of the team, and understanding team.

We want leaders. Nevertheless, how much time do you spend trying to develop leadership? How much time do you spend trying to get players to affect other players in a positive way? You have to serve other people to be a leader. You have to give of yourself and people have to think you have their best interest in mind. It is not about power. It is how you empower other people to affect others.

Leadership is important to everything. However, sometimes I think it is overrated. We had great leadership on our team this year, but we did not have anyone that needed to be led. Our 2009 team had one great leader on the team, and he affected everyone. I hoped every day that he did not get a headache. If he had a bad day, our whole team had a bad day. Everybody on the team fed off his energy. That was the problem. If you have multiple leaders, you have a better chance to be successful on a consistent basis.

Consistency in performance is what defines success. Team, leadership, respect, trust, and individuals make that happen. You have to work the individuals to make them do what you want to do.

On the second tier of our pyramid are positive energy and attitude. The first thing you want to do is define what you want to do. I ask that question of the players all the time. If they tell me they want to play in the NFL some day, we have a plan. The next question is "How is what you are doing now going to help you accomplish that goal?" That means he has to select a goal and take all the positive energy he has and put it toward that goal. Either you invest time doing that or you spend time doing something else that will not get you to the goal you set for yourself.

The next thing I want to know is "What are you selling today?" They project an air about how they sit, approach people, by the way they come out of the locker, and their entire demeanor as to what is on their minds. Did they fail a math test or did their girlfriend dump them today? I want to know if you are going to be positive and play with intensity. You need to be sharp mentally so we can get something accomplished and get better. I have had coaches on my staff who do not focus on what they want but what they do not want. They are not out there trying to win; they are trying not to get beat. There is a difference in that, and we do not want to play that way.

In the championship game, we had to throw the ball on first down. We knew LSU would be in an eight-man front and that running would be hard. I told our staff to trust the quarterback. If you show confidence in a player, he will always do better. You must have positive energy and attitude toward a goal or you cannot be successful. Negative energy brings everyone down. It is important to have an upbeat tempo at practices, preparation, meetings, and all related things.

You must be responsible for you own self-determination. That relates to accountability. This comes directly from Bill Belichick. What Bill Belichick is so good at is defining everything that goes on within his program.

When I worked for Bill Belichick at the Cleveland Browns, we had one sign in the entire complex. It said "Do Your Job." That means be accountable for your job. If you do not define what the expectations are, no one knows what to do. He defined what the janitor, secretaries, personnel employees, coaches, and anyone associated with the organization did. People that worked for him loved it. They knew what the expectations were, and they worked hard to fulfill them.

Everyone has self-imposed limitations. They come from your insecurities. I always tell the players this story. When I was a kid, I used to fish. I never caught anything. The man next to me caught everything. He threw the big fish back and kept the little fish. I asked him why he did that, and he told me he only had a nine-inch frying pan at home.

I ask that question of my players. "How big is your frying pan?" I want to know what they believe they can accomplish. When you watch the film of the game, it is never about the other team. It is all about what you did not do. You need to focus on what you control. You must believe in yourself and be accountable for the things you believe in.

The last thing is to play with a high standard all the time. That takes a tremendous amount of work. You must establish work ethics in the program. We are one of the hardest-working programs in the country. We have a fourth-quarter program that our players believe in. I missed it today. That is the first time since I went to Alabama that I missed the off-season program. People have wanted me to play golf at Pebble Beach and Augusta, but I would not go because it interfered with the off-season program.

My team comes first in the things I commit to do. It is important to get the work ethics established in terms of finishing, effort, toughness, and discipline to execute. You have to be in great condition to do that. A player loafs when he is tired. They make mental errors when they are tired. "Fatigue makes cowards of us all." Vince Lombardi said that. You are not going to play with toughness when you are tired. You must be well conditioned to work hard, and that must be established in your program. Our players have no problem with that fact. Our players believe they are going to win in the fourth quarter. They believe they will wear down the opponent. They see it happening in the games and embrace it when they do the work.

They make a commitment to the standard of what we want to accomplish. You cannot be a great competitor if you cannot overcome adversity. You have to define relentless for them because they do not understand that. I define it by comparison. You cannot kill Freddy Krueger from *A Nightmare on Elm Street*. That dude is relentless. I want the opponent to think our players are crazy. I want them to play every play with relentless effort. We want to do that repeatedly and dominate the opponent.

If you do not learn to overcome adversity, you will never have a great victory in your life. Great victory comes from overcoming adversity. You need to do all you can do to be the best you can be—to do whatever you choose in life. If you can do that, you will be successful.

When we lost to LSU in the first game, we had to do all those things I have just talked about to get into the national championship game. We had to finish the season playing to the highest standard possible to show we belonged in that game.

There was a feeling of resentment we had after the first game we had with LSU. When we got the opportunity to play the second time, people thought it might be a revenge type of game. Revenge is not a good motivator unless you can put it into perspective.

We have guest speakers come in to talk to our players every year. The week before the LSU game, I had a speaker address the team. He told them that if they see someone else's pain, they feel it more than if they had the pain themselves. When our players saw the pain their teammates had after losing the first game, it gave them incentive to play harder in the second game.

That is what you saw in the national championship game. When the other team cannot get across the 50-yard line, there is some relentless football going on. LSU had some good players, a good team, and they deserved to be in that game.

When we have a night game, I take the team to a movie. I try to pick an inspirational movie. The night before the national championship game, we went to see Red Tails. The spirit of that movie and the group of pilots in that movie were inspirational. What they had to overcome to gain the respect of their peers was phenomenal. They fought to the last man, last bullet, and last plane. They fought, they fought, and they fought. You have to do some of these things to get your players to resonate because they do not understand their feelings sometimes.

I want to talk some football. Do not let anyone tell you that winning is not important. Knowing how to win is the most important thing to know. Nothing I am talking about is about winning; it is about how to win. I am going to talk about the simplest thing. It is a cover 3 zone. We play what we call rip-Liz-match. The rip/Liz call is the direction of the safety dropping down. "Rip" is right and "Liz" is left. We play the coverage from a press-bail alignment from the corner. You can play it from the off in the alignment. The corner plays his drop off the divider in his zone. We base the divider on the distance from the safety.

If the top of the numbers is the divider and the receiver aligns inside that position, the corner plays outside leverage because the receiver is closer to the inside safety. If the receiver aligns outside that position, the corner plays with inside leverage because the receiver is farther away from the safety.

The corner has the #1 receiver and matches him unless he breaks immediately underneath. In that case, he makes an under call and zones off in his area. The safety or curl/flat defender is the seam runner. He keys the #2 receiver and reads his pattern. If the #2 runs vertical, he locks onto him and matches that pattern. If the receiver goes inside, he gives the under call and plays the curl/flat zone.

We have two linebackers inside who play the hook zones. They take the under calls from the safety and corner. If they drop and get no under call, they have a rule. They must take the #3 receiver through the zones. Those are the rules for what we call country cover 3.

If the offense comes out in a 2x2 formation, we make a call for strength of the set (Diagram #1).

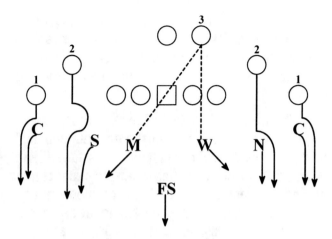

Diagram #1. Rip Seattle

We have a nickel back to the weakside opposite the strong safety. The first play we must stop in this coverage is the four verticals. We refer to that pattern as a Seattle. In that coverage, the corners lock onto the #1 receiver, the curl/flat defenders take the #2 receiver up the seam deep, and the free safety drops in his third. The linebackers get no under call and look for the #3 receiver releasing.

In the same formation, the #2 receiver runs a shallow cross to the inside (Diagram #2). The strong safety yells "under" to the inside linebackers and plays the curl/flat zone. The #1 receiver to the strongside runs an in pattern. The strong corner has the #1 receiver and has inside help from the strong safety in the curl area. The inside linebacker sees the under pattern from the #2 receiver and passes it to the backside linebacker. The shallow cross is the #3 receiver coming to the backside, and the inside linebacker plays him through if he does not get an under call from outside.

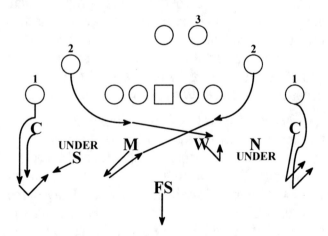

Diagram #2. Combination Pattern

If the #1 receiver to the weakside runs a comeback pattern, the corner matches the pattern. If the #2 receiver runs an under route, the nickel yells "under" and zones the curl/flat area. The shallow cross coming from the strongside ends up in the weakside curl/flat zone and is played by the nickel back. If the offense runs vertical routes, we are in cover 1 man. If they run crossing patterns, we are in zone. We can play the principles of the coverage and play any three-deep zone.

If we want to flood the coverage, we call Mable (Diagram #3). We may flood the coverage on all trips sets or all trips with no #4 receiver to the weakside. On this coverage, we flood the trips side with defenders. To the trips side, we are straight zone coverage with no pattern matches. The corner is running depth to the third and playing the vertical of #1 and #2 if they come. The nickel to that side is going to the flat zone. The strongside linebacker runs to the curl zone, and the backside linebacker takes the strongside hook zone. The strong safety rolls down to the weakside and plays the weakside curl zone. He is responsible for the first crosser. He also matches any pattern run by the #4 receiver coming out of the backfield. The backside corner is in man coverage on the #1 receiver.

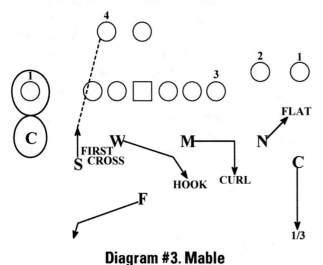

Diagram #3. Mable

If we do not want to play Mable because they have a #4 receiver weak, we check the coverage and run rip (Diagram #4). The corner matches the #1 receiver and the nickel plays curl/flat and matches the #2 receiver on vertical routes. The trips side linebacker has the #3 receiver through. To the backside, we are the same except we have inside linebacker help on the #4 receiver to the weakside.

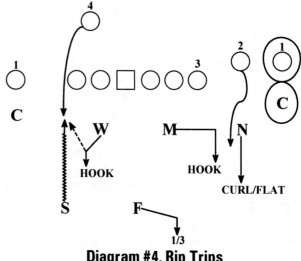

Diagram #4. Rip Trips

If the offense comes out in the empty set, we play a combination of both coverages. To the three-man side, we play Mable; to the two-man side, we play cover 1.

We can insert our safeties anywhere depending on the game plan. The three deep is three deep for us. If the offense motions to a quad set, we bring the safety down to that side (Diagram #5). The corner to that side has the deep in the divider. The nickel back buzzes to the flat and the safety plays the curl zone. The linebacker to that side has the inside hook zone. The backside linebacker has the #4 receiver and first crosser from the strongside. There is no #4 receiver to his side. The corner is cover 1 on the receiver and the free safety plays football and helps to that side.

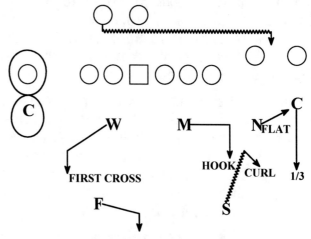

Diagram #5. Cover 3 Buzz

If there is no #4 receiver to the weakside, we will flood the coverage every time. There is no reason to leave anyone on that side with only one receiving threat.

Any time the corner sees the receiver stutter or skip at the line of scrimmage, he can make an under call to the strong safety (Diagram #6). He knows the #1 receiver is not going deep. We would rather have the safety playing the out or hitch and the corner on the smash 7 route by the tight end. He runs for depth in his divider. The strong safety runs under the #1 receiver. If the #2 receiver goes up the seam and vertical, the corner has coverage on that receiver. That helps us against a team that runs a smash concept with the hitch/flag combination. This is a game plan adjustment, and we do not do it every time.

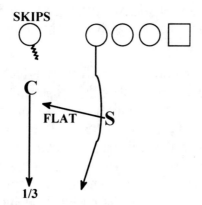

Diagram #6. Under Call

We have a technique we call corner (Diagram #7). We use this technique if the offense uses short motion or aligns with a tight split by the #1 receiver. We corner the set, and there is no matching of patterns. The corner takes the flat zone and the safety has the outside third deep zone. We do not worry about the Seattle route and roll the corner down.

In our 3x1 adjustments, we can play Mable or skate. When playing skate, we are in a cushioned man-to-man coverage with the #1, #2, and #3 receivers. On the backside, we play press-man coverage. We are matching patterns from an off position. If the defensive backs coach played cover 3 and got beat deep, it was all right.

However, if you played bump and run and got beat deep, they fired you. I go to the 1-on-1 drills every day. In those drills, the receivers go against the defensive backs. If we play off, they catch 100 percent of the balls. If we play press, they catch 40

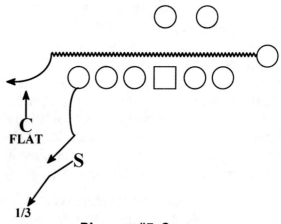

Diagram #7. Corner

to 50 percent of the balls. That tells me it is better to play press than off.

If you are a secondary coach, you will end up like me. You will be really nervous. Secondary coaches end up sleeping under some bridge after they are fired. If you coach the secondary, you have to have some guts and play press.

On third-down coverage, we play 2 Buster. The coverage is a five-under man cover 2 with self-adjusters. To play this coverage, you must have a three-receiver side. If the #3 receiver is behind the quarterback to the point we do not know which way he is going, we must check out of the coverage. The linebacker and the defender covering the #2 receiver has a you-me call on the #2 and #3 receiver. We base the call on which of the receivers is deepest. They play zone man-to-man coverage.

To the backside, we play a cut technique (Diagram #8). That means the linebacker over the tight end matches the pattern of the tight end if he

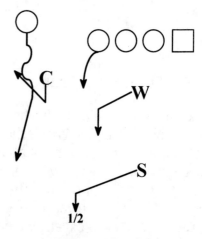

Diagram #8. Cut

goes vertical up the field. The corner sets down, plays a roll corner, and plays the flat. The safety to that side plays over the top of the coverage. The safety has the coverage on the #1 receiver if he breaks up the field. It is cover 2 match coverage. The two-receiver side is different from the three-receiver side. We can play anything we want on that side.

To the three-receiver side, the corner aligns as if he were playing quarter coverage. On the snap, he sinks inside the #1 receiver and plays him inside out (Diagram #9). However, if the #2 receiver runs to the flat, we play the coverage as a zone. The corner plays the new #1 receiver coming to the flat. The nickel back and the Mike linebacker have coverage on the #2 receiver. Depending on the split of the #2 receiver, the nickel makes a you-me call. That tells the defender who is taking the #3 receiver if he comes down the middle of the field.

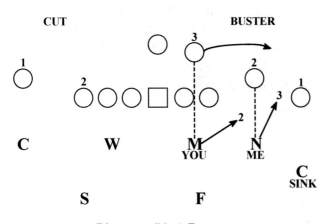

Diagram #9. 2 Buster

If there is a normal split with the #2 receiver, the nickel calls "me." That means he has the #2 receiver on a vertical pattern down the field. If the #2 receiver is in a wing position outside the tackle, the nickel makes a "you" call. The Mike linebacker has the #2 receiver and the nickel has the #3 receiver in the backfield.

If the nickel makes a "me" call, he has the #2 receiver in and out all over the field. However, if the #3 receiver goes immediately to the flat or flares, the call becomes an automatic "you" call. The nickel takes the back, and the Mike linebacker has the slot receiver even if he goes deep.

This coverage is self-adjusting and is not cat coverage. Cat coverage is the defensive backs

and linebackers pointing out their coverage men and saying "I got that cat." The offense picks the defenders if they run rub patterns. We adjust and switch to prevent the picks.

I want to show you this with a trips set (Diagram #10). The corner runs his sink technique on the #1 receiver. The #2 receiver aligns in the slot, and the #3 aligns at the tight end position. The nickel makes the "me" call to the Mike linebacker. If the offense runs the sail route, the receivers run a 9, 7, and flat route. The corner carries the #1 receiver up to 18 yards and zones back. The tight end runs the flat pattern and the nickel takes him on the automatic "you" call. The Mike linebacker matches the 7 pattern of the #2 receiver. The safety is over the top in half coverage.

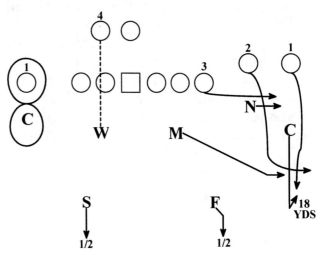

Diagram #10. 2 Buster vs. 3x1

To the backside of this set, we can play the single receiver in a number of ways. We can play the cut technique or we can dog the wide receiver. With the linebacker and the safety to that side, we can play match-man coverage on both receivers with the safety over the top.

Before I stop, I want to show you a bunch set. We play two techniques on the bunch (Diagram #11). We call this adjustment bingo. We play box or Buster. When we play box, we have a defender who takes the first inside breaker. We have someone who plays the first deep up the middle.

If the #1 receiver goes behind to the inside, we play box. If the #1 receiver remains, we play Buster with a "you" call because it is a tight split. That

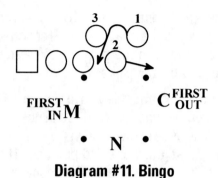

Diagram #11. Bingo

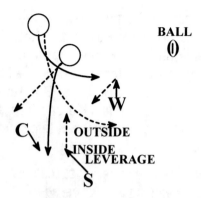

Diagram #12. Tango

means the nickel back takes the #2 receiver unless #3 comes to the outside. If this occurs, the Mike linebacker and nickel switch coverage and the Mike linebacker takes what is left inside. The safety plays over the top of the bunch.

The last thing I want to cover is a two-man stack release (Diagram #12). We call this technique tango. The linebacker has the first inside release, and the corner has the first outside release. The safety has the second inside or second outside playing with the leverage of the first release. That means that if the outside receiver releases inside and the inside receiver release up the field, the safety plays the receiver coming up the field with an inside release.

That was the leverage the linebacker had on that receiver.

I enjoyed visiting with you today. It is part of our professional responsibility to help each other as much as we can. If it were not for the good job you high school coaches do developing players and to inspire players to play our game, we would not have the opportunity to be college coaches. I know it is a long way to Alabama, but you are always welcome. We know what you do and the problems you have. I appreciate the job you do. I wish you the best of luck and thank you very much.

DEVELOPING THE COMPLETE WIDE RECEIVER

Clemson University

I am proud to be here representing Clemson and our players. Clinics are great, and it is a good opportunity to learn and share ideas. They are also a good place to establish some relationships with other coaches. Getting ideas from your peers is one way to develop and grow as a coach.

I am going to talk about developing a complete receiver. I hope I can give you some thoughts and that everyone can get something from it. There are things you can take back and apply in your scheme. They are drills, techniques, and fundamentals.

When I talk about a complete receiver, I am not talking about just catching the ball. I am looking for a player who takes pride in stance, start, release, break points, and route running, and who is knowledge about defense. He has to block, make yards after the catch, and secure the ball.

We are big on fundamentals and technique. That separates the good receivers from the great ones. The players we sign are all good. Something has to separate them. It can be work ethics, attention to detail, fundamentals, or technique. If you give me an average player with average talent who is committed, with great fundamentals and technique, he can play. It does not matter his speed. If he has great technique and fundamentals, he can play for you. You can take a receiver with great talent, but if he has none of the techniques and fundamentals needed, he will get you beat.

I want to start with these thoughts before we get into the meat and potatoes. We accomplished some of these things in the 2011 season:
- *ACC Champion* for the first time in 20 years
- *Atlantic Division champion* of the ACC for second time in three years
- *Earned first appearance in BCS Bowl* (Discover Orange Bowl) for the first time in 30 years

We were the first ACC school to defeat any AP-ranked teams in three consecutive bowl games. We beat Auburn University, who was ranked #19, #11 The Florida State University, and #10 Virginia Tech in our last three bowl appearances.

CLEMSON OFFENSE

- 6,171 yards of total offense—most in ACC history
- 33 touchdown passes—most in ACC history
- 1,952 passing yards—most in ACC history
- 170 points—most in ACC history
- Four first team all-conference players on offense
- Set Clemson records for passing yards, total yards, and total points

We got great quarterback production this year. Our quarterback was Tajh Boyd. He was a first-year starter and has a chance to be a big-time player. He passed for 3,943 yards with 33 touchdowns. He completed 310 passes out of 520 attempts. He rushed for 475 yards and five touchdowns.

In our offense, we assign numbers to our receivers. We have a 2 man, 3 man, 4 man, 5 man, and a 9 man. I have always been an X, Y, Z, and H coach in relationship to our receivers; however, we installed the numbers system because it allows us to tag our pass routes. Our 2 man this year was Sammy Watkins. He was the first true freshman to be selected an AP All-American.

When we talk about developing the complete player, we have three criteria for a Clemson receiver. Day one, when we meet with our team in the fall, I want them to know what it takes. When I meet with the recruits, I lay this all out for them. If they do not want to buy into these things, there is no need for them to come to Clemson. This is a non-negotiable item.

BASIC CRITERIA FOR CLEMSON RECEIVERS

- Great effort—consistency and confidence
- Intensity—concentration
- Aggressiveness—physical player

We cannot all be great players, but we can all want to be great players.

Our football team has to buy into the criteria. It is not simply for the receivers. We want great effort from every player on our football team. If you are going to be a football player, you must have consistency and confidence. If you have those things, you will give great effort.

Football is a game of intensity. If a player is laid back and lackadaisical, he cannot play. If he plays like that, he gets his butt whipped, misses assignments, and is not ready to play. You must play this game with intensity! If you are intense, you will have concentration. You have to focus to do your job.

At Clemson, we will be aggressive on both sides of the ball at every position. My kickoff man made three tackles this year and set an NCAA record. I love that. If you are aggressive, you will be a physical player.

The equation for us is: Consistency + Confidence + Concentration + Toughness = Playing Time

Every position in football starts with a foundation. You build your foundation from the ground up. It does not matter if you are a defensive lineman or a receiver; it all starts with the stance. As the receiver moves up in talent level, the margin for error becomes less and less. The little things make the difference. When you time a player in the 40-yard dash, you start the clock when he moves. If a receiver does not have enough stagger in his stance, as the ball snaps, the receiver drop-steps instead of moving forward.

If I have a fast receiver, who drop-steps before he runs his route, he loses a full second on his release. We want to maximize the efficiency of the receiver and gain the inches and seconds that lead to completions instead of interceptions.

STANCE—TWO-POINT

Legs and Feet

- Inside foot forward—feet shoulder-width apart

- Feet should be staggered—have enough stagger so you do not take a drop-step
- Both knees should be bent in comfortable position
- Concentrate weight on ball of front foot—enough weight so that you cannot false step

Body and Head

- Back straight slightly leaning forward—bend at the waist
- Head up, study the defense, and then look in at the ball—wide receivers move on sight, not sound
- Shoulders should be square to the line of scrimmage
- Arms should be in a comfortable position, up or down

Key Point: Knee over toe, chest over knee

Everyone coaches the stance differently. We coach the inside foot up on the ball. We do that for a particular reason. With the inside foot forward on the line, the receiver maintains a square shoulder position to the line of scrimmage as he looks in to the inside at the ball. If the inside foot is back and the receiver becomes lazy, his shoulder tilts inside. It takes time for him to square the shoulders for the release. Every fraction of a second counts in a completion.

We want the inside foot forward with the outside foot back. The receiver drives off the back foot and rolls over the front toe in his release. With the inside foot forward, it is not a natural move for the receiver to tilt the shoulders to the inside. They stay square to the line of scrimmage, which is what we want.

In the stagger, there is no exact hard rule. It varies from receiver to receiver, depending on his height. The key point is to have enough stagger to prevent the drop-step. The same thing holds true with the amount of weight on the front foot. We want enough so you do not false step or drop-step. Each receiver must find that position of balance in his stance. If there is a defender in the contact zone, the receiver wants his hands up in his stance.

The receivers move on sight and not sound. It is inexcusable for a receiver to be in motion or offside. He reacts to the movement of the ball and not the cadence of the quarterback. One of my pet peeves is the toe of the inside foot pointing outside. If he does that, the first thing he does is straighten the front foot to move out of his stance. We want the toe pointed downfield and not inside or outside.

The next step is the start. Every day in our agility period, we do stance and start. We get the proper stance, drive, and roll off the front foot. When we teach the start, I do not want to see the hips sink or the knees bend. That should be their position in the stance. The knees bent and the hips cocked for the takeoff. The only movement I want to see is forward.

RELEASES

We spend more time talking and drilling releases more than anything we do. If one defender can take your receiver out of the game, we are in trouble. The receiver must win the 1-on-1 battles.

Zone Coverage

When a receiver recognizes zone coverage, his release should be a straight line to get his proper depth as quickly as possible. No moves are necessary because the defender is concerned not with the receiver, but with covering a particular area on the field. The receiver should run and always threaten depth as though his route (knees bent, shoulders rolled forward, and arms pumping as though he is in a 100-yard dash event).

Important: The receiver cannot allow a defender responsible for an underneath zone to bump or force him out of his pattern. If by chance, the underneath defender forces you out of your route stem, you must get back on your original stem to allow for proper spacing.

Press Man Coverage

Versus man coverage, the release becomes more difficult. A clean release requires concentration at the line of scrimmage and quick, precise moves. The receiver has to understand what the defender is trying to do. The hands, eyes, and feet of a wide receiver must work together as one in order to get a clean release. In the stance, the receiver should narrow his base. He wants the weight placed more evenly on both feet to allow for more balance and

quicker release. He keeps a low center of gravity so he does not expose his entire body.

When I get a receiver from high school, he is generally a great athlete. He has not seen anyone get in his grill and lock him down. High school teams were not able to do that to him. That makes it hard for him to learn the fundamentals of hands, eyes, and feet working together. He never had to do it in high school. He does have to do it at our level.

The release has to be like a blink. When you walk around, you do not stop and make yourself blink. It happens automatically. The eyes must react that way in a release. You see it, and the hands and feet react to what you see. We must drill them to get the timing and coordination for it to become second nature. They see the defender, and they have a plan and a reaction to every move the defender has. We do it all in drill work. That builds the confidence to get the job done.

If the defender is in a semi-press coverage, the receiver can get in a normal stance. If there is space between the receiver and the defender, the receiver has to take up the space before he can execute a release move. If the defender's alignment is not tight press coverage, the receiver is wasting his time if he moves on space. He has to attack the defender and then make his release move. The receiver must learn to move on a stationary defender and a defender who is playing off him.

FEET

- Speed release—play low, and beat the defender with speed
- Single move—fake one way, and go another
- Double move—fake in the direction you want to go, shift weight to the other foot, and release the way you want to go
- Read steps—quick, choppy steps to read the defender's technique and then take the best release
- Squirt—start the defender upfield outside, get hips turned, and dip back underneath (used on a slant route)
- Shuffle—shuffle laterally to earn clean release versus heavy press
- Space—must be able to release in space with these techniques

The release is the game within the game. If the defender does the same thing every time, the receiver can beat him every time. The receiver has to know what the defender is trying to do and counter it. The receiver has to change his technique on his release. The receiver has to practice his technique throughout the game. He has to build his confidence of how to defeat the defender. The speed release is exactly what it says. The defender expects us to fake or do something else and the receiver gets low and runs by him.

When we drill the single move, we do it with our hands behind our back. We teach feet first and then incorporate the hands. On the single move, the receiver steps opposite of the way he wants to go. He does not turn his shoulders to that side. He steps in that direction with a threatening move with good body lean. The step to the opposite side is the same type move. He does not turn his shoulder to get in that direction. He makes a same decisive move to keep his shoulders square and get up the field.

We describe the upfield move as "knocking a hole in the upfield shoulder" of the defender. The double move is the most advanced move in football. If your receiver understands the double move, he can release on any defender. The double move is not two steps. It is the single move as the first step. The second move is a weight shift, not a step to the other foot. A receiver who can make the double move will freeze the defender.

We use the read step release against a defender who is trying to disguise what his technique is. On one occasion, he presses and bails out to the inside. One another alignment, he aligns outside and jumps to the other side. If we have a defender playing us in that manner, we use a read step release. The receiver uses a foot fire, which is a rapid movement of the feet. The defender reacts off the movement and gets to his technique. The receiver reacts to that technique.

Our receiver takes the best release he can get. If the defender aligns inside and the receiver has an inside breaking pattern, he cannot be hard-headed. He cannot try to force his way across the defender and bully his way into that area. He has to release on the defender and make him play his technique. We can get inside by using a read step and reacting to the technique of the defender.

The technique we use in that situation is a squirt release. With the defender aligned on the inside, the receiver has four yards to get inside the defender on his slant pattern. The first thing he has to do is threaten the defender with an outside move at the defender's outside shoulder. If the defender turns his hips outside on the first step, the receiver plants the outside foot, rips across his face, and runs the inside slant. The receiver takes the defender to the outside until he turns his hips in that direction. When that happens, he reacts and gets inside for the slant. If it does not happen until the fourth, that is fine with the receiver. The rip move to the inside with the arms is one motion like a club move.

HANDS/ARMS

- Swim—grab the back of arm or elbow of the defender as the defender attempts to grab or hit the receiver. The receiver then clubs the defender's arm and reaches over and past (swim) the defender with the other arm (tight swim).
- Rip—same technique as the swim, but he now rips past the defender with an uppercut technique instead of a swim motion
- Wash—two-handed wash motion
- Slam-and-go—used to knock the defender off balance and create some running room. Step into the defender high, but with body lean so you are not knocked off stride or backward.

Once the receiver has an edge, he must get long and lean up the field. "Knock a hole in his shoulder."

When the receiver does a swim move, he never gets his hand and arms outside the framework of his pads. He wants the swim done in a tight fashion. Never get the hand or arm up in the air. The swim works on the hands and arms of the defender. We want the work done below the shoulders and tight to the body. It is not done like a pass rush move. The swim move swims over the hands of the defender and not his shoulder. The target area for the receiver is to grab or punch between the defender's elbow and his wrist.

We use the slam-and-go technique as a change-up to give the defender one more thing to think about when he lines up. We want to come off straight into the defender and target his chin with our face mask. We want to jack him up and knock him off balance.

Once the receiver beats the defender, he wants to stack the defender behind him. If he cannot beat him with speed, it is essential that the receiver holds the line of his pattern and does not let the defender run him off it. That sets up the back shoulder stop or fade route.

RELEASE DRILLS

- Pop-up bag—used to teach the receiver to be physical with his hands while using a swim or rip technique (single, double, or squirt move)
- Extra defender—live work on the different releases that we will use
- Cover 2—used to teach the receiver to space release versus cover 2 and stretch coverage
- Hand shields—used to train the receiver to use his hands versus a press defender and to have proper targeting

When we first start to teach the drills, we start with a 1-on-1 release drill. The defender stands across from the receiver one yard from him. The defender takes his hands and extends them in front of the receiver. The receiver performs a release move and follows with a swim or rip move. The receivers target the elbow and works a swim or rip move on the defender. It is important that you teach these drills at a pace the receivers can learn. *Do not rush them into the drill.* Teach them at a slow pace, and gradually add speed to the drill.

The next thing we do is the same drill with the stand-up bags. These are pop-up bags, which react like Weebles®. They wobble, but they do not fall down.

The next drill is a read drill. We use the pop-up dummy with a coach or manager behind it. The receiver performs his read release. He foot-fires his feet, and the coach tilts the dummy one way or the other. The receivers react to the direction of the dummy and execute a release the opposite way the dummy tilts. If the coach tilts the dummy right, the receiver executes his release to the left side of the dummy.

When we do a receiver drill, we never do it without a simulated snap of the football. We have someone move a ball or someone pops a ball. We never do a drill on cadence. We never move them on sound because we do not play that way in a game.

We combine the two drills and have a two-dummy drill (Diagram #1). We have a pop-up bag at the line of scrimmage and a second dummy 10 yards down the field. There is a coach or manager holding the second dummy. The receiver takes a release on the first dummy. He releases either way. He squares up and runs at the second dummy. He has to use a space release on this dummy. The coach waits until the receiver is three yards from the bag and gives it a tilt one way or the other. The receiver has to make a second release off the reaction to the tilt of the bag.

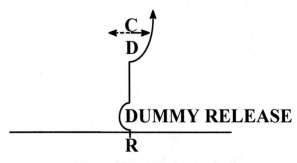

Diagram #1. Two-Bag Drill

We do a similar drill, making the receiver do a space release as his first move (Diagram #2). The receiver aligns at the line of scrimmage. He runs five yards to the first dummy. He does a space release on the first dummy. Five yards behind the first dummy is a manager or coach who extends the arms like the 1-on-1 drill. We use arm shields to prevent anyone from getting hurt. The receiver targets the elbow and performs a rip or swim move past the second defender.

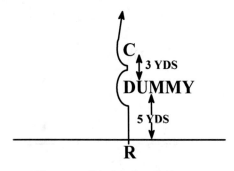

Diagram #2. Space Release

We do the same drill that the defensive linemen use (Diagram #3). It is a gauntlet drill with four stand-up bags. We set the bags two-and-a-half yards apart. The receiver comes off the ball and weaves though the bag, performing a release and hand movement at each bag. We work on coordinating the feet and hands together. Do not rush. Let them learn before they try to go fast. You have to crawl before you walk and walk before you run. We decrease the distance between the bags and do the same drill. That makes the receiver move his feet in a rapid fashion and perform his hand movement in traffic.

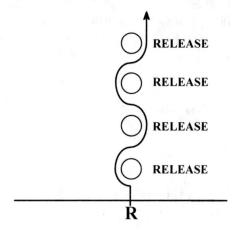

Diagram #3. Release Gauntlet

We work the squirt drill with two bags (Diagram #4). The receiver aligns with a bag on his inside shoulder. The second bag is two yards outside the first bag and four yards off the ball. The receiver releases off the first bag and pushes to the second bag. The second bag simulates the point at which the defender turns his hips. At the second bag, the receiver plants his outside foot and rips with his near arm to the inside of the dummy. We can put a ball in the drill and throw slant patterns.

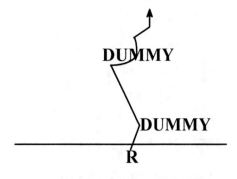

Diagram #4. Squirt Drill

We repeat the drill and bring the second dummy closer to the first dummy. It is two yards outside the first dummy and two yards deep. That forces the receiver to perform the first drill in a tighter area. His footwork is more difficult in that area. After we do the bag drills, we drill and execute them on live competition.

We do a redirect drill against a zone walk-off linebacker (Diagram #5). The linebacker wants to get a hand on the receiver or wall him off so he cannot get inside. We want to redirect off that defender. On this drill, we want to attack that defender and redirect a pattern off him. We set the drill with a wide receiver and a bag four yards to his inside. The receiver attacks the bag, pops it with his outside hand, and redirects his pattern up the field down the seam. The receiver works at full speed, plays with his hands, and makes a catch.

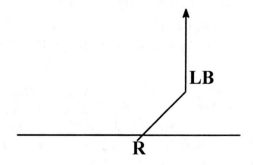

Diagram #5. Redirect Drill

The cover 2 release is similar to the redirect (Diagram #6). On the cover 2 drill, the dummy is set outside the receiver as if the corner rolls to the outside in his coverage. We have what we call a "100-percent protect release." The receiver does anything he can to get an outside release. If he has to run to the flat, he does it. If the corner wants to widen with the release of the receiver, that is

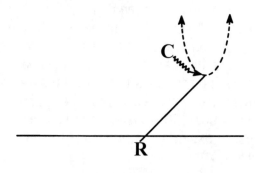

Diagram #6. Cover 2 Release

beautiful. Teams know we have the 100-percent rule. We work the redirect drill on the corner.

At other times, we may be able to release inside. We do the same thing as the 100-percent rule. We run at the corner and force him to widen. We want to put pressure on the safety. We widen the corner and redirect to his inside. When we redirect, we are on the landmark for the outside receiver on a four vertical pattern. We are not concerned with the corner; we want to get the pattern up the field and pressure the safety. When we go outside, we are in the hole from the half-field safety and the corner.

The next drills we use are hand shield drills (Diagram #7). These padded shields fit over the arms. It allows the handwork without anyone being hurt. We align the receiver and the hand shield defender one yard across from one another. The defender wearing the hand shields swings one hand shield at a time at the receiver. The receiver moves his feet, uses his swim-and-rip technique without moving downfield. It is a hand fighting exercise with the defender offering one hand shield and then the other. After three to four reps, the receiver uses one last escape move and goes up the field.

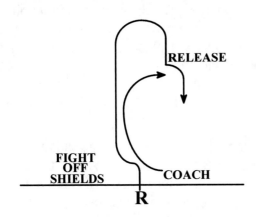

Diagram #7. Hand Shield Drill

We also use the hand shields as downfield movements. The manager or defender with a hand shield run with the receiver to his inside and stick the shield around his shoulders or at the waist. If the shield is around the shoulder area, the receiver lifts his arm and knocks the shield away. If the shield is around his waist area, he clubs down on the shield. That simulates knocking the hands of a defender off the receiver.

We take the drill one step further. The receiver works off the line of scrimmage, fighting his way past the hand shields. Once he gets free of the shields, he runs five yards, turns around, and faces the shield again back to where he started the drill.

ROUTE RUNNING—FIVE KEYS TO GOOD RUNNING

Speed

Speed off the ball (passes and runs) speed in and out of breaks. Knowing when to change the speed is the key. If the receiver is a 4.8-runner, then that is the speed he runs. If he is a 4.4-runner, he has to run at that speed. He runs at that speed off the line of scrimmage and into his breaks.

Leverage

It is very important to get leverage on the defender, especially against man coverage. Leverage is working for a head-up position on the defender. The receiver must try to get leverage by stemming for the outside shoulder of the defender (e.g., slant versus inside technique stem at inside shoulder to get leverage).

Influence

The receiver has the advantage because he knows where he is going. The receiver should turn the hips of the defender away from where he intends to make his final break. Eyes, fakes, jab step, and speed fluctuation will create separation against man coverage and air against zone.

Body Control

It is very important that a receiver keep his body under control while running routes, especially when trying to get in and out of breaks points. Receivers get into trouble when they slow down, rise up, drop their arms, or run routes with curves and wide turns. All these things will be picked up by good defenders and allow them to close on the route quicker. If the receiver keeps his body under control, he will be able to maintain his separation longer.

Defense

The receiver must understand defenses in order to know how and when to adjust his route against certain coverages. He has to know where he will get open, and how soon he will get open.

When the receiver breaks off the line of scrimmage, the defensive back's weight should be back because the receiver threatens him deep. If the defender does not respect the deep threat, we have lost the battle. That comes from speed off the line of scrimmage and influence on the defender.

You can stem off the line of scrimmage or downfield. Stemming will help the receiver get leverage on the defender. Stemming will tip off what coverage the defender is playing. If you stem at his inside and he runs outside, he is playing zone. The things that lead the receiver to his techniques are his eyes. He has to see the defenders and their movement. The tip-off to the break point is the raising of the body. The body and shoulders must stay down at all times.

The receiver has a number of objectives in his break point. He wants to gain an advantage and separation on the defender. He wants to decrease his angle to the ball and increase it for the defender. He gets body position on the defender and arrives at a certain place at the right time. His techniques to do that are the following.

TECHNIQUES

- Cause the illusion you are going somewhere other than where you end up.
- Thrust the head and shoulders forward.
- Lower the center of gravity.
- Keep your arms bent.
- Keep the elbows in near the sides of the body, and pump them each time you step with the opposite.
- Speed the feet as you lower the center of gravity, cut and drive off the foot opposite the direction of the cut.
- Accelerate just prior to the cut to create a deep feeling.
- Cut sharply and whip the head quickly toward the quarterback.

The break drill is a simple break point drill. The receiver aligns on a yard line. The coach stands two yards beyond the next yard line. The receiver breaks off the ball, and the coach gives the receiver

a number by a hand signal. That makes the receiver keep his eyes on the coach. They call out the number and break in or out on a square at the yard line in front of the coach. This is not a full-speed drill. We work on the techniques. We work the in and out cuts and the curl back cuts.

The next drill is a shadow drill (Diagram #8). We align a receiver and a defender side-by-side on a line. The defender is shadowing the receiver to his inside. The cut is an out cut. The receiver has the leverage he wants. He works down the field five yards and breaks out. The defender runs with the receiver down the field.

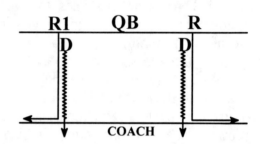

Diagram #8. Shadow Drill

The next thing we do in the shadow drill is to change the position of the defender. Instead of inside leverage, we place the defender in a trail position behind the receiver. The receiver has to make an evasive move at the cut to elude the shadow defender. He has to use some kind of double move.

The last thing we do with the shadow drill is to put the defender to the pattern side of the receiver (Diagram #9). The receiver has to make a move to get across the defender and back to the inside. He has to plant the outside foot and get under the defender.

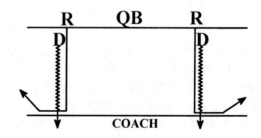

**Diagram #9. Shadow Drill—
Inside Leverage, Inside Break**

We go from that drill to a feel it drill (Diagram #10). We make the receiver perform a release off a dummy, come down the field, and turn back to the inside. We set a cone up and make the receiver touch the cone with his outside hand as he makes his plant. This emphasizes a low drive back to the inside. We work inside and outside comeback patterns.

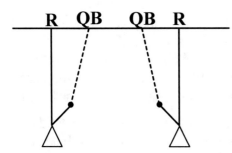

Diagram #10. Feel It

The push-off drill is a lean drill (Diagram #11). We put a dummy holder to the outside of the receiver. He presses the dummy into the receiver before the receiver releases off the line. As the receiver breaks off the line, the dummy holder pushes the dummy against the receiver, trying to make him adjust his route. The receiver leans into the dummy, maintains his course, and breaks at five yards.

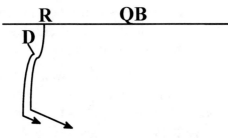

Diagram #11. Push-Off Drill

We work a number of cone drills to teach sharp breaking cuts. This is the square drill (Diagram #12). We like to start the drills off with a release on a dummy. The cones are set in a five-yard square. The receiver releases off the dummy and sprints to the first cone. He square cut to the second cone and continues on to the third cone. At the third cone, he plants and comes across the diagonal of the square, and the coach throws him a pass. You can change the pattern at the end to an out cut back to the starting cone.

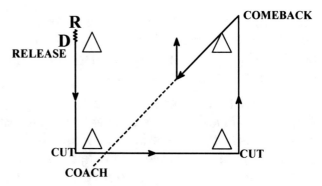

Diagram #12. Square Drill

The next drill is a simple cut drill (Diagram #13). We stagger cones at two-step intervals. The receiver starts at the first cone and runs at a 45-degree angle to the second cone. He plants and accelerates to the next cone and repeats the drill through four cones. At each cone, he cuts off his outside foot.

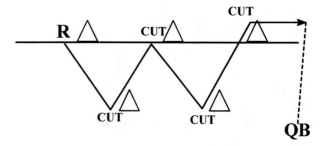

Diagram #13. Cut Drill

For the next drill, we change the configuration of the cones and combine the square drill with the cut drill (Diagram #14). We align four cones in the drill. Four of the cones are in the shape of the square. The fifth cone is in the middle of the square. The receiver starts at the first cone and does a square cut at the second cone. He sprints to the

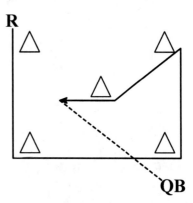

Diagram #14. Combination Drill

third cone and repeats the cut. He runs to the fourth and performs a comeback cut to the cone in the middle of the square. He breaks a square cut off the middle cone, and we throw him a ball.

We work the same drill as a sideline drill (Diagram #15). This drill works on the receiver keeping a low center of gravity and making sharp cuts. This is the cut drill working up the field with the last cut coming to the sideline. We throw the ball in this drill.

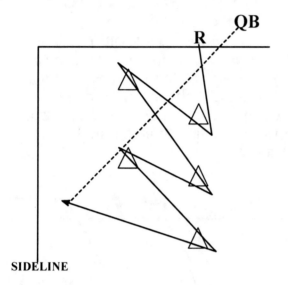

Diagram #15. Sideline Drill

The last drill is a throw-by drill (Diagram #16). This is a two-dummy drill. We align the dummies seven yards apart. The receiver releases off the first dummy and cuts off the second dummy. He runs to the second dummy, plants outside the dummy, and uses a club move across the face of the dummy to the inside cut. We throw the ball at the end of the drill.

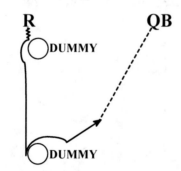

Diagram #16. Throw-By Drill

After we do the drills, we take the techniques to route running drills against live defenders. The technique receivers must become good at is the lean drill. With press coverage, the receiver has to lean against the defender to get separation. The thing that gives him the separation is the threat of getting deep on the defender. If the defender is not afraid of the receiver getting deep, he will never get open or separation.

In the live drills, we must perform all the techniques we learn. We must release and use whatever technique we need to beat the defender. You can always tell when the defender has bought the deep move because he has the lean in his body.

When we line our practice fields, we put an orange line up either side of the field parallel to the sideline. The line is four yards inside the sideline. That is no-man's land. No one runs inside that line on a deep pattern. That is where the quarterback throws the ball and the receiver goes to get it. You cannot run patterns in that area. We break into and catch balls in that area. The quarterback must have somewhere to throw the ball on the deep pattern to the sidelines. We do not want the ball thrown out-of-bounds.

On the deep patterns, the receiver wants to beat the defender. He wants to beat him and put the defender in a stacked position running behind him. That means, to get to the ball, the defender has to come over the top of the receiver.

We do all kinds of ball drills, which teach hand placement and ball security. They are simple drills you all have done. The emphasis points in the drill are to see it, squeeze it, and put it away. We work sideways down the line, throwing the ball to them. Then, we turn and come straight at the coach. The coach throws all kinds of throws. He throws low balls, high balls, and throws to the right and left. We want to emphasize catching in the hands with a soft touch. On the low balls, they have to bend the knees and get the little fingers together in their hand placement. On the high balls, they have to extend with their thumbs together.

We break them off the line and throw the ball over the outside shoulder. They must adjust and catch the ball. We also break them off the line and throw a back shoulder throw. That makes the receiver turn his head to the inside and catch the ball going to the outside. We put the quarterback directly behind the receiver and make the receiver catch the ball coming down over his head. We throw over the top of him.

We use high ball drills to make the receiver go up and rebound the ball at the highest point. You can make that a combative drill if you want. We do the same things with these techniques. We work against live defenders and throw all different types of balls.

The drill I like is a pole drill (Diagram #17). We have a flagpole in a stand. The receiver stands behind the pole and catches the ball in front of the pole. We align the pole between the receiver's eyes, and he has to extend his hands to the other side of the pole and catch the ball. When he catches the ball, the pole is between him and the ball. It is a great concentration drill.

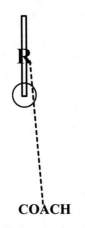

Diagram #17. Pole Drill

It is important to keep a drill checklist. List the drills you could possibly run and see if you are drilling the things your receivers need. List all your drills and check them off on the days you use them. It makes sure you drill the things the receivers are having trouble doing. Create the drills you need to do, but do not do drills for the sake of drilling. Make it apply to things that occur in the games. The drills must carry over on the field. If you cannot see the drill work on the field, you are doing the wrong drills.

We have a goal board that hangs in the receiver room. Our goals are no drops, no penalties, no missed assignments, no turnovers, at least three big plays, make a difference with blocking, and score.

We have a blocking chart we keep in our room. We want to know who is giving effort, who gets the key block, who makes a de-cleater blocker, and who gets the no-hitter. For every three de-cleaters, the receiver gets a cat's paw helmet sticker. You have to reward them for blocking. If they get a defensive lineman on the ground, that is an automatic paw. If they get a linebacker down, that is worth three paws.

You are always welcome at Clemson. When you come to our place, what you see is what you get. We recruit this area, and if you need anything, we can take care of you. I cannot make any promises, but we will work hard in everything we do. I appreciate the job high school coaches do. There is no greater responsibility than being called coach. A coach influences more lives in one year than most people do in a lifetime. Do not take the tag of a coach lightly. You have an opportunity to influence people for an eternity. Thank you very much.

ATTACKING MODERN DEFENSIVE COVERAGES

University of Louisville

I am going to speak about our passing game and the philosophy we apply in the offense. I am a West Coast passing game coach. I want to give you a little background of my career. I started at the University of Illinois with Mike White. That is where I learned the West Coast system. I believe wholeheartedly in that system. I am going to share with you the philosophy behind the system and some of the things we do, which I think are unique. What I want to talk about is how we attack coverages.

First, I want to give you an overview and some background so you will know where I am coming from. I will go into the methodology and teaching of the things we do. Finally, I will show you some plays and how to attack coverages. When we get to that point, I will talk about concepts and patterns we call multicoverage beaters. They can beat any type of coverage the defense plays.

There are only two fronts and two coverages in football. There are fronts that cover the guards and those that do not. There are coverages that have the middle of the field open and those that do not.

If you can keep it that simple and teach it, it takes all the complexities out of it for the players. When you can streamline the offense and make it simple is when you start to develop as an offense.

OUR OFFENSIVE PHILOSOPHY

• Balanced attack—50/50 run-to-pass ratio
• Multiple personnel groupings
• Multiple formation structures:
  ✓ Play from underneath center, shotgun, and pistol
  ✓ Motion game
  ✓ Shift game
  ✓ Shift and motion game

• Run game—downhill and physical:
  ✓ Inside zone
  ✓ Wide zone
  ✓ Gap scheme
  ✓ Pins and pulls
  ✓ Man scheme

We use elements of the read game to give our shotgun alignment credibility.

In championship football, if you look at the teams that played in the Super Bowl, BCS Championship, Division I AA, Division II, and Division III, they all have the same characteristic about winning the championship. The first characteristic is they do things. The second part is they had the ability to rush the football. The third thing was they played great in the special teams area. Their special teams were good at setting up scores.

A big part to having a balance in the offensive scheme is self-scouting. I spend a tremendous amount of time on Sunday looking at what we did in the game on Saturday. That gives me an insight into what the defensive coordinator in the next game will look at. We want to do the same things from week to week but present it in a different way. This past year, we were more of a passing team instead of being 50/50 run to pass. That related to what we could do. We were a young team with a young quarterback.

We want to be close in the balance of run to pass because we want the defense to defend both the pass and the run. We want to be multiple in our personnel groups. That is a huge part of allowing you to have multiplicity. We have as many as 12 personnel groups. How you utilize the personnel is a big part of the multiple plans. We can change the personnel groups but still run the same play with all of the groups. Doing that presents the defense with a different look at the same play.

We want to use multiple formations as well as be under center, in the shotgun, and in the pistol. Quarterbacks want to play in the shotgun and pistol sets. That is the best seat in the house for the quarterback. We want to be able to run the ball from the shotgun and pistol sets. We do not want to be known as a passing team in the shotgun and a running team under the center. We must have the same offense in the rush from the shotgun as we do under the center. Multiplicity starts with where we align our quarterback and our backs.

We use motions and shifts. I want to find out if the defense is a field defense. If it sets the front to the field, I want to use shifts and motions to manipulate how the defense aligns. We use shifts and motions to create mismatches or force personnel to do things they do not normally do. If a team has an openside linebacker and a closed side linebacker, we can shift or motion the tight end to the other side and make the openside end play the power game.

In our running game, we want to be a downhill, physical football team. We are a zone team. We run the wide zone and the knockout zone. Coach Dave Borbely, our offensive line coach, and I were introduced to that play at the University of Colorado when we worked there a number of years ago. We also run the inside zone and lead zone. We run the gap scheme power plays. The power game comes in off the inside zone play and the counter off that play. Pin and pull plays are zone blocking on one side of the line, with pulls and seals on the other side. Pins and pulls are a secondary thing for us, but they are a good complement to the scheme.

PASS GAME

We have a high percentage passing game that attacks the field horizontally and vertically while attacking an opponent's coverage structure:

- *Run action pass:* Naked (break contain pass)
- *Play-action pass:* pocket passes (three, five, seven steps)
- *Three steps:* Quick passing game
- *Five steps:* Possession passing game
- *Seven steps:* Crossing, intermediate, and deep horizontal passing game

- *Full sprint:* Break contain passing game
- *Screen game:* Rush control pass

The key to our multiplicity are plays that look the same yet are different.

We have a catalog we put together. This time of the year is my favorite as a coach. We sit in meetings and study ourselves and other people that are successful. We take what we do well and what other successful people did well last year and add that to the catalog. With all the different combinations of coverages in college football today, we have to prepare for whatever we get. We refined our offensive package and have it filled with coverage beaters for critical situations. We have coverage beaters that beat quarter coverages as well as cover 3 beaters. We mix and match these patterns to teams. If we play a team that is a fire-zone blitz team, we have a catalog of plays that beat that type of defense.

We want to attack coverages with multiple coverage beaters. No matter what coverage we see, there is an answer. That gets our quarterback locked in on how to make the read. This is simple football. In our passing game, we have a run action pass. That is our naked bootleg pass. We design it to break the containment of the defense and give us the run-pass option. When we run a play-action pass, we design it as a pocket pass. It is a pocket pass and has a three-, five-, and seven-step drop. We are multiple in our passing drops in the play-action scheme.

The three-step game is our quick passing game. When we use the five-step passing attack, it is a possession-type pass. We take the quick five-step drop and throw the ball on rhythm. When we hit the fifth step, the ball comes out. We ask the quarterback to be involved with our pass protection in his pass drops. He does not hold the ball and allow the sack. He gets the ball out.

The seven-step drop comes down to crossing routes and the intermediate game, which shows up on third-down passes. We also throw the deep horizontal stuff from the seven-step drop. Finally, we have a full sprint passing game. We want to break contain and have the option to pass or run the ball. However, we look to throw the ball first. This is important because I do not want the quarterback to sit back in a pocket with the same launch point. I do not like the defense to lock in on where the quarterback will be while throwing the ball. We chance up the passing attack, the launch point, and protections in all these passing schemes.

We have an active screen game. We use it as a rush control pass. In football today, the screen game is tough on defenses. We like the perimeter quick screens. These screens allow you to get the ball out quickly to combat the multiple coverages and rush schemes we see. The key to our multiplicity is to make the plays look the same, but they are different. Inside of all this is sequential football. That is where one play leads to another.

When I went to Miami of Ohio, it was the best experience of my life in college football. My next-door neighbor there was Weeb Ewbank. The head coach at Miami asked me to ask Coach Ewbank if he would speak at our spring coaching clinic. I asked him to speak, and from that, we established a great working relationship. He was retired at that time. He taught me about the West Coast offense.

He introduced me to Paul Brown, who, along with Bill Walsh, invented the West Coast offense in Cincinnati in 1968. Coach Ewbank and Coach Brown were education majors. They were teachers. At that time, I was a young coach and into the X's and O's of football. Coach Brown told me I was missing the main point with the offense. He told me it was not so much the play itself but how you teach it. That is what I am going to talk about tonight.

METHOD OF TEACHING: WHOLE-PART-WHOLE

- *Group installation:* concept overview
- *Position meeting:* detailing
- *Walk-through:* pre-practice
- *Individual:*
  ✓ Fundamental teaching and drills
  ✓ Technique teaching and drills
- *Small group drills:*
  ✓ 1-on-1
  ✓ 3-on-3
  ✓ 3-on-2
- *Large group drills:*
  ✓ 7-on-7

  ✓ Half ball
  ✓ 9-on-7 pass

The first thing we do is group installations. We teach the overview and whole part of the concept. At the University of Louisville, I teach the whole concept to the group. One voice teaches the play. I teach the whole concept and overview in this meeting because it is important for them to understand how all the pieces of the offense fit together.

From there, the meetings go to position meetings. The receiver coach, running back coach, and tight end coach in their position meetings teach the details of the play to their particular positions. They teach the same thing I just taught in more detail related to their positions. When I get into the explanation, you will hear me talk about timing and spacing as a big part of the scheme. The first thing Coach Ewbank taught me was timing plus spacing equals completions. Those elements are two of the equations that make this scheme work.

This is how Coach Brown said to coach the play. We install the whole play as a group. We break up into positions and teach in detail the parts of the play. We go to the practice field, walk through the play with group installation, and run the play against air. I give the quarterback a coverage key so he knows where to go with the ball. One of our graduate assistants acts as an action key for the quarterback. We get our spacing off him, and his reactions tell the quarterback where to throw the ball. For all you education majors in here, you recognize the whole-part-whole teaching method.

After we go through the walk-through, we get into individual periods and work on the fundamentals and technique teaching. That is where we learn what it takes to execute that particular play. We teach break points, protection, and the fine points of the play. The fundamentals and techniques are the things that make the play work.

I am a big John Wooden fan. I read everything I can find by him. He never worried about what the opponent did. He did not care what type of offense or defense they used. He wanted to be fundamentally sound. If they were fundamentally sound and they knew how to execute their offense and defense, they would be successful.

After we work in the individual period, we break into small groups and practice the fundamentals. They work the route against 1-on-1 coverage. They learn how to beat man coverage. We run every route in this scheme expecting man coverage and reacting to zone coverage. You begin the teaching session with man coverage. We do 1-on-1 drills with our receivers, backs, and tight ends to teach them how to beat man coverage. Man coverage is the biggest thing to disrupt the timing in the passing game.

Yet at the same time, man coverage is a big advantage for the quarterback. If the receivers beat man coverage, the results are big plays.

The next small group is 3-on-3. That is an inside pass skeleton drill. It is the three inside linebackers against the tight end, an inside receiver, and the back. This works the core of the read. The 3-on-2 drill is an outside receiver and inside receiver against a coverage scheme of three defenders. It could be a corner, Sam linebacker, and safety or nickel back or some other combination of coverage. In that drill, we always put a checkdown route into the play. We put a manager over the ball to give the quarterback somewhere to check the ball.

The 3-on-3 and 3-on-2 are the places where the quarterback begins to learn to read coverages. It is an awesome drill. We leave the small groups and advance to the large groups. One of the large groups we use is the 7-on-7 skeleton drill. We had a freshman quarterback this year, and we used two other drills that helped his development. These drills helped him become acquainted with the college game. We used a half-ball drill, which included the tight end, receiver, and back with the rush of the defense.

The drill I like is the 9-on-7 drill. The biggest and hardest thing we had to teach a freshman quarterback coming into the college game is how to use the checkdown pass. This drill is what teaches that skill. It is the 3-on-3 drill with the offensive line added. You add the rush and pressure and let the quarterback learn how to operate in the pocket. It teaches him how to work his possession and learn how to use the checkdown. That is the part of the drill I like.

- Team
  - ✓ Normal down pass: coverage
  - ✓ Normal down blitz pickup: pressure/stunt
  - ✓ Nickel down pass: coverage and twist
  - ✓ Nickel down blitz pickup: pressure/stunts
- Team Situational Football
  - ✓ Coming out
  - ✓ Red zone (overtime)/goal line/two-point play
  - ✓ Two minute/desperation

The next aspect of teaching the play is to take it to the team. Coach Charlie Strong does a beautiful job of setting up our practice schedule because it plays into exactly what we need. We have a normal down period going against coverages. The quarterback has to learn how to function and manage in the pocket. He has to learn how to push and slide in the pocket. The push in the pocket means to step up in the pocket. When the quarterback slides and moves in the pocket, he creates protection and throwing lanes in the defense. That is where the success of the quarterback comes from.

When we talk about a normal down situation, it is not a base defense. We use twists and blitzes on the defense. They twist, shout, and make noise along with the pressure. Normal down for us in today's football means fire-zone blitzing. There used to be fire-zone blitz with the secondary playing cover 3 behind it. The defense graduated to fire zones with cover 2 coverages, and today, they use it with man-free coverage. We must be good at beating pressure. We cover all the normal down passing on Tuesdays. We work normal down coverages, blitz pickups, pressure packages, and 7-on-7.

When our quarterback walks off the field on Tuesday, he has seen every situation that he will face during the game. We move from there into situational downs and distances. Situational downs to us are nickel and dime packages, coming out, red zone, overtimes, two-minute offense, desperation, and things of that nature.

I talked about how we teach it, how it began, and now I am going to give you the philosophy behind the play. When I was a young coach, I loved pass plays. I never met one I did not like. However, I did not get the play because I did not understand this aspect of it. Horizontal bracketing, vertical bracketing, and the checkdown are the West Coast passing game.

The first principle is vertical bracketing (Diagram #1). When Coach Ewbank showed me this at Miami, I could not believe I had never seen it. You take one single defender and attack his area of responsibility. If the defender is a middle hook player, we put a receiver under him and one on top of him. The receiver on top leverages the defender on top and to the inside. The underneath receiver leverages the defender underneath and to the outside.

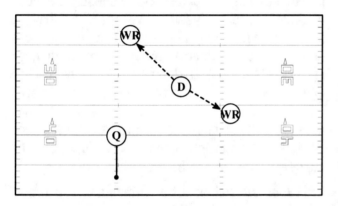

Diagram #1. Vertical Bracketing

We force the defender to make a decision of who to cover. I tell the quarterback, if you have ever played keep-away, you can play quarterback. Whichever receiver the defender covers, the quarterback throws to the other receiver. The thing the receivers have to understand is where they have to be and how to release on the defenders. The inside receiver has to release on top of and inside of the defender. The underneath receiver has to cross the face of the defender and sit down to the outside.

It becomes a simple game from there. It is pitch and catch. If the defender plays low, the quarterback throws high, and if he plays high, he throws low. It is not rocket science. It is simple, but the common sense principles of that concept are what get away from us. I like to watch teams and see what they do. What I see is teams attack coverage instead of individual players.

The next thing is horizontal bracketing (Diagram #2). The example is the same hook zone defender. Instead of going high/low, we set up inside and

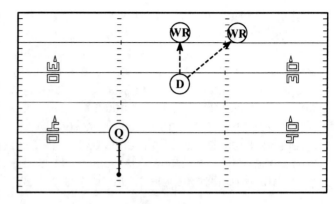

Diagram #2. Horizontal Bracketing

outside the defender. We force the defender to make a decision in his area of responsibility. If the defender plays the outside receiver, the ball goes to the inside receiver. The opposite occurs if the defender plays inside. It is not rocket science. It is common sense.

You have to put the aspect of timing with the throws. The quarterback has to deliver the ball on time. He has to throw the ball on time to the reference point of the play. You want to take advantage of the spacing and the defender as well as maximizing protection.

The checkdown is the hardest thing we teach (Diagram #3). However, it is also common sense. They pay defensive coaches to stop these types of things. That is where the zone blitzes come into play. They want to add defenders into their schemes. If we run the vertical bracketing scheme, the defense adds into its scheme. The read defender takes the low receiver, and the next adjacent defender takes the high receiver. The defense calls this adjustment an override. We take the third receiver, bracket him on the adjacent defender, and read him.

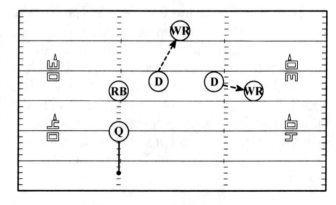

Diagram #3. Checkdown

When I sat down with Coach Ewbank, he asked me if I knew what K.I.S.S. meant. I said to him, "Keep it simple, stupid." He said it meant "Keep it simple and sound." He told me in this scheme, the defense has one defender and the offense has two receivers. That means we win. That is why you have to teach your receivers how to use spacing and show up on time.

Defensive coaches are smart. If the defense adds a defender, we add another receiver. If they have two defenders and we have three receivers, we still win. The checkdown pattern is tremendously important. It is important that the checkdown pattern be in close proximity to the ball. If the quarterback has five or six angry men coming after him, he has to know where the checkdown is. The obvious place for the checkdown is the place where we snapped the ball. The quarterback does not have to search for his man. He knows where his man is.

As the quarterback pushes up in the pocket, the checkdown pattern wants to get into the lanes of the quarterback's vision. If the quarterback cannot find a receiver, he can drop the ball off to the checkdown.

There are some misconceptions about the West Coast offense. Everyone thinks it is a dink-and-dunk ball control offense. There is that aspect of the offense. However, I have run this offense for 31 years, and the West Coast offense has a big ball on every play. You find those balls in what we call alerts. There is an alert on every play.

Alerts-Opportunity Ball

- *Technique alert:* big ball opportunity created by defender's technique
- *Coverage alert:* big ball opportunity created by coverage
- *Box alert:* free access throw created by structure and coverage

I will give you an example of the alerts, and we will start to look at the plays in a moment. If the quarterback comes to the line of scrimmage and reads bump coverage on a receiver, we can automatically signal to the receiver and send him on a go route. The quarterback gives the signal and the receiver knows it is the quarterback and him. You have to take the challenge. If the defense presses and bumps the wide receivers, you have to take the shot at the deep ball. If you do not, you play into the hands of the defense.

We spend time working on the fade. We work on executing the techniques. We work on walling off the defender, stacking him, and creating the leverage. In addition, we work hard on throwing the back shoulder fade.

The next alert is the coverage alert. The coverage alert we like is quarter coverage. We try to bait the safety into playing his area of responsibility and throw the post over the top of him. We have alerts for man coverage. We build concepts that come with a backside tag. We run route combinations to the field with a tag for the backside if we get man coverage into that area. That allows us to take advantage of a matchup we think we can win. An example would be a corner route.

The box alert is the last one. We run this from 3x1 and 2x2 formations. These are the 1-on-1 alerts. This is a free throw in a 1-on-1 with a corner and a receiver. This gives the quarterback a chance to read the entire field and take advantage of what the defense gives him. That is why this attack works so well. You should be able to execute no matter what the coverage is.

KEY ELEMENTS OF THE PASSING ATTACK

- *Timing*—quarterback's footwork
- *Spacing*—vertical or horizontal bracketing
- *Match-up*—attacking a single defender's area of responsibility with vertical or horizontal bracketing:
  - ✓ Creating match-ups better versus lesser
- *Man/zone conversion*—run versus man:
  - ✓ Sit in the voids zone
  - ✓ Rule: run every route expecting "man" and react to zone

Timing in the play is the quarterback's footwork. He is responsible for protection when we cannot depend on the five big linemen to protect him. He has to get the ball out on time. He has to learn how to sit and push up in the pocket. If he does that, he creates passing lanes. I love isolation routes where we match lesser defenders on better receivers. We try to get wide receivers on linebackers.

The man/zone conversion is important. Against man coverage, the receivers stay on the move and run. Against zone, they want to sit down in the windows of the zones.

KEY EQUATIONS

- *Timing:* protection
- *Timing and spacing:* completions
- *Timing and ball placement:* YAC (yards after catch)

The last point of ball placement leads to more yardage. If the quarterback can lead the receiver away from the defender, we can take a five-yard pass and turn it into a big play.

I am going to show you some of our three-step passes. This play comes from a 3x1 formation, which is user friendly for any coverage. We call the play dog/signal (Diagram #4). It is a right formation, and the dog call is the field concept. The signal call goes to the single receiver. The F1-receiver (outside field) takes an outside release and runs a go route. He must take a protection release and may never go inside. He runs this against cloud rolls by the corners or cover 2 rolls. He has to flush the corner, challenge the safety, and flush the coverage vertically.

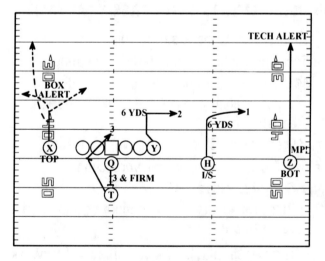

Diagram #4. Dog/Signal

The F2-receiver (second field) runs a six-yard speed-out route. The F3-receiver (third field) takes

the best possible release based on how the defense covers him. He runs a stick route, which is a six-yard out route. He walls off the C gap, pushes vertical to six yards, breaks out, and runs. The tailback has a check protection responsibility and releases. If there is no blitz, he runs a checkdown over the ball. The B1-receiver (outside boundary) receiver gets his route from a quarterback signal. This is a box alert signal. He can run a lion, lightning, Omaha, Frisco, or fade-go route. The lion is a three-step slant, lightning is a six-yard hitch, Omaha is a six-yard out, and Frisco is a five-step stop.

With a young quarterback, we called the signal route at the beginning of the season. As the season went by, the quarterback called some of them. We can adjust the fade route and call a fade back. The receiver runs the fade. On the quarterback's third step, he delivers the ball to the fade receiver's back shoulder. It does not matter what coverage we get—we are driving the bus.

The backside linebacker's movement gives the quarterback an insight as to the type of coverage he will see. If the linebacker retreats off the line of scrimmage, it is zone coverage of some kind. If he moves laterally, it is some kind of man coverage. If he moves forward, it is a blitz. When we see the blitz coming, we like to throw into the void created by the blitzing linebacker.

We teach the play by evaluating the backside linebacker to get a tip of the coverage. If he is in the box or tight to the box with the corner off, we think the B1-receiver is where we can to go with the ball. On the third step, the quarterback throws the hitch or speed-out to the backside.

If we see a cloud or any type of 2-on-1 to the B1-receiver, we go to the field patterns. If he goes to the field, the quarterback looks at the flat defender. If he flashes outside, the quarterback throws to the F3-receiver. If the flat defender hangs and waits for the tight end, he throws to F2-receiver. If the area is muddy or our quarterback cannot find a receiver, he sets his feet and goes to the checkdown to the tailback. I tell him he has to see the receiver before he can throw.

I have a section in my position manual of rules to live by. As of last count, there were 52 rules in the manual. In that manual are 52 rules that can help the quarterback. One of those rules deals with full field reads. If the quarterback chooses to work to the field, he stays to the field. He reads one, two, three, and the ball comes out. If he cannot find anything through his third choice, he throws the ball away.

Our offensive formations are 2x1, 2x2, 3x1, or 3x2. In addition, we declare the field open or closed. If there is a safety in the middle of the field, it is closed. If there is no safety in the middle, it is open. That is how we teach the offense to the players and the quarterback.

I want to show you some of our coverage beaters. The first one is a double formation. It has the strength to the left or into the boundary. We double call the play, which gives a concept of patterns to each side. The call is Omaha/dragon. We have the combination of routes to the left and a combination of routes to the right. The sides correspond to the middle of the field being open or closed. If the middle is open, we work the boundary or Omaha combinations. If the middle is closed, we work the dragon combinations. If the coverage is cover 2, we work the boundary combinations.

I want to go on to a 2x2 set. This play is Omaha/dragon (Diagram #5). This a left formation, so the Omaha combination goes to the left and the dragon goes to the right. The dragon is the F1-receiver running a slant pattern or a speed-out. If he gets press coverage, he converts the pattern to a go. The F2-receiver in the dragon runs an arrow route. The arrow route aims at a point three yards on the boundary, but we want to settle at the top of the numbers. This pattern gains depth as he runs to the boundary. The tailback has check protection and gets out on a box route. The Omaha is the B2-receiver running the stick route and the B1-receiver running a speed-out speeding back at four to six yards or converting to a go against press or man coverage.

The defender we want to isolate is the curl/flat defender. The good thing about three-step football is the quarterback can make the decisions before the ball snaps. However, he has to read after the pre-snap read for the disguised secondary. The quarterback reads the coverage from the outside going to the inside. If we read cover 2 or cloud coverage, the outside receivers run go routes. The corner becomes the flat defender and the player the quarterback reads.

If the corner drifts out with the go route, the quarterback throws the arrow route going to the flat. If the corner rolls hard to the flat, the quarterback throws the ball into the hole up the sideline to the outside receiver. If the play gets muddy for the quarterback, he has the checkdown over the ball.

When the quarterback chooses a side to work, we want the shortest and surest routes. In the case of a young quarterback, those throws are to the boundary.

Teams will play split coverages. They will play a cloud look to the boundary and a quarter look into the field. With this offense, it does not matter which side the quarterback chooses; it works both ways. The quarterback does not use a full field read.

This next concept is a dragon/thunder combination (Diagram #6). This is a 2x2 formation with the strength left or into the boundary. The strength is our tight end side. That is the dragon side of the pattern. The B1-receiver runs the three-step slant to the inside. The B2-receiver runs the arrow route to the sideline. The tailback has the check protection/checkdown route over the ball. The fieldside is the thunder side of the combination. The F1-receiver runs an under route. He pushes vertical and comes inside across at a depth of six yards.

The F2-receiver runs a shave route. There is no set depth or steps to the pattern. The receiver

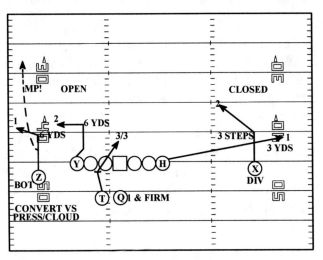

Diagram #5. Omaha/Dragon

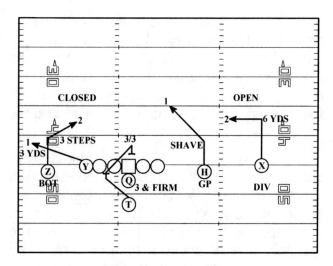

Diagram #6. Dragon/Thunder

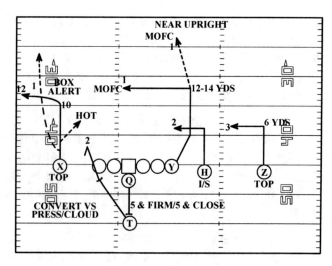

Diagram #7. Crash

shaves through the inside shoulder of the defender and keeps a high angle. His job is to stay away from the curl/flat defender. The curl/flat defender is generally a walkaway linebacker to his side. He wants to find the void in the defense.

The F2-receiver runs a shave route. He drives through the inside shoulder of the hook defender and tries to drag him with him. He wants to open up the inside for the under route. If the hook defender releases him and rallies to the "under" route coming into his area, the F2-receiver settles and stops in the seam in the middle. The dragon side is the closed side and the thunder side is the open side. We work cover 2 to the thunder concept. We work cover 3 to the dragon concept.

I want to show you a five-step passing play. This is a concept I really like. This is one of the staples in the five-step passing game. We build the concept in a 3x1 set to beat multiple coverages. The play call is crash (Diagram #7). When we call a crash concept, the back protection goes to the one receiver side. The B1 or X-receiver runs a speed-out at 12 yards. He is the hot receiver. In the diagram, the pattern is a slant. According to the scouting report, it could be a hitch depending on how they skip out of their blitz. The term skip means how the defense drops the defensive end off the line of scrimmage in the zone blitz scheme. If he gets any kind of press or bump coverage, he turns his pattern into a go.

To the fieldside, we run a crash combination. The F1-receiver runs an under route at six yards. He pushes vertical up the field, separates from the

corner, and settles. His job is to key the walkout defender. If the defender works toward him, he crosses his face. If the defender is inside and walling off the F2-receiver, he sits down and stays away from the walkout defender. We do not want him in his proximity.

The F2-receiver runs an under or crash route and stays on the move. If the Mike linebacker rallies to him, he crosses his face and keeps on the move. The F3-receiver runs the seam down the middle of the field. He makes that decision on whether the middle is open or closed. He gets a pre-snap read but must make the decision when he reaches 12 yards deep. He runs 2 yards inside the hash mark. If the middle is open, he continues down the seam, aiming for the near upright of the goal post. If there is a safety in the middle of the field, he curls away from the Mike linebacker, trying to find a lane for the quarterback.

The tailback has one job. He has a check protection responsibility. If he gets out, he runs a break route, which means he sits down outside the Will linebacker. This is one of the plays we can use a multiple tag for with a backside receiver. If the quarterback is confused with the coverage, he goes to the key on the Mike linebacker. He plays keep-away with the Mike linebacker. If the Mike takes the F2-receiver, he has the F3-receiver. He works high/low off the Mike linebacker to the checkdown. However, on this play, the checkdown is not over the ball.

We use the spin/curl combination, and it has been good for us (Diagram #8). This is a 2x2 formation

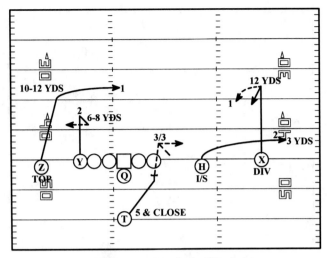

Diagram #8. Spin/Curl

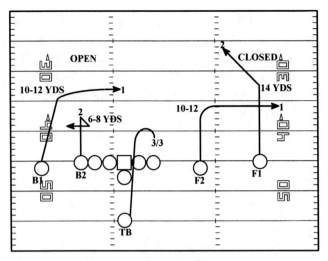

Diagram #9. Spin/Hornet

with the tight end to the boundary. The B1-receiver runs a 12-yard quick dig. He wants to get his pattern into the hash mark at 12 yards. The B2-receiver runs a work route. He releases inside and keys the inside linebacker. If the linebacker drops for depth under the dig route, he works to six yards and hooks up. If the linebacker comes to him and attaches to him, he does a snag route and works outside. That opens up the dig over the top.

On the spin route, the key defender is the first inside linebacker. The spin concept is the open middle option for the quarterback. The checkdown pattern is over the ball. If the second linebacker tries to get involved to the spinside, the checkdown is open.

To the field, we run the curl combination. The F1-receiver runs the 12-yard curl pattern, coming back to 10 yards. We want him to find the window depending on the drop of the curl/flat defender. The F2-receiver runs the arrow pattern. This is the closed combination side. The key defender is the curl/flat defender.

When we get into our 2x2 formation, we see a lot of quarter coverage across the board and cover 2. We run the spin/hornet combination against that type of defense (Diagram #9). We run the spin combination to the boundary side. On the fieldside, we run a hornet combination. The F1-receiver runs a seven-step post route. The F2-receiver runs an out at 10 to 12 yards. The key on this play is the field safety in the quarter cover. We want to bait the safety to go for the out pattern. If the safety attacks the F2-receiver on the out pattern, we throw the post behind him.

The out is the first choice, the post is the second choice, and the checkdown is the third choice.

We have another boundary concept we use with the curl combination. We call this smack/curl (Diagram #10). The curl combination to the field is the same. To the boundary, we run the smash combination. We worked on the linebacker in the spin concept; this concept works on the corner. We want to isolate the corner.

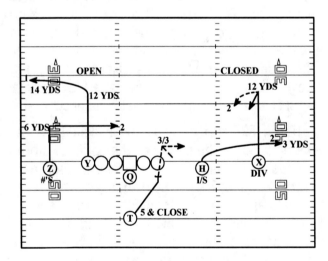

Diagram #10. Smash/Curl

The checkdown pattern in the middle keeps the Mike linebacker from cheating outside on the under route. We work to the out first and the under second.

I put this one in because I think four verticals is a good concept, but you must have some multiplicity to run it. This is our switch/stop concept off the four verticals scheme (Diagram #11). This comes from a 3x1 set. The F1-receiver runs a stop route at 14 yards. That converts to our go route versus cloud coverage. If the coverage has two high safeties, the F2-receiver stays down the middle of the field. If there is one high safety, he gets to his landmark at two yards outside the opposite hash mark.

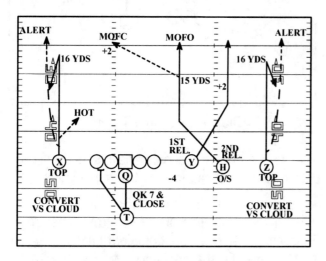

Diagram #11. Switch/Stop

The F3-receiver switch-releases with the F2-receiver and runs the seam route two yards outside the hash mark. The tailback runs his check protection and gets out into the box. The B1-receiver has the same route as the outside receiver to the other side. He runs a 14-yard stop pattern. Against a cover 2 or cloud roll, this becomes a four-vertical route. This pattern is good against quarter coverage.

If the F2-receiver finds the middle open, he runs right down the middle of the uprights on the goal post. The quarterback can make the boundary safety dance with his eyes. We make him stay to the field and throw to the boundary or draw him to the boundary and throw to the field. You teach the quarterback to use his eyes as a weapon. The tailback has an option route over the ball.

The last one is probably my favorite. We call this play lefty (Diagram #12). The F1-receiver runs a seven-step speed post with an aiming point at the near upright of the goal post. The F2-receiver runs a diagonal route through the middle of the field. If there are two high safeties, he runs at the boundary safety's alignment. If there is one high safety, he runs through the safeties inside shoulder. The

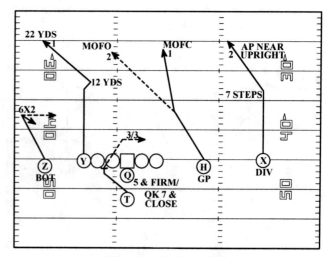

Diagram #12. Lefty

B1-receiver runs a wide departed hitch. He is six yards deep and two yards from the sideline. If there is a cloud or press coverage, he works back inside.

The B2-receiver runs a 12-yard corner with an aiming point at 22 yards on the sideline. If the hitch route is open, we take it right now. However, he is not the primary receiver. We are looking for a deep completion. If the coverage is cover 2, we are going after the boundary safety. The B2-receiver runs the corner route and stays high and deep. The F2-receiver has a big job. He has to win his release off the walkout linebacker and get over the top of the Mike linebacker.

After he gets into the middle of the field, he has to know whether it is open or closed. If it is open, he wants to replace the boundary safety. If the safety is on the hash mark, he runs at him and threatens him. If the safety is off the hash, the receiver replaces him. If the middle of the field is closed, the receiver stays down the middle of the field. He has to run through the inside shoulder of the middle safety. His job is to make the middle safety take him.

If the middle is open, the boundary safety is the key. The quarterback has the corner route as his first choice and the middle post as his second choice depending on what the safety does. If the field is closed, the quarterback throws to the F2-receiver as his first choice or the F1-receiver as his second choice.

I am out of time. Thank you for your attention.

DEFENDING THE SPREAD OFFENSE

The Ohio State University

Thank you. It is a pleasure to be back in this area. It was funny when Coach Meyer told me that I did not have a recruiting area in Ohio. He told me my recruiting area was North Carolina, South Carolina, and Georgia. I thought, "Here we go again, battling the SEC and the ACC for all the athletes." I am very fortunate to be a part of the staff at Ohio State. It is a great staff. It is fun to walk into the defensive room every day and see Luke Fickell and Mike Vrabel. It is great to bounce ideas off those coaches. Luke and I went through the same thing last year as interim head coaches, and Mike has three Super Bowl rings.

It is fun to go in there and talk football every day. We feel like we have many good things going on at Ohio State. What I want to do today is give you some insight into what we look for in a high school athlete. I also want to talk about some of the drill work we use to get players ready to play. I am going to coach the defensive backs at Ohio State and focus on the safeties. We will have a corners coach, and I will tie it all together there.

I want to talk to you about defensive back philosophy and fundamentals. However, I want to start talking about what we look for in athletes at Ohio State. I always talk about core values. That is one of Coach Meyer's big things. The core values are non-negotiable at Ohio State. Either a player has these cores values, or he does not play at Ohio State. Coach Meyer talks to the entire team about core values, and we talk to the individual players about them in our position meetings.

When I go into a high school and talk to the head coach about a prospect, I will ask some frank questions about the player. I will ask the coach if he smokes marijuana, whether he smokes dope, or uses any kind of drugs. We do not want a dope smoker in our program, and I will ask the coach if he

does. There are certain things I am going to ask, and I am going to give you several of them right now.

CORE VALUES

- Competitive excellence
- Communication
- Student of the game
- Like the game (will attack)
- Production

I want to know if he will compete. You will know when I come into your office what I am going to ask. Is he a *competitor*? As a defensive back, will he fight every day to be the best defensive back he can be? Will he fight in the classroom? I talk about grinders in the classroom. The player does not have to be a 3.0 GPA student in the classroom. He can be a 2.4 or 2.3, but he grinds every day in the classroom. He hangs in there and works with his teachers trying to get it done. I have seen a bunch of those types of players, and I love them. I was that kind of student, too.

We talk about competitive excellence at Ohio State. We want to know if the player has the tools to win when we call his number. We want to know if the defensive back has the tools to stop the best receiver on the opponent's team in a critical situation. Does he have the tools and competitive excellence to go make the play and win the game?

We want to find out if we have a competitor. Does he like the war? Does he like the preparation it takes to get into the war? We want a competitor who will accept the challenge of playing in the intensity of the game.

We want a player who is a *communicator*. When a player comes to junior day, if I have not had any previous relationship with the player, I probably will not know much about him. Even though I may have watched high school tape, I will not know much about him. However, I am going to sit down and talk to him. I want to sit down and see if he will talk to me. I want to see if he will look me in the eye and communicate with me or will he hang his head and mumble.

There is one thing I know about defensive backs. If they cannot communicate, the other team's band is going to play after the score. It is essential for the defensive backs and linebackers to talk and communicate on every down. Those players have to communicate and have some personality.

The other aspect of communication is the player talking to his teachers in the classroom. If a player makes a bad grade on a test or paper, he has to immediately talk to the teacher and get the situation corrected. They have to get the classroom going in the right direction. They cannot wait until the end of a semester to try to correct a problem. These players have to take the initiative and verbally get things done. I think this is important in the core values of a person.

We look for players who are *students of the game*. How many of you coaches are in your school all day? If you are in your school all day, you get the chance to see your players each day. You have the chance to work with their class schedules. However, we have boundaries with respect to the amount of time we can spend with our players. If a player does not come in on his own to study the game, it will be hard for him to be successful.

We get our players for 20 hours a week. In the off-season, we get them for eight hours a week. In most cases, the strength coach wants them for those eight hours. When does the player have time to watch game film, technique tapes, cut-ups of his position, and related films? He must come in on his own and be a student of the game. If he treats preparation as his high priority, he will be successful. If he gets himself ready to play, that will be the most important thing he can do as a football player. He can do that before he steps on the field.

The day of the player showing up and dominating is over. As you go to the higher levels of our sport, many players can play the game. The edge for the player is to be a student of the game and be prepared to handle the teaching involved with the game.

We look for players who *actually like the game.* I have used this for the last 15 years of my coaching career. In the game of football, the ball is the issue. I want one player on defense who understands that the ball is the issue. He is the player who finds a way to be around the football. If they throw it or run, it, he is around the ball. He is breaking up passes or intercepting them in the secondary. He makes tackles at the point of attack. He attacks the ball.

When I talk about defensive backs, I do not simply mean safeties. I am talking about the corners also. I want corners who will attack the ball. I am not one of those coaches who says corners do not tackle.

At the defensive back, we must have players who are productive players. As a defensive coach, we grade our players. A player may play only eight plays out of 65 plays on the tape. We want to know what he did on those eight plays. We want to know if he affected the game in the eight plays. If he was in a position to make a play, did he make it or not? You must know who is making plays for you. If a player plays 30 plays, he must do something. He may not make any mistakes in assignment, but if he is not making plays that affect the game, he is not productive.

We are in the off-season program right now. We are looking at the players in that program. We are in an evaluation-friendly profession. We have a deal in the off-season called "win or lose." The deal is whether the player was whipped or not. There are eight drills with points assigned to each one. There are not degrees of defeat. Were you whipped or not? We evaluate the drills and post the results. One player goes against another player. You cannot argue the results because we arrive at the results by a point total.

We can make this thing more than it is. We can find out who will compete, fight, and attack. You must put some form of measurability on them to declare a winner. You can measure production. If you can get a player on your campus and in your program who does not know his statistics, I do not want him in my room. I want the players who know how many yards they ran for or how many interceptions they had. They can tell you and are proud of the fact. We want these qualities in the players we recruit.

I want to get into some drills. There are coaches who like X's and O's, but I am a fundamental coach. You can put X's and O's anywhere on the paper. If you do not play with fundamentals, none of the X's and O's in the game matter. I am not a guru with all the answers. I am a fundamental coach.

We talked about this in our defensive meeting yesterday. What is the most important thing a defensive football player has to do? If you listen to all the talking heads on ESPN and the numerous sports shows, they have all the answers. The most important thing in defensive football is tackling. If you cannot tackle, you cannot play defense. You have to teach tackling, and you have to start teaching it now. You have to teach it every day. You can practice tackling every day without even hitting the players. Tackling is about body position and putting yourself in good position to tackle.

I am going through some drills that will help you teach young men to play. We do a drill we call "speed to power tackling" (Diagram #1). This drill is relative to where the defensive backs play. The players align at the hash marks five yards apart on a yard line, and the coach is at the numbers. The coach starts the drill with a movement. The players sprint toward the coach to get in position. The sprint part of the drill we call speed.

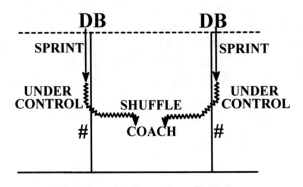

Diagram #1. Speed to Power

The coach makes another move that signals the players to come under control. The players come under control, gather their feet, and get into a fundamental football position. We call this the power stage of the drill. In the power stage, you sink the hips, get all the cheats in the ground, and start shimming the feet. You get the chest over the knees and knees over the toes. That puts you into a position to tackle.

The coach makes the final move with his hands, and the players shuffle into him from each side. They do not cross their feet, and they keep their shoulders square to the coach. You can do this drill every day you have your players. It does not require any equipment.

We conduct this tackling drill because the defensive backs must master it. This is an open field tackling drill (Diagram #2). We place the cones to represent a running back. The defensive back uses the speed and power drill to get into position on the running back. When we do this tackling drill, we look for the fundamentals of tackling. We do not want them to cross over with their feet as they come under control. We do not want the feet to come out of the ground very far. We want to keep the pads square on the ballcarrier. A good running back will attack the leverage of the tackler when he gets his feet out of the ground or crosses over with them. The running back will take advantage of that and break outside.

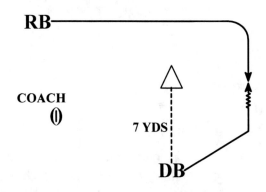

Diagram #2. Open Field Tackling

The tackler mirrors the speed of the running back. The tackler uses the speed stage of the drill when the ballcarrier is using speed. When the ballcarrier slows his speed to make a move on the tackler, that is the time the tackler comes to balance and gets his pads square with the ballcarrier.

The tackler wants to run fast in the speed stage. He comes to balance and gets under control in the power stage. To make the tackle, he must have his pads square with the ballcarrier. He wants to keep his feet close to the ground and squeeze the ballcarrier. On a field turf field, you should see the small rubber pellets coming out of the ground from the shimming of the tackler's feet.

In an open field tackle, the tackler does not want to get his chest or shoulders too far over the knees. The tackler in the open field wants to stay higher and show his chest. I want the tackler to be vertical in his approach to the ballcarrier.

If a linebacker is playing downhill and filling into his fit, his shoulder and lean can be more forward and more bent over the knees. That is because the linebacker works in a tighter space with more traffic. It is the opposite for the defensive back. He tackles in space and must be able to move from side to side. He cannot do that with his weight too forward.

The next thing we talk about with the defensive backs is leverage. Defensive backs have to get off blocks and make tackles. They have to understand leverage and how to keep it. Leverage plays a role in the running game as well as the passing game. The defensive back has to know his run fit is the running game. We work block escape and getting off blocks every day in practice.

DEVELOPMENT DRILLS

- Tackling
- Block escape
- Backpedal
- Transition
- Play the ball in the air

At the beginning of practice, we do drills called development drills. The development drills are drills we work on daily. In the block escape drill, it is all right to rep the hand placement and pad level in a fit or dummy drill. You have to learn that first. We do those drills at the beginning of practice. We work them against a one-man sled. We work on the punch, lock out, shed, and tackle. The defensive back punches the one-man sled and gets his hand placement on the dummy. He locks out and lifts the sled as the second part of the drill. He disengages and makes his rip move to the outside of the sled and performs a form tackle on another player.

However, you must do these drills live at full speed to learn how to play blocks. You must do live stalk drills against the receivers. In the stalk drill, the defensive back must have his hands up and into the receiver's chest (Diagram #3). We want the thumbs up and the hands inside the receiver's hands. We

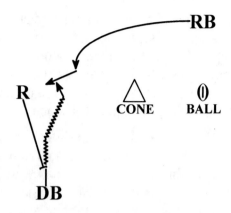

Diagram #3. Stalk Drill

want to press the receiver away by extending the arms. In a dummy drill with a shield, the defensive back does not get to pull the receiver in a violent manner. In the live drill, the defensive back pulls the receiver across his body in the opposite direction that he wants to go. The back wants to disengage from the receiver by taking him the opposite way the defender wants to go.

The defensive back has to engage the receiver, stun him with a punch, violently disengage by throwing him across, and make the tackle on the ballcarrier. When we do this drill, the live part of the drill is the disengagement of the block followed by a form tackle at the end.

The low shed drill simulates the beginning of a play (Diagram #4). We align three small bags on the ground. The defensive back steps over the bags and gets ready to take on the blocker. We tell them to dip and rip. You need a dummy holder with a pad so the defender can dip and rip through the outside of the blocker. After he gets past the blocker, he has to square back up to prepare for the tackle.

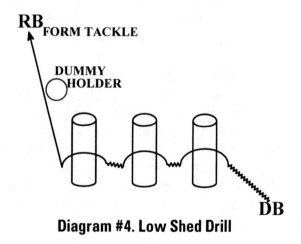

Diagram #4. Low Shed Drill

The situation the defensive back can encounter is an offensive tackle as a lead blocker with the running back eight yards behind him. If the defensive back takes on the offensive lineman, it is like an elephant taking on a mouse. If the defensive back uses the dip and rip technique, the offensive lineman will never block him. They cannot get that low to block the defensive back. The defensive back gets his pads under the pads of the blocker, gets low, plays up, and squares his shoulders.

The finish to this drill is the tackle. There are two ways to finish the drill. You can strike, wrap up, and drive the ballcarrier back, or you can do the same thing and take the ballcarrier to the ground. The object of the drill is to dip and rip under the blocker instead engaging the blocker, who outweighs him by 150 pounds.

The defensive back has to make plays out of his transition (Diagram #5). We started this last Thursday in our off-season program. This skill is a defensive back breaking into coverage with a coverage drop. We hand the ball off, and the defensive back has to transition from his drop into an attack mode and make the tackle. The problem the defensive back has is there is space on either side of the ballcarrier.

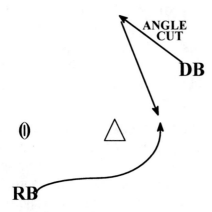

Diagram #5. Transition Drill

He has to make a tackle in space. The first thing he has to do is get his chest out and not get top heavy with his posture. He has to pin a hip of the ballcarrier. He cannot square up on the belt buckle of the ballcarrier. If he does that, he gives the ballcarrier two ways to go. We want to give the ballcarrier one way to go. To do that, the defensive back has to pin a hip of the ballcarrier.

To pin a hip means the defensive back attacks with outside or inside leverage and forces the ballcarrier to go only one way. When the defender does that, he has to know where his help is. If he has the rest of the defense pursuing from the inside, the defensive back pins the outside hip of the ballcarrier. That sends the ballcarrier back into the pursuit. If the ballcarrier is too far away from the pursuit and close to the sideline, the defensive back pins in the inside hip and makes the ballcarrier break to the sideline. That way, the defender uses the sideline as the pursuit and drives the ballcarrier out-of-bounds.

The transition drill is the same drill we did in beginning, except the ballcarrier can cut both ways. We do not take the ballcarriers to the ground, so there is no one being hurt. You can do this drill every day. You can do this drill in a gym. The defensive back has to close the ground between him and the ballcarrier as quickly as he can. In the drill, the defensive back wants to get under control, pin the hip, shuffle the feet, and squeeze the ballcarrier. As the ballcarrier breaks, the shuffle is to get the tackler's shoulder square.

The defensive back wants to shuffle the feet into the tackle. If he crosses over with his feet, there are no power angles left in his knees and ankles. If he crosses over with his feet, he has lost the ability to make a play if the ballcarrier breaks the opposite direction.

The tackler can put his head across the ballcarrier once he makes his final break and attempts to get by him that way. Until that time, the tackler wants to stay square with the ballcarrier. That includes the speed part of the drill. As the tackler closes the distance between the ballcarrier and him, he keeps the shoulders as square as possible. If the ballcarrier tries to cut back on the tackler, he can press him immediately and make the tackle.

If the tackler shuffles and the ballcarrier tries to cut back, the defender can plant his outside foot in the ground and attack him. If the tackler crosses over, he cannot make the tackle on a cutback run. Spend time getting your players into positions they will encounter in a game. Do it with a number of different drills teaching the same things. You have to practice those positions.

When you teach players to backpedal, you must teach safeties as well as corners. When we talk about backpedal, we tell our players that the transition from backpedal to a forward move on the ball is what leads to their chance to play at the next level. If they want to make some money, they must learn this skill. The difference between the players who make it in pro ball and the ones who do not is the transition.

I am a two-step coach. We have a plant step and a drive step. When we backpedal, we want the feet brushing the ground. We want them close to the ground and not off it. If the defensive back wants to break to the left, he plants his right foot. He wants that foot planted at a 45-degree angle to the inside. That allows his hips to open to the left. He gets his left foot on the ground and breaks at a 45-degree angle. There are seven cleats on the bottom of the average football shoe. When he plants his foot, we want all seven studs in the ground. He cannot be on his toe. We say that every day. We want all seven cleats in the ground.

The plant foot is not outside the butt cheek of the defensive back. He has to keep that foot under him. He does not want his weight going backward. He wants it on the plant foot and transferred to the drive foot immediately. The drive foot has to go to the target. We want our defensive back to do that in the mirror at night when they are home. The movement is not that complicated, but it requires repetition to make it second nature.

The defensive back cannot think about his footwork when he tries to cover a receiver. It has to be ingrained and second nature. We rep the movement so it becomes second nature and something the defensive back does not have to think about as he transitions on a break. When we transition from backpedaling to the drive, we want the drive foot in front of the body, not under it. If it is under the body, the defensive back has lost a step. We want a positive step to the target.

We teach the plant and drive steps in a W drill (Diagram #6). We work the drill off the sideline. The defensive back starts facing the coach at the sidelines. On movement, he backpedals down the yard line. When he reaches the bottom of the numbers, he transitions and drives back to the sideline at a 45-degree angle. When he reaches the

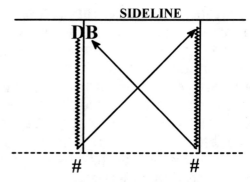

Diagram #6. W Drill

sideline, he backpedals up that line until he hits the bottom of the numbers. He plants and transitions back to his starting point. When they hit the line, they backpedal again and repeat the drill.

If the defensive back has to gather himself as he transitions, his weight is too far back in his backpedal. The transitions of the weight should not cause the defensive back to stop his momentum before he changes direction. His transition should be constant and fluid. The second thing they have to do is keep their eyes up. You cannot let the defensive back drop his eyes to look at his feet. The eyes of a defensive back control everything he does. You can do this drill anywhere. You can do it in the gym or on the grass.

You have to give defensive backs tools to put in his toolbox. The angle cut is one of those tools. One of the things any defensive player has to learn is to keep his shoulders square. If the defender can play with his shoulders square, he can go in a number of different directions.

In the last two weeks, I discussed the technique of bailing out of coverage for the defensive back. If a defensive back is in press coverage, he sometimes bails out of that coverage. That means he opens his hips and runs out of the coverage. When the receiver breaks off the line of scrimmage running vertical, he can break in any number of directions. If the defensive back opens his hips on the bail out, he can only be efficient on the inside cut. He cannot stop the speed-out or the comeback to the outside.

As long as the defensive back stays square, he can play both outside and inside on breaking patterns. The technique of playing defensive back is trying to stay square as long as possible. The defensive back cannot stay square if the receiver is going to run by him. In that case, he has to open his hips and run.

When we talk though this part, I want to talk about angle cuts. If the safety has a quarter read from the #2 receiver to the #1 receiver, he has to stay square. If the #2 receiver runs to the flat and the safety turns his shoulders to the flat, he gets beat on the post cut of the #1 receiver. If the safety can angle cut and keep his shoulders square, he can play the entire route combination. This skill is to angle cut and transition to keep the shoulders square.

In the footwork of the defensive back, we want to be efficient with every angle or move we make. When you teach footwork drills, you cannot go at full speed from the start. You must slow down the drill and let the players get comfortable with what they are doing.

An important thing for the defensive back to do is to be able to control his backpedal. Some backs have only one speed in backpedaling. They go as fast as they can. If they try to slow down, they are too slow. The ability to control the speed is a plus, especially deep into the field. When a defensive back can control his speed, he can speed up or slow down, and nothing changes with the upper body. It all has to do with controlling the revolutions in the feet.

While backpedaling, the defensive back eventually has to turn and run (Diagram #7). We teach this on a line. We backpedal and hip-turn into a running position, running along a line. When we teach this part of the technique, we teach pulling the elbow to the side of the turn through to get the hips turned the other direction. When we open the hips to the right, the right elbow has to pull hard to get the body to start to turn. As the hips open to the right, the left knee has to move inside to unlock the hips.

When we do our drills, we do everything on a line. When we open the hips, we want the left foot to be back on the line as quickly as we can. To open the hips to the right, we press the right toe, throw the right elbow, bend the left knee inside, and unlock the hips. That allows the left foot to come through and get back on the line running the other way.

If the back cannot get his hips unlocked, he will step off the line and run horizontal. If the receiver runs vertical and the defensive back runs horizontal, the receiver wins the race. The back, as he turns with his right foot, wants to step past 180-degree position with his right foot. That allows the left foot to hit the line.

In the development of our defensive backs, they are taking baby steps. We are working on all these things right now. We want them to snap their head around to get the body going in the right direction. The body follows the head.

We have to disguise the coverage we plan to play in the secondary. If the offense knows what you do, they can pick you apart. That means defensive backs must be able to get into areas of the field rapidly. They have to angle cut to get into a responsibility and backpedal when they get there. You can work the angle drop drill, slow the speed, and get into the pedal. All the drills relate to footwork and are all connected. One drill builds on the other one.

We work an angle drop drill (Diagram #8). We align the defensive back on one line. On the signal, he opens his hips and angle drops into his area of responsibility. He angles drops to the next line. Once he gets to that line, he converts the angle drop into a pedal.

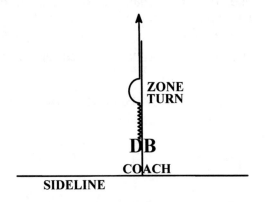

Diagram #7. Backpedal to a Zone Turn

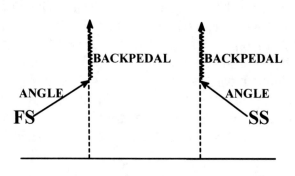

Diagram #8. Angle Drop to Backpedal

You can angle drop, pedal, and zone turn in the same drill. When you drill defensive back, the positions you put them into will be the same ones they see in the games. When you develop your drills, work on a coverage drop and add a speed turn to the drill. If you work the entire off-season on these drills, you can take the skills directly to the field.

If a player wants to play safety, he must have the ability to break off the hash marks and overlap the ball. When he plays the ball, he has to high point the ball. With the ball in the air, he has to go get it. The ball is his. Some players struggle with that part of playing the ball.

If you want to teach that skill, you can do it before practice. Take the defensive back and put them on their backs. Make them lie down with their backs on the ground. They bend the knees and put their feet flat on the ground. The coach stands in front of them, facing their knees, and throws them a ball. To catch the ball, the backs have to reach up and extend their arm. Make them catch the ball over their heads, to the right of their heads, and to the left of their heads.

You can do this in the off-season, during spring practice, or anytime. You can do the drill with tennis balls. This improves their eye/hand coordinator. Safeties who do not highpoint the ball panic when the ball gets close to their hands. You have to build confidence in the safeties to go up and get the ball. You can do that with that simple drill. I love football players who play center field on the baseball team. They can run, go up, and high point the ball.

I found out something that is important to college coaches. You have to show players NFL tapes. Show them making plays and show them pro players making the same plays. They will see the difference. High school coaches should find some college tapes to show their players. Find films that fit your situation, and cut them into your films. The videos that are available today are outstanding. The video machines used today are phenomenal. You can put together just about any type of film you want. If you are behind the times in your video capabilities,

you are behind the times in your coaching. You have to take film and teach your players. They cannot all learn with X's and O's drawn on the board. Some of them learn best from seeing the correct technique. We want players who play with their shoulders over their knees and their knees over their toes. Those are the players making plays.

If I come into your school to recruit, I have a preconceived notion of what I am looking to find. I know if a player can play, he can play. It does not matter if he is 5'8" or 6'4". I want a player who can play like a 6'1" safety. If I ask to meet him, it is not to try to talk to him about Ohio State. I want to see how long his arms are. If the back is 5'10", I have to know how long his arms are. Basketball players who come out for football all want to play receiver. If you play with a 5'10" player, he must have long arms and have a great vertical.

If you tell me you have an in-the-box safety, my response is: there is no box. On 75 or 80 percent of the snaps, you must play from sideline to sideline. If a coach has a linebacker who is 6'2", 215 pounds, and all he does is make 50 tackles a game, he cannot play for us. If a coach tells me he has a 6'2", 215-pound safety, I give the tape to the linebacker coach. Coach Fickell may see his potential.

At defensive backs, we look for players who can run and are athletic. If we recruit a corner with size, we will take him. He has a place he can fall. He can always play safety. If we recruit a safety, we can take him because he has a place to fall. He can always go to linebacker. We try to evaluate players in other sports. Coach Meyer likes players who run track. When we try to evaluate player, we like to see them play other positions on the football team, play basketball, or run track. If he runs track, you can judge the straight-line speed. As a defensive safety, you hit the jackpot if you get a player who plays an option quarterback on the football team, center field on the baseball team, and point guard on the basketball team.

Thank you, coaches. I appreciate what you do. If you want to come to see us, we would love to have you.

2012
COACH OF THE YEAR CLINICS
Football Manual

Featuring lectures from several of America's most renowned coaches. Edited by Earl Browning.

$29.95 • 291 pages • 978-1-60679-218-6

Also available:

2006	2007	2008	2009	2010	2011

1-58518-969-3	978-1-58518-073-8	978-1-58518-719-5	978-1-60679-062-5	978-1-60679-104-2	978-1-60679-171-4
304 pp. • $24.95	288 pp. • $24.95	272 pp. • $24.95	288 pp. • $29.95	313 pp. • $29.95	295 pp. • $29.95